GERMAN IDEALISM

German Idealism is one of the most important movements in the history of philosophy. It is also increasingly acknowledged to contain the seeds of many current philosophical issues and debates. This outstanding collection of specially commissioned chapters examines German idealism from several angles and assesses the renewed interest in the subject from a wide range of fields.

Including discussions of the key representatives of German idealism such as Kant, Fichte and Hegel, it is structured in clear sections dealing with:

- metaphysics
- the legacy of Hegel's philosophy
- Brandom and Hegel
- recognition and agency
- autonomy and nature
- the philosophy of German romanticism

Amongst other important topics, *German Idealism: Contemporary Perspectives* addresses the debates surrounding the metaphysical and epistemological legacy of German idealism; its importance for understanding recent debates in moral and political thought; its appropriation in recent theories of language and the relationship between mind and world; and how German idealism affected subsequent movements such as romanticism, pragmatism, and critical theory.

Contributors: Frederick Beiser, Jay Bernstein, Andrew Bowie, Richard Eldridge, Manfred Frank, Paul Franks, Sebastian Gardner, Espen Hammer, Stephen Houlgate, Terry Pinkard, Robert Pippin, Paul Redding, Fred Rush, Robert Stern.

Espen Hammer is Professor of Philosophy at the University of Oslo and a Reader in Philosophy at the University of Essex. He is the author of *Adorno and the Political* (Routledge, 2006).

GERMAN IDEALISM

Contemporary Perspectives

Edited by Espen Hammer

LONDON AND NEW YORK

First published 2007
by Routledge
2 Milton Park Square, Milton Park, Abingdon, OX14 4RN

Simultaneously published in the USA and Canada
by Routledge
270 Madison Ave, New York, NY 10016

Routledge is an imprint of the Taylor & Francis Group, an informa business

Typeset in Goudy by
Taylor & Francis Books
Printed and bound in Great Britain by
Antony Rowe Ltd, Chippenham, Wiltshire

British Library Cataloguing in Publication Data
A catalogue record for this book is available from the British Library

Library of Congress Cataloging in Publication Data
A catalog record for this book has been requested

ISBN10: 0-415-37304-2 (hbk)
ISBN10: 0-415-37305-0 (pbk)
ISBN10: 0-203-03083-4 (ebk)

ISBN 13: 978-0-415-37304-3 (hbk)
ISBN 13: 978-0-415-37305-0 (pbk)
ISBN 13: 978-0-203-03083-7 (ebk)

CONTENTS

CONTRIBUTORS

Frederick C. Beiser is Professor of Philosophy at Syracuse University. He is the author of *The Fate of Reason: German Philosophy from Kant to Fichte* (1987); *Enlightenment, Revolution, Romanticism: The Genesis of Modern German Political Thought* (1992); *German Idealism: The Struggle Against Subjectivism, 1781–1801* (2002); *The Romantic Imperative: The Concept of Early German Romanticism* (2003); *Schiller as Philosopher: A Re-Examination* (2005); and *Hegel* (2005). He is also the editor of *The Cambridge Companion to Hegel.*

J.M. Bernstein is University Distinguished Professor of Philosophy at the New School for Social Research. Among his works are: *The Fate of Art: Aesthetic Alienation from Kant to Derrida and Adorno* (1992); *Recovering Ethical Life: Jürgen Habermas and the Future of Critical Theory* (1995); *Adorno: Disenchantment and Ethics* (2001); and *Against Voluptuous Bodies: Late Modernism and the Idea of Painting* (2006). He is also the editor of *Classical and Romantic German Aesthetics* in the Cambridge History of Philosophy series.

Andrew Bowie is Professor of Philosophy and German at Royal Holloway, University of London. His books include *Aesthetics and Subjectivity: From Kant to Nietzsche* (1990); *Schelling and Modern European Philosophy: An Introduction* (1993); *From Romanticism to Critical Theory. The Philosophy of German Literary Theory* (1997); and *Introduction to German Philosophy: From Kant to Habermas* (2003). His book, *Music, Philosophy, and Modernity,* will be published by Cambridge University Press.

Richard Eldridge is Charles and Harriett Cox McDowell Professor of Philosophy and Religion at Swarthmore College. He is the author of *On Moral Personhood: Philosophy, Literature, Criticism, and Self-Understanding* (1989); *Leading a Human Life: Wittgenstein, Intentionality, and Romanticism* (1997); *The Persistence of Romanticism: Essays in Philosophy and Literature* (2001); and *An Introduction to the Philosophy of Art* (2003). He is also the editor of *Stanley Cavell* (2003).

Manfred Frank is Professor of Philosophy at the University of Tübingen. He is the author of numerous books, among them *Das Individuelle Allgemeine.*

Textstrukturierung und -interpretation nach Schleiermacher (1977); *Was ist Neostrukturalismus?* (1983); *Die Grenzen der Verständigung. Ein Geistergespräch zwischen Lyotard und Habermas* (1988); and *Selbstgefühl: Eine historisch-systematische Erkundung* (2002).

Paul Franks is Associate Professor of Philosophy at the University of Toronto. He is the author of several articles on Kant and post-Kantian idealism as well as *All or Nothing: Systematicity, Transcendental Arguments, and Skepticism in German Idealism* (2005). He is also an Associate Editor of the International Yearbook of German Idealism.

Sebastian Gardner is Professor of Philosophy at the University College London. He is the author of *Irrationality and the Philosophy of Psychoanalysis* (1993) and *Kant and the 'Critique of Pure Reason'* (1998). He is also the co-editor of *Art and Morality* (2002). His book, *Fichte, Schelling and Early German Idealism*, will be published by Routledge.

Espen Hammer is Reader in Philosophy at the University of Essex and Professor of Philosophy at the University of Oslo. He is the author of four books, including *Stanley Cavell: Skepticism, Subjectivity, and the Ordinary* (2002) and *Adorno and the Political* (2005), and the Norwegian translator of Immanuel Kant's *Kritik der Urteilskraft*. He is also a co-editor of *Stanley Cavell: Die Unheimlichkeit des Gewöhnlichen*. He is completing a book on modernity and time-consciousness.

Stephen Houlgate is Professor of Philosophy at the University of Warwick. His publications include *Hegel, Nietzsche and the Criticism of Metaphysics* (1986); *An Introduction to Hegel. Freedom, Truth and History* (2005); and *The Opening of Hegel's Logic: From Being to Infinity* (2006).

Terry Pinkard is Professor of Philosophy at Georgetown University. He is the author of *Hegel's Phenomenology: The Sociality of Reason* (1994); *Hegel: A Biography* (2000); and *German Philosophy 1760–1860: The Legacy of Idealism* (2002). His translation of Hegel's *Phänomenologie des Geistes* will be published by Cambridge University Press.

Robert Pippin is the Evelyn Stefansson Nef Distinguished Service Professor in the Committee on Social Thought, the Department of Philosophy, and the College at the University of Chicago. He is the author of several books, including *Kant's Theory of Form* (1982); *Hegel's Idealism: The Satisfactions of Self-Consciousness* (1989); *Modernism as a Philosophical Problem: On the Dissatisfactions of European High Culture* (1991); *Idealism as Modernism: Hegelian Variations* (1997); *Henry James and Modern Moral Life* (2000); and *The Persistence of Subjectivity: On the Kantian Aftermath* (2005).

Paul Redding is Professor of Philosophy at the University of Sydney. He is the author of *Hegel's Hermeneutics* (1996); *The Logic of Affect* (1999); and *Analytic*

Philosophy and the Return of Hegelian Thought, to be published by Cambridge University Press.

Fred Rush is Associate Professor of Philosophy at the University of Notre Dame. He has written several articles on Kant, Hegel, critical theory, and aesthetics. He is completing a book on the philosophical significance of early German romanticism and its relation to Kant and Kierkegaard. He is also the editor of *The Cambridge Companion to Critical Theory* (2004).

Robert Stern is Professor of Philosophy at the University of Sheffield. He is the author of *Hegel, Kant and the Structure of the Object* (1990); *Transcendental Arguments and Scepticism: Answering the Question of Justification* (2000); and *Hegel and the 'Phenomenology of Spirit'* (2002). Stern edited G. W. F. *Hegel: Critical Assessments* (1993) and *Transcendental Arguments: Problems and Prospects* (1999). He is also the editor of the *European Journal of Philosophy*.

ACKNOWLEDGEMENTS

First, I would like to thank the contributors to this volume. They have all done a marvellous job.

Many people have helped shape this book. I am especially grateful to my colleagues in the philosophy department at Essex University whose interest in the significance of Kant and post-Kantian idealism has never failed to inspire. Thanks to Richard Eldridge for providing some very helpful comments on the introduction. I would also like to mention Tony Bruce at Routledge. It was he who initially came up with the idea for this book. Gordon Wells must be thanked for his translation of Manfred Frank's article from German. And I acknowledge the financial support of the Arts and Humanities Research Council in the form of a research grant in the autumn of 2005.

One of the chapters has previously been published: 'Brandom's Hegel' by Robert Pippin first appeared in *European Journal of Philosophy* 13 (3): 381–408 (2005). I thank the editor and publisher for permission to reprint this material.

INTRODUCTION

Few trends in contemporary philosophy seem stronger and more influential than the resurgence and revival of themes and arguments that owe their origin to thinkers associated with German idealism. Not only has scholarship (particularly in the Anglo-American context) on figures such as Kant, Fichte, Schelling and Hegel become more sophisticated, prestigious and creative than it has been for a long time, but the innovative uses to which idealist motifs have recently been put have changed the nature of many philosophical debates. Drawing on strong readings and reconceptualizing traditional arguments, philosophers working in fields as different as epistemology, philosophy of language, political theory, ethics and aesthetics have opened new intellectual vistas while reinvigorating others.[1] For central thinkers of our time such as Robert Brandom, Stanley Cavell, Jürgen Habermas, John McDowell, Hilary Putnam, and many others, Kant and Hegel are household names whose writings have served as a basis for the development of their own work.

It is tempting to speculate why this resurgence has taken place. One simple but not quite sufficient reason may be that it responds to a long-standing and vigorous rejection of the German tradition. Certainly, in the first two or three decades after the Second World War, virtually all of the most highly valued and recognized work in Anglo-American philosophy was 'analytic', with interest in German idealism largely classified (and not seldom denigrated) as 'mere' historiography. Although Kant was widely considered to be a figure worthy of serious engagement, the idea that his arguments could contribute directly to contemporary debate struck many professional philosophers as being implausible, if not downright unthinkable. While Kant's work admittedly did play an important role in areas such as the philosophy of mathematics, philosophy of religion, aesthetics, and, through the work of Peter Strawson and others, in debates surrounding the nature and scope of transcendental arguments, the subsequent idealists, among them Fichte, Schelling and Hegel, were almost completely ignored by those in the philosophical community who did not restrict their research to historical issues. Arguably, this tendency has been present throughout the history of the analytic movement and was there from the very earliest moments of its inception. Indeed, the almost instinctive distrust of the later idealists among post-war analytic philosophers has a strong historical precedent in the fact that the origin of anglophone analytic philosophy in figures such as Bertrand Russell and G.E. Moore to a considerable extent was predicated on their dismissal of British idealism (represented by Bradley, Green and others) and its Hegelian roots.[2]

In the heydays of post-Second World War linguistic analysis and analytic Kantianism, the 'historical' Kant was dismissed for supposedly committing himself to a supernaturalist or, in some cases, 'faculty–psychological' account of the mind, and for lapsing into a self-defeating skepticism with regard to the possibility of objective knowledge. (If we can't have knowledge of the thing in itself, of what is real, then what is there for knowledge to be?)[3] His account of the transcendental ideality of time and space seemed to imply some kind of extreme version of subjective idealism, and he had not yet discovered the true philosophical significance of language and logic. However, if Kant was seen to be in trouble, it could not, many philosophers felt, compare to the intellectual depths that, for example, Hegel had fallen into. The general consensus seems to have been that Hegel was a pre-critical metaphysician whose 'dialectics' and 'system' could lay little or no claim to intellectual seriousness.[4] From the negation of one proposition by another, no third determinate proposition follows: the very notion of dialectics, philosophy teachers liked to point out, is simply a complete non-starter. Moreover, the very ambition of creating a philosophical system capable of organizing a priori knowledge into a coherent and self-sufficient whole seemed to suggest, again problematically, that philosophy enjoys a privileged epistemic role in relation to the empirical sciences.[5] A related charge was that the German idealists appeared to have shown little understanding and appreciation of the methods and achievements of mathematically based natural science. How can their penchant for a priori, totalizing philosophies of nature ever be squared with the prestige of sober scientific research?

For the earlier generation of logical positivists, the notion of synthetic a priori judgment was enough to make them reject both Kant and the subsequent German idealists. If, as they argued, analytic judgments provide the only form of a priori knowledge there can be, then synthetic judgments are bound to be a posteriori and hence grounded in experience. From this distinction a division of labor arose: while philosophy should restrict itself to conceptual clarification, only empirical science can embody genuine claims to knowledge about the world. However, when Quine's influential attack on the analytic/synthetic distinction started to make its impact in the 1950s, the basis for this division of labor began to weaken, leading many philosophers to give up the idea that their discipline had any unique claim to knowledge or rationality; hence naturalism now became the preferred metaphilosophy (or ontology) of many practitioners working in fields such as philosophy of mind or epistemology. For the most radical ontological naturalists, not only is natural science the exclusive source of rational claims about nature, but what natural science is engaged in is to tell us *what there is* in a deep, ontological sense.

Currently a dominating ideology not only in many leading Anglo-American philosophy departments but in much popular debate as well, naturalism poses a considerable challenge to its skeptics. One of its starkest implications is that philosophy as a distinct discipline or *Fach* is a thing of the past. According to this paradigm, the task of those who still call themselves philosophers is to interpret the results of specific scientific theories and then apply those interpretations to problems that previously occupied traditional philosophers. Thus, interpretations of Darwinian accounts of evolution, for example, are used to formulate views about the operations of the human mind, about morality, or about action. All such naturalistic views inevitably make reference to law-like propositions aiming to provide causal explanations of a given set of phenomena.

Since naturalism disposes of no means to articulate normative commitments, it seems to remain incapable, however, of justifying itself in a non-circular manner; and it generally seems unable to acknowledge the existence of normative notions such as truth, validity, and correctness, as well as accounting for the activity of applying concepts and making judgments. Most significantly, naturalism either squarely opposes, or takes as metaphysical or pre-rational, the view that human beings are agents who freely and responsibly relate to normative expectations and structures. It thus asks for revisions of everyday conceptual schemes, holding that we should see concepts such as thinking, willing and feeling as belonging to an illusory 'folk psychology.'[6] It is hard to think of a philosophical outlook that is more contrary to that of Kant and German idealism. For precisely this reason, however, much of today's resurgence of this older tradition may be seen as representing a battle-cry against current variations of naturalism and scientific realism. A central concern for thinkers such as McDowell, Brandom and Putnam is to show that while science is a perfectly legitimate, admirable and important endeavor, scientism, the confusion of scientific with philosophical claims, is not. If purged of its speculative metaphysical aspirations, German idealism can inspire the formulation of views that show nature and freedom to be compatible with one another.

To be sure, if we expand the focus to include continental Europe, and Germany in particular, then the picture (however schematic) looks rather different. In no major twentieth century German school of philosophy did the distinction between history of philosophy and philosophy as such ever establish itself as binding. Virtually all of the leading thinkers of this tradition, including Husserl, Heidegger, Adorno, Gadamer and Habermas, have formulated their views in close *rapport* with the idealist tradition in which they found themselves.[7] Moreover, all these thinkers have developed their projects in sharp opposition to both positivism and naturalism. While their interpretations and assessments of Kant and German idealism have varied enormously, there was never a moment when this section of the larger Western tradition was found to be of no use or somehow intellectually questionable. Not least as a result of the influence wielded by Habermas and his associates, many current German philosophers have looked to analytic philosophy for inspiration; yet despite the import of Anglo-American pragmatism and speech act theory, Habermas himself continues to view himself as essentially a left-Hegelian thinker with a strong orientation towards Kant.

We must therefore distinguish between the German and the Anglo-American interest in Kant and German idealism. Whereas, today, the German interest tends to be dominated by systematic and constructive scholarship (Dieter Henrich, Manfred Frank and others), as well as the reception of post-analytic thinkers like McDowell and Brandom, the Anglo-American interest is, as already mentioned, more strongly divided between historiographic scholarship and systematic appropriation. There is, however, another important difference. Since most of the impetus for bald naturalism has come from British and American universities, its proponents have been viewed as stronger, and therefore more important to oppose, than has been the case on the European continent, where philosophy has been significantly less influenced by naturalism. In purely intellectual terms, it is not difficult to recognize the dialectic which, in the Anglo-American context, got started when analytic philosophy, as initially defined through the methods and convictions of logical positivism, began to dissolve *qua* research paradigm, while at the same time being radicalized in its aims and commitments by the rise of new forms of naturalism: It set the stage for so-called post-analytic philosophy, which, while taking Quine's and Davidson's critiques of logical positivism onboard, is deeply hostile to the naturalist alternative.

'For me, at least, almost all the problems of philosophy attain the form in which they are of real interest only with the work of Kant.'[8] The sentence is from a lecture given by Putnam in 1987. Only a few years later, in the preface to the now celebrated *Mind and World*, McDowell wrote the following tribute to Brandom:

> The way I put things here bears substantial marks of Brandom's influence. Among much else, I single out his eye-opening seminar on Hegel's *Phenomenology of Spirit*, which I attended in 1990. Thoughts Brandom elicited from me then show up explicitly at a couple of places in these lectures, but the effect is pervasive; so much so that one way that I would like to conceive this work is as a prolegomenon to a reading of the *Phenomenology*, much as Brandom's forthcoming *Making it Explicit: Reasoning, Representing, and Discursive Commitment* is, among many other things, a prolegomenon to his reading of that difficult text.[9]

In his 2002 *Tales of the Mighty Dead: Historical Essays in the Metaphysics of Intentionality*, Brandom grants Kant and Hegel a central status as forerunners in the development of his own brand of inferentialism. These are extraordinary claims coming from thinkers previously positioned within the analytic tradition. What they suggest is the possibility of an extensive *rapprochement* between, on the one hand, the legacy of Kant and German idealism and, on the other, the concerns and orientations of recent analytic philosophy. (One can easily turn elsewhere in philosophy and find parallel developments. In the domain of moral and political philosophy, for example, its most influential practitioner of the last thirty years, John Rawls, looked to the German tradition when, trying to determine the philosophical nature of his particular brand of proceduralism, he introduced the important notion of 'Kantian constructivism.'[10])

Central to all of these thinkers is that the works of Kant and Hegel are understood to offer cogent alternatives to naturalism in the sense that they contain resources with which to demonstrate that human beings are both natural creatures and, as such, responsive to reason-giving and normative claims. However, they also provide a viable point of view from which to consider humans as epistemic subjects. For these thinkers, the Kantian idea that knowledge has conditions that determine what it means for a representation to count as objective has been immensely valuable, leading Putnam to formulate his doctrine of 'internal realism' and McDowell to trace Hegel's elaboration of it in the direction of 'absolute idealism.'[11] Yet while philosophers such as Putnam, McDowell, Brandom and Rawls apply ideas from the German tradition in order to engage directly with debates in analytic philosophy, there is a new generation of Anglo-American scholars, represented by people like Henry Allison, Karl Ameriks, Paul Guyer, Christine Korsgaard, Béatrice Longuenesse, Terry Pinkard and Robert Pippin, who have applied the rigor of analytic philosophy to interpreting Kant and Hegel, thereby contributing significantly to the resurgence of interest in these thinkers. Typical of much of this work is that while downplaying the metaphysical commitments displayed by the German idealists, it tends to focus, sometimes exclusively, on their alleged insights into the nature of agency, knowledge and rationality.

One persistent issue in the interpretive debates arising from these encounters with German idealism is whether the 'new' Kant and, especially, the 'new' Hegel are adequately interpreted when reconstructed within a post-metaphysical framework. The word 'deflationary' is occasionally used to describe these readings, suggesting that they deliberately refrain from taking someone like Hegel's claim to possess metaphysical knowledge of the essence of reality seriously. It may in fact be argued that much of the new scholarship offers Kantianized versions of Hegel. In Pippin and Pinkard, for example, much of the gist of Hegel's project has to do with the attempt to provide a social epistemology that, while remaining committed to Kant's account of rational self-legislation, bases its normative orientation on criteria derived from concrete historical communities rather than individual minds. 'The upshot of idealism,' writes Pinkard, 'is an understanding that, as self-legislated, our normative authority is always open to challenge, which means that "we" are always open to challenge; and that the only challenges that can count are contained within the "infinite" activity of giving and asking for reasons.'[12]

While attractive as an account of the constitution of normative authority, the notion of reason-giving and its indefinite temporal extension may sound more in line with contemporary theories of rationality (Habermas, Rorty, Brandom) than with Hegel's dialectics, which, according to more traditional readings, seeks to uncover the structure and essence of reality in some deep metaphysical sense. If that is the case, however, then what is the real value of such deflationary readings? If they do not capture Hegel's project in its entirety but at best select and highlight some aspects of it to the detriment of others, then are they legitimate? If they are not legitimate as interpretations of Hegel, then are they at least valuable as contributions to contemporary thinking about rationality? I think the answer to the last question must be a clear and resounding 'yes.' Yet we still need to ask whether postmetaphysical interpretations of what to many appear to be a metaphysically oriented movement are acceptable. Frederick Beiser, for one, has argued that they are not, and that what is required is a more historically sensitive approach according to which a thinker must be studied with reference to questions posed in his own intellectual environment, rather than an orientation towards questions arising from contemporary philosophy. Others find that 'strong' readings of classical philosophers – readings which do not observe a strict distinction between interpretation of textual meaning and applications of the text in various other contexts – are not only perfectly legitimate but necessary in order to bring philosophy forward. (Of course, few interpreters will ever admit to offering strong readings in this sense.)[13]

As in the case of the difference between naturalists and anti-naturalists, the debate (internal to the resurgence of German idealism) between historicists and proponents of anti-metaphysical or deflationary approaches often reflects different attitudes towards philosophy as such. For the historicist, philosophy is first and foremost a hermeneutic endeavor: it consists in the painstaking interpretation of authoritative texts, without much regard for contemporary intellectual concerns. The extent to which an allegedly authoritative text succeeds in addressing us in a genuinely authoritative fashion is a function of our ability to reconstruct it *on its own terms* and on the basis of its own historical presuppositions. The historicist seeks more than anything else to avoid making history a mere screen for the projection of our own prejudices. For the anti-historicist, however, philosophy is first and foremost a disinterested search for ahistorical truth; hence historical studies are to be understood as *means* to articulate and arrive at such truths, but not as ends in themselves. They may be considered excellent means, encouraging the philosopher to work on them throughout their entire careers, yet the way in which the texts are laid out and read will differ from that of the historicist, who insists on treating the reading of them as an end in itself.

None of the major figures associated with the revival of themes originating in German idealism falls easily into either of these two camps.[14] None of them distinguishes rigorously between historical and conceptual claims. However, the differences – between the Anglophone and the German reception, as well as between the various practitioners within the Anglophone world – cannot be denied. As with all the other issues I have been broaching, they create tensions that will be explored in this book.

The contributions to this book

Metaphysical questions are central both to the interpretation of German idealism and to accounting for the relevance of this movement today. The author of the first essay, Sebastian Gardner, is skeptical of antimetaphysical (or deflationary) approaches to German idealism. In his view, however, the anti-metaphysical readings of someone like Hegel are not, or at least not primarily, suspicious because they fall short of taking the texts and their context properly into account, but because, given their philosophical presuppositions, they do not seem to hold up well argumentatively against bald scientific naturalism. Gardner starts by arguing that the analytic rejection of idealism in the early twentieth century did not really spring from a refutation of idealism on its own terms so much as from a sense of the superiority of logical analysis. Later, with Quine and others, the adoption of a scientific/naturalistic world-view made idealism seem even more unpalatable. The fundamental difficulty with naturalism, however, is its rejection of values – or at least its subordination of them to the ways in which human organisms respond to the requirements placed on them by the natural world. As soft naturalism runs to the rescue with philosophers like Brandom and McDowell, it agrees with naturalism that speculative metaphysics is impossible but, in part since bald naturalism is now the default position, has difficulties showing that there are phenomena that 'have substantial reality, but do not owe it to the hard natural facts.' If, in particular, the soft/hard naturalism dispute can be transformed into an appearance/reality contrast, then the hard naturalist wins. In his conclusion, Gardner recommends that rather than reading German idealism along deflationary lines, we would be better off taking its strong claims to being *idealistic* at face value. Hegel's *Geist*, for example, should not be seen as in some sense arising from nature, but as being *sui generis* and prior to it.

Kant's account of principles that are constitutive of the very possibility of epistemic practices makes up the heart of his transcendental philosophy. Against Humean skepticism and methodological naturalism, Kant argues that such principles are both necessary and universally valid. In his paper, Paul Franks looks at how certain thinkers in the post-Kantian generation, in particular Salomon Maimon, responded to Kant's criticisms of Hume, and he compares this response to similar ones offered by certain modern analytic philosophers, in particular Quine. According to Franks, what Maimon realizes is that Kant underestimates the challenge of methodological naturalism, insofar as he regards it as revisionist. It is perfectly possible to agree, as Hume himself seems to do, with Kant's claim that these principles are ineliminable while adopting an anti-realist attitude towards their constitutive function. If the principles are only practically necessary for our epistemic practices, but do not justify those practices, then they are themselves unjustified, and their objective validity is open to doubt. There is therefore no 'fact' – such as that of the existence of sciences founded on synthetic a priori principles – that naturalism cannot account for and is not compatible with. Moving on to the twentieth century, Franks detects the same dialectic in Quine's response to Carnap. There is a continued stand-off between transcendental philosophy and methodological naturalism. Without drawing any strong conclusions, Franks considers some of the ways in which this stand-off has been dealt with in post-Kantian idealism and in contemporary analytic philosophy.

Like Gardner yet internally to the interpretation of given historical texts, Beiser attacks antimetaphysical and deflationary accounts head-on, arguing that they radically misrepresent the nature of German idealism. In the hands of interpreters such as Peter Strawson, Jonathan Bennett, John Rawls, Robert Pippin and Terry Pinkard, German idealism has ended up being sanitized and purged of its metaphysical commitments. This has occurred, Beiser argues, as the result of these interpreters' subscription to an 'analytic method' of interpretation. According to this method, the interpreter should restrict himself to rationally reconstructing the arguments he detects, and he should do so in accordance with the standards of argumentation and basic ontological commitments of today's analytic philosophy. The consequence, however, of applying the analytic method is that the readings that emerge become anachronistic, tailored to contemporary philosophical fashions, and thus potentially limiting. Like the proponents of the analytic method, Beiser demands close attentiveness to the possible *truth* of historical utterances; yet unlike them, and in agreement with the historicist tradition, he thinks that this activity should be combined with rigorous scrutiny of the historical figure's intention and historical context. In order to know *why* someone like Hegel makes a claim or advances an argument of a specific form, we need to individuate him as an author and show how he responds to particular issues and questions that arise in his own cultural and historical context.

In contemporary scholarship on Kant and Hegel, the notion of autonomy is both central and disputed. On Fred Rush's view, the extension of Kantian ideas of autonomy into a Hegelian framework, which often occurs in deflationary readings, has the unfortunate consequence of occluding some of the most interesting aspects of Hegel's ethical and political thought. Indeed, if the tendency among Anglo-American Hegel-scholars today is to push Hegel in the direction of Kant, then Rush wants to promote the view that 'a better indicator for what is of continuing interest in Hegel's political thought is Marx.' One upshot of this is that the appeal, common to the many Kantian readings of Hegel, to 'the sociality of reason' appears to be too superficial and too predicated upon a prior acceptance of liberalism. What is needed is a more ambitious account of group agency. Rush is not claiming that the demands of modern individualism have no place in Hegel. He is, however, proposing that Hegel holds an organic view according to which individual agents are to a large degree determined in their thought and action as the result of an overall rationality. Their identities come about in terms of their functional roles in the social whole. Individuals are free, but not because they are self-legislating beings. The values they are able to count as authoritative will be those with which they have identified because they are constitutive of the social and historical structure within which they exist. Ethical argumentation is then not about testing which precepts or values one may freely and rationally accept but about bringing into consideration how or whether they cohere with the more general form of ethical life from which they issue. To be free is to reflectively know oneself and one's function as part of an overall, rational structure.

My own paper looks at how certain crucial themes from Kant and German idealism are being negotiated today in the work of Jürgen Habermas. Like his mentor, Theodor W. Adorno, Habermas strongly criticizes what he sees as totalizing idealist tendencies in Hegel. The notion of the absolute subject, he argues, cannot be defended on contemporary, postmetaphysical grounds. In order to make Hegel relevant for contemporary thought his philosophy needs to be 'detranscendentalized' – even if this should turn out to violate the spirit and letter of Hegel's text. In my view, this reading is not adequate. There is more to Hegel's procedure of immanent critique than Habermas eventually acknowledges; and the *Phenomenology of Spirit* can be read productively without a metaphysical conception of the absolute subject. In Habermas's later development of formal pragmatics, Kant becomes a much more important source of inspiration than Hegel. Again, I criticize this turn and argue that Hegel has arguments that call into question the Kantian side of Habermas's position. At the end of my essay, I turn briefly to Adorno in order to exemplify a form of immanent critique that can genuinely lay claim to a Hegelian heritage.

Robert Brandom is another contemporary figure whose work is indebted to the German idealist tradition. Although the parallels between Habermas's and Brandom's accounts of rationality and language are evident, they do not, however, agree in their interpretation of Hegel.[15] While Habermas understands Hegel as predominantly a metaphysical thinker, Brandom draws on him in order to articulate his pragmatist account of discursive commitments. Stephen Houlgate, however, takes issue with Brandom's reading. Focusing on Brandom's inferentialism, Houlgate argues that, while similar in certain ways to Hegel's view, it differs in philosophically fundamental ways that Brandom fails to recognize. Brandom argues that concepts are inferentially articulated and, in particular, that formal rules of inference such as those studied in formal logic are to be understood as reconstructions of the ways in which these rules operate pragmatically in everyday speech. According to Houlgate, Hegel agrees that concepts are inferentially articulated and thus by claiming that such-and-such is the case commits one to other propositions that ultimately make sense within historically mediated networks of holistically structured semantic unities. However, on Houlgate's reading, Hegel would not see the pragmatics of speech as fundamental and self-sufficient; rather, it is the a priori concepts and categories explored in Hegel's *Logic* that make linguistic activity and intelligibility possible in the first place. The *Logic* uncovers the basic concepts and categories that structure thinking (and linguistic activity), yet in doing so it also uncovers the necessary and universal structure of the world itself.

In his own discussion of Brandom, Robert Pippin takes himself to be following Kant in holding subjective processes and meaningful claims about objects to be 'reciprocally sense-dependent'. One important upshot of transcendental idealism is that talk about objects is dependent on the conditions for representing them. Since these conditions determine what can be represented *überhaupt*, the problem of fit, which Houlgate brings up, between subjective processes and the a priori structure of the world does not seem to arise. However, Pippin is not primarily focusing on metaphysics but on whether Brandom can be said to succeed in inheriting Hegel's brand of idealism. (After all, since Pippin and Brandom both take themselves to be building on Hegel, their differences are bound to be instructive.) Unsurprisingly, Pippin and Brandom agree on many of the central issues occupying them. They both subscribe to a Hegelian view of normativity. All forms of intentional behavior depend on the capacity to take a stance, and undertake commitments, in a normative space. Moreover, both take normativity to depend on processes of mutual recognition within concrete communities. Pippin offers many interesting comments on Brandom's approach, some of them less critical than others. Perhaps the most far-reaching ones have to do with Brandom's understanding of the sociality of reason. According to Pippin, Brandom fails to distinguish between undertaking a commitment in the sense of merely satisfying the socially endorsed criteria for doing so, and undertaking a commitment in the sense of being normatively engaged in a more genuine way which is recognized as such by the individual. Brandom thus fails, he argues, to allow the distinctly Hegelian problem of the positivity of norms to emerge.

Despite his influence on the Jena romantics and on thinkers such as Schelling, Nietzsche and Husserl, Fichte has for a long time been a neglected figure in the Anglophone reception of German idealism. According to a widespread but not always well-founded view, the *Wissenschaftslehre*, Fichte's doctrine of knowledge on which he labored throughout his philosophical career, represents an extreme and unattractive form of subjective idealism that fails to account for the mind-independence of the external world as well as for the existence of other minds. Focusing on Fichte's theory of recognition, Jay Bernstein presents a rather different picture. In contrast to the methodological individualism of the Cartesian and Kantian tradition, Fichte sees the transcendental ego as dependent on social recognition. As Bernstein reads him, recognition most fundamentally takes place in socialization and education. While often seen as a philosopher of the inner and the ideal, Bernstein also highlights the importance of the human body in Fichte. Anticipating Wittgenstein, Fichte argues that other minds exist as embodied: his account of recognition presupposes an ongoing reference to the inherent expressiveness of the human body.

Like Bernstein, Terry Pinkard sees recognition as fundamental to human agency: 'To be an agent (or a subject) is to be *recognized*, that is, to be granted a normative status by others.' However, whereas Bernstein is primarily interested in the actual process of recognition and how it illuminates our constitutive relations to others, Pinkard turns more explicitly towards morality and politics, drawing on Hegel in order to criticize and modify what he considers to be the shortcomings of the influential Kantian picture of the liberal individual. How, he asks, can we come to terms with the 'unvoiced antinomy' in Kant's work between, on the one hand, accounting for the constitution of our normative status by referring to our dependence on a mixture of animality and sociality, and, on the other, seeing us as self-originating sources of normative claims? One of Kant's great achievements is to have made the binding character of practical obligations a function of reflective endorsement. An end has value for me, or matters to me, because of the reasons I can put forward for favoring its adoption. It is in taking myself to be in possession of good reasons that I assert my normative authority. On Pinkard's Hegelian conception, we should not so much reject this view as we should accept that Kantian rationality must be embedded in a particular set of social practices and intersubjective relations on which one depends when asserting one's normative authority. In seeking to overcome the Kantian antinomy, the Hegelian suggests that the concept of the liberal individual amounts to an abstract fantasy when considered outside of a specific practical, social, and institutional order.

Paul Redding's contribution also deals with Hegel's moral and political thinking. In a reading that draws on contemporary theories of rationality and moral action, he follows Hegel's intricate critique of Fichte's account of the role of conscience in moral judgment, arguing that the latter's extreme internalization of the self-legislating will makes it impossible to account for the truth of the authority which the will claims to have. Rather than being located within the solitary individual's conscience, normative authority can only be established in the socially concrete conditions of ethical life. Like Pinkard, Redding understands the crucial process of intersubjective recognition in terms of a pragmatics of reason-giving. At the end of his paper he compares his own approach to such a pragmatics with that of Brandom.

Robert Stern looks at the apparent irreconcilability between McDowell's and Pippin's approaches to Hegel. In his moral philosophy, McDowell places a lot of emphasis on the idea that values are part of the fabric of the world – not the world as it is in itself, but the world as it exists for us human beings, or what McDowell sometimes calls 'second nature'. As a result of socialization and a degree of receptivity, values can be perceived as having an objective existence and authority, beyond mere willing and desiring. Pippin's Kantian rejoinder to this view is essentially that, for Hegel, values can only be adopted as binding for an agent insofar as they are self-chosen. The key to validity is self-legislation. On Pippin's view, McDowell's position, insofar as it is at odds with Hegel's commitment to a modern conception of autonomy, appears to be reactionary. Stern's claim is that while these seem like very distinct positions, there is a lot of common ground between them in Hegel's own thinking. According to Stern, we may in particular profit from reconsidering the early Hegel's critique of the view that moral goodness is to be assessed in light of a command or imperative of some sort.

Following Richard Rorty, Richard Eldridge raises some of the classical questions of epistemology and argues that this discipline no longer deserves to occupy the center-stage when assessing philosophy's claim to cultural significance. Yet while Rorty links the fate of philosophy inextricably to epistemology, arguing that the end of epistemology should spell the end of philosophy (as we know it) as well, Eldridge wants to see philosophy transformed along lines staked out by such figures as Aristotle, Hegel and Wittgenstein. Rather than focusing on representation in terms of the relationship between mind and world, philosophical work should be geared towards the ways in which human agents position themselves within a community of speakers. To make a claim is to lay claim to a certain position within a social field that calls for recognition by other individuals who themselves are recognized as rational. Moreover, every judgment is an act of normatively structured positioning; thus judging presupposes what Kant called spontaneity – the act of freely determining something as something in accordance with rules for which one carries a degree of responsibility. On Eldridge's account, there is always a play between the individual agent and the community – between individual acts of self-determination and the instituted set of rules that governs particular practices of discourse and justification. By way of conclusion, he suggests that art is capable of holding this play up before us. Art dramatizes the ineradicable human tension between freedom and givenness, autonomy and heteronomy.

Eldridge has argued elsewhere that romanticism can philosophically be understood as emphasizing the unavoidability of this tension.[16] According to the German philosopher Manfred Frank, however, what is distinctive about early German romanticism, in particular, is the belief that the activities of the subject and its awareness of itself must rest on a 'transcendent ground' that can never be made into an object of knowledge. In his essay, Frank distinguishes this idea from what he thinks of as the fundamental principle of German idealism, namely that the structures of reality can be traced back to, and be shown to derive from, the operations of the human mind. The conception of an absolute foundation is then developed by tracing its treatment in some of the major figures of this movement, in particular Novalis. There must be an absolute foundation, they argue, because otherwise the process of justifying the existence of consciousness will run into an endless regress. However, since the foundation cannot itself be justified, it must be ascertained in some non-discursive fashion. This is the point at which Novalis, for example, starts to introduce a notion of 'endless striving', an impossible yet imperative search to connect with the foundation of one's own existence for which art has been seen to serve a fundamental role. According to Frank, the legacy of this idea can be traced from the early German romantics to twentieth-century thinkers such as Heidegger, Wittgenstein, Adorno, Musil and Derrida.

German idealism contains a wealth of resources for thinking about issues such as autonomy, agency and rationality. However, many of its friendly and romantically oriented critics, including Jacobi, Schelling and Adorno, have argued that for the idealist vision of rational self-determination to be possible, it is necessary that something else which can never be the object of full conceptual mastery is in place. While for Jacobi, there must be an element of cognitively unassured faith, for Schelling there must be a concept-transcendent 'Ground', and for Adorno a layer of mimetic–expressive behavior. Andrew Bowie explores some of these claims, suggesting that 'the conception of freedom as self-determination does not do justice to the more expressive dimensions of human existence, which are not adequately grasped by thinking in terms of giving reasons and taking normative stances'. Rather than merely being active and self-determining, reason has a receptive and passive dimension that fails to be acknowledged in much idealist thinking. Bowie brings this thought to bear on the wider issue of whether there may be some kind of complicity between, on the one hand, reason in its idealist configuration and, on the other, the degenerated, instrumentalist forms of reason that, according to Adorno and others, have been an essential aspect of modernity. If that is the case, however, then perhaps the bourgeois optimism implicit in the rationalist vision of reason-giving that we find in much of the current renaissance of German idealism needs to be tempered and a more radical critique of reason be brought back to the table.

Notes

1 For parallel discussions of this trend, see Nicholas S. Smith (ed.) *Reading McDowell: On Mind and World* (London/New York: Routledge, 2002) and Katerina Deligiorgi (ed.) *Hegel: New Directions* (Chesham: Acumen, 2006). Other important studies include Karl Ameriks (ed.) *The Cambridge Companion to German Idealism* (Cambridge: Cambridge University Press, 2000); Karl Ameriks, *Kant and the Fate of Autonomy: Problems in the Appropriation of the Critical Philosophy* (Cambridge: Cambridge University Press, 2000); Sally Sedgwick (ed.) *The Reception of Kant's Critical Philosophy: Fichte, Schelling and Hegel* (Cambridge: Cambridge University Press, 2000); Andrew Bowie, *Aesthetics and Subjectivity from Kant to Nietzsche* (Manchester: Manchester University Press, 2003); Terry Pinkard, *Hegel's Phenomenology: The Sociality of Reason* (Cambridge: Cambridge University Press, 1994); Robert Pippin, *Idealism as Modernism: Hegelian Variations* (Cambridge: Cambridge University Press, 1997).

2 Robert Brandom formulates this point in more general terms. See his *Tales of the Mighty Dead: Historical Essays in the Metaphysics of Intentionality* (Cambridge, Mass.: Harvard University Press, 2002) p. 1:

> Analytic philosophy in its youth was viscerally hostile both to historical philosophical enterprises and to systematic ones. For that movement of thought initially defined itself in part by its recoil from the excesses of philosophical programs tracing their roots back to Hegel, for whom history and system jointly articulate the form of reason itself.

I encourage the reader to note that I refer to the origin of anglophone analytic philosophy and not to analytic philosophy as such. In his *Origins of Analytical*

Philosophy (Cambridge, Mass.: Harvard University Press, 1993) p. 1, Michael Dummett insists that 'a grave historical distortion arises from a prevalent modern habit of speaking of analytical philosophy as "Anglo-American". ... this terminology utterly distorts the historical context in which analytical philosophy came to birth, in the light of which it would better be called "Anglo-Austrian" than "Anglo-American".' See also Michael Beaney, *The Bonds of Sense: An Essay in the History of Analytic Philosophy* (Oxford: Oxford University Press, 1990).

3 See for example Peter Strawson's brusque remarks about Kant's doctrine of transcendental idealism in *The Bounds of Sense: An Essay on Kant's Critique of Pure Reason* (London: Methuen, 1966) p. 16. What Kant meant by this doctrine was that 'reality is supersensible and that we can have no knowledge of it' (ibid.). H.A. Prichard's comment in *Kant's Theory of Knowledge* (Oxford: Clarendon Press, 1909) pp. 78–79 is just as scathing. According to his interpretation, Kant makes knowledge impossible by rejecting that it means *to know something as it really is*.

4 Michael Rosen, a distinguished Hegel-scholar, sums up this sense when claiming that nothing is alive in Hegel's logic. See Rosen, *Hegel's Dialectic and Its Criticism* (Cambridge: Cambridge University Press, 1982) p. 179.

5 An influential statement of this view is Karl Popper, 'What is Dialectic?' in *Mind* 49 (1940) pp. 403–26. Popper ends the article with the following statement.

> The whole development of dialectic should be a warning against the dangers inherent in philosophical system-building. It should remind us that philosophy should not be made a basis for any sort of scientific system and that philosophers should be much more modest in their claims. One task which they can fulfill quite usefully is the study of the critical methods of science.

6 The writings of Stephen Stich and of Paul and Patricia Churchland have been particularly influential in this regard.

7 The history of modern French philosophy is again very different from both the Anglo-American and German traditions. In the aftermath of French neo-Kantianism, Hegel, mediated by Alexandre Kojéve, exerted a tremendous impact on the existentialist generation (Sartre, Merleau-Ponty and others). For the structuralist and poststructuralist generations (Lévi-Strauss, Foucault, Derrida and others), however, German idealism, and in particular Hegel, became the epitome of everything they wanted to reject. Recently, as the popularity of poststructuralism has been waning in France, there has been a strong upsurge of interest in Kant. For what may still be the best recounting of this development, see Vincent Descombes, *Modern French Philosophy*, trans. L. Scott-Fox (Cambridge: Cambridge University Press, 1980). See also Gary Gutting, *French Philosophy in the Twentieth Century* (Cambridge: Cambridge University Press, 2001).

8 Hilary Putnam, *Realism with a Human Face* (Cambridge, Mass.: Harvard University Press, 1990) p. 3.

9 John McDowell, *Mind and World* (Cambridge, Mass.: Cambridge University Press, 1994) p. ix.

10 John Rawls, 'Kantian Constructivism in Moral Theory', *Journal of Philosophy* 77 (1980) pp. 515–72.

11 Putnam, *Realism with a Human Face*, pp. 30–42 and *Reason, Truth and History* (Cambridge: Cambridge University Press, 1981); John McDowell, *Mind and World*, pp. 44–45.

12 Terry Pinkard, *German Philosophy 1760–1860: The Legacy of Idealism* (Cambridge: Cambridge University Press, 2002) p. 367.

13 Brandom is an exception. In *Tales of the Mighty Dead*, p. 111, he writes that:

the methodology pursued here is explicitly *reconstructive*. It approaches the conceptual contents of textual claims by a method of selection, supplementation, and approximation that locates those contents by means of a grid that, except in limiting cases, is always too coarse to place them exactly. A reading of this sort addresses a particular target set of claims, concepts, and distinctions. In all the essays considered here, that target includes some philosopher's claims about intentional or semantic phenomena, and the particular conceptual apparatus that philosopher deploys to discuss those phenomena. Picking out such a target may involve selection of passages and claims within the texts being considered.

14 Alasdair MacIntyre has argued that the kind of contrast I draw between historicism and anti-historicism is misleading: there is an alternative, which consists in acknowledging that conceptual and historical/empirical claims are largely inseparable. While I largely sympathize with this point, I do think it is instructive for the purpose of distinguishing between different contemporary orientations towards German idealism to draw this contrast. See MacIntyre, 'The Relationship of Philosophy to its Past', in Richard Rorty, J. B. Schneewind and Quentin Skinner (eds), *Philosophy in History* (Cambridge: Cambridge University Press, 1984) pp. 31–48.

15 Habermas outlines what he takes to be the similarities and the differences between their views in 'From Kant to Hegel: On Robert Brandom's Pragmatic Philosophy of Language', in Habermas, *Truth and Justification* (Cambridge, Mass.: MIT Press, 2003) pp. 131–74.

16 Richard Eldridge, *The Persistence of Romanticism: Essays in Philosophy and Literature* (Cambridge: Cambridge University Press, 2001).

Part I

German Idealism, Naturalism and Metaphysics

1

THE LIMITS OF NATURALISM AND THE METAPHYSICS OF GERMAN IDEALISM

Sebastian Gardner

'In einem schwankenden Zeitalter scheut man alles Absolute und Selbständige; deshalb mögen wir denn auch weder ächten Spaß, noch ächten Ernst, weder ächte Tugend noch ächte Bosheit mehr leiden.'

Nachtwachen von Bonaventura, Dritte Nachtwache

One issue above all forces itself on anyone attempting to make sense of the development of German idealism out of Kant. Is German idealism, in the full sense of the term, metaphysical? The wealth of new anglophone, chiefly North American, writing on German idealism, particularly on Hegel – characterized by remarkable depth, rigour, and creativity – has put the perennial question of German idealism's metaphysicality back under the spotlight, and in much of this new scholarship a negative answer is returned to the question.

Recent interpretation of German idealism owes much to the broader philosophical environment in which it has proceeded. Over recent decades analytic philosophy has enlarged its view of the discipline's scope and relaxed its conception of the methods appropriate to philosophical enquiry, and in parallel to this development analytically trained philosophers have returned to the history of philosophy, the study of which is now regarded by many as a legitimate and important (perhaps even necessary) form of philosophical enquiry. At the same time, it remains the case that the kinds of philosophical positions most intensively worked on and argued about in non-historical, systematic analytic philosophy are predominantly naturalistic – and thus, on the face of it, not in any immediate and obvious sense receptive to the central ideas of German idealism. A primary impulse in recent work on German idealism has been, however, to indicate the consonance, unobvious though it may be, between German idealism, or portions thereof, and some of the leading strands in major systematic positions explored and defended within analytic philosophy. Characteristic of interpretations of German idealism exhibiting this tendency are claims such as the following: that the apparent baroque speculative metaphysics of German idealism, correctly understood, amounts to a richness of conceptual explanatory apparatus that is altogether innocent of the postulation of supernatural entities; that the ontological commitments of German idealism are no different from those of many contemporary naturalistic positions, and perhaps even compatible with a robust physicalism; that the relation of German idealism to religious ways of thinking, superficial appearances to the contrary, is no more intimate than that of many analytic naturalisms; that one of the essential, defining insights and metaphilosophical principles of German idealism consists in the idea that normativity is irreducible and occupies a position of ultimate explanatory priority; that the fundamental motor of German idealism lies in the concern to validate and give adequate form to and validate the modern conception of individual autonomy, a post-theocentric concern which is ours just as much as that of German thinkers in the 1790s and 1800s; that German idealism is to a great extent a radical deepening and extension of Kant's Copernican revolution (or 'epistemological turn'), the necessity of which (in some form) as a corrective to naive empiricism, is widely accepted in the later analytic tradition; that, in a similar fashion, German idealism pursues Kant's thesis of the primacy of practical reason, in a way that makes a crucial and favourable difference to the meaning of its apparently metaphysically formulated claims, and which forges a direct connection with the American pragmatist tradition; that in any case the contributions of German idealism to moral, political and social theory stand independently from its putative metaphysics; and so forth. The notion that in these ways and others German idealism can be shown to provide a significant historical resource for progressive, non-metaphysical contemporary philosophical developments has provided a powerful stimulus to the flowering of recent scholarship in that area.[1]

Accordingly, one task is to measure the new interpretations of the German idealists at the level of historically informed close textual exegesis. My intention here is, instead, to attempt to put the new development in perspective by taking a step back and offering a critical view of certain leading elements in our present philosophical situation, which has in turn, I will suggest, direct relevance for our understanding of German idealism. What I am supposing therefore for present purposes, in accordance with proponents of the new interpretations of German idealism themselves, is that what should be taken to count for us as the correct interpretation of German idealism is not something that need be determined altogether by the texts and historical data taken in independence from critical reflection on our present philosophical situation: in other words, that we should not seek to isolate the task of answering such questions as that of in what sense German idealism is metaphysical, from the task of determining what our present philosophical orientation should be, just as, conversely, German idealism (and all other historical resources) should contribute to forming that orientation.[2]

The end of idealism and the ascent of naturalism

To begin, I want to engage in a brief historical exercise, to set our present philosophical situation in relief by drawing the contrast with the outlook that prevailed at the beginning of the twentieth century. To bring alive the historical fact of the extraordinary transformation in the philosophical landscape of the English-speaking world over the last hundred years, a now little read but highly pertinent paper by Norman Kemp Smith serves well.

In 'The present situation in philosophy', his inaugural lecture at Edinburgh in 1919, Kemp Smith gives a universal typology of philosophical positions, and explains how, in his view, the balance of argument lies between them.

There are, in Kemp Smith's account, only three basic types of philosophical position: 'idealism', 'naturalism', and 'skepticism'. Naturalism he defines as the view that 'man is a being whose capacities, even in their highest activities, are intelligible only as exercised *exclusively in subordination* to the specific requirements of his *terrestrial* environment'.[3] Idealism by contrast treats man as a 'microcosm' of a larger reality and measures him 'against standards for which it [man's natural environment] cannot account'.[4] Its 'supreme concern is to show that the aesthetic and spiritual values have a more than merely human significance', and that 'intellectual and spiritual values' – where intellectual means: pertaining to theoretical reason – 'stand on the same plane of objectivity, and thereby justify parity of treatment'.[5] Idealism, he says, is 'probably the philosophy of the great majority of men',[6] and Kemp Smith considers that the overall tendency in the history of philosophy has been towards it.[7] Skepticism – which Kemp Smith also calls 'agnosticism', and under which heading he includes also nineteenth-century positivism – is a kind of pseudo-position, not on a par with idealism and naturalism: it has, he says, no 'engine-power' and is 'at most, a kind of Greek chorus, commenting ironically on the course of the action'.[8] It has affinities with both naturalism and idealism – with the former because it leads smoothly into the view that '[t]hought is an instrument developed through natural processes for the practical purposes of adaptation',[9] and with the latter because it upholds a distinction of reality and appearance which opens the way to 'idealist teaching'. Skepticism thus resolves itself ultimately, according to Kemp Smith, into either naturalism or idealism.

So it is the great antagonism between idealism and naturalism that lies at the heart of all philosophy, and here there has been, Kemp Smith thinks, some change: whereas until recently idealism predominated, by virtue of its appeal to 'moral, social, religious' considerations, the nineteenth century (through the growth that it witnessed of the human sciences) has seen the development of a 'very greatly strengthened' naturalistic position that 'can now profess to meet idealism on more equal terms within its own field, that of our specifically human activities'.[10] This fortified naturalism is further strengthened by having shed its positivistic elements: it now 'claims to be realistic', 'dealing with reality' not in the manner of Mill or Huxley but 'as apprehending it face to face'.[11]

However, the opposition remains as sharp as ever: the naturalist holds that we are parts of the Universe which are simply 'more complex', 'more completely unified than is the Universe as a whole', while the idealist interprets the Universe as a whole in the light of this 'part'.[12] And although the decision between naturalism and idealism has become marginally less easy to make, Kemp Smith considers that idealism retains its edge, for two reasons, both having to do with values. First, because naturalism must hold that our values *have* value 'only by reference to the detailed contingencies of terrestrial existence',[13] only idealism is compatible with the claim for their absoluteness. He writes: 'Now since the only basis upon which idealism can rest this far-reaching conclusion' – namely that man (purposive self-consciousness) is the model for grasping the Universe as a whole – 'is the contention that spiritual no less than intellectual criteria have an absolute validity, idealism must stand or fall according to its success or failure in upholding this latter position, in face of the counter-arguments of the naturalistic philosophies.'[14] Second, Kemp Smith believes that the best that naturalism can achieve is a sideways-on view of values: the naturalists, he says, 'keep their eyes off the human values' in so far as they 'approach them only through the study of our natural and economic setting, or through analogies derived from the study of animal behaviour', with the result that 'they do not study them at all'.[15] The two criticisms are of course connected: Kemp Smith believes that to take a non-sideways-on view of values, to look them in the face, *is* to view them as absolute, as beyond all natural contingency.

Kemp Smith's outlook was in its day quite the opposite of idiosyncratic. The era which he represents was at the time of his lecture fast disintegrating – only three years later Roy Wood Sellars would write: 'we are all naturalists now'[16] – but it had enjoyed a remarkable hegemony. As the philosophical journals of the period show very clearly, British and American philosophers had for several decades shared exactly Kemp Smith's view of the philosophical geography.[17]

The nature of the historical change is therefore clear: once upon a time idealism seemed without doubt philosophically superior to naturalism, whereas we now think, more or less, the exact opposite. Indeed, our conviction of the correctness of naturalism is so well entrenched that Kemp Smith's broad category of naturalism is no longer particularly meaningful for us: for us it does not pick out a unified philosophical outlook but merely points towards a wide variety of differentiated positions which, we would say, have it in common just that they reject supernaturalism and restrict metaphysics to explicating empirical theory of the natural order.[18] In order to give the term naturalism, or naturalization, a job to do, it has become common to use it much more narrowly than Kemp Smith, with the result that at least some of the arguments that now go on between self-described naturalists and anti-naturalists look, from Kemp Smith's point of view, like arguments within the naturalistic camp. Similarly, the term 'idealism' hardly serves any longer for us, as it did for Kemp Smith, to express a unified philosophical programme worth speaking of under one heading – we do not find it helpful to suppose that a single philosophical thought is working itself out in the history of philosophy from Plato through Berkeley to Kant and the German and British idealists.

In this way, the victory of what Kemp Smith means by naturalism has been followed by a kind of self-effacement: because naturalism in its own eyes contrasts with nothing philosophically significant, the designation ceases to express a credo and falls away. From Kemp Smith's point of view, however, this is a mistake: it is as if naturalism has sought to consummate its victory by concealing it, by dissolving the concepts needed to express what was at issue in its original struggle with idealism.

Recognition of the extraordinary contrast between how the philosophical world looked a hundred years ago and how it looks to us now raises the question of what it was exactly that came to persuade philosophers that idealism in fact possesses none of the strengths supposed by the generations for whom Kemp Smith speaks. There is no space to argue the point here, but I suggest that it is very plausible to regard idealism as having faded out of anglophone philosophy without having ever been expelled by force of argument: the new logical apparatus and method of conceptual analysis opened up possibilities that called to be explored, and this was felt to require a clean break with the existing idealist establishment, which had become complacent and uncreative, but idealist philosophy was not *refuted* by logical discoveries or application of the method of analysis. A proper critique of idealism would have required a detailed reconstruction of idealist philosophy, which is just what no longer seemed worthy of attention.[19] This point, assuming it to be correct, should lead us to reconsider the perspective articulated by Kemp Smith. Can we recapture the philosophical state of mind that gives idealism the authority it had for him?

The axiological problems of naturalism

A crucial component of Kemp Smith's outlook is his view of naturalism as incompatible with the claims of value. The subject of naturalism and value is of course very large, but for the purpose of retrieving the motivation for Kemp Smith's outlook it will suffice to concentrate on some relatively obvious historical points.

What should first be recalled is a basic historical fact about the experience of naturalism, namely that throughout the greater part of the modern period, naturalism was thought to present an immediate intellectual threat. Reconceiving ourselves as parts of the natural order, relating to ourselves in the way that we relate to natural objects, involves, it was felt, a profound self-devaluation. In the seventeenth century, the term 'naturalist' was employed most frequently to signify a willingness to think the unthinkable. Nor was this just the view of theists. Proponents of naturalism *themselves* accepted that the basic *prima facie* axiological meaning of naturalization is negative: an acceptance of human devaluation is present in writings by naturalists all the way from la Mettrie and d'Holbach to Freud, who states that psychoanalysis administers to the human ego the third blow of humiliation, following those delivered by Copernicus and Darwin (and Darwin himself had said the same of his own discoveries).[20]

In addition to emphasizing all of the compensating material and social goods to be delivered by a scientifically orientated culture, naturalists have sought to turn the devaluative impact of naturalism to their own advantage, suggesting that the blow to our self-esteem is not simply epistemically needful but also salutary, of moral benefit.[21] Thus la Mettrie argues that humbling ourselves through the doctrine that we are machines is a commendable, indeed a thoroughly Christian exercise of self-abnegation. Freud does something analogous, suggesting that the psychoanalytic naturalization of the human personality is a step out of narcissistic immaturity towards psychological *Aufklärung*. Nietzsche tells us that returning to the hard text of *homo natura* is a necessary first step towards the recovery of health. Even Hume, who is almost completely comfortable with the implications of naturalism for morality, acknowledges that there is a case to be answered, and his reply to the lover of virtue, Francis Hutcheson, is that the Humean account of morality in terms of sympathy at least shows morality's inescapability – Hume urges Hutcheson to exchange his sense of the dignity of value for an assurance of its psychologically binding motivational power.

In connection with this observation, I want to indicate two historical patterns which stand out when we consider in general terms the relation of naturalism to value.

The first is the increased *independence of theoretical reason* from practical reason in the account which is given of the justificatory basis of naturalism. In the case of the materialist *philosophes*, naturalism is presented in a *visionary* spirit – as heralding a new era, as the road to the Good. This dimension is regarded, furthermore, as *essential* to the appeal of naturalism – without this connection to the Good, it is not supposed that the argument against anti-naturalism, against religion, could be won. By the time we get to Freud, however, let alone Quine, naturalism is conceived as resting *exclusively* on theoretical reason and as *immune* to non-theoretical attack – it is assumed that nothing *could* be shown regarding the axiological implications of naturalism that would give us reason to reconsider our commitment to it: we have ceased to think that naturalism is essential for the realization of our interest in value, and do not believe that it would be an option for us to reject naturalism even if it were to prove thoroughly inimical to our value-interests.[22]

The second pattern relates to a well-recognized difficulty which is encountered in the naturalistic explanation of value, especially moral value. Naturalism tends to do one of two things. *Either* value is resolved by the naturalist into something that has ready and immediate empirical intelligibility, typically pleasure or desire-satisfaction. This form of value-naturalism is associated with optimism regarding the prospect of human fulfilment. *Or* alternatively, and conversely associated with a pessimistic outlook, naturalism generates explanations of value that refer to complex psychological, social, biological-evolutionary, etc., causal processes, the discovery of which is dependent upon empirical theory, and which are remote from ordinary axiological understanding – as in Nietzschean, Freudian and neo-Darwinian explanations of morality. Naturalism is thus constantly threatened with missing the mark in one of two opposite ways: either the naturalistic account of value is too shallow to be credible as a reconstruction of our pre-philosophical understanding of value, or its account of value is deep but in a way that is alien to and undermines our axiological self-understanding. The historical shift has been from the salience of the former case to that of the latter: while there is a strong association of earlier naturalism with utilitarianism, when contemporary naturalism makes itself felt in thinking about morality, it is in connection with theory-driven causal explanations of value which carry *prima facie* revisionary implications.

The second pattern is of course related closely to the first: as naturalism becomes increasingly the property of theoretical rather than practical reason, its non-attunement with ordinary views of value comes to the fore.

The next point to be made is that, it seems fair to say, we have ceased to be much preoccupied with the axiological character of naturalism *in general*: we argue about the cogency of particular attempts to naturalize moral and other species of value, but we do not pose the question of what naturalism *as such* implies regarding the very possibility of value *as such*.

This may be brought out by attending to Dewey, who began his philosophical career as a Hegelian and who shares with the earlier founders of American pragmatism a keen appreciation of the attractions of idealism. In an influential critique of contemporary idealism published in the *Philosophical Review* for 1906, 'Experience and objective idealism', Dewey accepts that the issue of value is paramount. Like Kemp Smith, Dewey recognizes idealism as a unified tradition which goes back to Plato yet receives its optimal formulation in modern neo-Hegelian idealism, and regards idealism's claim to be able to do justice to the existence of purpose and value in experience as one of its cornerstones. Dewey argues accordingly, not just that idealism fails in this regard (its a priori structures are, he claims, conceived incoherently), but that the 'thoroughgoing empiricism' which he recommends in its stead is able to show that the 'one constant trait of experience from its crudest to its most mature forms is that its contents undergo change of meaning, and of meaning in the sense of excellence, value'.[23]

This feature of Dewey's engagement with idealism makes his outlook remote from that of the present day, for Dewey *accepts* that the philosophical authority of naturalism is conditional upon what service it renders to our interest in inhabiting a world in which we can take value to be realized, and believes that our value-orientation is in fact what most gives us reason to be naturalistic. Dewey thus belongs to the tradition of humanistic, Enlightenment, value-grounded naturalism which holds, with d'Holbach and la Mettrie, that our value-interests *alone* make it rationally necessary to think of ourselves as natural through-and-through.[24] Our present view, by contrast, is that naturalism is a *fait accompli*, setting limits to what we can allow ourselves to think, the only question which remains being that of how much of the value-riddled 'manifest image' can be retained alongside or within the scientific image and on what sorts of terms – naturalism functions in present anglophone philosophy as a default and restraining presupposition.

The purpose of drawing attention to this historical change is to bring to light the deep alteration that has occurred in our view of what needs to be, and what can be, argued for in this context. One who these days objects to moral naturalism is obliged to identify some feature of moral thinking that makes it conceptually resistant to naturalistic analysis, while on the earlier outlook, reflected in Kemp Smith's claim that values are 'absolute', it is taken as an immediate philosophical datum, virtually an axiom, that a deep axiological problem surrounds the *bare idea* that our metaphysical status is that of a natural object. On the earlier view, the notion that we are in essence of a kind with the objects that we experience as composing nature is held to be axiologically problematic quite apart from whatever more concrete, more technical problems may face particular forms of ethical, aesthetic, etc. naturalism. These latter, relatively shallower problems are ones that naturalists are prepared to countenance as *prima facie* challenges for their position, and they allow themselves to be argued about; the existence of the deeper axiological problem, by contrast, cannot be argued for from 'neutral' premises that the naturalist could accept.[25]

What I now wish to suggest is that, just as the replacement of idealism by naturalism is not a historical development underwritten by philosophical reason, the same is true, connectedly and in parallel, of the development whereby naturalism has come to be experienced as axiologically acceptable. On the view which naturalists themselves take, this process has been one of the continued adjustment of our ideas about ourselves to the facts that we discover about reality: the experience of naturalization is like that of waking from a dream, where the initial discomfort of confronting hard reality fades along with the dreams of the night and is rewarded eventually by the bright daylight of reason and reality. On the opposing view, that of Kemp Smith, the process appears rather as one of desensitization, a kind of forgetting, which may be supposed to operate at two levels. Outside philosophical reflection, it occurs through a sort of *dissociation* – we accept a high degree of naturalism in our official conceptual or *reflective* self-representation, while *living as* non-natural beings. (Thereby fulfilling a prediction of Nietzsche's, who suggested that we may evolve 'a double brain', 'one to experience science and one to experience nonscience'.[26]) Precisely because the non-naturalistic dimension of our self-experience is deeply buried in the fabric of unreflected life, it is easy for us to overlook it in reflection. Second, on a philosophical plane, it occurs through the absence of any *determinate* conception of an alternative. Because the determinate forms of non-naturalistic conception suggested by the history of philosophy (early modern metaphysics, Cartesian dualism, Kantian noumenalism) appear at most a hair's breadth away from religious supernaturalism, a non-naturalistic conception appears possible only in so far as it is *in*determinate, and this indeterminacy then gets converted into a conviction of the *emptiness* of any non-naturalistic alternative. Once it is accepted in the theoretical sphere that naturalism must be true, it appears pointless to ask whether or not naturalism is axiologically possible at the deeper level which is of concern to Kemp Smith.

I think this allows us to recapture the state of mind evidenced by Kemp Smith when he refuses to countenance the idea that values might have a sufficient explanation in 'the detailed contingencies of terrestrial existence': we should regard his statement that our values are 'absolute' not as a contentious, metaphysically inflated claim, but simply as a reiteration of the longstanding negative view of the feasibility of naturalism from an axiological point of view.

It will be clear that nothing that has been said by way of elucidation of Kemp Smith's attitude counts in any sense as a *proof* that our value-interests extend beyond what any naturalism can satisfy – my intention has been only to indicate that a question mark may be put over the assumption that they *can* be satisfied by naturalism. The naturalist may of course respond by drawing a distinction between *extravagant* and *moderate* demands in the sphere of value, insisting that once we have achieved maturity – once we have stopped asking for heaven on earth, once it has been realized that the death of God is a problem only in adolescence – we will be able to appreciate how moderate value-demands, at least, can be satisfied within naturalism. I believe this is a common view. My observation is just that it is deeply unclear how we should set about measuring our value-needs and determining whether the recommendation of moderation makes sense, and that the historical record supports the idea that there is a puzzle here which contemporary naturalism cannot really be said to have engaged with. Nevertheless, when all is said, it is true that the existence of the deeper axiological issue which motivates Kemp Smith cannot be established conclusively, and for that reason, although it is imperative that we continue to remain aware of how deep the problem of value for naturalism may go, no account of our present interest in German idealism should rely directly or exclusively on it.

The limits of naturalism

Whether or not the deeper axiological problem is agreed to be genuine, there is in any case acceptance on the part of many within the naturalistic camp that at *some* level there is a problem to be faced regarding naturalism's implications for value. This brings us to an important distinction which has been conspicuously missing from the discussion so far. Up until now I have, following Kemp Smith's map of the terrain, left out of the account the various kinds of contemporary position which describe themselves as naturalistic whilst opposing themselves sharply to naturalism's reductionist, physicalist, scientistic, scientific-realist forms.[27] What is called rich, non-reductive, or soft naturalism formulates itself in reaction against the presumption that nature consists of nothing but the hard physical bare-bones of things: it presents itself as correcting what it regards as an overly restrictive, unnecessarily austere conception of the natural order which other naturalists have, mistakenly, extrapolated from natural science. By relaxing the boundaries of the natural it tries to show that, appearances to the contrary, there is nothing within naturalistic commitment *as such* that threatens the value-interests of natural consciousness. We can have 'symphonies as well as atoms', as one naturalist put it.[28] According to this outlook, given that we must be naturalists of some sort, our value-interests give us reason to be soft naturalists.

The issue of soft naturalism is potentially decisive for our attitude towards German idealism. If its prospects are good, then it is highly plausible that Kemp Smith and the other idealists of his generation were wrong to draw up the battle lines in their exclusive, either-idealism-or-naturalism fashion, and at the same time, that the new interpreters of German idealism are right to downplay the metaphysical commitments of German idealism and to propose German idealism as a resource for contemporary soft naturalists to draw on.[29] Now the exploration and defence of soft naturalist possibilities is central to contemporary philosophical enquiry, and can hardly be said to be heading towards a negative conclusion. Nevertheless, I think that reasons can be given for thinking that there are limitations to what can be achieved in its sphere. To begin, two preliminary observations.

First, it is important to recognize that the originally negative or reactive character of soft naturalism, its formulation as a *correction* to hard naturalism, is not accidental to it. This will be seen to have implications for how the burden of argument is divided. Soft naturalism qualifies *as* naturalism because it rejects speculative metaphysics, and the ultimate historical source of this rejection can be nothing other than modern philosophy's incorporation of the great epistemological achievement of natural science. In this sense the starting point of soft naturalism, as much as that of hard naturalism, is the conception of nature that arises out of natural science, and it is safe to say that, ever since the disappearance of romantic *Naturphilosophie*, this conception can only be an austere one. Soft naturalism thus accepts the priority of at least the *appearance* that nature has of being intrinsically value-indifferent, and it takes its initial bearings from this apparently authoritative starting point, even as it subsequently rejects it. This is not to say anything the soft naturalist will disagree with but merely to describe how soft naturalism comes to enter the field of philosophical debate. It means, however, that as a consequence of the primacy of hard naturalism, in the sense just explained, soft naturalism has its work cut out for it: what it needs to do is persuade us that it is not *merely* a negatively defined position, that it amounts to *more* than a mere statement of the *obstacles* to hard naturalism, which can claim to express the initial, default trajectory given to philosophy by natural science.

The second and related observation is that the distinction between soft and hard naturalism is for us well articulated, and that we are highly sensitized to the danger of fudging the issue by merely stipulating a harmony between the *Lebenswelt* and reality as disclosed by natural science. Dewey throws this feature of present-day philosophical consciousness into relief. Much in Dewey's statements of his position initially seems to resonate with contemporary soft naturalism, but closer examination reveals that Dewey is not a good advertisement for its coherence. Dewey's claim is that it is in the very nature of experience to form ever higher 'unities', which, simply in virtue of being unities, possess *value*, in the strongest sense. Yet the ground of this tendency to unity and value is, on Dewey's account, baldly Darwinian – biological functions take the place of the idealists' a priori metaphysics. Dewey talks as if it is no surprise to discover in nature the very same kind of purposiveness that we claim for human activity. We think, however, that he ought to be surprised at this fact, if it is one.[30] This is why the generation of American naturalists to which Dewey belongs, and for whom Dewey was the leading figure, looks to us now a mere phase in the development of anglophone naturalism, in which the naturalistic impulse had announced but not yet clarified itself.

We can now ask how the two forms of naturalism compare with respect to basic philosophical plausibility, and what soft naturalism can say in criticism of hard naturalism or regarding its own advantages, in order that we should prefer it.

To begin I want to consider briefly the argumentative resources available to soft naturalism. Usually soft naturalism seeks to establish itself by means of anti-reductionist arguments, and this strategy raises several questions.

In the first place, the criteria for reducibility need to be considered. If reducibility is what is to decide between soft and hard naturalism, then the two forms of naturalism need to agree what considerations count as relevant to determining whether or not a given phenomenon is reducible to the bald natural facts privileged by the hard naturalist. But if that is so, then it seems that the substantial, doctrinal disagreement between the two kinds of naturalism will inevitably show up methodologically, as an argument over criteria, over what does and does not count as relevant to determining reducibility. And if it is not possible to design criteria which will avoid begging questions, and yet also allow determinate conclusions to be reached, then anti-reductionist arguments will not suffice to establish soft naturalism securely. To the extent that the incumbent, default conception of nature is the austere one, this outcome is to the disadvantage of soft naturalism.

Second, there is the question of what exactly is, or would be, achieved in any case through a successful demonstration of irreducibility. The hard naturalist holds that the reality of phenomena in the *Lebenswelt* – those that do have genuine reality – derives from the hard natural facts to which they reduce, while these facts derive their reality in turn from the nature of the basic stuff or structure that exhausts reality. Hard naturalism thereby answers the metaphysical question concerning what gives the phenomena their reality and what this reality consists of. If, then, it is demonstrated successfully by the soft naturalist that such-and-such a phenomenon is not reducible to the natural facts austerely conceived, this conclusion is *not an end* of the enquiry, but rather a *reaffirmation* of an explanandum, i.e. a restatement that the phenomenon stands in need of metaphysical explanation. Irreducibility arguments, if successful, yield *data* that do not interpret or explain themselves, but call for interpretation: the soft naturalist needs to say something on the subject of *why there should be, in general*, phenomena that have substantial reality, but do not owe it to the hard natural facts. Conclusions of irreducibility cannot stand without further, vindicatory interpretation, and the issue for soft naturalism is where this can come from.[31] The idealist has to hand an independently formed, positive and contentful concept of the status to be accorded to phenomena that have been shown to be irreducible to the hard natural facts, which can play this role.[32] The soft naturalist is not in the same position. And it should be plain that for the soft naturalist to answer here, that the reality of irreducibles 'derives from the natural order broadly conceived', would be to merely draw attention to the further difficulty facing soft naturalism, of specifying the principle of unity of this order.

Soft naturalists have a strategy which is relevant in response to these points, which I will come to in a moment, but if, as I will argue, it proves ineffective, then the limited force of anti-reductionist argumentation remains a serious problem for soft naturalism.

The point just made concerning the unity of nature raises a further issue of considerable importance. Hard naturalism converts the epistemological privilege of modern natural science into a philosophical position which is 'as good as metaphysical' in the sense of securing completeness of explanation in principle; it enjoys the formal advantages of a monistic metaphysical system, exemplifying, as Hegel appreciated, the virtues of Spinozism.[33] In addition, hard naturalism gains through evolutionary theory the capacity to ground itself epistemologically, and may even claim to be in the Kantian sense a thoroughly 'Critical' philosophy.[34] There are several things that hard naturalism need not assume in order for it to be able to lay claim to these virtues, and these are all points commonly made by proponents of hard naturalism, in response to critics who charge it with implausibility. To rehearse some of the most important: Hard naturalism need not subscribe to any doctrine that presupposes a closed concept of the physical, nor take any particularly demanding view of the unity of science; it need not suppose that the different sciences will ever actually form an absolute unity, nor that, if this goal of ultimate completion is not achieved, we will be able to explain why we have not achieved it. Finite natural creatures need not expect to be able to nail down natural reality comprehensively. What is essential for hard naturalism is only the regulative or methodological thought that all of the sciences should be understood as converging on one and the same complete theory, conforming to the broad pattern of explaining bigger things in terms of smaller things, forming interfaces between theories and seeking integration in ways that will allow maximally continuous lines of explanation to run from the smallest things to the biggest things, and so on. No significant difference is made to the trajectory or standing of hard naturalism by the peculiarities of quantum mechanics or cosmological discoveries, nor by the complexities of the relation between the organic and inorganic realms.

The position of soft naturalism is very different. It seems both essential that it should provide some positive and contentful characterization of the natural order – of that which it identifies as the overarching unity containing both the objects of natural science and the objects which hard naturalism excludes: the genuine whole and order of things to which it says we belong – and at the same time very difficult to see how it can provide this. Without it, however, the hard naturalist will understandably object that soft naturalism is a non-naturalistic position under a misleading name. The overarching characterization will, furthermore, need to be accompanied by an explanation for why the unitary natural order should be such as to exhibit a split, between the entities that natural science can get hold of and those that it cannot. Put slightly differently: to designate reality as nature creates *prima facie* the expectation that nature is to be understood as 'tightly' as possible, not directly on account of any metaphysical commitment such as to materialism, but because of the difficulty of seeing how the affirmation that something is gained for explanation by designating reality as nature can be combined with a denial that interests of explanation require nature to be conceived in hard naturalistic terms. Soft naturalism does not contest the intelligibility of a natural order conceived in the terms of hard naturalism: it does not deny that there could be such a thing as the physical order without human subjects to occupy it, rather it grants that the austere concept of nature comprises a totality complete in itself, and its departure from this picture consists in *adding* items not implied by the hard physical totality. This means that what it calls 'nature' cannot amount to a totality of the same, non-aggregative sort as that of the hard naturalist.[35] (Idealism, by contrast, is able to posit a complete totality, one that includes the items that the soft naturalist wishes to include in nature.) This leaves a tension between the monistic tendency which soft naturalism derives from its being a *naturalism*, and the pluralism needed to rationalize its merely aggregative conception of the totality of what it calls nature.

Soft naturalists are aware that they cannot hope to match the formal virtues of hard naturalism. Their response is to decline to compete on traditional grounds of systematic unity and completeness of explanation and to propose a different view of the demands of philosophical explanation, invoking meta-philosophical or methodological principles which allow philosophical explanation to legitimately call a halt at an earlier point than the hard naturalist supposes is permissible. Typically appeal is made to a conception of philosophical enquiry as having a broadly descriptive or phenomenological goal, in relation to which, it is claimed, the entities excluded by hard naturalism qualify as real;

or to allegedly inescapable necessities of representation, which are said to underpin our attribution of reality to the disputed phenomena and to override the explanatory considerations pressed by the hard naturalist. In addition, soft naturalists characteristically claim the adequacy of the modest, conservative, apologetic philosophical aim of defending our commonsensical convictions against objections.[36] All of these are essentially different formulations of a single idea, namely that philosophical vindication of the phenomena can be provided by something other than ontological grounding and which instead involves essential reference to the subject or to a 'perspective' relative to which internal, perspectival reality can be claimed for the phenomena.[37] In this way the soft naturalist hopes to persuade us that the point at which soft naturalist explanation ends, is one at which the demand for further explanation, whether it comes from the hard naturalist or from the supernaturalist, is ill-conceived, reflecting an illusion of unfilled explanatory space.[38] For this reason, soft naturalists do not regard irreducibility arguments as limited in their significance in the way that, I suggested, the hard naturalist must view them as being.

The soft naturalist's perspectival, explanation-circumscribing conception is exposed to several sorts of criticism. The first focuses on the tension created within soft naturalism by its weakening of the demands of philosophical explanation. The rationale of soft naturalism lies in its insistence on the reality of phenomena that it regards hard naturalism as putting in jeopardy, and this makes less sense if the conception of reality claimed by soft naturalism is weakened in the profound way implied by the repudiation of a need for ontological grounds. Thus while the original motivation of soft naturalism suggests that it accepts the traditional conception of the task of philosophy as furnishing sufficient legitimating grounds, the resort to perspective appears to withdraw from that conception, obscuring the intention of metaphysical vindication.

This can be seen more concretely by considering hard naturalist responses to the various ways in which the soft naturalist specifies the perspectival conception. If the reality claimed by soft naturalism for its objects bears the qualification 'as determined by descriptive or phenomenological enquiry', then what it offers an account *of* is ultimately, in relation to the harder reality claimed by hard naturalism for its natural-scientific ontology, mere *appearance*: the soft/hard naturalism opposition resolves itself, it will be claimed, into an appearance/reality contrast, and the argument is at an end, with hard naturalism as the victor. Similarly, the soft naturalist idea of default to common sense involves, it will be objected, a misreading of how the debate stands: the hard naturalist has precisely raised a question mark over the identification of common sense rather than natural science *as* the default position, so the issue cannot be decided merely by reasserting common sense as the measure of reality. The hard naturalist, after all, does not allow common sense and science to merely contradict one another, but offers accounts of why common sense receives the appearances that it does: there will be a hard naturalist explanation for the manifest image of the world, which will subsume it under the scientific. Again, regarding any appeal by the soft naturalist to necessities of representation, it will need to be said what sort of ground these are envisaged as having, whether empirical or trans-empirical.[39] The latter seems immediately and unacceptably idealistic, but the former takes us back to the interpretation of soft naturalism as concerned with mere appearance and can again be accommodated by the hard naturalist.

More generally, a question mark hangs over the soft naturalist's employment of the concept of perspective. When soft naturalism rationalizes itself in this way, it commits itself to endorsing, as coherent and valid, a form of explanation which is susceptible to a great deal of further development, which it of course receives in the hands of the idealist. In order to preserve its distance from idealism, soft naturalism must ensure that its employment of the concept of perspective is kept as metaphysically light as possible, and this creates a problem. Consider the following application of the perspective idea by P. F. Strawson, in the context of a discussion of the apparent conflict of the perspective of scientific determinism with that of human responsibility:

> the error lies ... in the attempt to force the choice between them. The question was: From which standpoint do we see things as they really are? and it carried the implication that the answer cannot be: from both. It is this implication that I want to dispute ... the appearance of contradiction arises only if we assume the existence of some metaphysically absolute standpoint ... But there is no such superior standpoint – or none that we know of; it is the idea of such a standpoint that is the illusion ... We can recognize, in our conception of the real, a reasonable relativity to standpoints that we do know and can occupy.[40]

Jennifer Hornsby, another philosopher working within the Strawsonian soft naturalist tradition, defends the autonomy of personal level explanation by appealing to a conception of the philosophy of mind as an essentially *reflexive* form of enquiry, in contrast with the *non*-reflexive character of philosophy of *psychology*: answers to questions in the philosophy of mind, Hornsby says, 'are meant to cast some light on ourselves (on persons), and on our place in the world'.[41]

The appeal to perspective or reflexivity, I suggest, in both cases cancels itself out. Strawson's claim is of course not just that our powers of representation are conditioned differently in different contexts: the soft naturalist's claim is one about the *reality* of objects of representation and the metaphysical value of our powers of representation. So even though Strawson rejects 'the existence of some metaphysically absolute standpoint' as an illusion, he nevertheless reverts to a higher perspective, which, whether 'metaphysically absolute' or not, is what allows it to be seen that our existence has this dual-perspective structure (ordinary and scientific) and *from which* it can be affirmed that the objects of *both* perspectives are *equally* real. And this is essential for soft naturalism to offer itself as a rival form of naturalism: if the soft naturalist did not claim knowledge of 'our place in the world' – if he did not lay claim to a perspective on our perspectives, through which the latter are validated – then he would not be contradicting the hard naturalist. The reflexive move – the reference back to the reality of such-and-such to *our* concepts, *our* practices, taken on their own – thus misses the point: the hard naturalist will reasonably reply that it is not in doubt that our concepts and practices weigh with *us*, but that the whole issue concerns what it *means*, in the *overall* scheme of things, for something to be a practice of ours. What are *we*, the hard naturalist asks, such that the fact of a representational practice's being ours is supposed to raise its status, not merely in the trivial sense of its having status in *our* eyes, but in the sense of its ranking alongside the hard reality of natural science. The metaphysical significance of the soft naturalist's use of the first person plural has to be *shown*, not merely asserted.

Exactly this point is made eloquently by Hume, in the different but analogous context of the argument from design. Hume objects that, without a prior assurance of our own supernatural status for which deism would need to be presupposed, the deist's selection of *thought* as the basis or archetype of the design of the cosmos is arbitrary and unjustified:

> But allowing that we were to take the *operations* of one part of nature upon another for the foundation of our judgement concerning the *origin* of the whole [. . .], yet why select so minute, so weak, so bounded a principle as the reason and design of animals is found to be on this planet? What peculiar privilege has this little agitation of the brain which we call *thought*, that we must thus make it the model of the whole universe?[42]

The soft naturalist's attribution of metaphysical significance to our conceptual needs and practices parallels exactly the attribution of importance to thought by the deist; the soft naturalist is attempting, as it were, to run the argument from design on ourselves.

If this is correct, then soft naturalists are not entitled to appeal to perspective in order to support their affirmative view of the force of irreducibility arguments.

One important dimension of the disadvantage at which soft naturalism finds itself in the argument with hard naturalism concerns the handling of axiological considerations. The original motive for soft naturalism, as I introduced it, was axiological, but if the soft naturalist does appeal to axiological motives in the argument with hard naturalism, then it will be necessary to clarify how these are to be taken as operating: Is the reason for taking axiological motives as a ground for favouring soft over hard naturalism, that there actually *are* axiological facts in the natural world, or does it lie just in our *interest* in reality's being such as to contain such facts? The hard naturalist will be moved by neither claim: the first begs the question of there actually being such facts, while the second is philosophically irrelevant (it concerns merely the wishes of a piece of organized matter). So it seems that, although soft naturalism is axiologically motivated, it cannot represent itself *as* being so motivated in its engagement with hard naturalism. Again, this goes back to its originally reactive character: the soft naturalist began with a conception of the natural order shaped by natural science, and then tried to *expand* it to include value; he did not work *from* a prior, rich conception of nature, *to* the reality of value. The idealist, by contrast, is able to legitimate the axiological motivation of his position by affirming at the outset that there are sources of philosophical rationality independent of the form of theoretical reason that yields naturalism.

In conclusion, I think the correct view of the balance of argument between the hard and the soft naturalist is that soft naturalism is unable to make significant argumentative headway against hard naturalism or to give us convincing reason for preferring it over hard naturalism. Suppose, however, we take the more generous view that soft naturalism does succeed in at least holding its own, such that the argument between the two positions ends in a stand-off. Another question then opens up: namely, whether, even if soft naturalism can sustain itself on the *one* side against hard naturalism, it can in so doing sustain itself also on its *other* flank, i.e. against *idealism*. At many points in the preceding discussion it has transpired that the trajectory which soft naturalism is forced to take due to the pressure exerted by hard naturalism is proto-idealist, and that idealism is able to meet hard naturalism on its own terms in exactly the way soft naturalism cannot: idealism can meet the traditional demand to conceive complete totality, offer a theory of subjectivity and objectivity that explains why perspective bestows 'real' reality on its objects, translate axiological motives into philosophical reasons, and so on. Hence, it may be suggested, when idealism is added to the picture, soft naturalism ceases to look like the median-point between scientism and supernaturalism that it represents itself as being, and appears instead a merely provisional position that expresses either a moment's hesitation before proceeding down the road of hard naturalism, or the moment of drawing back in the face of hard naturalism that leads us to reverse direction altogether.

The interest and interpretation of German idealism

I have argued that a question mark hangs over the form of naturalism which appears best equipped to satisfy our value-interests – soft naturalism either loses the argument with hard naturalism or converts itself into idealism – and that the limitations of naturalism can be seen to correspond to the strengths of idealism, which can justifiably claim to overcome the axiological limitations of hard naturalism while avoiding the structural weakness of soft naturalism. Kemp Smith's assessment of the 'present situation of philosophy' is to that extent borne out.

Now I want to return to the question with which I started, of German idealism's metaphysicality and its new non-metaphysical mode of interpretation. The questions that would need to be addressed in any comprehensive discussion of the metaphysical *vs.* deflationary issue are multiple and highly complex. What follows is restricted to pursuing, in the context of German idealism, issues which emerged above in the context of assessing soft naturalism, my overall contention being that deflationary interpretations of German idealism reveal themselves to be structurally problematic in the same way as soft naturalist positions. The argument divides into three stages.

Stage 1

If what was argued in the previous section is correct, it follows in the first place that soft naturalistic positions should not be taken – as, I affirmed, there would be a case for doing, if such positions proved coherent and robust – as 'models' to which it would be desirable to discover that German idealism approximates, and in the direction of which German idealism should be nudged.

From this alone it does not follow that German idealism should be interpreted in a metaphysical manner. There are nonetheless considerations deriving from the preceding discussion which cast doubt on the cogency of the non-metaphysical, deflationary approach. These emerge if we attend to two ideas which have been particularly prominent in the new interpretations of German idealism.

The first is that German idealism's conceptual and theoretical richness can be understood in terms of a commitment to irreducible concepts, schemes of explanation, principles of reasoning, patterns of justification, etc., to which no matching ontology corresponds, allowing the ontological facts to be conceived as austerely as the naturalist wishes.[43]

The problem which this approach presents is the same as that presented by the soft naturalist's appeal to perspective. If the import of the claims of idealism is qualified as non-ontological, then inevitably it must seem that this is due to a recognition of their essentially reflexive and thus *subjective* significance. The question is then what reply can be made to the hard naturalist's objection that German idealism has been reduced to at best a mere, non-vindicatory *expression of perspective*, which leaves the field free for an ontologically committed non-idealist account which will explain (away) this perspective as a function of ontological facts which falls outside the limited purview of subjectivity. In order to meet this threat, it appears necessary for the idealist to reassert a correlation between the ontological and the conceptual/explanatory orders: the ontological order cannot be allowed to be indifferent to what we think, and the conceptual richness of idealism must be regarded as echoed in it. While this of course does nothing to refute the naturalistic view, it does something else, of crucial importance, to meet the naturalist's challenge: it meets the demand that a reason be given for thinking that things in the ontological domain are *not* as the naturalistic explanation says they are. The requisite internal connection and parallelism of thought and being may either be regarded as a core principle defining the idealist position, or secured by way of a claim about our *metaphysical status* as thinkers and explainers, from which it will follow that whatever counts for us as a correct explanation, necessary conceptualization, etc., must, on account of what we as cognizers are metaphysically, carry ontological significance. Either way, we are brought back to what can only be described as a metaphysical understanding of idealism.

The naturalistically irreducible conceptual schemes of German idealism, the new interpretations have highlighted, are pervasively concerned with the status of the normative. Accordingly, the second idea prominent in recent interpretation is that it is one of the deepest and most important insights of German idealism that we should hold fast to the distinction of normativity from nature, affirming that normativity 'comes out of' nature in some highly restricted, causal but not constitutive sense – namely, we are natural beings *before* we are normative beings; nature is required to set the stage, to provide a platform for our normativity – but denying that its emergence can be grasped from the natural side of the distinction. What we should think instead, it is proposed, is not that our normativity emerges out of nature in a 'metaphysical' manner, on the basis of any ontological grounds, but that it comes forth as a historical, normative-developmental achievement – this achievement being, again, no alteration in the ontological fabric of the universe, but a matter internal to our thinking. As Terry Pinkard puts it, defending a non-metaphysical interpretation of Hegel: 'we establish or *institute* our freedom from nature by virtue of a complex historical process in which we have come to see nature as inadequate to agency's (that is, *Geist*'s) interests'; previously we took nature as our norm (we 'made nature normative for ourselves'), but we came to see this norm as inadequate and thereupon grasped the true character of normativity as *autonomy*; it is Hegel's insight that *Geist*, normativity aware of itself as such, is 'a *self-instituted liberation* from nature'.[44]

The problem here lies not directly in the fact that the 'emergence' of normativity is left unexplained from the side of nature, since the claim is precisely that there is no explanation to be got from that quarter, nor in the apparent paradox created by speaking of a 'self-instituted emergence'. Rather it has to do, again, with the further consequences that ensue in the context of the argument with naturalism. The hard naturalist will claim, once again, that no reason has been given for thinking that there is not a naturalistic explanation to be given for the emergence of normativity from nature, in the light of which it will be seen that *what* emerges is not *Geist*/normativity as Hegelians conceive it – something with *real* autonomy – but simply our *representing ourselves* in *geistig*, normative terms. The sophisticated naturalist may grant, furthermore, that an *appearance* of autonomy and absoluteness is built into the perspective of *Geist*/normativity, and then claim that it is this which leads to the (illusory) view that *Geist*/normativity is independent from nature in the strong, 'absolute' sense affirmed by Hegelians; the paradox of self-instituted emergence is thus resolved, in a way that acknowledges the (mere) appearances.

Stage 2

So, I have suggested, there is a difficulty for the deflationary view which results from its non-ontological construal of idealist explanation and the sort of account which it gives (and, by virtue of its repudiation of extra-naturalistic ontological grounds, is bound to give) of the emergence of Spirit/normativity. However, since the difficulty as just presented emerges only when idealism is set in confrontation with naturalism, it may be thought that the non-metaphysical Hegelian, perhaps less impressed by hard naturalism than I have suggested is appropriate, may choose to leave his position exposed in this way. Be that as it may – I will return shortly to the question of whether, even with this concession made, all is well with the deflationary interpretation – it should be noted next that Hegel himself has an explanation for the emergence of Spirit/normativity, which supplies exactly what is needed to block the naturalist's objection, and which appears so clearly ontological as to make his idealism unequivocally metaphysical. In the final section of the *Encyclopaedia's Philosophy of Nature*, Hegel affirms that nature as such has a telos, aim, goal, namely Spirit:

> The goal of Nature [Ziel der Natur] is to destroy itself and to break through . . . Nature has become an other to itself in order to recognize itself as Idea and to reconcile itself with itself . . . Spirit, just because it is the goal of Nature

And Hegel insists with complete clarity that this should be understood to mean *not just* that Spirit emerges from nature (nor just that when it does so Spirit will *represent* itself as the goal of nature) but that it does so because and only because Spirit was, in addition, *there all along*:

> Spirit has thus proceeded from Nature . . . But it is one-sided to regard spirit in this way as having only *become* an actual existence after being merely a potentiality [Aber es ist einseitig, den Geist so als *Werden* aus dem Ansich nur zum Fürsichsein kommen zu lassen]. True, Nature is the immediate – but even so, as the other of spirit, its existence is a relativity . . . spirit is no less *before* than *after* Nature, it is not merely the metaphysical Idea of it [er ist ebenso vor als nach der Natur, nicht bloß die metaphysische Idee derselben]. Spirit, just because it is the goal of Nature, is *prior* to it, Nature has proceeded from spirit: not empirically, however, but in such a manner that spirit is already from the very first implicitly present in Nature which is spirit's own presupposition [Als der Zweck der Natur ist er eben darum *vor* ihr, sie ist

> aus ihm hervorgegangen, jedoch nicht empirisch, sondern so, daß er in ihr, die er sich voraussetzt, immer schon enthalten ist]. But spirit in its infinite freedom gives Nature a free existence and the Idea is active in Nature as an inner necessity; just as a free man of the world is sure that his action is the world's activity. Spirit . . . wills to achieve its own liberation by fashioning Nature out of itself [will sich selbst befreien, als die Natur aus sich herausbildend].[45]

This passage amplifies a claim made in the Introduction to the *Philosophy of Nature*:

> Nature is the first in point of time, but the absolute *prius* is the Idea; this absolute *prius* is the last, the true beginning, Alpha is Omega [Die Natur ist in der Zeit das Erste, aber das absolute Prius ist die Idee; dieses absolute Prius ist das Letzte, der wahre Anfang, das A ist das Ω].[46]

This, on the face of it, goes flatly against the deflationary view, which does, in emphasizing the temporal–historical order as the ground of normativity, regard Spirit 'as having only *become* an actual existence after being merely a potentiality', and thus, in Hegel's terms, one-sidedly fails to see that 'spirit is no less *before* than *after* Nature'.

Now the deflationary Hegelian may object that to take Hegel's way of expressing himself in this passage in traditional metaphysical terms is not to gain anything on the argumentative front, since the metaphysical account requires us to accept the possibility of Spirit's ontological productivity, a metaphysical 'explanation' which works only if we are willing to saddle Hegel with the sort of crazy platonism that exposed his system to understandable ridicule. Why prefer, the deflationary Hegelian asks, the supernaturalistic extravagance of a Spirit that quasi-theistically creates nature, to the perhaps awkward but considerably more modest and much less incredible notion of normativity's self-institution?

To take up this question fully would be to embark on a whole new discussion – of whether (and if so, how) Hegel can be thought to have offered any metaphysics in the wake of Kant's critique, of the relation between Hegel's 'speculative' philosophical propositions and the statements of traditional metaphysics, of the relation between the metaphysical and the transcendental, and so on. Within the narrower confines of the discussion that I have been pursuing, the following two points may however be made.

In the first instance, there is at least one immediate reason why one might choose the metaphysical over the deflationary interpretation of Hegel's account of the relation of Spirit to nature. On the metaphysical reading of Hegel's story, the *explanans* lies *outside* and *prior to* nature, such that at the point where nature is posited into existence, there is nothing which the positing ground, Spirit, can be thought to *contrast* with – nothing in this pure philosophical space to *interfere* with its intelligibility (in a way similar to the first and second principles of Fichte's 1794 *Grundlage*). The deflationary reading, by contrast, asks us to think of the self-positing of normativity as conceptually original while situating the 'event' of normativity's self-origination *in a pre-existent context* – that of nature, which has a character of its own, one which is alien if not *opposed* to normativity. In this formal sense at least – quite aside from the matter of its vulnerability to the naturalistic claim to be able in principle to explain (away) the appearance of *Geist*'s autonomous self-institution – the allegedly more 'straightforward' deflationist explanation is in fact the more demanding.[47]

The second point is broader. Whether it is true that what the metaphysical account requires us to accept is something which is 'incredible' from a point of view which should be regarded in the context at hand as philosophically authoritative – this is a claim which a proponent of the metaphysical account should be keen to contest. In appealing to the inherent craziness of any broadly 'platonistic' option, the deflationist is asking us to endorse a measure of philosophical credibility which has no doubt become instinctive for us, but which, I have tried to suggest, historical reflection allows us to distance ourselves from, and which, if left to its own devices, can be seen to lead to the impasse of either axiologically unacceptable hard naturalism or inherently problematic soft naturalism. It is also of high relevance to recall that the German idealists themselves emphasized the necessity with which their positions would appear to ordinary, naturalistic consciousness as an 'inversion' of common sense, an 'inverted world';[48] so, it may be suggested, to take at face value the *appearance* which German idealism gives of 'incredible' metaphysicality is to endorse as adequate the limited standpoint of the *gemeinen Verstand* which German idealism specifically argued needs to be overcome.

Stage 3

Now I want to return to the question of whether, even when the threat of naturalism is held aside, and the Hegel-exegesis-associated issues raised above are bracketed, the non-metaphysical position is stable.

A crucial idea found in deflationary interpretation, intimated earlier but not spelled out, is that the distinction between the normative and the natural/non-normative should be regarded as *itself a normative distinction*.[49] This is a corollary of the claim that *Geist*/normativity is self-instituting. Its importance for the non-metaphysical view lies in its implication that normativity presents no *explanandum* from the point of view of nature and hence leaves no explanatory gap from that angle.

It needs to be considered what is involved in the claim that the nature/normativity distinction is 'itself normative' needs to be considered. What is meant by this is not of course just that the drawing and employment of the distinction – 'thinking in terms of a nature/normativity opposition' – is a conceptual act of ours and thus has a normative character, for this is trivial. Nor is it simply being pointed out that the nature/*Geist* distinction holds for us normative beings and not for nature, to which distinctions apply but *for* which no distinctions hold in the relevant sense. Rather the intention is to claim normativity as the *root explanation* for *why there is* (and not merely: why *we think in terms of*) a distinction of nature from normativity. It is because the existence of the distinction is self-explained from the side of normativity, that the emergence of normativity can be regarded as not unexplained from the side of nature, and the naturalist's objection that, in the absence of sufficient efficient causal conditions, a miracle has been invoked, can be regarded as met: to think that an explanation from the side of nature is needed, it can be retorted, is to be looking for explanation in the wrong place, to misunderstand the nature/norm distinction and the concept of *Geist*. Yet, at the same time as it is insisted that this account does no violence to natural law or the integrity of nature, equally there is no intention to suggest that the naturalist is right after all, i.e. to concede that all of the facts are natural facts: the non-metaphysical account continues to maintain that the existence of *Geist*/normativity is *real* and its distinction from nature a distinction within reality, not merely a congenial representation of our situation, a tale that we tell ourselves.

Clearly this is a complex combination of claims, and it is at this point, I suggest, that the deflationary account appears – as suggested previously, but now in a different argumentative context and in a deeper respect – to reproduce the difficulties of soft naturalism.

As has been seen, the concept of perspective or point of view is essential to the articulation of the deflationary position, which operates with a picture composed of two sides, nature and normativity, the point of view of only one of which, that of normativity, it says we must take up (we 'take it up' in so far as we come to the realization that we must already occupy the point of view of normativity in order to entertain the picture at all). In saying this, however, to emphasize the point made a moment ago, the deflationary theorist does not mean to suggest any *relativization* to points of view – which would (among other things) make Hegel's *Geist*/nature duality into a *dualism* of the (for Hegel) untenable Kantian sort. The idea is thus not that 'normativity exists from its own point of view but not from that of nature'. Rather it is that, if we are to grasp things correctly – if we are to make *un*relativized sense of the two-sided picture – the point of view which is properly to be assumed is the normative and not the natural one. This point corresponds therefore to that at which, it was seen earlier, Strawson's appeal to perspective, in his defence of human responsibility, is seen to require a higher perspective sanctioning our dual-perspective outlook.

But if this is correct, then the deflationary Hegelian must be understood as maintaining a deep and important, non-trivial sense in which normativity has (and, again, not merely: is *represented* by us as having) *primacy over nature* – not a temporal, but a logical or conceptual primacy. Normativity has primacy in so far as the nature/normativity distinction is one not given by nature but determined by normativity, so that normativity encompasses nature by virtue of distinguishing itself from nature and nature from itself, whereas nature does not, symmetrically, encompass normativity. It follows that there is a sense in which, on the deflationary account, there is a *normative explanation of nature*, which is in a good sense its *real* explanation: nature *is*, in reality, that which stands under and answers to the *normatively self-instituted* distinction of nature and norm.

Now the naturalist and the metaphysical Hegelian will insist in unison that to think this *just is* to think of *Geist*/normativity as something that has reality apart from nature and so it *just is* to say that *Geist*/normativity 'has always been' ('platonistically') distinct from nature, meaning that the 'historical achievement' emphasized by the deflationary Hegelian can only be the *epistemic* one of our having *come to recognize* normativity's (trans-epistemic, metaphysical) distinctness from and priority over nature. This, the naturalist and metaphysical Hegelian may further suggest, was effectively implicit in the original formulation that normativity is self-instituting: to think that normativity can *rightfully* claim to be self-authorizing, that it is *capable* of being its own real ground, that it is *able* to constitute or construct itself *into reality*, is necessarily to accord it a metaphysical reality beyond that which is attributed to 'our concepts' in the sense of mere representations.

The deflationary Hegelian may retort that all of this is a gross misconstrual, which trades on a confusion of different senses of 'primacy', because the only sense in which, on the deflationary view, normativity has primacy over nature does not stretch to nature's *existence*: this restriction, it will be insisted, distinguishes firmly deflationary primacy from primacy in the platonistic metaphysical sense.

Now there are two observations to be made at a general level about the deflationist's use of the distinction of ontological from non-ontological matters.

The first is that it is unclear what rationalizes the restriction of *Geist*'s primacy to non-ontological respects. If *Geist*/normativity has primacy over nature in all conceptual, explanatory, etc., dimensions, and the claim that the distinction of nature from norm is normatively generated does more than merely report our representational dispositions, then it is fair to ask why it should be denied that nature exists for normative reasons, i.e. because it *should* exist, as Hegel maintains. The formal properties of *Geist*/normativity appear to cast nature into the shade as an inferior, non-autonomous kind of thing, a mere dependent correlate, and this contrast seems to demand conversion into an ontological relation. Why not accordingly take *Geist*'s explanatory, etc. primacy as a reason for regarding it as being in consequence *vor der Natur*? In virtue of what is *Geist* not ontologically prior? What *makes it true* that its primacy is non-ontological? How indeed can it be *known* that it does not enjoy ontological primacy?

Granted, the claims of explanatory and ontological primacy are logically distinct, but the question is what can be thought to hold us back from moving from the former to the latter, from taking the step that Hegel takes. It seems that what alone would give reason for holding back is some notion that the ontological and conceptual orders are positively dislocated from one another, but it is hard to see how this idea can be supposed to find a home in the context of German idealism, or how invoking it could avoid rendering the whole explanatory apparatus of German idealism merely subjective.

It must also be emphasized in this context that, at the point where normative grounds are held to be in any real sense prior to natural states of affairs, we are already just about as remote from naturalistic common sense and philosophical naturalism as it is possible to get: the autonomous, spontaneous normative grounds of the deflationary Hegelian are from the commonsensical standpoint every bit as strange, as 'metaphysical', as the platonistic grounds from which deflationary interpretations wish to distance Hegel. So while it should be left open that there may perhaps be internal interpretative reasons for identifying *Geist* with some sort of non-ontological grounding – e.g. perhaps it can be argued that it is a requirement of post-Kantian transcendental explanation, a part of its logic, that philosophical explanation be ontologically neutral – it is highly doubtful that there is anything to be gained by doing so from the point of view of accommodating realistic common sense or the naturalistic orientation of contemporary philosophy.

The first observation leads to the second, which is that it is in any case not clear what has become of the ontological/non-ontological distinction in the present context. The previous objection accepts at face value the deflationist's description of his position as non-ontological. But should we do so? The deflationary view, while seeking to respect the absoluteness of German idealism which the metaphysical interpretation so clearly conserves, but without ontologizing it, insists on a distinction between the conceptual and the ontological which, if it is not to render its idealism 'one-sided' and non-absolute, involves an escalated claim for the status of 'the conceptual'. And plausibly, the deflationist's idealism becomes hard to distinguish from that of the metaphysical interpretation to the degree that it empowers the conceptual order: if the so-called conceptual order has ultimate, fundamental, comprehensive explanatory position, then plausibly it is no longer conceptual *as opposed to* ontological.[50] So while again there is, of course, no strict logical necessity forcing the deflationist to identify the conceptual order with the ontological, it seems that what cannot be claimed is at least that the non-ontologicality of *Geist*/normativity is of the same plain, familiar, everyday kind as we have in mind when we talk ordinarily of such and such as being a 'mere epistemic' or 'merely conceptual' matter. In those ordinary contexts, our grasp of what makes the relation in question *merely* epistemic or conceptual is underpinned by a picture that we have of our situation in which a secure distinction is drawn between things on the one hand and their representations in mundane subjects on the other. At the limit point where this very picture is first introduced or 'set up' for us, however, the contrast of ontological and conceptual matters is not yet available;

which makes it hard to see what makes it right to describe the order of *Geist* as 'non-ontological'.

This last point suggests an explanation for how it may come to seem as if the deflationary view is entitled to claim an unproblematic ontological innocence. Matters will appear thus if there is a confusion of transcendental and empirical distinctions of nature from norm. It can seem, if we follow Pinkard's presentation of the nature/normativity distinction as the 'product' of an historical development, as if the nature/norm distinction is *just another* distinction drawn in thought. To think that the *transcendental* self-institution of normativity as such out of nature can be regarded as metaphysically innocuous in the manner of, or intelligible in the same way as, the instituting of some *particular* nature-involving norm – as when, for example, it is decided that a certain metal will count as 'money' and a distinction is thereby instituted between the stuff's natural being and its social exchange value – would however surely be a mistake. The latter, empirical-level sort of distinction does not impinge on our conception of the natural world and the realm of concepts as two distinct orders, but it is hard to grasp how the former can be thought not to do so, i.e. how the ordinary conception of an independently existing nature or ontological order counterposed to a distinct normative conceptual order can be supposed to remain unaltered, once it has been claimed that there is a real, non-trivial sense in which the latter encompasses the former. It is consequently rather as if, in drawing its distinction between the normative/conceptual and the natural/ontological orders, with a view to immunizing idealism from ontological commitment and thereby distinguishing itself from the metaphysical view, the deflationist wishes to treat the distinction of Thought and Being as merely a further distinction drawn within Thought, something which, Kant and the German idealists are clear, it cannot be.

Conclusion

I have argued that the considerations which can be argued to give idealism its definite philosophical advantage over naturalism are at the same time considerations which support its metaphysical rather than deflationary interpretation. We should prefer the metaphysical to the deflationary interpretation if we wish to ensure that the liberation of *Geist* from nature is true and complete, that normativity does not end up being reabsorbed into nature, and because the deflationary interpretation in any case reveals itself to be less stable than (to the extent that it holds itself distinct from) metaphysical idealism – it stands in relation to the metaphysical interpretation in the same relation as soft naturalism stands to hard naturalism. My suggestion is that it is a mistake to locate German idealism on the 'post-metaphysical' side of the fence conceived and erected by naturalism and that the answer to the question with which I began – irrespective and in advance of whatever more particular conclusions we may come to regarding the ontological status of the absolute *Ich*,

Geist, the Absolute, etc. – should be that German idealism is 'in the full sense' metaphysical: not to make this 'admission' is to agree to play the game by rules which obscure the interest that German idealism presently holds for us.[51]

If this is correct then, in line with Kemp Smith's view, the 'extremes' – *either* hard naturalism, *or* metaphysically construed idealism – are all that remain.

Notes

1 Although I have talked here (and for brevity's sake will continue to do so) of 'German idealism' as if it were a single uniform quantity, it is of course above all mainly Hegel and Fichte who are in question, with Schelling serving often as a foil, as showing what German idealism would be, were it metaphysical. If the eventual conclusion of this paper is correct, however, this contrast is not accurate.

2 Thus what I am concerned with here is the species of interpretation of German idealism which is intended to count as a (systematic, analytical) 'reconstruction', in which considerations of contemporary philosophical interest are to the fore and an interest is declared in 'salvaging' the parts of philosophical systems deemed 'worth saving'. What conditions apply to interpretation in the more strictly historical sense, and how the line is to be drawn between 'reconstructive' and historical interpretation, are matters about which I here remain neutral. For historically minded criticism of one (Klaus Hartmann's) non-metaphysical interpretation, see Frederick C. Beiser, 'Hegel, a non-metaphysician? A polemic', *Bulletin of the Hegel Society of Great Britain* no. 32, 1995, 1–13; the issues of 'reconstructive and/or historical' raised there are pursued in Terry Pinkard, 'What is the non-metaphysical reading of Hegel? A reply to Frederick Beiser', *Bulletin of the Hegel Society of Great Britain* no. 34, 1996, 13–20, and Beiser, 'Reply to Pinkard', *Bulletin of the Hegel Society of Great Britain* no. 34, 1996, 21–26.

3 Norman Kemp Smith, 'The present situation of philosophy', *Philosophical Review* 29, 1920, 1–26: p. 25.

4 Ibid.

5 Op. cit., p. 15.

6 Op. cit., p. 2.

7 Op. cit., p. 4.

8 Op. cit., p. 7.

9 Op. cit., pp. 10–11.

10 Op. cit., p. 6.

11 Op. cit., p. 14.

12 Op. cit., p. 18.

13 Op. cit., p. 20.

14 Op. cit., p. 19.

15 Op. cit., p. 24.

16 Roy Wood Sellars, *Evolutionary Naturalism* (Chicago: Open Court, 1922), p. i.

17 See the St Louis Hegelians' *Journal of Speculative Philosophy*, and *Mind* and the *Philosophical Review* up until about 1910.

18 Important for this is the distancing of naturalism from a dogmatic materialism, and a shift of emphasis from metaphysical claims to methodological claims.

19 When charges of ground-level logical fallaciousness and conceptual confusion were levelled against the idealists, as they were by Moore, Russell, Cook Wilson and others, the analytical machinery that was appealed to, or the interpretation of its philosophical significance directing its application, came laden with assumptions that begged the major questions against idealism. See Peter Hylton, *Russell, Idealism, and*

the Emergence of Analytic Philosophy (Oxford: Clarendon, 1990). Nor was the target adequately specified: much of what was rejected in the *name* of idealism consisted in an identification of idealism with a Berkeleyan subjectivism that the whole tradition from Kant onwards had strained to refute.

20 The period from Rousseau to romanticism, in which man's naturalization had the wholly positive, elevated significance of a spiritual rehabilitation or re-enthronement through joining with or rejoining Nature (for an excellent account of which, see Alexander Gode-von Aesch, *Natural Science in German Romanticism* (New York: AMS Press, 1966), esp. ch. 4), is however no counter-instance to this generalization, since the Nature of romanticism was itself supernaturalized: the aesthetic and *naturphilosophisch* conceptions which were needed to maintain the axiologically positive interpretation of naturalization were historically revealed to be not 'genuinely naturalistic' after all.

21 In Spinoza's theological variant, naturalization of the world vindicates itself by the intellectual love of God that it makes possible: naturalization purifies our vision and thus makes God accessible. Schopenhauer's system has a similar structure.

22 Thus in the case of soft naturalism, discussed below, the situation is not that it is held that our value-orientation gives us reason to be *naturalists*, but that it gives us reason – given that we *can only* be naturalists – to be *soft* naturalists.

23 John Dewey, 'Experience and objective idealism', *Philosophical Review* 15, 1906, 465–81: p. 479.

24 See for example Dewey's polemical essay 'Antinaturalism *in extremis*', in Yervant Hovhannes Krikorian (ed.) *Naturalism and the Human Spirit* (New York: Columbia University Press, 1945), pp. 1–16, in which naturalism is claimed to be *necessary* for the realization of value, and a hefty portion of the evils suffered by humanity are attributed to anti-naturalism.

25 Articulations of the deeper, 'nihilistic' axiological problem in naturalism may be found in Jacobi, Schopenhauer, Nietzsche and Heidegger. Schopenhauer's metaphysics of purposeless purposiveness is, as it were, a representation in the language of metaphysics of the axiological situation which follows from naturalism. Nietzsche's view in *The Genealogy of Morals* (I argue in 'Nietzsche, the self, and the disunity of philosophical reason', in *Nietzsche on Freedom and Autonomy*, Ken Gemes and Simon May (eds) (Oxford: Oxford University Press, forthcoming)) is that our inability to resolve ourselves successfully back into nature in Enlightenment fashion leaves us high and dry in a position of reflexive unintelligibility. A very early and eloquent criticism of (Hutcheson's sentimentalist) naturalism in moral theory is John Balguy, *The Foundation of Moral Goodness: or, A Fuller Inquiry into the Original of our Idea of Virtue*, Part I, 4th edn, in A *Collection of Tracts Moral and Theological* (London: Pemberton, 1734), pp. 39–103, esp. pp. 45–46 and 57–58. Balguy probes the contingency which issues from naturalistic foundations, and suggests that while naturalized morality may retain practical force, it sacrifices our reflective sense of its purposiveness: naturalism inevitably deprecates the 'Honour' and 'Dignity' of morality.

26 Friedrich Nietzsche, *Human, All Too Human: A Book for Free Spirits* (1878), trans. Marion Faber (Lincoln: University of Nebraska Press, 1996), vol. I, § 251, p. 154.

27 Though Kemp Smith has an inkling of the distinction, indicated by his account of a newly 'strengthened' naturalism.

28 John Herman Randall, Jr., 'Epilogue: the nature of naturalism', in Yervant Hovhannes Krikorian (ed.) *Naturalism and the Human Spirit* (New York: Columbia University Press, 1945), pp. 354–82: p. 369.

29 What might be held to interfere with this conclusion is, as I have indicated, the deeper axiological problem, which it may be maintained, even soft naturalism is unable to resolve, but for the reasons given above, I hold this aside.

30 Dewey is not unconscious of the possibility that the programme of naturalism contains two potentially conflicting vectors, but his confidence that it will not split is unsupported. The reason why soft naturalism looks easier to Dewey than it really is, lies in his historical proximity to idealism: idealism is the position he thinks he needs to dislodge, and austere reductive naturalism – having challenged idealism earlier in the nineteenth century but, Dewey believes, lost the argument – is not on his horizon. Consequently, though he sets himself the goal of differentiating naturalism from idealism, he lacks a clear view of what this requires.

31 Soft naturalism is liable to interpret the challenge posed to the internal perspective of natural consciousness by the austere conception of nature as if what were at issue were *only* the question of reduction. But establishing relations of logical equivalence is not the hard naturalist's ultimate target, and the challenge is not met but merely deferred by a demonstration of irreducibility. The real task for soft naturalism is to *ground* its irreducibles. To stop at conclusions of irreducibility is to substitute for the metaphysical question of the unity and constitution of reality, the much more limited, parochial question of the inter-relations of elements within that order according to our presently existing concepts of them.

32 Conclusions of irreducibility may be taken up by the idealist as *confirming* metaphysical conceptions which have been formed independently of whatever premises have been employed in the demonstration of irreducibility: for the idealist, it is no surprise to (re)discover, by way of the sorts of arguments offered by soft naturalists, that intentionality, normativity, etc., are irreducible.

33 See Hegel's remarks on d'Holbach's materialism, defending it (as speculative, an attempt to express subject–object identity) against Reinhold's dismissal, in *The Difference Between Fichte's and Schelling's System of Philosophy* (1801), trans. H.S. Harris and Walter Cerf (Albany, N.Y.: State University of New York Press, 1977), pp. 114 and 177 [*Differenz des Fichteschen und Schellingschen Systems der Philosophie*, in *Werke. Auf der Grundlage der Werke von 1832–1845 neu edierte Ausgabe*, Eva Moldenhauer and Karl Markus Michel (eds) (Frankfurt am Main: Suhrkamp, 1979) (Theorie-Werkausgabe), vol. 2, pp. 46 and 118]; and Hegel's critical but appreciative discussion of the *philosophes* in *Lectures on the History of Philosophy*, vol. 3, *Medieval and Modern Philosophy*, trans. E.S. Haldane and Frances H. Simpson (Lincoln: University of Nebraska Press, 1995), p. 382 [*Vorlesungen über die Geschichte der Philosophie*, in *Werke*, vol. 20, pp. 288–89].

34 See Vittorio Hösle and Christian Illies, 'Der Darwinismus als Metaphysik', in *Die Philosophie und die Wissenschaften* (Munich: Beck, 1999), pp. 46–73.

35 The point is not that soft naturalism lacks a concept of nature from which the non-austere elements can be *deduced*, but that it lacks a contentful concept that can *unify* the 'parts' of what it calls 'nature'.

36 Philosophical defence of common sense on this view requires only negative philosophical work, the exposure of mistakes made by those whose picture of reality departs from common sense.

37 For reasons of space I cannot provide these attributions with the extensive illustration which could be supplied, but I assume they will be familiar to readers of the literature in philosophy of mind.

38 P.F. Strawson, *Skepticism and Naturalism: Some Varieties. The Woodbridge Lectures 1983* (London: Methuen, 1985), pp. 39 ff.; 'The non-reductive naturalist's point is that there can only be a *lack* where there is a *need*' (p. 41).

39 Regarding this distinction, see Mark Sacks, *Objectivity and Insight* (Oxford: Oxford University Press, 2000), ch. 6.

40 Strawson, *Skepticism and Naturalism*, pp. 37–38.

41 Jennifer Hornsby, 'Personal and sub-personal: a defence of Dennett's early distinction', *Philosophical Explorations* 3, 2000, 6–24: p. 15. See also, e.g. Richard Moran, *Authority and Estrangement: An Essay on Self-Knowledge* (Princeton, N.J.: Princeton University Press, 2001), pp. 34–35.

42 David Hume, *Dialogues Concerning Natural Religion* (1779), Henry D. Aitken (ed.) (New York: Hafner, 1948), pt. II, pp. 21–22.

43 See Robert Pippin, 'Naturalness and mindedness: Hegel's compatibilism', *European Journal of Philosophy*, 7, 1999, pp. 194–212.

44 Terry Pinkard, 'Speculative *Naturphilosophie* and the development of the empirical sciences: Hegel's perspective', in Gary Gutting (ed.) *Continental Philosophy of Science* (Oxford: Blackwell, 2005), pp. 19–34: pp. 23 and 30. See also Pinkard's 'Response to Stern and Snow', *Bulletin of the Hegel Society of Great Britain* nos. 49–50, 2004, pp. 25–40, where nature's otherness to the normative order is said to be a matter of our having made it so (p. 31), the 'distinction of the normative and the non-normative' being 'itself a *normatively* established distinction' (p. 34). See, again, Pippin, 'Naturalness and mindedness', and also *The Persistence of Subjectivity: On the Kantian Aftermath* (Cambridge: Cambridge University Press, 2005), p. 292.

45 *Philosophy of Nature* (*Part Two of the Encyclopaedia of the Philosophical Sciences, 1830*), trans. A.V. Miller (Oxford: Oxford University Press, 1970), § 376 Zusatz, p. 444 [*Enzyklopädie der philosophischen Wissenschaften im Grundrisse. Zweiter Teil: Die Naturphilosophie*, in *Werke*, vol. 9, pp. 537–38].

46 Ibid., § 248 Zusatz, p. 19 [p. 29].

47 In this connection, see Christoph Halbig's comment in 'Das "Erkennen als solches": Überlegungen zur Grundstruktur von Hegels Epistemologie', in *Hegels Erbe*, Christoph Halbig, Michael Quante and Ludwig Siep (eds) (Frankfurt am Main: Suhrkamp, 2004), pp. 183–63: p. 160 n23.

48 See for example Fichte, '[First] Introduction to the Wissenschaftslehre', in *Introductions to the Wissenschaftslehre and Other Writings (1797–1800)*, trans. and ed. Daniel Breazeale (Indianapolis: Hackett, 1994), pp. 2–35: p. 5 ['Erste Einleitung in die Wissenschaftslehre', in *Johann Gottlieb Fichtes sämmtliche Werke*, ed. Immanuel Hermann Fichte, 8 vols (Berlin: Veit & Comp., 1845–46), vol. 1, p. 421]; and Hegel and Schelling, 'The Critical Journal of Philosophy, Introduction: On the essence of philosophical criticism generally, and its relationship to the present state of philosophy', trans. H.S. Harris, in George di Giovanni and H.S. Harris (eds) *Between Kant and Hegel: Texts in the Development of Post-Kantian Idealism* (Indianapolis: Hackett, 2000), pp. 272–310: p. 283 ['Einleitung. Über das Wesen der philosophischen Kritik überhaupt und ihr Verhältnis zum gegenwärtigen Zustand der Philosophie insbesondere', *Schellings Werke. Nach der Originalausgabe in neuer Anordnung*, Manfred Schröter (ed.) (München: Beck, 1927), vol. 3, p. 521].

49 See Robert Brandom, 'Freedom and constraint by norms', *American Philosophical Quarterly* 16, 1979, pp. 187–96, esp. p. 193: 'the difference between the social and the objective is a difference in how they are treated by some community (by *us*) rather than an objective matter about which we could be right or wrong [. . . it is] itself a social difference'.

50 I argue for a view of Fichte's metaphysicality parallel to the view proposed here regarding Hegel in 'The status of the Wissenschaftslehre: transcendental and ontological grounds in Fichte', *Internationales Jahrbuch des Deutschen Idealismus* 5 (forthcoming).

51 Some clarifications and caveats are in order. First: I have not offered an account of how 'metaphysical in the full sense' should be understood, since I have intended the phrase simply to carry the meaning usually intended by the deflationary theorist. As I envisage matters, we have *first* to get clear whether we intend to follow the deflationary programme, that is, what we think of its principled self-opposition *ab initio* to

what it calls 'metaphysical interpretation' of German idealism; the question of what (certainly complex and very different) understandings and senses of 'metaphysics' are actually in play in Fichte, Schelling and Hegel, belongs to a later stage of enquiry, which I have not embarked upon. Second: What I have called 'the deflationary interpretation' is, of course, arguably just one version thereof, but I have tried to focus on elements that I suppose will be shared by all or at least many of its instances. It also goes without saying that my discussion bears on the positions of non-metaphysical Hegelians only on a single front, and that I have not begun to attempt to engage with the subtle and complex arguments with which those views are supported. Third: Although I have, following Kemp Smith, emphasized the role of axiological considerations, which must surely figure in any plausible interpretation of German idealism, what I have not intended to suggest, and would not wish to argue, is that the axiological is the *only* angle from which the present-day philosophical interest of German idealism can be demonstrated. See Frederick C. Beiser, *German Idealism: The Struggle Against Subjectivism, 1781–1801* (Cambridge, Mass.: Harvard University Press, 2002); and Paul Franks, *All or Nothing: Systematicity, Transcendental Arguments, and Skepticism in German Idealism* (Cambridge, Mass.: Harvard University Press, 2005).

Acknowledgement

I am grateful to audiences at the Goethe-Universität Frankfurt am Main, the University of London and the University of Essex for comments on earlier drafts of what developed into the present paper, and to the Arts and Humanities Research Council and the Philosophy Department of University College London for research leave that enabled its completion.

2

FROM QUINE TO HEGEL: NATURALISM, ANTI-REALISM AND MAIMON'S QUESTION *QUID FACTI*

Paul Franks

Why, roughly a century after analytic philosophy's triumph over various post-Kantian traditions, does German idealism seem – at least to some philosophers who have inherited the analytic tradition – of contemporary significance once again?[1]

An illuminating answer, so it seems to me, would focus, not initially on *theses* or *themes*, but rather on *problems*. It would begin by tracing detailed analogies between the problems confronted within analytic philosophy today and the problems motivating German idealism. These analogies would then serve to explain the parallels between the strategies available for addressing contemporary problems and the strategies available to the first post-Kantian generation. My goal here is to contribute to an account of this sort. I will focus on one of the two major problems to which German idealism may be seen as responding – namely, naturalism – leaving the other – nihilism – for discussion elsewhere.[2]

Maimon and the contested matter of fact

I will start by discussing the naturalistic challenge to Kantianism, a challenge issued in its most interesting version by Salomon Maimon – a Lithuanian Talmudist, kabbalist and sometime wandering beggar who wrote some of the most provocative, profound and seminal works of the 1790s before his untimely death in 1800.[3]

Maimon's challenge arises in the first place from consideration of the success of transcendental philosophy in responding to Humean skepticism, a skepticism that presupposes what I shall call *methodological naturalism*. So we need to understand the skeptical doubt that arises from this naturalism, as well as the transcendental response to that doubt, before we can adequately characterize Maimon's challenge.

Methodological naturalism is the view that the methods of natural science are the only methods appropriate for understanding anything, including epistemic practices such as natural science itself. Notice that both rationalism and empiricism may be seen as methodologically naturalist in this sense, differing primarily in what they take the methods of natural science to be. Notice also that, while a methodological naturalist is likely to be a substantive naturalist – someone who is committed to the existence only of natural entities – a substantive naturalist need not be a methodological naturalist.

From methodological naturalism, Humean skepticism may be said to arise as follows. (I am concerned here with Maimon's account of the skeptical upshot of Hume's arguments. Whether he is right about the interpretation of Hume is a question I set aside for the purposes of this paper.) When asked to justify a belief in some empirical yet unobserved matter of fact, we soon find ourselves attempting to justify an inference from observed matters of fact by appealing to some principle supposed to express a metaphysical necessity or strict universality, such as the principle that every event has some cause from which it follows according to a law. Now it is possible, using the methods of natural science, to *explain* how we come to formulate such a principle, through mechanisms such as habituation and imaginative projection. But it is impossible, using these methods, to *justify* such a principle. In short, a naturalistic explanation of our epistemic practices is available, but this explanation will involve no naturalistic *reduction* of epistemic justification. Consequently, if epistemic warrant consists in being able to give a justificatory account of reasons for holding a belief – that is, if we take what is now called an *internalist* view of knowledge – then it follows that, not only do we not *know* anything about empirical yet unobserved matters of fact, but also that *we do not have any warranted beliefs about them*. This conclusion threatens to undermine our philosophical sense of the worth both of our everyday epistemic practices and of natural science itself.

To this skeptical conclusion, transcendental philosophy of the kind in question may be said to respond as follows. It is quite true that the principles in question cannot be justified by the methods of natural science. But this is because the principles play a special epistemic role, and when this role is understood it will be seen that the principles can be justified in another way, employing uniquely philosophical methods not available to natural science. What the principles do is *constitute* the very possibility of epistemic practices, including natural science. Without *presupposing* the principles, there would be no epistemic practices at all, and of course there would be no natural science.[4]

It is important to note the *reciprocal relationship*, emphasized by Kant, between constitutive principles and what they constitute. On the one hand, the principles in question *constitute* the possibility of experience. That is, they underwrite the justifications we can give for beliefs about the empirical world – as, for example, the principle of causality underwrites inferences from observations to beliefs about unobserved matters of fact. On the other hand, experience returns the favor. For these principles cannot be derived from concepts alone or from observations. So they stand in need of justification. And this justification is provided by experience, the actuality of which shows that the principles constitutive of its possibility must also be actual. I will call this *the reciprocity claim* of transcendental philosophy.

Hume is correct, then, to demand justification for what we may now call constitutive principles. He is also correct to see that no such justification can be given by means of the methods of natural science.

Where then, if anywhere, does Hume's error lie? Only in his failure to see that another – non-naturalistic or transcendental – method is available for the philosophical justification of constitutive principles, hence for an explanation of the possibility of our epistemic practices, including natural science itself, and that this method does *not* undermine our understanding of these practices as involving genuine justification. Once we have found such a method, we need no longer be troubled by Humean skepticism, and we need no longer take seriously Hume's own naturalistic proposal. In Kant's words:

> to the synthesis of cause and effect there attaches a dignity that can never be expressed empirically, namely, that the effect does not merely come along with the cause, but is posited **through** it and follows **from** it. The strict universality of the rule is therefore not any property of empirical rules, which cannot acquire anything more through induction than comparative universality, i.e., widespread usefulness. But now the use of the pure concepts of the understanding would be entirely altered if one were to treat them only as empirical products.[5]
>
> The empirical derivation [of the categories] . . . to which both of them [i.e. Locke and Hume] resorted, cannot be reconciled with the reality of the scientific cognition *a priori* that we possess, namely that of **pure mathematics** and **general natural science**, and is therefore refuted by the fact [*durch das Faktum*].[6]

The first passage says, in effect, that, because of the strictly universal character of constitutive principles, for which there can be no naturalistic reduction, it follows that to adopt naturalism would be to propose a *revision* in our use of the concepts defined by these principles. To this point the second passage adds, in effect, that if we are confronted with a choice between, on the one hand, a naturalistic view that cannot account for the reality of the knowledge we claim of mathematics and the foundations of physics – a view that instead of accounting for our epistemic practices, proposes to revise them – and, on the other hand, a non-naturalistic view that succeeds in accounting for the reality of the knowledge we claim – a view that is *not* revisionist – then *it is obvious that we should prefer the latter, transcendental epistemology*. Methodological naturalism, we might say, is ruled out by a principle of conservatism that should be uncontroversial: "if it ain't broke, don't fix it."

However, Maimon believes that Kant misinterprets Hume and consequently underestimates the challenge of methodological naturalism. As we have seen, Kant thinks that, because Hume cannot offer a naturalistic reduction of the reality of our cognition, Hume must propose a *revision* of our epistemic practices. Here is Maimon's direct reply:

> One cannot build with certainty upon the commonest use of the understanding. The [commonest usage] distinguishes itself excellently from the scientific use of the understanding insofar as the latter seeks the *ground* and the *mode of origination* of some given *knowledge*; [while] the former satisfies itself with this *knowledge in itself* and its application in common life; thus the common human understanding can deceive itself and believe itself to be in possession of a cognition which has no *objective ground*. As an example, you bring forth the proposition that all alterations must have a cause, and you say that the concept of cause would be wholly lost if one were to [explain] it as Hume did, etc., because it contains necessity and strict universality. But friend! Here you are doing the honorable Hume a great injustice. He derives from association of ideas and custom, not the *concept* of cause, but only its supposed *use*. Thus he doubts only its *objective reality*, since he shows that the common human understanding could have arrived at belief in the *use* of this concept through the confusion of the merely *subjective* and *comparatively universal* with the *objectively* and *absolutely universal*.[7]

In other words, Hume proposes no significant *revision* of our epistemic practices. He regards our practice of causal inference – our *use* of the concept of cause – as natural and ineliminable. However, on Maimon's interpretation, Hume proposes what we should nowadays call an *anti-realist* account of some *beliefs* involved in that practice. In particular, he proposes an *error theory* of *justification*: we cannot help engaging in causal inferences from observations to beliefs about unobserved matters of fact, and we cannot help believing that these inferences are justified by the strictly universal principle of causality. But this unavoidable belief in the justified status of our inferences is *false*. A methodologically naturalist *explanation* of the *use* of a concept may therefore be adequate even though it falls short of *justifying* the *conceptualization* itself.

On this view, Kant has underestimated the viability of methodological naturalism. For Kant thinks that there are only three epistemological options worth considering:

1) *methodologically naturalistic reductionism*, which is ascribed to Lockean empiricists and Leibnizian rationalists, who seek to account for the reality of our cognition by employing only the empirical and conceptual methods of natural science;
2) *methodologically naturalistic revisionism*, which Kant ascribes to Hume, and which is motivated by the failure of the reductionist program; and
3) *Kant's own program*, which seeks to account for the reality of our cognition by employing a transcendental method suitable for the justification of

> constitutive principles within philosophy, but not for the justification of either the empirical or conceptual beliefs with which we are concerned in ordinary cognition or in natural science.

However, Kant has missed a fourth alternative. Namely, the methodological naturalist can happily concede Kant's transcendental argument that constitutive principles constitute the possibility of experience and that these principles are consequently ineliminable and unrevisable. But the naturalist can then proceed to take what we should nowadays call an *anti-realist* attitude towards the constitutive function of these principles – for example, by adopting an error theory of the belief in the principles' justificatory role, as described above. But there are also other ways to be anti-realist. One could view supposedly constitutive principles, for example, as merely *instrumental* rules of inference, whose use involves no doxastic commitment to their objective validity.

In short, the Humean naturalism envisaged by Maimon accepts the first half of the transcendental philosopher's reciprocity claim – the argument that constitutive principles underwrite the justifications without which experience would be impossible, and indeed that they are indispensable to our current epistemic practices – but rejects the second half – the argument that our current epistemic practices actually amount to experience, and that the actuality of experience justifies the principles that constitute its possibility. For the Humean naturalist proposes to explain in fully naturalistic terms the very epistemic practices which the transcendental philosopher describes in supposedly non-naturalizable terms such as "justification." Thus the Humean naturalist denies the actuality of what the transcendental philosopher calls "experience," which is not merely perceptual experience, but a body of knowledge that integrates perceptions into a view of the world.[8]

The existence of this fourth alternative dramatically alters the dialectical context in which Kant assesses his own transcendental program. For the naturalist who adopts anti-realism with respect to the constitutive function of the principles is not proposing any revision of our epistemic practices. Consequently, the principle of conservatism does not obviously count *against* such a naturalist and *for* the transcendental philosopher who seeks to be a realist about our putative cognition. Indeed, Maimon argues in effect that the principle of conservatism could be seen to favor anti-realist naturalism, because it makes use only of methods already used successfully in natural science.[9] If the transcendental philosopher can claim to be a *cognitive content conservative*, then the anti-realist naturalist can claim to be a *methodological conservative*.

So Kant is mistaken: there is no "fact" by which naturalism is refuted. Indeed, this is one way to understand Maimon's famous objection that Kant begs the question *quid facti*: Kant's transcendental deduction proceeds on the assumption that we are actually in possession of sciences founded on synthetic a priori principles for which methodological naturalism cannot account, but this is an assumption that the methodological naturalist need not and should not grant.[10]

Now, this does not mean that, in Maimon's view, methodological naturalism vanquishes transcendental philosophy. For Maimon agrees with Kant that we are in possession of a science of pure mathematics for which methodological naturalism cannot account.[11] With respect to physics, however, the situation is at best a philosophical standoff. *Both* a methodologically naturalist but anti-realist account *and* a transcendental yet empirically realist account remain unrefuted options. Accordingly, both should be pursued. Transcendental philosophy – which, for Maimon, becomes the transcendental logic of mathematics – should continue to investigate the necessary conditions for the possibility of general natural science – that is, of a thoroughgoing mathematization of sensibly given objects.[12] On the other hand, methodological naturalism should continue to develop methodologically conservative accounts of our cognitive practices, and should remind transcendental philosophy of the extent to which general natural science is not a "matter of fact" but remains an unrealized hypothesis. In Maimon's memorable exegesis of the adversarial relationship between humanity and the serpent in Genesis 3:15:

> The critical and skeptical philosoph[ies] stand approximately in just the same relationship as man and the serpent after the fall, where it says: He (that is, man) will tread on your head (that is, the critical philosopher will always disturb the skeptical philosopher with the necessity and universality of principles required for scientific knowledge); but you (serpent) will bite him on the heel (that is, the skeptic will always tease the critical philosopher with the fact that his necessary and universal principles have no use).[13]

German idealism is, in significant part, an attempt, often with the help of resources adopted and adapted from Maimon, to respond to this standoff – if not to resolve it in transcendental philosophy's favor, then at least to find a way for transcendental philosophy to stand its ground without compromising itself. To understand the contemporary appeal of German idealism, it will help to understand the analogy between the situation characterized by Maimon and the state of analytic philosophy in the wake of Quine.

Quine and the contested fact of the matter

Quine begins one of his major essays on Carnap by noting that despite his self-proclaimed empiricism, Carnap is in a crucial sense post-Kantian:

> Kant's question "How are synthetic judgments *a priori* possible?" precipitated the *Critique of Pure Reason*. Question and answer notwithstanding, Mill and others persisted in doubting that such judgments

> were possible at all. At length some of Kant's own clearest purported instances, drawn from arithmetic, were sweepingly disqualified (or so it seemed . . .) by Frege's reduction of arithmetic of logic. Attention was thus forced upon the less tendentious and indeed logically prior question, "How is logical certainty possible?" It was largely this latter question that precipitated the form of empiricism which we associate with between-war Vienna – a movement that began with Wittgenstein's *Tractatus* and reached its maturity in the work of Carnap.[14]

Indeed, Kant also seems to regard the question of the possibility of logical certainty as prior and even as exemplary. In the preface to the B edition of the *Critique*, he notes that logic attained its scientific status and, as he notoriously adds, its completeness, because in matters of logic the understanding must deal only with its own form, which it can know a priori.

This explanation of certainty with respect to a priori judgments is the model for Kant's explanations of the possibility of knowing the synthetic a priori principles of mathematics, experience and morality. In every case, *knowledge of the a priori is knowledge of the forms of our own faculties*. Logic is the easiest case because it is unconditionally general and applies to every possible judgment just in virtue of its being a judgment, so that no further account of the applicability of logical form is required. The challenge, as Kant sees it, lies in the extension of the model to sciences that involve the a priori applicability of form to sensibly given objects. Members of the Vienna Circle – several of whom, including Carnap, had begun their careers in proximity to some version of Neo-Kantianism – call themselves empiricists, not because they are attracted by the empiricism of Locke, Berkeley and Hume, but rather because they reject this extension and the concomitant notion of synthetic a priori judgment. This is, to be sure, a significant departure from Kant, whose transcendental idealism is intended to explain the possibility of synthetic a priori judgment and merits little consideration if there is no such possibility. But it can coexist within a framework that remains crucially post-Kantian insofar as it regards science as possible only with the contribution of logical form, which is neither empirically given nor reducible to mere "relations of ideas."[15]

Carnap himself develops several post-Fregean versions of Kant's account of the possibility of logical certainty. Moving away from Frege and, with the help of Wittgenstein's tractarian notion of tautology, closer to Kant, Carnap regards logic as entirely *formal*. Adopting what he takes to be the truth in Poincaré's conventionalism, he departs from both Frege and Kant, proclaiming that there is not *one* logic, but *many* – a plurality over which reigns a Principle of Tolerance.[16] In each case, however, logical form will be, so to speak, constituted by those propositions that are entirely formal – that is, by the *analytic* propositions, which now take over what remains of the constitutive function formerly ascribed to Kant's synthetic a priori principles. After Carnap's semantic turn, we may say that a set of analytic propositions express the *meanings of terms*, and constitute *truths in virtue of meaning*, hence *objects of a priori knowledge* – all relative to a given language.[17]

Since philosophy deals with the plurality of logical forms, it lacks substantive commitment. Thus it is distinct both from natural science and from every sort of metaphysics – whether pre-Kantian or Kantian – that commits the amphiboly of confusing logical form with ontology. Thus Carnap's project remains opposed to methodological naturalism, although it does not serve as his explicit target in the way that Hume is Kant's target or in the way that psychologism – of which more will be said later – is the target of Neo-Kantians such as Cohen and Windelband, and of logicists such as Frege.

It is possible, then, to formulate a Carnapian version of transcendental philosophy's reciprocity claim: a specific set of analytic propositions constitutes the possibility of those epistemic practices possible with the use of the relevant set of meanings, while the value of the epistemic practices can alone validate the choice of just these analytic propositions.

It is also possible to formulate an analogue of Maimon's methodologically naturalist response to such reciprocity claims: appropriate the first half of the claim, by giving a methodologically naturalistic account of linguistic *use* that treats as a merely *practical* necessity what non-naturalistic philosophy treats as a *constitutive* necessity, while rejecting the second half by treating as a merely *practical* necessity what non-naturalistic philosophy treats as a *constitutive* necessity which grounds epistemic practice and is thereby justified. One strand of Quine's critique of Carnap – the indeterminacy of translation thesis[18] – may be seen as just such a response. Indeed, it is a striking radicalization of Maimon's response: whereas Maimon limits his combination of naturalism and anti-realism to categorial concepts such as the concept of causation, Quine gives a naturalistic account of the usage and an anti-realist account of the constitutive functions of *all* concepts.[19]

Quine's thesis is best divided into two. First, there is the Non-Supervenience Thesis: the thesis that translation – hence synonymy, hence meaning, and hence intentionality in general – does not so much as supervene on and is therefore not determined by facts determinable with the help of naturalistic methods. Intuitively speaking, and setting aside for current purposes a proliferation of distinct formulations, X supervenes on Y if and only if there can be no change or variety in X without some change or variety in Y. According to Quine, "manuals for translating one language into another can be set up in divergent ways, all compatible with the totality of speech dispositions, yet incompatible with one another."[20] Indeed, "Two such translations might even be patently contrary in truth value."[21] Yet facts about speech dispositions – about verbal behavior – are the only naturalistically discernible facts relevant to the learning and study of language: "In psychology, one may or may not be a behaviorist, but in linguistics" – and of course Quine means: in *scientifically respectable linguistics* – "one has no choice."[22] Thus there can be translational variety where there is no naturalistically discernible variety, and so translation does not supervene on naturalistic facts. Since there can be incompatible homophonic translation manuals that are equally compatible with all naturalistically discernible facts just as easily as there can be such manuals in the case of distinct languages, it follows that synonymy in general – hence meaning or intentionality in general – does not supervene on naturalistic facts.

As Quine notes, this is of a piece with "Brentano's thesis of the irreducibility of intentional idioms."[23] But here the road forks: "One may accept the Brentano thesis as either showing the indispensability of intentional idioms and the importance of an autonomous science of intention, or as showing the baselessness of intentional idioms and the emptiness of a science of intention."[24] Quine takes the second option, and it is this that leads him to speak of indeterminacy: there is no "objective matter" – no "matter of fact" – for two empirically equivalent yet incompatible translation manuals to be right or wrong about.[25] Thus Quine supplements the Non-Supervenience Thesis with what may be called the Anti-Realist Thesis.

He hastens to add that translation nevertheless goes on and should go on, and that intentional idioms are *practically* indispensable. What he proposes is not a thoroughgoing revision of our daily practice, but rather the adoption of a "double standard":

> If we are limning the true and ultimate structure of reality, the canonical scheme for us is the austere scheme that knows no quotation but direct quotation and no propositional attitudes but only the physical behavior and constitution of organisms ... But if our use of canonical notation is meant only to dissolve verbal perplexities or facilitate logical deductions, we are often well advised to tolerate the idioms of propositional attitudes.[26]

In other words, we should tolerate talk of meaning and intentionality where it is useful, as it is in everyday life and sometimes in a philosophically more sophisticated version of everyday life. From ontology, however, understood as the theory of the real, this sort of talk should be rigorously excluded. Thus Quine's methodological naturalism about use is accompanied by anti-realism about meaning, and the radicalization of Maimon's skepticism is complete. The Kantian distinction between the empirical and the transcendental, both of which are to be taken seriously in their own terms and from the proper standpoint, is replaced by the adoption of a "double standard" that treats only the methodologically naturalistic with genuine seriousness.

Why draw Quine's lesson rather than Brentano's? Or some Kantian or German Idealist version of the moral that the study of intentionality must employ methods other than those of the natural sciences? For that matter, why not, like Maimon, pursue both the naturalistic and non-naturalistic lines of inquiry, letting each moderate the pretensions of the other?

Quine's reasons for promoting the Anti-Realist Thesis may be discerned from his various, much-discussed arguments for the Non-Supervenience Thesis. What I want to argue is that these reasons support a Maimonian approach as much as they support a Quinean one. This is not because, as Quine acknowledges, his reasons cannot be expected to amount to logically compelling proofs. Rather, it is because, just as, according to Maimon, transcendental philosophy cannot avoid begging the question against methodological naturalism, so do Quine's considerations beg the question in favor of methodological naturalism, and indeed of Quine's physicalist brand of methodological naturalism.

Quine's earlier discussions focus on what has come to be called "the argument from below."[27] He employs the expository device of a radical translation situation, in which the linguist must construct a translation manual without the help of either established tradition or helpful interpreter, in order to focus our attention on what he takes to be the naturalistically discernible facts of the matter. These facts may be said to determine translations of observation sentences, taken as wholes with respect to which speakers' dispositions to assent and dissent do not vary significantly with collateral information. However, as soon as the linguist begins to segment observation sentences into terms – thus, as soon as she begins to assign to speakers intentions to refer to determinate objects – it is necessary to formulate "analytical hypotheses" linking terms in the speaker's language to terms in the linguist's language. It is here, with what Quine later calls the inscrutability of reference, that the Non-Supervenience Thesis enters the story, and the extent of translational variability increases inversely with the degree of observationality.

The problem is that this argument is formulated in a way that *presupposes* the Anti-Realist Thesis. That it does so is evident from Quine's attitude towards holistic interconnections *within* the totality of the speaker's linguistic dispositions. Far from ignoring such connections, Quine emphasizes them, and philosophers who have developed our understanding of them may rightly be said to build on Quinean insights. But the more the linguist is allowed to exploit the holistic structure of language, the more determinate translation becomes:

> Even highly observational sentences do not derive what we ordinarily think of as their meanings only from the links between patterns of sensory stimulation and our dispositions to assent to and dissent from them. Their links with other expressions in the language, hence with the speaker's theory of the world, are also relevant.[28]

Surely it is question-begging to assume that any considerations relevant to the determination of inner-linguistic links are not objective matters of fact.[29]

In his later discussions, Quine shifts the weight onto what has come to be known as the "argument from above," an argument that was always present but was not at first given the same emphasis.[30] To bring out the difference between the indeterminacy of translation and the under-determination that pertains to any theory, including the physical theories that he privileges, Quine focuses on "the radical translation of a radically foreign physicist's theory."[31] In other words, he turns directly to the consideration of highly non-observational sentences. Here the linguist has *two* choices to make. The first is the physicist's choice: she must herself make an observationally underdetermined choice between empirically equivalent physical theories. Then she must make an additional choice about which of the empirically equivalent theories to attribute to the scientifically minded foreigner. Consequently there is a lack of determinacy in translation that goes beyond the under-determination of physical theory by observation.

This argument has the advantage of bringing out the importance of Quine's physicalist brand of methodological naturalism. But it has the same defect as the "argument from below." Namely, it begs the question of anti-realism by assuming that only the links between stimulation patterns and dispositions with respect to observation sentences, and not links betweens items within the speaker's language, count as objective matters of fact. Indeed, as Kirk points out, the exclusion of inner-linguistic connections is particularly striking here, since nobody could hope to tell which sentences belong to the theory, or what the theory is, without paying attention, not only to dispositions to assent or dissent to observation sentences, but also to higher-order dispositions, such as dispositions to revise first-order dispositions under certain circumstances.[32]

No surprise, then, that the Non-Supervenience Thesis has been more attractive than the Anti-Realist Thesis. For the former can be liberated from the latter, and can be supported by a far shorter argument emerging from Quine's discussion. As McDowell points out, even the identification of assenting and dissenting behavior requires the formulation of analytical hypotheses, so translation is under-determined even in the case of observation sentences.[33] This can be taken to show something about Quine's methodological naturalism:

> That meaning is indeterminate with respect to "empirical significance" has no tendency to show, what would indeed be interesting, that meaning is indeterminate, period. That would require that we have an ineliminable freedom of play when we look for a kind of understanding that takes us outside the ambit of "empirical significance": a kind of understanding that involves seeing how the phenomena of our subjects' lives can be organized in the order of justification, the space of reasons. If meaning is indeterminate in this interesting sense, that is not something one could learn at Quine's feet.[34]

But here Maimon's line seems just right. The methodological naturalist and the methodological non-naturalist cannot avoid begging the question against each other. The former will claim the advantage of methodological conservatism, the latter that of content conservatism. No end is in sight to the old enmity between human heels and serpentine fangs.

Some available options

If the analogy developed so far has been sufficiently illuminating, then it should pay off in the form of further detailed analogies between post-Kantian responses to Maimon's reinvigoration of methodological naturalism and contemporary analytic responses to Quine's parallel move. Here I want to introduce a few such payoffs, without claiming that these exhaust the range of options.

One early post-Kantian response to the standoff between transcendental philosophy and methodological naturalism was to revise both Hume's and Kant's conceptions of naturalistic methodology. What we need, in this view, is a discipline of anthropology or psychology that is methodologically distinct from physics, but which nevertheless counts as an equally legitimate science. Such responses were developed by the contemporaneous figures for whom the German Idealists have the most contempt: figures such as Carl Christian Erhard Schmid, Jakob Friedrich Fries and Friedrich Ernst Beneke, for whom the term "psychologism" seems to have been coined.[35]

Thus, according to Fries, Kant correctly identifies the transcendental *subject matter* of philosophy, which aspires to "cognition of the possibility and applicability of *a priori* cognitions."[36] But Kant errs in thinking that the achievement of transcendental cognition also involves a *method* that is distinctively transcendental and a priori. Fries calls this error "the transcendental prejudice," which consists in the assumption that deduction must consist in inferential proof (*Beweis*). This leads Kant to develop inferential deductions of synthetic a priori principles from the actuality of the experience they enable, which cannot escape from a "logical *circle* in the *proofs*."[37]

Kant's error is in fact an instance of a still more widespread confusion that Fries calls "the rationalist prejudice": the assumption that *all justification is inferential*. This has misled philosophers into thinking that every science must take the form of Euclidean geometry, and that all the sciences must form a hierarchy, in which the basic principle of each lower science is provable within a higher science, and in which philosophy must be the highest science of all.[38] Indeed, Humean skepticism arises, in Fries's view, from the very same prejudice, plus the insight that the principle of causality cannot be inferentially proven. Instead of seeking a novel, non-naturalistic method for the inferential proof of synthetic a priori principles, the transcendental philosopher should abandon the underlying prejudice.[39]

Fries intends to reconstruct Kant's philosophy, by acknowledging that what Kant calls transcendental cognition is "really psychological or, better, anthropological cognition," and by developing an appropriate method *that makes no pretension whatsoever to justificatory force*.[40] This is *analogous* to the method of the existing natural sciences. Thus Fries writes:

> one has also cast on my philosophical deductions the aspersion of circular proof, but they are not circular, for they are not proof at all. They belong rather to a theory of these cognitions, and the analogous situation is manifest without any difficulty in all inductions in physics. For example, from individual facts I discern the phenomena of electricity, and lead them back to their universal laws; then I assume these laws as principles of a theory of electricity, and explain from them once again those facts with which I began. Only once my reasoning goes, in preparatory fashion, along the regressive path, does it subsequently go along the progressive path of the system. In an entirely analogous way, we proceed from the observation of our cognition, showing thereby how human cognition is created, elevating ourselves to a theory of the same, showing which principles, according to this theory, must lie in our cognition, and now deriving once again the individual cognitions and judgments from these principles.[41]

The "individual facts" with which Fries begins are what he and others call "facts of consciousness" (*Tatsachen der Bewusstsein*), such as its unity. These are doubly universal: first, they concern the content or structure of any state of consciousness whatsoever; second, they are recognizable as true by anybody who merely reflects on her own conscious states and acts. We may say, then, that Fries replaces Kant's metaphysical expositions and deductions with *inductive identifications* of the facts of consciousness, and he replaces Kant's transcendental expositions and deductions with *explanations* of these facts in terms of a priori principles.

It is impossible not to recognize here a forerunner of a currently prominent post-Quinean strategy: retain Quine's methodological naturalism while rejecting his physicalism, thus insisting on the irreducible plurality of natural sciences, and hence on the variety of naturalistic methods. Of course there are crucial differences, both in the general conception of science and in the specific, foundational concepts of the projected science of mind. Still, the hopes for cognitive psychology expressed by, say, Fodor, surely echo Fries's ambitions for a post-Kantian psychology that would naturalize what was worth preserving in transcendental philosophy without incurring any skeptical consequences.[42]

Of course, the facts of consciousness approach developed by Fries is anathema to the German Idealists. Though their alternatives have significant commonalities, they are also significantly different. For present purposes, the most important differences concern the possibility and status of a philosophy of nature, the issue over which Fichte and Schelling, abetted by Hegel, had a sharp disagreement in the early 1800s.

Let us start with Fichte, who appreciates not only the force of Maimon's anti-realist challenge but also the power of the resources made available by Maimon's contributions to transcendental philosophy. Recall that the methodological naturalist may appropriate what the transcendental philosopher treats as categorial necessities by redescribing them as no more than practically indispensable. We may think of Fichte as taking them back again: if we press hard enough on the idea of *the primacy of the practical*, then these practical indispensabilities may be just what transcendental philosophy needs! In his Jena *Wissenschaftslehre*, Fichte proceeds to rethink the theoretical in terms of the practical, so that the fundamental conditions of the possibility of experience are reconceived as anticipatory versions of normative principles that play an essential role in the moral life. At the deepest level lie anticipatory versions of what Kant calls *Wille* and *Willkür*: the inescapability of responsiveness to the summons of another, and the freedom to choose how to respond.[43]

At the same time, Fichte reconfigures transcendental idealism so that it is surprisingly close to the anti-realism of Maimon's naturalistic challenger. For Fichte, there are necessary conditions of the possibility of experience that are ideal in the sense that, like Kantian ideas of reason, they cannot be empirically realized. Yet, like Kant's idea of freedom, Fichtean ideas can have effects within the empirical world. Thus the absolute I and God are efficacious ideas, but not in any sense realities. Indeed, the only realities are natural objects of empirical knowledge: "all objects necessarily occupy space, that is, they are material."[44] There can be no transcendental realities, no things in themselves.

What, then, distinguishes Fichte's idealism from naturalistic anti-realism? Fichte is prepared to agree with Maimon and hence with Hume that the imagination plays an essential role in experience. It is involved, not merely in the schematization of the categories, but also in the generation of the categorial form and, indeed, even of the sensible matter of cognition. Its activity is regulated by the aforementioned ideas. However, Fichte rejects the anti-realist characterization of the imagination as generating "deception." Every deception must contrast with the possibility of truth. If the imagination is practically indispensable in the sense that *rational agency is impossible without it*, then there is no alternative, and so there is no deception.[45] Instead, the imagination should be understood in transcendental terms, as constituting the possibility of experience, both formally and materially.

Of course, this is hardly a *refutation* of naturalistic anti-realism. For it is not true that there is *no* alternative. It would be more accurate to say that there is no alternative that preserves the content of our self-understanding as rational agents. In short, the transcendental philosopher still claims content conservatism, to which the methodological naturalist will oppose methodological conservatism, and the standoff continues. Fichte is well aware of this. He hopes, however, to have made fully explicit what was implicit in Kant's philosophy: that it is not only science but also rational agency that is at stake.

Brandom is a contemporary proponent of an analogous strategy. Though he typically appeals to Hegel rather than to Fichte, much of what he appreciates in Hegel is in fact Fichtean,[46] and the lesson he learns from Quine's Non-Supervenience Thesis is a Fichtean overcoming of the dualism of theory and practice:

> Carnap and the other logical positivists affirmed their neo-Kantian roots by taking over Kant's two-phase structure: *first* one stipulates *meanings*, *then* experience dictates which deployments of them yield true theories ... Quine rejects Carnap's sharp separation of the process of deciding what concepts (meanings, language) to use from the process of deciding what judgments (beliefs, theory) to endorse ... There is only one practice – the practice of actually making determinate judgments. Engaging in that practice involves settling all at once both what we mean and what we believe ... The actual *use* of the language settles – and is all that *could* settle – the *meanings* of the expressions used.
>
> Hegel is a pragmatist also in this monistic sense. He aims at a conception of experience that does not distinguish two different kinds of activity, one of which is the application of concepts in (determinate) judgment and action, and the other of which is the institution or discovery of those concepts (by "judgments of reflection").[47]

In other words, if use is all that could determine meaning – if there is no alternative, or at least no alternative that preserves meaning – then meaning is just as determinate as use enables it to be, and there is no "meaning in itself" of which use falls short. Meaning may not be a natural reality, susceptible to investigation with the help of naturalistic methods, but it can be accounted for by non-naturalistic methods, and there is consequently no need to adopt Quine's disparaging "double standard."

Neither Fichte nor Brandom says much about nature. They accept the dichotomy of nature and rational agency or meaning, and seek to develop the only – or, at least, the optimal – account of the conditions and structure of rational agency of meaning, leaving nature to its own devices. But this is just the bone of contention between, on the one hand, Fichte and, on the other hand, Schelling and Hegel, who insist that the transcendental account of rational agency must be accompanied by an account of nature that explains how it is possible for natural beings to be rational agents.

After all, despite all Fichte's efforts, the success of his ambitious project would still leave methodological naturalism, radicalized by Maimon, intact and unfriendly to rational agency. As long as natural psychology or anthropology are obliged to account for acknowledgments of normative principles and of inferences in terms of mechanisms whose explanation involves no notion of validity whatsoever, the naturalistic serpent can still bite the transcendental philosopher's heel. And this remains the case: while Fichte derives some principles constitutive of organic and inorganic nature, he does so only insofar as the natural world is assumed to provide the background and the instruments for rational action. Only the human world, not the natural world, can be said to incarnate reason. Consequently, naturalistic thinking remains unaccommodating to rational agency.

One can see the attraction of a more direct approach, in which one seeks to understand nature in general as the incarnation of reason – so that even inorganic nature is, in a phrase drawn by Hegel from Schelling, "petrified intelligence" – with the consequence that no natural scientific explanation is adequate unless it can be placed within a framework that renders rational agency intelligible.[48] Idealisms of this sort, unlike those of the Fichtean variety, are aptly characterized as forms of realism about ideas.

McDowell's naturalism of second nature adopts a more modest analogue of this strategy. Its goal is not to give a positive account of the possibility that natural beings can be rational agents, but rather to dissolve the sense that this is an impossibility:

> Given the notion of second nature, we can say that the way our lives are shaped by reason is natural, even while we deny that the structure of the space of reasons can be integrated into the layout of the realm of law.[49]

Of course, it is far from clear that the methodological naturalist is *obliged* to think in terms of second nature at all. But McDowell's aim is not, I think, to resolve the standoff. It is, rather, to enable the transcendental philosopher to sleep with an easy conscience.

Could anything resolve the standoff? Maimon's view is that pure mathematics is not susceptible to naturalistic methods. Certainly mathematics is a hard case for methodological naturalism, and it deserves closer consideration than it has so far received from the contemporary proponents of analogues of German idealism.

Another alternative is to develop a closer analogue to the nature-philosophies of Schelling and Hegel. The maximally ambitious Schellingian program is to reform natural science itself, showing that it does a better job by its own lights if it employs concepts of proto-rationality to explain how first nature gives rise to second nature. The more modest – but still ambitious – Hegelian program aims to employ distinctively philosophical methods to *interpret* the results of natural science as contributions to an account of the proto-rationality of nature, and hence of the naturalness of reason.[50] In both cases, of course, it would have to be shown that it is impossible to take an anti-realist attitude to proto-rationality. And it is unclear what would show this. Schelling's program has the advantage of downplaying the distinction between the methods of natural science and the methods of philosophy, making the former more like the latter in a way that would seem to render an anti-realist attitude towards some methods and not others arbitrary. But this maximalist program is unattractive in an age of specialization, when philosophers are highly unlikely to contribute to physics and vice-versa.

The merits of these options require discussion elsewhere. Meanwhile, Maimon continues to be a helpful guide, not only to post-Kantian philosophy, but also to its post-Quinean descendant. If you cannot defang the serpent, you must learn how to treat snakebites, and how to walk with swollen heels.

Notes

1 I dedicate this paper to the memory of Burton Dreben, who suggested to me – some two decades ago, before the analytic resurgence of German idealism made its public appearance – that Quine was the Hegel of contemporary philosophy. I did not know – sitting in his office in Emerson Hall – exactly what Dreben meant, and I do not know how he would respond to the argument developed here. But I took what Dreben said as an encouragement of my graduate student ambitions, and I am still responding to his – ever provocative – pedagogy.

2 For the problems motivating German idealism, see Paul Franks, *All or Nothing: Systematicity, Transcendental Arguments, and Skepticism in German Idealism* (Cambridge, Mass.: Harvard University Press, 2005).

3 For further discussion, see Franks, "What should Kantians learn from Maimon's Skepticism?", in G. Freudenthal (ed.) *Salomon Maimon: Rational Dogmatist, Empirical Skeptic* (Dordrecht: Kluwer, 2003), pp. 200–32.

4 See Immanuel Kant, *Critique of Pure Reason*, trans. and eds. Paul Guyer and Allen Wood (Cambridge: Cambridge University Press, 1998), A737/B765: "no one can have fundamental insight into the proposition 'Everything that happens has its cause' from these given concepts alone. Hence it is not a dogma, although from another point of view, namely that of the sole field of its possible use, i.e., experience, it can very well be proved apodictically. But although it must be proved, it is called a **principle** and not a **theorem** because it has the special property that it first makes possible its ground of proof, namely experience, and must always be presupposed in this."

5 Ibid., A91–92/B124.

6 Ibid., B127–28.

7 Salomon Maimon, *Gesammelte Werke*, V. Verra (ed.) (Hildesheim: Georg Olms, 1970), vol. 7, p. 58. Translations from Maimon are mine.

8 Maimon sometimes refers to experience "in Kant's sense." Following Kant's *Prolegomena*, Maimon believes that the "empirical propositions" discussed by Kant in the *Critique* are judgments of experience claiming necessary connections among sensuously given objects. See Franks, "What should Kantians learn?"

9 See Maimon, *Gesammelte Werke*, vol. 4, p. 239n.: "It is a well-known proposition, which Newton lays at the foundation of his philosophy of nature, that one should assume no new principle for the explanation of a phenomenon, which may be explained from other, long since known principles."

10 See Kant, *Critique*, A84/B116–17. Kant explicitly draws on Roman law as practiced in Germany, but Maimon perhaps draws, and Quine certainly draws, on the distinct British common law tradition, on the basis of which Bacon and Boyle had built an epistemology of experimentation. For Kant's usage, see Dieter Henrich, "Kant's Notion of a Deduction and the Methodological Background of the First Critique," in Eckhart Förster ed., *Kant's Transcendental Deductions* (Stanford, Calif.: Stanford University Press, 1989). On Bacon and Boyle, see Rose-Mary Sargent, *The Diffident Naturalist: Robert Boyle and the Experimental Philosophy* (Chicago, Ill.: University of Chicago Press, 1995).

11 See, e.g. Maimon, *Gesammelte Werke*, vol. 4, pp. 214–15n.:

> Hume doubts, not perception as a fact in itself, but merely its objective necessity and universal validity, and he explains the appearance of necessity on a subjective basis in accordance with a law of association of ideas . . . My skepticism concedes the concept of objective necessity and doubts only its actual use with respect to objects of perception. If I am asked whence I have the concept of objective necessity, then I answer that I find objective necessity in the

objects of mathematics and their relations. If I am asked further what is the criterion of this objective necessity which I attribute only to the objects of mathematics, but not to the objects of perception, then I answer that this criterion is completely obvious. The objects of perception presuppose a condition in the subject if their relations are to be known as necessary. In contrast, the objects of mathematics presuppose no such condition in the subject. When I think the straight line necessarily as the shortest, I may represent it for the first time, or I may already have repeated its representation often. In contrast, the judgment, "Fire melts wax necessarily," is available to me for the first time only after a frequent repetition – dependent either on chance or on my will – of this perception, and it is therefore here only a subjective necessitation, but no objective necessity.

12 See Maimon, ibid., vol. 5, p. 19:

> Without the *Godhead* the world cannot be *thought* but, without the world, the *Godhead* cannot be *known*. Without *philosophy*, no *science in general* is possible, because it determines *a priori* the form of a *science in general*. Without presupposing some other science, *philosophy* can have no significance whatsoever for us.

13 Maimon, ibid., vol. 4, p. 80.

14 W.V.O. Quine, "Carnap and Logical Truth", in Quine, *The Ways of Paradox* (Cambridge, Mass.: Harvard University Press, 1966), p. 107.

15 There has been much recent scholarship on Kantian and Neo-Kantian aspects of Carnap's thinking. See, e.g., Michael Friedman, *Reconsidering Logical Positivism* (Cambridge: Cambridge University Press, 1999).

16 See Rudolf Carnap, *The Logical Syntax of Language* (Chicago, Ill.: Open Court, 2002), p. 51.

17 See, e.g. Carnap, *Meaning and Necessity* (Chicago, Ill.: University of Chicago Press, 1956).

18 I am leaving out of consideration here those arguments for indeterminacy that depend on the inextricability of meaning and belief, or on the role of normative principles in translation or interpretation. These arguments can be rendered independent of methodological naturalism, and I will consider them elsewhere.

19 There is of course no suggestion here that Quine ever read Maimon, or even heard of him.

20 Quine, *Word and Object* (Cambridge, Mass.: MIT Press, 1960), p. 27.

21 Ibid., pp. 73–74.

22 Quine, "Indeterminacy of Translation Again," in *Journal of Philosophy*, 1987, vol. 84, no. 1, p. 5.

23 Quine, *Word and Object*, p. 221.

24 Quine, *Word and Object*, p. 221.

25 Quine, *Word and Object*, p. 73. While Maimon is anti-realist about the *justificatory role* and hence the *justified status* of Kant's transcendental principles, leaving open the possibility that they are *true*, Quine seems to foreclose the analogous possibility that meanings truly exist, and is accordingly closer to revisionism than Maimon. The underlying difference is that Quine believes that we have a natural science uncommitted to meanings, whereas Maimon does not believe that we have a natural science uncommitted to causes, though he believes that *if* we had a natural science, it *would* be non-causal.

26 Quine, *Word and Object*, p. 221.

27 See Quine, "On the Reasons for the Indeterminacy of Translation," in *Journal of Philosophy*, 1970, vol. 67, no. 6, p. 173.
28 Robert Kirk, "Indeterminacy of Translation," in R.F. Gibson Jr. (ed.) *The Cambridge Companion to Quine* (Cambridge: Cambridge University Press, 2004), p. 167. For a seminal discussion of the point, see Gareth Evans, "Identity and Predication," in Evans, *Collected Papers* (Oxford: Oxford University Press, 1985).
29 Kirk draws a slightly different moral: "It is question-begging to assume that the totality of behavioral dispositions falls short of fixing what those links are." My formulation avoids Quinean talk of "behavioral dispositions."
30 See Quine, *Word and Object*, pp. 75–76.
31 Quine, "On the Reasons," p. 179.
32 Kirk, "Indeterminacy," p. 170.
33 John McDowell, "Anti-Realism and the Epistemology of Understanding," in McDowell, *Mind, Knowledge, and Reality* (Cambridge, Mass.: Harvard University Press, 1998), pp. 338–40.
34 McDowell, *Mind and World* (Cambridge, Mass.: Harvard University Press, 1994), pp. 156–57.
35 See Johann Eduard Erdmann, *Grundriss der Geschichte der Philosophie* (Berlin: W. Hertz, 1870), vol. 1, p. 636. See Wilhelm Windelband, *Geschichte der neueren Philosophie* (Leipzig: Breitkopf & Härtel, 1880), pp. 386–97, for criticism of Fries as psychologistic. For earlier criticism of "psychological idealism" in Kant and Fichte, see Hegel, *Werke* (Frankfurt am Main: Suhrkamp, 1970), vol. 1, pp. 303, 305, 307.
36 Jacob Friedrich Fries, *Neue oder anthropologische Kritik der Vernunft* (Aalen: Scientia Verlag, 1967), vol. 1, p. 28. Translations from Fries are mine.
37 Fries, *Neue Kritik*, vol. 1, p. 25.
38 Fries, *Neue Kritik*, vol. 1, pp. 21–25.
39 Fries, *Neue Kritik*, vol. 1, p. 27.
40 Fries, *Neue Kritik*, vol. 1, p. 29.
41 Fries, *Neue Kritik*, vol. 1, p. 26.
42 For a classic argument, see Jerry Fodor, "Special Sciences," in Fodor, *RePresentations* (Cambridge, Mass.: MIT Press, 1981). For more recent reflections, see Fodor, *The Mind doesn't Work that Way: The Scope and Limits of Computational Psychology* (Cambridge, Mass.: MIT Press, 2001), and *Hume Variations* (Oxford: Oxford University Press, 2003).
43 Fichte's second Jena presentation illustrates this line of thought better than his first. See Franks, *All or Nothing*, pp. 313–25.
44 J. G. Fichte, *Sämmtliche Werke* (Berlin: Walter de Gruyter, 1971), vol. 1, p. 247. Translations from Fichte are mine.
45 Fichte, *Werke*, vol. 1, p. 227:

> It is accordingly taught here that all reality – self-evidently *for us*, for it cannot be understood otherwise in transcendental philosophy – is merely brought forth by the imagination. One of the greatest thinkers of our age, who – so far as I understand – teaches the same doctrine – calls this a *deception* of the imagination. But every deception must contrast itself with truth, every deception must let itself be avoided. So if it is proven, then, as it should have been proven in the present system, that on that act of the imagination is grounded the possibility of our consciousness, our life, our being for ourselves, i.e., our being an I – then that act cannot be removed if we should not abstract from the I, which is an abstraction, insofar as it is impossible for that which does the abstracting to

abstract from itself. Therefore it does not deceive, rather it gives truth, and the only possible truth.

46 This is not to deny that there are distinctively Hegelian features of Brandom's thinking. I hope to discuss these in an essay on holism and nihilism in German Idealism and in post-Quinean analytic philosophy.
47 R. Brandom, *Tales of the Mighty Dead* (Cambridge, Mass.: Harvard University Press, 2002), pp. 214–15.
48 Hegel, *Werke*, vol. 9, p. 24.
49 McDowell, *Mind and World*, pp. 87–88.
50 For the distinction, see Alison Stone, *Petrified Intelligence: Nature in Hegel's Philosophy* (Albany, N.Y.: SUNY Press, 2005), pp. 86–89.

3

DARK DAYS: ANGLOPHONE SCHOLARSHIP SINCE THE 1960S

Frederick Beiser

Of ventriloquists and dummies

Since the end of the Second World War, the predominant concern of Anglophone scholarship on German idealism has been to emasculate, domesticate and sanitize it, to make it weak, safe and clean for home consumption. The great dead German idealists – almost always Kant and Hegel, almost never Fichte, Schelling or Schopenhauer, who are beyond the pale – have been refashioned into English gentlemen or American niceguys. Kant and Hegel are remade in the image of Anglo-American philosophical culture – like Renaissance paintings of Biblical scenes – with scant interest in what they were in their own culture. Such domesticization has one great advantage: we need not worry about how the German idealists challenge our own ways of thinking.

The heart of this domestication programme has been the tendency to read the *metaphysical* themes and issues out of German idealism.[1] Writing under the shadow of positivism, pragmatism or ordinary language philosophy, Anglophone scholars have had great difficulty in accepting the legitimacy of any form of metaphysics. Since they have had to make German idealism palatable to an academic audience influenced by these trends, they have had no choice but to underplay its metaphysics. Many are the spurned metaphysical themes: Kant's transcendental idealism, his transcendental psychology, his noumenal–phenomenal dualism, his practical faith in a transcendent God; Hegel's absolute idealism, his concept of an infinite spirit, his speculative *Naturphilosophie*. All these themes were of prime importance to Kant and Hegel; but they have been read out of them because they are of little importance to us. Rather than the real Kant and Hegel, what we get instead are dummies. The late Paul Kristeller would complain about the ventriloquist's approach to the history of philosophy, where an interpreter only reads his views into an historical figure.[2] Nowhere has ventriloquism been pursued with more vigour and rigour than with contemporary interpretations of Kant and Hegel.

For all the diversity and complexity of contemporary Anglophone scholarship on German idealism, its anti-metaphysical direction has been persistent and pervasive. It first appears in P.F. Strawson's influential account of Kant's first *Critique*, *The Bounds of Sense*, which appeared in 1966. Famously, Strawson rejected Kant's transcendental idealism and 'the imaginary subject of transcendental psychology'; and all he could salvage from Kant was something like his own 'descriptive metaphysics'. For generations of Oxbridge students, Strawson's interpretation was the model for how to do history of philosophy. The same anti-metaphysical tendency surfaces in John Rawls's interpretation of Kant's moral philosophy, which he first sketched in *A Theory of Justice* (1971) and then elaborated in lectures at Harvard and Columbia.[3] Rawls saw Kant's ethics chiefly as an anticipation of his own theory of justice. Since, however, he saw no use for Kant's dualisms or transcendental idealism, he advocated 'detaching' them from the rest of his philosophy. Rawls's work became the inspiration for a whole generation at Harvard, who duly followed his lead in trying to find anticipations of Rawls in Kant. Finally, the same anti-metaphysical bent emerged in the 'non-metaphysical' interpretation of Hegel, which became very popular in the 1980s. Although this approach was first fostered by Klaus Hartmann in Germany,[4] its most vocal and prominent advocates have been in the Anglophone world, most notably Robert Pippin, Terry Pinkard and Allen White. They stress Hegel's affinity with the Kantian tradition and his interest in epistemological issues, and downplay his Spinozistic metaphysics and speculative *Naturphilosophie*.[5] The non-metaphysical interpretation of Hegel has proven especially popular among scholars of Hegel's moral and political philosophy, who are eager to salvage some meaning for it independent of Hegel's metaphysics.[6]

The anti-metaphysical tendency of Anglophone scholarship has been based upon a specific hermeneutic, a certain method of interpretation, which has been widely practiced by analytic philosophers. This method is entirely a-historical. It has little interest in the genesis or context of a text, still less in the nuances of meaning in the original language. These are deemed historical details, irrelevant to philosophical content.[7] The chief aim of this method is to reconstruct 'the arguments of a philosopher', to assess their value as solutions to apparently *eternal* problems, though these problems usually turn out to be only the latest fads and fixations. This method assumes that texts are self-contained and self-illuminating wholes, as if their meaning should be fully apparent to the intuitions of a contemporary Anglophone reader. When their meaning is not obvious, one resorts to guesswork and asks 'What could this possibly mean?'; where the suggestions are meant to be logically exhaustive, though they usually reveal the limits of the philosophical culture of the interpreter. When the guessing is over, target practice begins; the hapless historical figure becomes an 'Aunt Sally', whose chief fault is not being one of us. This shoot-first-and-ask-questions-later approach has been practiced with most *élan* by Jonathan Bennett, whose *Kant's Analytic* and *Kant's Dialectic* are the *non plus ultra* of the genre. His description of the methodology of these works says it all:

> The author believes that we understand Kant only in proportion as we can say, clearly and in contemporary terms, what his problems were, which of them are still problems and what contribution Kant makes to their solution.[8]

It is a remarkable, and indeed embarrassing, fact that some of the most notable practitioners of this method seem to have scant conception of the chief alternative to their own. They show little awareness of, or scant interest in, the historical methodology developed and practiced in the late nineteenth and early twentieth centuries by Wilhelm Dilthey, Rudolf Haym, Benno Erdmann, Erich Adickes and Ernst Cassirer. Their method is the very antithesis of the contemporary Anglophone one: it insists on understanding and assessing a text in its own terms, according to the author's intentions and historical context. *Pace* the suggestions of Strawson and Bennett,[9] it was never reverential or deferential to historical figures; rather, they were criticized from within, according to their own standards and assumptions. These German scholars fully recognized that the best criticism only emerges from the deepest sympathy, from the most plausible reconstruction of an author's meaning. It is an enormous pity that their work has not been better known in the Anglophone world. In many respects they provide a model for how to approach and understand a text historically. Their achievements dwarf anything produced in the Anglophone world. They stand to their Anglophone counterparts as men to boys.

What is so wrong with the analytic method? It suffers from two irreparable flaws. First, it is anachronistic. Rather than understanding the past in its own terms, it is understood entirely in contemporary terms. Kant and Hegel are read as if they were participants in *our* discussions and concerns; but there is no interest in *their* discussions and concerns. So we learn much about what they *ought to have said*; but we learn little about what they meant in their own context. There is nothing wrong with this in principle; it can even be illuminating in bringing out the relevance of an historical figure to our concerns. There should be no taboo against the counterfactual exercise of imagining what Kant or Hegel might have said if they knew of our contemporary issues, or even of revising or reformulating their theories so that their relevance is made clear. The only problem is that, all too often, these imagined or revised Kants and Hegels are still presented as the actual, historical Kant or Hegel. For all their logical finesse, practitioners of the analytic approach are remarkably unsophisticated about the status of the entities they revise and reinvent in contemporary terms. Strictly speaking, they are only fictions; but seldom is this admitted; they would like us to believe that it is the actual, historical Kant or Hegel who is doing the talking. But perhaps this is all we should expect of ventriloquists, whose whole art consists in deception?

Second, the analytic method is *philosophically* limiting and blinding. The more we make a past thinker conform to our own concerns and preconceptions, the more he becomes like us, and so the less we broaden our horizons and get outside the limits of our own era. We learn most from past philosophy only when we see how it *differs* from our own. In philosophy, as in anthropology, what is most interesting and exciting is the different. A past intellectual milieu is fascinating in the same way as another culture. We learn new problems, new ways of thinking, different concepts, and even a different language. The analytic method presents us with a false dilemma: anachronism or antiquarianism. It assumes that the past has to be forced into our own terms to get philosophical relevance from it; hence historical research on its own has a merely doxographic or antiquarian value. But this is to assume that our own culture and epoch has a monopoly on ways of doing philosophy, and that we never can escape our own intellectual horizons.

Nowhere are these mistakes more apparent than in Anglophone interpretations of German idealism. Both are committed as soon as we read the metaphysics out of German idealism. This is not only anachronistic, but also philosophically blinding, because it is precisely the metaphysics of German idealism that is so challenging to our own ways of doing philosophy. Analytic philosophers like to focus on specific issues and to settle questions piecemeal; they are suspicious of grand theories which seem speculative and to multiply commitments beyond necessity. But this way of doing philosophy often begs fundamental questions. It was the great merit of the German idealists that they never shirked such questions, and that they fully recognized one's answer to them determined one's philosophical commitments all the way down, prescribing answers to all specific questions.

In the following sections I want to show some of the ways in which reading the metaphysics out of German idealism has been philosophically blinding and has only begged fundamental questions. I will examine each of the tendencies above; I will then conclude with some more positive suggestions about what must be done.

Kant, the *Jolie Laide*

P.F. Strawson's interpretation of Kant in *The Bounds of Sense* was a milestone for Anglophone interpretations of German idealism. It set the precedent for domesticating German idealism, for making it philosophically jejune and palatable to tastes weaned on positivism and ordinary language philosophy. Strawson's antiseptic reading of Kant, which removed all traces of transcendental psychology and idealism from the core of Kant's enterprise, perfectly illustrates the philosophical vices of the analytic approach. The price of accepting Strawson's interpretation is that we cannot take seriously the sceptical problems that Kant attempted to address in the *Critique of Pure Reason*. It was a virtual premise of Strawson's interpretation, which was heavily influenced by the ordinary language philosophy of the 1960s, that such problems are illusory. For this point Strawson provides no justification or explanation in *The Bounds of Sense*. It is noteworthy, though, that Kant himself believed that he could preserve common sense beliefs with his own empirical realism – a point Strawson fails to appreciate by conflating Kant's idealism with Berkeley's; it is also noteworthy that Kant attacked the attempt to resolve sceptical problems by appealing to common sense – a critique that Strawson would have done well to heed.

Strawson lays down all his cards in the very beginning of *The Bounds of Sense* by making his graphic distinction between the two faces of the *Critique of Pure Reason*. There is the pretty face, which is Kant's account of the structure of possible experience; and there is the ugly face, which is his transcendental psychology. While Strawson honours Kant for his investigation into the limits of experience, he insists that his transcendental psychology is 'incoherent in itself' and that it 'masks rather than explains the real character of his enquiry'.[10] Kant's proper concern in the *Critique of Pure Reason*, Strawson tells us, was to investigate the 'limits of what we can conceive or make intelligible to ourselves, as a possible general structure of experience', or to determine 'the set of ideas which form the limiting framework of all of our thought about the world and experience about the world.'[11] Unfortunately, however, Kant was led astray by a psychological analogy: that the way the world appears to us is determined by our psychological constitution. Understandably but wrongly, he conceived the limiting or necessary general features of experience to have their source in our faculties or cognitive constitution. So Kant's basic error was this: 'Whatever necessities [he] found in our conception of experience he ascribed to the nature of our faculties.'[12]

For Strawson, the biggest wart on the ugly face of the *Critique* is transcendental idealism. Transcendental idealism is the doctrine that we know only appearances, and that behind them lies some unknowable thing-in-itself. Such a doctrine is the direct result of Kant's transcendental psychology, Strawson argues, the evil fruit of his mistaken equation of conceptual limits with psychological faculties. Because Kant reads the necessities of our concepts of experience as necessities of psychological constitution, he thinks that they provide conditions to which our experience of the world must conform, so that we cannot know the world in itself prior to the application of these conditions.[13] So, in Strawson's view, transcendental idealism arises from the combination of two errors: first, the identification of the limits of our conception of the world with our faculties; second, the assumption that how the world appears to us is determined by our faculties. Strawson regards these as 'errors' not because they are erroneous in themselves, but because he cannot accept the conclusion from combining them: namely, that we cannot know reality but only the appearances of things. This clashes too violently with his common sense realism. When Strawson, like G.E. Moore, holds his hand before his face in broad daylight there can be no doubt about it: it is a *real* hand!

Kant would not have been impressed by Strawson's reasons for rejecting transcendental idealism. He would have explained that Strawson confuses *empirical* realism – a common sense standpoint – with *transcendental* realism – a philosophical *explanation* of that standpoint. But let us leave aside the merits of Strawson's common sense realism. We need to examine more closely his diagnosis of the basic error of transcendental idealism. We need to raise two more specific questions. First, is it a mistake to think that how we perceive the world is determined by our psychological constitution? Second, is it an error to assume that conceptual necessities have something to do with our psychological constitution?

Regarding the first question, it has to be said that in a straightforward sense – the kind beloved by ordinary language philosophers – it is not a mistake at all. It is just a fact of ordinary experience and science that the way things appear to us does depend on the faculties with which we perceive them. Since this is a point that Strawson himself has to concede,[14] there is no quarrel here. The more contentious issue concerns the second question, specifically, Kant's alleged conflation of conceptual necessities with psychological constitution. What confusion is this exactly? It is indeed a mistake to conflate logical with psychological necessities, as if logical entailments between propositions were somehow descriptive of how people think. Much of the plausibility of Strawson's antiseptic interpretation rests on this simple point; but the problem is that it is hardly a mistake that Kant can be accused of committing. Kant himself was a sworn enemy against all forms of psychologism, a fundamental fact that Strawson never ponders. What is not so plainly a mistake – and what is really at issue here – is Kant's assumption that there is a psychological explanation for the fundamental principles and concepts by which we understand the world. Rather than an error, this seems to be straightforward common sense. For if I constantly and inevitably interpret my world according to the assumptions that it consists in a world of enduring things, or that there are causes for events, then surely there must be some psychological explanation for it. The *validity* of these assumptions is of course independent of this explanation; but there must still be some psychological explanation for them; and since these assumptions are so basic for my interpretation of the world, these facts must be basic too; they must answer to my basic psychological constitution.

Strawson could defend himself by saying that 'basic ideas and conceptions' amount to only fundamental beliefs, and that these are not something so deep-going about our psychological constitution that they determine how things appear to us. They are not on par with, say, having five senses. If we had completely different basic ideas and conceptions, then the world would still appear to our senses as it does now. The problem with this defence is that it presupposes a very sharp distinction between concept and sense, thinking and sensing, which Kant himself provisionally accepts but eventually undermines in the Transcendental Deduction. There he argues that how we *perceive* the world also depends fundamentally on how we *conceive* it, namely, that we perceive things in a single space and time because they conform to the concepts of causality and reciprocity. Kant is perhaps wrong here; but at the very least Strawson has begged another fundamental question.

At this point it should be plain that Strawson is in trouble. If it is a fact that our psychological constitution determines how the world appears to us, and if it is also a fact that our fundamental principles are based on that constitution, then the question is inescapable: To what extent do these principles correspond with the world itself? This is a difficult question, to be sure, and there is no guarantee from what has been said so far that Kant's transcendental idealism is a plausible answer to it. But the chief point here is only that the question is perfectly meaningful, and that it cannot go away simply by confidence in our ordinary language and our naive realism. Indeed, the whole nasty issue of the thing-in-itself already raises its hoary head at this point, because we want to know whether there is a discrepancy between reality itself and our ways of conceiving things.

If Strawson's account of Kant's epistemological enterprise is to be coherent at all – if he is to exclude entirely transcendental psychology and its resultant transcendental idealism – then he has to interpret the *Critique* strictly as a *second-order* enquiry into the logical structure of our discourse about the world. Its task will be to find the fundamental presuppositions of such discourse. This means that all the portions of the *Critique* worth salvaging must be translatable into the formal mode of speech. But such a pedantic and sterile reading of Kant's project is bought at a very steep price; for the only way to avoid all first-order questions about the world itself is to abstract from the whole issue of truth itself. Kant would have to consider simply *the logic of our discourse*, and would not be able to ask whether this discourse is true. He would be able to determine, for example, that the principle of causality is fundamental to our ordinary discourse about the world; but he would not be able to ask about whether it is really valid.

But if this is all the *Critique* does, then it loses most of its philosophical interest: namely, Kant's reply to scepticism. The transcendental deduction is really concerned with the conditions of the truth of these fundamental principles, not simply with the role they play in our ordinary and scientific discourse. But if we are concerned with the truth conditions of our basic principles, then it becomes impossible to abstract from the ontological question of what these principles are true. Clearly, the question 'Under what conditions is this true?' is inseparable from 'Of what in the world is this true?' Epistemology and ontology become closely intertwined.

Kant himself did not think that it is possible to separate the justification of our fundamental concepts from transcendental idealism. Indeed, he regarded transcendental idealism as the underpinning of the whole argument of the Transcendental Deduction, which attempts to justify the application of synthetic a priori principles to experience. As he explains in the Summary Representation of the A Deduction and in §27 of the B Deduction, the synthetic a priori principles of the understanding apply to experience only if the objects of experience are appearances, that is, objects whose existence and form depend upon the cognitive activities of the subject perceiving them

(A 128–29). If *per contra* these objects were things-in-themselves, there would be no guarantee that these principles apply to them, 'which is precisely what the skeptic wishes most' (B 168). Since these principles are a priori, i.e. universal and necessary, they cannot be derived from perception, and so they must originate in the understanding itself. But if the principles arise from the understanding, there is no reason to assume – barring some miraculous pre-established harmony – that they apply to things-in-themselves, which *ex hypothesi* have an existence and essence independent of them. Even if we reject Kant's argument here, the fundamental problem remains: How do synthetic a priori principles apply to experience if they are not derived from it? If these principles claim universality and necessity, how are they true of the world, which never provides evidence for such a claim?

Such was the problem that Kant pondered in the 1770s, and that eventually led to his transcendental idealism. Whether we accept transcendental idealism or not, it is hard to deny that we face a problem here of the first importance. Strawson's willingness to abstract from this whole issue reveals, I believe, the influence of Oxford ordinary language philosophy upon him. He seems to think that everything is in order as it stands with ordinary discourse, and that Kant gets in trouble when he attempts to step outside it and ask critical questions about it.[15] But this, I suggest, is not the misery but the glory of the *Critique*.

Jack Rawls falls in love with *Zwittermensch*

Sometime in the mid 1970s, John Rawls began to work intensively on Kant's moral philosophy, making it the focus of his lectures and seminars at Harvard.[16] The motivation came from his conviction that Kant had been the inspiration for his own theory of justice. The culmination of this new interest was his 1980 Dewey lectures at Columbia, which were published as 'Kantian Constructivism in Moral Theory'. The task of these lectures was, as Rawls himself put it, 'to set out more clearly the Kantian roots' of the theory of justice as fairness.[17]

It is obvious that Rawls's enterprise was not meant to be historical. Rather than reconstructing the historical Kant, he simply wanted to show the relevance of Kant for his own conception of justice. Rawls was very cautious not to confuse his Kant, who anticipated the procedural theory of justice, with the historical Kant; and so he warned his listeners 'the adjective "Kantian" expresses analogy rather than identity'.[18] More precisely, the adjective meant only that Rawls's doctrine 'sufficiently resembles Kant's in enough fundamental respects so that it is far closer to his view than to other traditional moral conceptions that are appropriate as a benchmark of comparison'. This is all fair enough. It is perfectly legitimate for Rawls to compare Kant with his own theory, and it is indeed illuminating, bringing out the continuing relevance of Kant's moral philosophy for contemporary concerns. Rawls's lectures and seminars have been the inspiration for a whole generation of students at Harvard, who have greatly increased the level of philosophical sophistication in Kant scholarship. If Kant's ethics remains vital today, this is chiefly because of their work.[19]

There was, however, always a fatal equivocation behind Rawls's approach to Kant. Rawls was not always so careful to distinguish the actual, historical Kant from the Kant he appropriated for his theory of justice. Somehow, the real and genuine Kant was the one who had conceived – if through a glass darkly – his own constructivist theory of justice. What did not anticipate this approach was chaff and dross, the product of historical accident and irrelevant to philosophy. The rational core of Kant's doctrine was his constructivism; his mystical shell was his transcendental idealism and noumenal–phenomenal dualism, which could and should be detached from 'the structure of Kant's doctrine'.[20] This equivocation is most apparent in *A Theory of Justice* itself.[21] Here Rawls is at first very cautious to stress that the Kantian interpretation of justice as fairness does not amount to 'an interpretation of Kant's actual doctrine'. But he then assures us that 'the characteristic structure' of Kant's 'moral conception' becomes 'more clearly discernible' if we drop Kant's dualisms. Rawls insists that Kant's dualisms should not be interpreted 'in the sense that Kant gave them', but that they should be 'recast and their moral force reformulated within the scope of an empirical theory'. One wonders, though, how the actual structure of Kant's theory can be revealed by detaching it from his dualisms and transcendental idealism? The equivocation is plain: on the one hand, Rawls is frankly and explicitly revisionary; on the other hand, he claims to reveal Kant's actual moral conception, to lay bare the structure of Kant's theory as found in his texts.

The question is irrepressible: '*Who* is Rawls's Kant?' We know it is not the actual, historical Kant, who was entangled in his dualisms and transcendental idealism, and whom Rawls explicitly and frankly declines to reconstruct. But it is not a strictly or entirely a philosophical or ideal Kant either, because Rawls claims to reveal, at least to some extent, the moral conception of, and clarify the structure of the reasoning of, the actual, historical Kant. So the truth of the matter is that Rawls's Kant is a *Zwittermensch*, neither an historical reality nor a philosophical fiction. The best way to understand him is in terms of the very noumenal realm Rawls wants to eradicate. For Rawls's Kant is the *noumenal* Kant, i.e. his better self, what he ought to have said if he were wise enough to leap beyond eighteenth-century Prussian culture to grasp the theory of justice.

However we characterize Rawls's Kant, his equivocation has been fateful. Kantian ethics, which is now a field of philosophy in its own right in the US, has been essentially the pursuit of a completely imaginary subject: Rawls's *Zwittermensch*. The conviction underlying so much of this scholarship is that if we only formulate constructivist assumptions precisely enough we will finally reveal Kant's noumenal self. This new and growing field is as equivocal as its subject matter: it is neither fish nor foul, neither scholarship nor philosophy.

Rather, it is a monster: scholarship distorted by philosophy, philosophy obscured by history. The attempt to understand Kant's ethics in its actual historical context – to clarify Kant's intricate relations with the competing moral theories of his contemporaries and immediate predecessors in the German tradition (Schiller, Wolff, Baumgarten and Achenwall) – has not advanced a single step under Rawls's tutelage.[22] Given his equivocation, it should be apparent why.

The crucial question remains: How does Rawls's revised Kant relate to the historical Kant? The extent to which Rawls's constructivist interpretation of Kant is accurate is a difficult and intricate issue, which I cannot begin to pursue here, and which has not been investigated sufficiently by Rawls's students, who have been content with, or unsuspicious of, his equivocation. Suffice it to say here that there is powerful and abundant evidence that the discrepancy between Rawls's revised Kant and the actual, historical Kant is vast. The distance is easily measurable as soon as we ask: What happens if, as Rawls advises, we detach Kant's transcendental idealism or noumenal realm from his moral philosophy? First of all, we would have no means of dealing with the metaphysical issue of determinism that led to Kant's transcendental idealism in the first place. To be sure, transcendental freedom is not an issue for Rawls, who thinks that we can talk about moral freedom apart from this issue. But here Kant would beg to differ with him. For Kant refuses to separate the issue of transcendental freedom from moral freedom, and never ceased to stress how moral freedom depends on the possibility of transcendental freedom. Here again we see how revisionist readings of German idealism arise from a reluctance to face metaphysical issues. We tear apart the unity of Kant's system – as Rawls bids us – only with eyes blinded or averted to the deeper philosophical issues it attempts to address. More significantly, if we eliminate Kant's noumenal realm from his moral philosophy, it becomes impossible to conceive of a normative structure valid independently of deliberation and choice. Of course, it is precisely this structure that Rawls wants to remove through constructivism;[23] but this would be doing violence to Kant's deepest 'moral conceptions', and indeed 'the whole structure' of his moral philosophy. There is plenty of evidence that Kant would never have accepted the Rawlsian thesis that the moral law is a construction of free and rational agents; for Kant insists firmly and frequently that the moral law has a binding validity independent of what all agents choose or decide. Consider the following.

1) Kant thinks that the moral law is a fact of reason, which is simply given to us, and which we know through a kind of intellectual intuition.[24]
2) Kant insists that no being, not even God, is an author of moral laws, since they cannot originate from choice but are practically necessary.[25]
3) Kant is consistently and constantly antivoluntarist, stressing that God commands laws because they are good and not that they are good because God commands them.[26]

Why does Rawls not want to recognize this more objective side of Kant? He insists that it would be a form of heteronomy.[27] Rather than subjecting himself to a law of his own creation, the agent would submit to a law given from outside. Yet Rawls's worries here come from a confusion of Kantian *Willkür* with *Wille*, or Rousseau's *volonté générale* with *volonté de tous*. Since Kant identifies the will with practical reason or the moral law itself, there can be no heteronomy.

I do not pretend that these texts amount to anything near a refutation of Rawls's interpretation. Far from it. Rawls has his own sensitive reading of them, which I cannot engage now. Nevertheless, these points should be sufficient to show that, in important respects, Kant's texts are more intricate than Rawls's one-sided constructivist reading permits. The historical Kant was indeed much more complex than any simple form of constructivism. Kant's moral theory was neither constructivist nor intuitionist, neither rationalist nor voluntarist, but rather a very subtle synthesis of both. It was a careful attempt to steer between two opposing traditions in the eighteenth century, namely, the voluntarism of Hobbes and Pufendorf, and the rationalism of Leibniz and Wolff. Precisely in what this synthesis consists – what exactly Kant accepts and what he rejects from these opposing parties – remains an outstanding desideratum of Kant scholarship.

One final word. In exposing Rawls's equivocation I do not wish to convey the impression that he was not an historically sensitive reader of philosophical texts. The very opposite is the case. We should take Rawls's word for it: he struggled to understand past thinkers as they understood themselves, and he did his best to present each thinker in his strongest light.[28] About his lectures, he once wrote: 'I always took it for granted that the writers we were studying were much smarter than I was.' At the very least, Rawls's practice was more sophisticated than his Oxbridge counterparts. Yet the fact remains: on one crucial point Rawls's historical conscience deserted him. Kant was simply too important for him not to be claimed for a theory of justice. It will take some time before we get Kant out of his mighty embrace.

The owl of Minerva, stuffed

One of the most remarkable developments in the history of philosophy since the 1960s has been the Hegel renaissance. After James's 1908–9 Gifford Lectures, and after Russell's, Moore's and Dewey's public disavowal of their shameful absolute idealist past, Hegel became the pariah of the Anglophone intellectual establishment. From the 1920s to the 1950s, except for exercises in excoriation, an interest in Hegel had to be private and secret, something better read in the loo. But *tempus rerum imperator!* The radicalism of the 1960s brought with it an interest in the historical and philosophical roots of Marxism, which inevitably led back to Hegel. Since Hegel scholars had to legitimate their new interest in a scholastic and intolerant intellectual environment, they cleaned and scrubbed, pruned and trimmed, until their man was respectable by the standards of the day.[29] Hegel, who made the beginning and end of his philosophy the absolute, somehow became a category theorist, a Kantian epistemologist, even an ordinary language philosopher. Somehow, the absolute evaporated, turning into a second-order attribute of his system, its claim to absolute validity.[30]

Anyone with even a passing acquaintance with Hegel should be astonished by such a remarkable transformation. But let us examine how Hegel became a dummy. Spokesmen for non-metaphysical interpretations of Hegel are well-informed and begin with perfectly plausible premises. Almost always they presuppose a very definite conception of metaphysics: the Kantian conception of metaphysics as a priori reasoning about the unconditioned, or as speculation about transcendent entities, such as God or the soul. They want to distance Hegel's philosophy from the pre-Kantian rationalist tradition of Leibniz, Wolff and Baumgarten, whose reputation Kant shattered in the *Critique of Pure Reason*. To do so, they often stress Hegel's allegiance to the Kantian tradition, especially the importance he gave to the critique of knowledge.

So far, so good. In this respect they are perfectly correct. Hegel did not want his philosophy to relapse into the dogmatism of the pre-Kantian tradition, and he firmly believed that any philosophy after Kant would have to satisfy the demands of critique. Yet it scarcely follows from these points that Hegel is not a metaphysician at all. Still less do they imply that his philosophy was a social epistemology, a radical version of transcendental idealism, or a second-order investigation into the logic of our categories. Advocates of the non-metaphysical interpretation have thrown the baby of metaphysics out with the bathwater of pre-Kantian dogmatism.

Hegel's philosophy is indeed a metaphysics, though not in the Kantian sense of speculation about transcendent entities. It was a metaphysics in the classic Aristotelian sense of an enquiry into being as being, an investigation into what is first in the order of being or substance. The textual evidence for this point is overwhelming, though it lies in places Anglophone scholars have scarcely bothered to study: namely, in Schelling's and Hegel's collaborative Jena writings.[31] The main aim of Schelling's and Hegel's philosophy during these formative years was to revive the classical Aristotelian project. Hence they state expressly that the goal of philosophy is to know '*das An-sich*' or '*das Absolute*', which is their clumsy German prose for Aristotle's '*ousia*' or Spinoza's '*substantia*'. To be sure, Hegel will later break with Schelling around 1804, bringing their joint metaphysics to an abrupt end. But Hegel never renounced the conception of philosophy behind their project. He split with Schelling over the means for acquiring knowledge of the absolute, specifically his method of intellectual intuition, which he found unpardonably dogmatic and esoteric; but he never foreswore the attempt to know the absolute. Indeed, his later Jena years are dominated by the search for the proper methodology to know the absolute. It was in these years (1805–6) that Hegel developed his project for a phenomenology of spirit, which would be a critical introduction and foundation for metaphysics.

Although Hegel attempted to provide a critical foundation for metaphysics, this has been a point lost on his neo-Kantian successors. Neo-Kantianism grew out of a reaction against Hegel's grand metaphysical project, which was viewed as a relapse into dogmatism. With the rapid rise of the natural sciences in nineteenth century Germany, Hegel's and Schelling's *Naturphilosophie* began to seem like so much reckless a priori speculation. The cry '*Zurück zu Kant!*' was meant to make philosophy viable again by keeping it within the confines of the critique of knowledge. Philosophers, if they wanted their own legitimate task within the academic division of labour, would now have to investigate the logic of the natural sciences. For worse rather than better, this reaction to Hegel has been profoundly influential for twentieth century interpretations of his philosophy. For Kant scholars, this has been reason to be suspicious of Hegel, whom they continue to regard as a reckless metaphysician. For Hegel scholars, however, this has been reason to underplay, ignore or deny the metaphysical dimension of his thought, which would have been unacceptable to the philosophical public. The non-metaphysical interpretations of Robert Pippin and Terry Pinkard are indeed still inspired by this neo-Kantian mentality. Hence they stress the epistemological dimension of Hegel's thought, and want to cast aside his Spinozist metaphysics or speculative *Naturphilosophie*.[32] They are fully aware of, and indeed emphasize, some of Hegel's departures from the Kantian tradition, especially his more social and historical conception of knowledge.[33] Nevertheless, they still see Hegel's philosophical project as fundamentally an epistemological enterprise in the Kantian tradition, whether it is grounding norms socially or whether it is developing the implications of his transcendental idealism.

The neo-Kantian tradition, and the Hegel scholars who have inherited its values and assumptions, have prejudged Schelling and Hegel because they have never cared to investigate why they turned toward metaphysics in the first place. It is one of the ironies of philosophical history that Schelling and Hegel believed they had no choice but to return to metaphysics to resolve the intractable *aporia* of Kantian epistemology. It had become clear to many thinkers in the late 1790s that it was impossible to resolve the problem of the transcendental deduction – 'How do synthetic a priori concepts apply to a sensible manifold when they are not derived from it?' – from Kant's original starting point, namely, his dualism between understanding and sensibility. Kant's dualism was so drastic and severe – the understanding is spontaneous and beyond the world of space and time, whereas sensibility is passive and within the world of space and time – that it made it impossible to explain how there could be any correspondence between such heterogeneous faculties. The only way to resolve the problem of knowledge in the face of such unbridgeable dualisms – so it seemed to Schelling, Hegel and many others in the 1790s – was to re-examine the concept of nature behind them. They rightly saw that the premise behind such dualisms was the mechanical conception of nature, which seemed to place the entire mental realm outside of nature. If it could be shown that nature is not mechanical, this would completely recast the entire problematic of epistemology. Rather than seeing the mind as something outside nature yet somehow mysteriously knowing it, perhaps it could be regarded as part of nature itself. Sure enough, by the late 1790s, the mechanical conception of nature was rapidly crumbling in favour of a more organic conception, which saw the essence of matter as force or energy rather than inert extension. According to this new paradigm, the mental realm is only the highest degree of organization and development of the organic powers of nature; the mental and physical differ only in degree rather than kind: the mental is the invisible form of the physical, the physical the visible form of the mental. Armed with this new conception of nature, the transcendental deduction seemed to pose much less of a problem. For now there was no need to explain a mysterious harmony between heterogeneous realms.

This history, of which only the crude outlines could be told here,[34] has been almost entirely forgotten by the neo-Kantians, who could make their naive demand to return to epistemology only because they had forgotten its *aporia* in the 1790s. It should be the task of future Hegel scholarship not to prejudge Hegel's turn toward metaphysics. Rather than casting it aside from post-Kantian intuitions, it should investigate it within its original context. This means examining the context behind the development of Schelling's and Hegel's *Naturphilosophie* in the 1790s and early 1800s.

The final refuge, the last redoubt, of the non-metaphysical interpretation has been Hegel's social and political philosophy. Here, it has seemed to many, we can clearly extricate Hegel's teachings from his metaphysics. Surely, even if we jettison that metaphysics, Hegel still has much to say of value about social and political philosophy. Indeed, the metaphysics that surfaces in his social and political writings seems to be accidental to their content. It seems as if Hegel pushes their content into a metaphysical vocabulary because of a metaphysical agenda strictly irrelevant to his social and political concerns.

Of course, Hegel would have protested vehemently against such an interpretation. His motive would be not simply to protect the integrity of his system, but to stress how fundamental concepts and issues in social and political theory ultimately presuppose a metaphysics. It is no accident that his first publication in social and political theory – his 1802 *Naturrecht* essay – begins with a polemic against legal positivism, which attempts to resolve issues in a piecemeal fashion and by casting aside all metaphysics. We cannot determine the nature of justice simply by examining cases and precedents, Hegel argued, because we need to know whether the traditions behind these cases and precedents are just themselves. The whole question of the foundation of law and justice cannot be pursued independently of metaphysics, because the classical question whether justice is based on command or nature forces us to re-examine the meaning of nature itself. The prevalence of voluntarist theories of value since the Enlightenment have simply presupposed a mechanical concept of nature, which places value outside it.

Nowhere is the need for metaphysics in social and political theory more evident, Hegel believed, than with the concept of freedom itself. No less than Kant, he denied that we can separate the political concept of freedom from the classical metaphysical issue of freedom versus determinism. Whether we adopt a Kantian or Spinozian response to this issue makes all the difference to our social and political theory. Hegel's famous demand in the *Philosophy of Right* that we reconcile ourselves to the necessity of nature and history is replete with political implications; yet it grew out of his Spinozist conception of freedom.

Complacency versus despair

What is to be done? Where should research on German idealism be heading if it is to make substantial progress? How should we proceed if we are to understand the German idealists themselves and not simply rehash contemporary attitudes toward them?

First, we should not listen to the counsel of complacency. This advises us that anachronism is unavoidable, so that we need not trouble ourselves to understand the past in its own terms. Its rationale goes something like this: 'that to understand a historical figure is to reconstruct him in our terms, because we are inextricably caught inside our own philosophical culture and cannot get beyond its way of understanding things'.[35] The problem with this advice is that it stretches the point. It is of course true that our understanding of the past is conditioned by our own culture and that this imposes severe limits upon our comprehension of the past. A perfect understanding of a past culture in terms of how the participants understood it themselves is an ideal we probably will never attain. But does it follow that we cannot even *approach* it? Is it really the case that further intensive research into the language, social and political values, the traditions of discourse of another culture, will bring us nowhere closer to understanding the past? The problem with the counsel of complacency is that it presents us with the stark choice: everything or nothing, perfect understanding or perfect ignorance.

Second, we should not heed the counsel of despair. This tells us that we avoid anachronism only through antiquarianism. It claims that meaning is so bound to a specific historical context that we should not attempt to judge whether what people said in the past is true.[36] The past can teach us no lessons because its context differs too much from our own. All that we can do with the past, then, is to describe and reconstruct it like detached observers. This advice is also guilty of exaggeration. Although it is true that each historical context is unique, it does not follow that no generalizations can be made from it, still less that its participants thought entirely in such local terms. To appreciate the past we have to take seriously its own claims to solve general problems.

It seems to me that, in this respect, there was always something right about the analytic method. Its chief purpose was always to reconstruct and appraise arguments in the hope that this should tell us something about the truth, or at least shed some light on a general philosophical problem. I think that historians of philosophy should not abandon this ambition, which is a crucial and characteristic feature of the history of philosophy. We can understand a philosophical text only if we understand it internally according to its logical geography, which involves such factors as: 1) the formal structure of its arguments, i.e. what are their premises and whether the conclusion follows from them; 2) the meanings of its central terms; 3) its hidden premises; 4) its main principles; and 5) its internal coherence or consistency. To understand the internal structure of the text involves more than just knowing the author's intention and context. But in attempting to draw the outlines of this logical geography we are also, inevitably, testing the theory and evaluating it. Historical contexts are never so uniquely individual that a philosopher cannot draw useful comparisons with his own context; and philosophical problems and theories, unlike scientific ones, are never so completely antiquated that we cannot learn philosophy from the past. The history of philosophy differs from the history of science precisely in that philosophers continue to learn from their past in ways that scientists do not; it is a notorious fact that philosophy cannot make the kind of progress that natural scientists do, and that philosophers must forever keep their horizons open so as not to lapse into dogmatism.[37]

But if the end of the analytic method is admirable, the means of realizing it have been paltry. What too few analytic philosophers who treat an historical figure realize is that their reconstruction of an argument should not replace historical investigation but should result from it. If we are to reconstruct an argument with any accuracy, and if we are to appraise it with any fairness, we must investigate it in its historical context. To assume that we can completely understand an argument from its exposition in a single text is like thinking we can enter into a court room and fully understand an argument in a court case without knowing anything about the opposing arguments or the history of the case. To evaluate an argument before the basic historical legwork has been done is the philosopher's version of shooting first and asking questions later.

While reconstruction and appraisal of argument has been the chief end of the analytic method, it should not be the sole end of the history of philosophy. The single-minded pursuit of this end among analytic historians of philosophy has often blinded them to, or taken them away from, other fundamental tasks crucial to the understanding of a philosopher. Assume that we have achieved a completely accurate historical reconstruction of an argument, and that we have accurately and fairly assessed it. Does it follow that we have fully understood the philosopher? Hardly. We need to know two more important kinds of facts. First, how the philosopher is similar to, and different from, his contemporaries and predecessors, i.e. what he took his own distinctive contribution to be to the discussions and disputes of the past. Second, why the thinker made it, or what purpose he had in devising it. Each point deserves a little explanation. One of the basic desiderata of historicist tradition was *to individuate* an author, i.e. to determine precisely his position *vis-á-vis* his contemporaries and predecessors. It was regarded as important to ascertain the author's unique place in the conversations and controversies of his day. If we think a doctrine is unique to an author that was in fact common to his age, or, if we assume that something is common that is in fact unique to him, we cannot be said to know *the* author, him or her as opposed to anyone else. Understanding the individuality of an author is often one of the most laborious tasks of historical research; it demands knowing, in detail, the positions of other thinkers in the past and precisely what they said on specific occasions.

To no small degree, Anglophone research on German idealism has been deficient in just this respect. It is fair to say that most contemporary Kant and Hegel scholars cannot identify what is characteristic of their positions *vis-á-vis* their contemporaries. Scholarship on Hegel constantly praises Hegel for ideas and arguments that were *Gang und Gäbe* for the romantic generation. It is not true that Hegel's characteristic project was his attempt to fuse Fichte with Spinoza, or to combine communitarianism with liberal freedoms; for such were the ambitions of all *Frühromantik*. Regarding Kant, the situation is even more dire. Most Kant scholars cannot state precisely how Kant's philosophy differs from that of Wolff, Baumgarten, Tetens or Lambert for the simple reason that they never read these thinkers. Yet there is no escape from the fact that the precise meaning of some of Kant's central doctrines depends upon understanding exactly how they differ from these figures. Nowhere is this more evident than with regard to Kant's distinction between understanding and sensibility, which is so crucial for his philosophy as a whole. This distinction can be fully understood only by contrasting it with Baumgarten's position in the *Metaphysica*, a masterpiece as good as forgotten by the average Kant scholar.

Another fundamental desideratum of historical research in the history of philosophy is to determine *why* a thinker made the argument in the first place. We need to know his purpose in making the argument, the role that it plays in his life. We have to investigate the social, political or religious values that made him put it forward.[38] Seeing the motivation or purpose behind an argument does not invalidate it, still less does it necessarily relativize it, as if it were of interest or value only within its historical context. But it is essential to understand it, for no one could be said to understand an argument, let alone an author, unless he knows why it was made, the specific role that it plays in his life and culture. To abstract from these purposes or intentions is to fail to see how much philosophy matters, how much it plays a vital role in the life of a culture. One of the naivetés and sterilities of the analytic method is that it treats arguments as if they were made *solely* to get to the truth, as if they matter only in an academic context.

Here too Anglophone research on German idealism has been lacking. Only very recently has there been sufficient research into the details of Kant's biography that have allowed philosophers to identify some of his most basic social, political and religious values.[39] The relevance and application of some of these details for an understanding of Kant's moral, religious and political thought still remains to be explored. In the case of Hegel the situation is more obscure. There has been much detailed investigation, chiefly by French and German scholars, into Hegel's social and political context.[40] However, much of this research has been limited to defining the background to Hegel's mature political philosophy, the context behind the 1820 *Philosophy of Right*. Much work remains to be done on Hegel's social and political philosophy before his years in Prussia. The great work by Franz Rosenzweig, *Hegel und der Staat*, was a promising and pioneering effort, though his lead has not been appreciated or followed in the Anglophone world.

A few parting words for final clarification. It is not my intent to diminish, still less banish, interpretations of German idealism that understand and appraise them in contemporary terms. Strawson, Bennett and Rawls have made important contributions to our understanding of Kant, just as Pippin, Pinkard and Hartmann have made significant advances in our appreciation of Hegel. Even when they have been wrong or confused they have added to the conversation, they have aided the struggle for accuracy and clarity. There are only two evils to avoid: conflating philosophical reconstruction with historical reality, and assuming that the analytic method is the *only* way to do the history of philosophy. It is these two errors that have been so pernicious and that have seriously hampered research on German idealism. Fortunately, they are easily avoided. All we need to see light after these dark days is to cultivate a little intellectual tolerance.

Notes

1 I use the term 'metaphysics' here in a broad contemporary sense, so that it covers all grand philosophical theories, or more precisely 'any enquiry that raises questions about reality that lie behind or beyond those capable of being tackled by the methods of science.' (See Simon Blackburn, *Oxford Dictionary of Philosophy* (Oxford: Oxford University Press, 1994), p. 240.) The term is somewhat problematic because Kant would not have regarded his transcendental idealism as metaphysics.

2 I owe this anecdote to Bonnie Kent, a student of Kristeller's.

3 See, John Rawls, *A Theory of Justice* (Cambridge, Mass.: Harvard University Press, 1999), pp. 221–27; 'Kantian Constructivism in Moral Theory', *The Journal of Philosophy*, 1980, 77, 515–72; and *Lectures on the History of Moral Philosophy*, Barbara Herman (ed.) (Cambridge, Mass.: Harvard University Press, 2000).

4 See especially Klaus Hartmann 'Hegel: A Non-Metaphysical View', in A. MacIntyre, (ed.) *Hegel: A Collection of Critical Essays* (New York: Anchor, 1972), pp. 101–24. Regarding his wide following in the Anglophone world, see the anthology edited by Tristram Engelhardt and Terry Pinkard, *Hegel Reconsidered* (Dordrecht: Kluwer, 1994).

5 See especially Robert Pippin, *Hegel's Idealism* (Cambridge: Cambridge University Press, 1989); Terry Pinkard, *Hegel's Dialectic* (Philadelphia: Temple University Press, 1988), and Alan White, *Absolute Knowledge: Hegel and the Problem of Metaphysics* (Athens: Ohio University Press, 1983).

6 For this non-metaphysical approach to Hegel's moral and political philosophy, see especially Allen Wood, *Hegel's Ethical Thought* (Cambridge: Cambridge University Press, 1990), Paul Franco, *Hegel's Philosophy of Freedom* (New Haven: Yale University

Press, 1999), Frederick Neuhouser, *Foundations of Hegel's Social Theory* (Cambridge, Mass.: Harvard University Press, 2000); and Z.A. Pelczynski in 'An Introductory Essay' to T.N. Knox's edition of *Hegel's Political Writings* (Oxford: Oxford University Press, 1964), pp. 3–140.

7 Bennett confessed to his 'very limited' knowledge of German in the preface to his *Kant's Dialectic* (Cambridge: Cambridge University Press, 1974). This seems like refreshing honesty; but in the preface to his *Kant's Analytic* (Cambridge: Cambridge University Press, 1966) he tells us that he is out of sympathy with previous writers on the *Critique*. When, however, he lists the writers he has learned from, he mentions virtually every English scholar before him. Who were these previous writers?

8 See the back cover of *Kant's Analytic*. Presumably, Bennett endorsed this description if he did not write it. In any case, it closely fits his own account of his method in 'Response to Garber and Reé' in *Doing Philosophy Historically*, ed. Peter Hare (Buffalo: Prometheus, 1988), pp. 62–72.

9 See Bennett's comments in 'Response to Garber and Reé', pp. 66–67. See also Strawson's review of Bennett's *Kant's Analytic*, where he praises Bennett's methodology for making Kant our contemporary, and claims this as a way of saving him from 'the wrong kind of respect'. 'Bennett on Kant's Analytic', *Philosophical Review* 77 (1968), p. 332. Both Strawson and Bennett seem to regard the older historical interpretations as too sympathetic and reverential.

10 Peter Strawson, *The Bounds of Sense: An Essay on Kant's Critique of Pure Reason* (London: Methuen, 1966), p. 16.

11 Ibid., p. 15.

12 Ibid., p. 19.

13 Ibid., p. 21.

14 'We know that to any being who is a member of the natural spatio-temporal world of science and everyday observation the spatio-temporal objects of that world can sensibly *appear* only by *affecting* in some way the constitution of that being. The way in which objects *do* appear, what characteristics they appear as having, depends in part upon the constitution of the being to which they appear. Were that constitution different, the same things would appear differently' (p. 39).

15 Strawson writes in his preface to *The Bounds of Sense: An Essay on Kant's Critique of Pure Reason*: 'He [Kant] seeks to draw the bounds of sense from a point outside them, a point which, if they are rightly drawn, cannot exist' (p. 12).

16 For the background, see Herman's foreword to Rawls's *Lectures*, pp. xi–xix.

17 'Kantian Constructivism', p. 515.

18 Ibid., p. 517.

19 See Christine Korsgaard, *Creating the Kingdom of Ends* (Cambridge: Cambridge University Press, 1996); Thomas Hill, *Dignity and Practical Reason in Kant's Moral Theory* (Ithaca: Cornell University Press, 1992); Barbara Herman, *The Practice of Moral Judgment* (Cambridge, Mass.: Harvard University Press, 1993); Susan Neiman, *The Unity of Reason: Rereading Kant* (Oxford: Oxford University Press, 1994); and Onora O'Neill, *Constructions of Reason* (Cambridge: Cambridge University Press, 1989). See too the Rawls *Festschrift*, Andrews Reath, Christine Korsgaard and Barbara Herman (eds), *Reclaiming the History of Ethics* (Cambridge: Cambridge University Press, 1997).

20 See Rawls 'The Basic Structure as Subject', *American Philosophical Quarterly* 14, 1977, 159–65: 'To develop a viable Kantian conception of justice the force and content of Kant's doctrine must be detached from its background in transcendental idealism and given a procedural interpretation by means of the construction of the original position.'

21 *A Theory of Justice*, pp. 226–27.

22 I have documented the failure of contemporary Kant scholarship with regard to Schiller in my *Schiller as Philosopher: A Re-Examination* (Oxford: Oxford University Press, 2005), pp. 169–90. That the same could be done with other contemporary figures almost goes without saying.

23 'Kantian Constructivism', pp. 523–24.

24 *Kritik der praktischen Vernunft*, V, 47. See too the first section of 'Über den Gemeinspruch: Das mag in der Theorie richtig sein, taugt aber nicht für die Praxis', VIII, 287–88.

25 See the Collins Lectures, XVII, 282–83; and *Metaphysik der Sitten*, VI, 227.

26 See, for example, KrV, B 847.

27 'Kantian Constructivism', p. 559.

28 See Rawls's description of his own teaching cited in Herman's foreword to Rawls's *Lectures on the History of Moral Philosophy*, pp. xvi–xvii.

29 Not that every scholar surrendered to this. One important exception was Charles Taylor's magisterial *Hegel* (Cambridge: Cambridge University Press, 1975), which found more acceptance among the general public than Hegel scholars. Another voice in the wilderness has been Adriaan Peperzak, *Modern Freedom: Hegel's Legal, Moral and Political Philosophy* (Dordrecht: Kluwer, 2001), pp. 1–52.

30 For the most breathtaking of these gymnastics, see Stephen Bungay, 'The Hegelian Project', in *Hegel Reconsidered* (Dordrecht: Kluwer, 1994) pp. 19–42.

31 It might seem arrogant to say this, given that some of Hegel's Jena writings have been translated and widely available for some time. Among these writings are Hegel's *Differenzschrift*, *Glauben und Wissen* and the *Naturrecht* essay. However, Anglophone attention has focused chiefly on these texts at the expense of other important writings, most notably Hegel's and Schelling's collaborative work, *Fernere Darstellung aus dem System der Philosophie*, an untranslated work crucial for an understanding of the Jena project. Hegel's writings during this period have to be read in conjunction with Schelling's works, which they were meant to defend. Crucial are Schelling's 1801 *Darstellung meines Systems* and 1802 *Bruno*, which are rarely read by Anglophone Hegel scholars.

32 See Pippin, *Hegel's Idealism*, pp. 4, 5, 61, 66.

33 See Pinkard, *Hegel's Phenomenology: The Sociality of Reason* (Cambridge: Cambridge University Press, 1994), pp. 1–19.

34 I have attempted to tell this story in more detail in Frederick Beiser, *German Idealism* (Cambridge, Mass.: Harvard University Press, 2002), pp. 368–72, 506–28, and in my 'Kant and the *Naturphilosophen*', in *The Romantic Imperative* (Cambridge, Mass.: Harvard University Press, 2003), pp. 153–70.

35 This is the essence of Richard Rorty's defence of Jonathan Bennett's methodology. See Rorty, 'The Historiography of Philosophy: Four Genres', in *Philosophy in History*, Richard Rorty, J.B. Schneewind and Quentin Skinner (eds) (Cambridge: Cambridge University Press, 1984), pp. 52–53.

36 This is the message of Quentin Skinner and James Tully, who think that the historian should bracket the whole question of truth. See Quentin Skinner 'A Reply to My Critics' and James Tully's 'The Pen is a Mighty Sword' in *Meaning and Context: Quentin Skinner and his Critics*, James Tully (ed.) (Cambridge: Cambridge University Press, 1988), pp. 20–22, 256.

37 Here again I take issue with Rorty, who thinks that the history of philosophy is precisely on par with the history of science. See his 'Historiography', pp. 49–56.

38 In this regard I accept many of Skinner's arguments. See his 'Meaning and Understanding in the History of Ideas', *History and Theory* 8, 1969, 3–53 (reprinted in *Meaning and Context*, pp. 29–67); and his 'Motives, Intentions and the Interpretations of Texts', in *On Literary Intention*, D. Newton de Molina (ed.) (Edinburgh:

Edinburgh University Press, 1976), pp. 210–21 (in *Meaning and Context* pp. 68–78). It is a sad fact that Skinner's methodological views have not had more following outside the realm of political theory.

39 I refer, of course, to Manfred Kuehn's *Kant: A Biography* (Cambridge: Cambridge University Press, 2001). The fact that Kuehn is a German, and that his work is so recent, only vindicates my argument. The same holds for another work of great merit, Arsenig Gulyga's *Immanuel Kant* (Frankfurt: Insel, 1981) (first Russian edition 1977).

40 I refer especially to the work of Jacques D'Hondt, *Hegel secret* (Paris: Presses Universitaires de France, 1968) and *Hegel en son temps (Berlin 1818–1831)* (Paris: Editions Sociales, 1968).

Part II

The Legacy of Hegel's Philosophy

4

HEGELIANS – YOUNG AND YOUNGER

Fred Rush

Nearly a half-century ago P. F. Strawson inaugurated reconsideration of Kant's theoretical philosophy within a recognizably contemporary Anglophone framework,[1] and the same may be said of the 1975 publication of Charles Taylor's *Hegel* relative to its subject matter.[2] Since Taylor's work, there have been a number of treatments of Hegel, many of which claim, on Hegel's behalf, insights with contemporary significance.

One can divide this recent reconsideration of Hegel roughly into three branches. The first of these seeks application of Hegel at the intersection of the fields of the philosophy of mind and epistemology. Here the work of John McDowell and, especially, Robert Brandom is at the forefront.[3] The influence of this 'Pittsburgh School' on the mainline philosophy of mind has been, all told, minimal. Nowadays, the philosophy of mind and epistemology operate cleanly within standard, commonly accepted paradigms that prefigure what can count as well-formulated philosophical questions, as well as what would qualify as acceptable sorts of answers to such questions. This uniformity of 'framework' cuts across the many divisions between the main camps, e.g. Davidson, Kripke and Chomsky.

Aesthetics is a second forum in which Hegel has made a contemporary reappearance. Arthur Danto's analysis of the 'transfiguration of the commonplace' and his claim that the art of Warhol constitutes an 'end of art' are crucially indebted to Hegel.[4] Yet, in the philosophy of art as well, Hegelianism has not won the day – at least not in the United States and Britain. Nelson Goodman's nominalism, Kendall Walton's 'make-believe', or even Stanley Cavell's blend of Emerson, psychoanalysis and screwball comedy have claimed more adherents than has Danto's Hegelianism.

I want to concentrate on a third strain of contemporary Anglo-American reconsideration of Hegel, which has found a home in ethics and in social and political theory. Here I believe the impact of Hegel is potentially much greater than in the two strands just mentioned. Typically, reconsideration of Hegel in social and political theory has taken the form of advancing a view of his work that can be shown to be compatible with core elements of liberal democratic theory. For instance, there is a range of interpretations of Hegel's concept of freedom that seeks to accommodate one of several liberal views on the nature of freedom and ideas of subjectivity that support those views. Not all liberal concepts of political subjectivity can be made commensurate with Hegel's views in this way of course – e.g. those that would arrogate to subjective preference a basic role in political rationality, etc. will be ruled out presumptively. Much renewed interest within liberal theory for Hegel's views on freedom has focused, rather, on extending Kantian ideas of *autonomy* in new ways. But why would one look to Hegel as a Kantian helpmate? Well, one might find it worthwhile to investigate whether certain Hegelian doctrines are promising ways to add back into Kant's ethical and political theory a richer account of intersubjectivity in order to respond to what have, by now, become standard objections to Kant, e.g. those of 'particularists' such as Bernard Williams and Alasdair MacIntyre.[5]

I want to discuss whether the most promising aspects of Hegel's thought to develop in contemporary political theory are those that fit best with liberal theories with Kantian provenance. I shall argue that this is not the most promising way to develop Hegel. I shall suggest instead that the most interesting aspects of Hegel's ethical and political thought are ones that are the most un-Kantian. I claim that a better indicator for what is of continuing interest in Hegel's political thought is Marx. What I shall stress when making this claim is not that some form of Marxist socialism is superior to liberalism as a matter of political doctrine (although I believe that is true). It is rather that Marx's views of what is valuable in Hegel afford insight into how to think of political theory as emerging from political practice. It is only in this context that one will be able to determine whether Kantian ideas of autonomy have further life.

Prima facie it may seem odd that one be concerned with drawing a single line extending from Kant to Hegel in terms of the concept of autonomy, for the simple reason that Hegel is quite critical of Kant's specific account of autonomy, even if he praises Kant's account of freedom in many places. In fact, Hegel never uses the precise term 'autonomy' to characterize his own views on freedom.[6] To the contrary Hegel's work is replete with charges that Kantian autonomy is an impoverished mode of what Hegel calls 'ethical life' (*Sittlichkeit*) and, surely, that should make one wary of arguing for a connection of Kant and Hegel along such lines. This does not mean of course that Hegel's account of freedom does not feature elements derived from Kant's concept of autonomy as a historical matter, perhaps even 'obviously' so.[7] In fact, Hegel's dialectical understanding of the structure of the history of philosophy leading up to his own views dictates this result. So, the most able writers on Hegel's ethical and political philosophy are not plainly wrong to emphasize Kantian autonomy as an important precursor to Hegel's own views on freedom.

Moreover, it is possible, and perhaps even desirable, to develop positions out of the work of historical figures without those positions being ones that those figures would have endorsed. So, perhaps Hegel's views are 'Kantian' in senses that neither he nor Kant would have recognized. For example, there are no objections to presenting some views in ethics as being Kantian, even though they were not actually expressed by Kant. (This is not, of course, to say that the question of whether such views were Kant's is philosophically idle – much of interest can come from an investigation of such questions, and of the fair limits in calling a position 'Kantian' if Kant would not have held it.) But one does not have to make special appeal to the license in the philosophical reception of the history of philosophy in order to make the case for a strong general connection between Kant's conception of autonomy and Hegel's ethical and political thought. Hegel's charge that Kantian *Moralität* is an impoverished form of Hegelian *Sittlichkeit* contains within it a silver lining for the Kantian.[8] Hegel's view of how theoretical worldviews like *Moralität* and Hegelian *Sittlichkeit* relate to one another is such that autonomy cannot be so impoverished to be of no substance to ethical life. Kantian autonomy can be enriched by Hegel, be suitably transformed and offered a place in Hegel's own conception of ethical and political well-being. The questions become: (A) what is this transformation? and (B) what does it offer to the Kantian liberal?

I

Even though there have been many developments in Hegel scholarship in the thirty years since the publication of Taylor's study, it is remarkable how much Taylor's interpretation has formed the terms of debate. Two lines of influence are prominent. The first of these concerns the question of the metaphysical nature of Hegel's project or, more precisely, whether the project is metaphysical at all.[9]

But before I discuss this topic I would like to turn quickly to the second strand in Taylor's influence, one that is related to the 'metaphysical question' but is conceptually distinct from it. This is the issue of the sense in which Hegel's philosophy is 'transcendental'. Taylor's book appeared at a time when there was a renewed interest in transcendental arguments in Anglo-American philosophy and was the first to suggest that at least part of Hegel's work might be seen through the lens of transcendental argumentation. Other scholars, such as Frederick Neuhouser and Robert Pippin, have endorsed a broader application of this interpretative strategy.[10] It is a delicate matter as to whether transcendental argumentation might not be developed away from this 'classical' Kantian model and allow for even more non-metaphysical versions of it, and there was a strong push in German idealism after Kant in just this direction. My own view is that interpreting Hegelian dialectic as a kind of transcendental procedure is hopeless for the simple reason that such an interpretation of Hegel severely underestimates the sort of response Hegel thinks is due to the philosophical skeptic. As recent scholarship has shown, Hegel took skepticism to be a position to refute and held Pyrrhonism to be the kind of skepticism that required such a response – in comparison with which he thought Cartesian and Humean skepticism a walk in the park.[11] Transcendental argumentation is a philosophical strategy that has as one of its main goals a circumvention of skeptical concerns by regressive argumentation back to necessary conditions for the possibility of some alleged 'fact' whose possibility then can be 'deduced' from the conditions posited. But Hegel responds to skepticism by attempting to refute it. The structure of this response is highly complex – nothing less than the whole of Hegelian dialectic – but whatever *that* is, it is not a set of arguments that take as given certain *facta* that provide grist for the transcendental mill. Hegel's system is supposed to be presuppositionless, after all.

I turn now to the more germane issue of the significance of non-metaphysical interpretations of Hegel for resulting strands of Hegelianism. Taylor identifies the central question of Hegel's philosophy as one of giving content to the idea of self-determination [*Selbstbestimmung*] as foundational in an account of freedom. Self-determination surely is the idea in Hegel correlative to autonomy in Kant.[12] Taylor interprets self-determination as a type of 'super-autonomy', where determination by anything 'given' to one is inimical to freedom. Because Hegel also rejects the standard Kantian account of autonomy that requires the source of normative authority to lie exclusively within the scope of individual agency abstracted from social context, Taylor argues that Hegel ascribes the property of autonomy *cum* self-determination to a super-individual agency, i.e. *Geist*. Now, the phrase 'super-individual agency' permits several interpretations. I concentrate on two of them. Perhaps the most historically straightforward, and certainly the most classically metaphysical, is the idea of a super-individual *individual*, i.e. God. There are numerous passages in Hegel that can be cited in support of this attribution, although it is often very difficult to tell whether Hegel is asserting this as *his* view of the matter or, instead, is offering the traditional concept 'God' as a possible, but less than fully perspicacious, gloss on *Geist*. In any case, a question remains as to how, precisely, the freedom of this entity impacts on human freedom. Does Hegel, according to Taylor, hold that *Geist* and only *Geist* is free without qualification, and that humans, if free at all, are so only derivatively? This interpretation would be contentious; for every passage one can cite to the effect that super-human *Geist* is free, there is a passage where Hegel attributes freedom to humans without qualification and, more to the point, without qualification to individual human *subjects*. Yet the suggestion most conspicuously on offer in Taylor's work on Hegel is that humans are free only *pro tanto*, i.e. free (and thus self-determining) to the extent that they are the necessary vehicles for *Geist*'s freedom. There are drawbacks to the interpretation. It may be little consolation *to me* that I am free, or self-determining, derivatively, if my philosophical intuition concerning freedom as autonomy requires freedom at the individual level *simpliciter* (one might call this 'Kierkegaard's Complaint'). Being even a necessary vehicle for freedom does little to lessen this impact.

Such challenges have led other Anglophone commentators to embrace non-metaphysical (or at least less metaphysical) interpretations of Hegel's philosophy – ones intent upon preserving senses in which subjects are free *qua* subjects. For instance, the very influential account of Robert Pippin, which follows Taylor in holding that Hegel's central problematic has to do with a radical version of autonomy (and is more or less transcendental)[13], demurs to the idea that Hegelian freedom operates primarily at a super-individual level, arguing instead that it is human collective rational agency that is the necessary and sufficient condition for self-determination. For Pippin, Hegel's great insight is that rationality and freedom are products of and answerable to the shared practices of communities at points in their histories, such that individual human freedom (autonomy) is preserved as basic.[14] One of the main attractions of this move is that it offers a way around one of the central elements of the metaphysical view that is problematic by contemporary lights: i.e. the teleology that drives Hegel's account of self-determination. But there are problems that can mitigate its appeal. I mention two main difficulties.

The first problem, and one that I shall return to a bit later in more detail in what follows, is that one will have to give an account of 'collective agency' that does not replicate what was objectionable with Taylor's 'super-individual individual' account, i.e. that the agency to which freedom 'really' attaches is not both individual and human. Collective agency is just as much a danger to individual autonomy as is the concept of God as the bearer of autonomy. A second problem is that this interpretation of Hegel at first may seem to allow for a very great degree of ethical pluralism and this does not augur well for it as an interpretation of Hegel, for whom norms must be grounded in universalistic standards and practices. The idea of normativity so crucial to Hegel and to many recent accounts of his thought seems in danger of evaporating if one makes the assumption – and this is certainly still a mainstream view in autonomy theory – that normativity requires an account of objectivity based in universalism. What is Hegel's candidate to replace Kant's various statements of the ground for morality and morally informed political life if not an *a priori* constraint like teleologically-driven history? History itself must be rationally ordered so that its main value-forming products – societies – are also rational. But history being rationally structured is not a sufficient condition for reason itself to develop historically in such a way that rational communities become ever more rational – a result that both Hegel and Pippin require. Reason itself must be historical. According to Hegel reason itself must develop by being historically instantiated in various cultural 'shapes', each of which discovers inadequacies in its conception of reason and freedom and corrects for them. Without some sort of strong structural principle that guarantees a step-wise isomorphism between thought and world this is not plausible. 'Inferentialist' accounts of normativity, such as those of Dewey and Brandom, that are resolutely non-metaphysical do not capture the status of this structuring principle for Hegel and, as Pippin allows, such appeals to contemporary accounts of normativity in Hegel interpretation 'can seem like pretty thin gruel' if ascribed to Hegel.[15] I am not convinced that interpreters of Hegel in the non-metaphysical tradition have yet found a way to beef up the recipe. If one allows that there is a panlogicist principle in Hegel, one will be thrown back upon a quasi-secularized version of the metaphysical view with something like 'human culture' in the place of 'God'.[16]

II

'Autonomy' does not of course have anything like an unequivocal meaning.[17] In everyday speech 'autonomy' might just mean 'deciding for oneself', which fits rather nicely into standard liberal frameworks based in what Isaiah Berlin classifies as 'negative' concepts of liberty.[18] But this run of the mill idea of autonomy is not the one that has come to play a central role in contemporary debates about morality and political life. There is a more conceptually loaded idea of autonomy – actually many of them – that descend from Kant. According to Kant, autonomy requires more than selecting or legislating a course of action for oneself. For Kant, the authority according to which an action is endorsed must originate from 'within one'; it must also be 'self-given'.[19] The relevant 'one' here is *not* any particular person – neither you nor I – it is rather one's rationality, or rationality as such. Kant is not interested at all in autonomous *selves* and never, to my knowledge, applies the term 'autonomy' in connection with the concept of an individual self. It is *reason* that is autonomous for him, and individuals act autonomously precisely to the extent that they are able to submerge their individuality in favor of acting out of reason alone. In many cases, what one wants to do and what one should do, will converge, and Kant even hopes that the potential for such convergence may be developed characterologically. But the fact that desire and duty may diverge is always present and sometimes keenly felt – in fact, it is felt *as* being riven between one's inclinations and reason. This tension between empirical and rational nature abides in each agent; indeed, for Kant it is constitutive of finite agency. For these reasons one might call Kant's concept of autonomy 'regulated reflexive autonomy'. It is 'regulated' because the exercise of autonomy involves endorsement of potential action in terms of *rules*. It is 'reflexive' because the ultimate source for the rules is rationality as such, as it is present in all rational beings.

Kant develops this account of autonomy in his ethical writings, and his political theory has a complex relation to it. Depending on whether one thinks that Kant's political theory requires something like autonomous ethical agents as political agents or not, one can interpret Kant as allowing for a sense of political autonomy that draws from its ethical counterpart or one can interpret him as allowing that something like base-line negative liberty is all that political freedom requires (i.e. that a politically free state need not be composed of morally good, Kantian agents but rather might be established by a 'nation of devils').[20] I hold the former interpretation, but deciding the point is not germane here. For, whatever Kant's views on the matter were, it is a cardinal point of Hegel's ethical and political theory that ethical and political agency cannot be Balkanized in the way the second interpretation of Kant allows. Although Hegel clearly demarcates between ethical and political freedom, he holds that the former is an underdeveloped form of the latter. Autonomy, if it is to have a place in Hegel's thought, will have to run the gamut of ethical *and* political life.

As is well known, modern concepts of individual autonomy such as Kant's have roots in two primary sources: (1) early modern political ideas of self-governance that take states as the effective political actors and (2) the religious debates of the Protestant Reformation.[21] Even though Kant is perhaps the first thinker to explicitly broaden the idea of autonomy to include individual moral agency, his insistence on an impersonal source and measure for autonomy is in keeping with the first of these antecedents. Kant's claim is that autonomy is a property of impersonal reason and not of individuals *per se*; this is one reason why German Idealists after him found it inviting to give greater scope to the idea that human freedom issues from a source that is essentially non-individualistic and impersonal. It would not be mistaken at all to see Hegel and the post-Kantian Idealists before him to be reclaiming for themselves versions of the original political orientation of the concept of autonomy as that might be refracted through Kantian lenses. If this way of thinking about the connection of pre-Kantian, Kantian, and post-Kantian concepts of autonomy is more or less correct, Hegel's statements that he can find a place in his account of social and political freedom for a refurbished notion of autonomy can be seen (as Hegel undoubtedly saw them himself) as a cumulative progression in German idealist thought leading up to Hegel.

It almost goes without saying that Idealists from Fichte onwards build into their basic accounts of freedom several elements that Kant would have certainly considered egregiously heteronomous. For instance, although there are faint antecedents in Kant for mutual recognition (*Anerkennung*) as an important ethical concept (e.g. the idea of a 'Kingdom of Ends'), nowhere does Kant allow that mutual recognition between ethical agents is constitutive of ethical agency, as do Fichte and Hegel.[22] Recognition is a vivid example of a core Hegelian ethical and political category that resists easy analysis under Kantian autonomy-based moral theory, where the autonomy in question is that of individuals unto themselves. Hegel accords intersubjectivity such a central role in his account of ethical reasons that one might quite reasonably think that the main Hegelian bar to a recognizably Kantian idea of ethical agency is Hegel's emphasis on collective agency as it is embedded in his idea of 'Spirit' (*Geist*) – the very idea that calls for explanation in non-metaphysical accounts of Hegel in a way that does not spoil individual freedom.

Let us recall that one difficulty with the non-metaphysical view is that it does not *eo ipso* produce a version of Hegelianism that accords individuals freedom. In the versions of this general approach that substitute historical rationality as a whole for *Geist* as a super-individual individual, one might still hold that communities are the true bearers of freedom and not their constituents. What more has to be added to the non-metaphysical account to avoid this result? Invocation of autonomy theory cannot do the work unaided, for the question of *who* has the autonomy is still at issue.

Thinking of social groups as exercising agency that is not reducible to the aggregate agency of individuals was not new in Hegel's time. Montesquieu, Smith and, of course, Rousseau took the idea of irreducible group agency seriously. Smith's version of the idea is too steeped in negative liberty to be a serious contender for the sort of group agency that is relevant to Hegel's account of political freedom. The more classicizing Montesquieu might look to be a better candidate but, from the Hegelian perspective, Montesquieu's communalism must be rejected as a retreat into pre-modernity that insufficiently takes into account the demands of modern individualism. Hegel's own account of freedom is an attempt to reformulate ethical and political particularism in a way that accommodates what he takes to be advances in modern notions of individual freedom.

Hegel's model of the relation of individual wills to society at large is organic, following from his more general account of the dialectical relation of universals and particulars in the overall ontological structure he calls 'the Concept'. Hegel's conception of ontology is perhaps too arcane to be of much contemporary interest and, although it may be impossible to fully detach his political views from that structure, exposition of his views for my limited purpose does not require extended comment on it. The main idea is that individuals and social wholes are 'reciprocally determining' in the way that parts of an organism and the organism as a whole are related. Two features of Hegel's idea that society is an organism need to be kept in mind when one is asking the question of how this proposal could possibly be related to freedom as self-determination. The first of these is that, although the parts of an organism have their identity (their 'determination' [*Bestimmung*]) in terms of their functional roles in the whole and their value to the whole in terms of its overall proper function, the parts each relate functionally to the whole in their own ways.[23] Their contributions to it are *theirs* and the contributions being theirs is constitutive of their individuality. This is just to reiterate that, in Hegel's view, organic structure cannot allow for reduction of whole to part *or* of part to whole. Second, as Neuhouser emphasizes, the way humans are parts of the whole of society is quite particular.[24] My eyes, for seeing and visually orienting my body with reference to other things, etc. cannot, so to speak, rise above their function in order to survey the whole of which they are a part. But humans are reflective beings that do have this capacity, as well as many interests in exercising it. The relevant interest here – which Hegel treats as endemic to being human – is to be free, where part of being free is to know oneself as being free. This of course departs substantially from Kant, who holds that (A) we cannot 'know' that we are free in any sense of 'know' that would count according to acceptable canons of empirical knowledge, or even a priori knowledge as it relates to theoretical matters; (B) that we cannot know, in even an extended sense of the word, that we have acted in *any* specific case out of the moral law; and (C) that we cannot know (we can only profess a rational faith outlined by the complicated machinations of the Kantian doctrine of the *summum bonum*) that moral action is empirically effective in the world. For Kant, we can be free without knowing ourselves to be. In fact, even if we are free we cannot know ourselves to be so. Hegel rejects this account across the board and the rejection has to do with a very general concern to dispute the cognitive gap between inclination and morality that informs Kant's ethics. For Hegel not only must we know ourselves to be free if we are to be so, we can demonstrate that being free makes the world free.[25] Freedom as well as rationality pervades the entirety of what there is.

Hegel's account of what it means to be a reflective part in such an overall structure also does not credit the Kantian idea that rationality requires completely distancing oneself from social structures. One must be reflective within the structure, and this capacity to reflect on the structure from within increases as the structure that is reflected upon becomes more and more rational overall. Note that this idea that being a human subject in ethical and political society includes reflection crucially changes the idea of organic organization away from its biological roots. For the reciprocity now involves advancing degrees of reflective awareness by the parts of the structure of the whole and, thus, of one's place as a part in it. That is, the whole is made up of parts, which parts are able to assess the proper functions of both the whole and the parts. The rationality of this part-whole structure must also run in the direction of whole to part for Hegel. One need not posit an intentional being at the level of universality in order for the rationality to run in this way however. Hegelians will urge that whole to part rationality is not intentional and thus cannot be a matter of *assessment* of the proper functioning of the parts in any straightforward sense. Rather, societies as wholes at a given time *express* certain levels of rationality and, therefore, certain reciprocal rational relations that exist between themselves and their constituents. Societies can only be progressively changed if their historical circumstances (i.e. their stations in overall rationality) allow them to be changed. No individual or group of individuals could have made thirteenth-century France republican. There simply were not conceptual and material resources available to do so.

The agents for such change are individuals, although the precise meaning or impact of the agency is not always maximally open to the reflective capacities of the agents. This idea of the 'cunning of reason' (*List der Vernunft*) in Hegel has set the teeth of many of his critics on edge because the idea of history operating behind one's back seems to be explicable only on a metaphysical view of Hegel that accords primacy to teleologically directed group agency at the expense of individual freedom. But an advocate of Hegel as an autonomy theorist can reply that the idea of unintentional individual agency can be accommodated on the organic model without the idea that human individuals are bereft of freedom. The idea is a rather simple one, once one accepts the organic model. Being unaware of the free consequences of one's actions can be conceived as the dawning awareness of one's newly increased reflective capacity relative to society (and thus of one's new advance in freedom). Clear, explicit thought for Hegel follows from action; rather than preceding action, it follows from it.

The worry I have just discussed is a species of a more general concern common to thinkers as diverse as Hayek, Popper and Berlin. It has seemed that thinking of the relation of individual to society in an organic way entails that individual freedom is unreal because, at the limit, the thesis might commit one to the claim that processes of belief- and desire-formation are so impinged upon by implicit and implacable social forces that it is merely those forces that are expressed in individual action. No philosopher in the history of the reception of Hegel's political thought, including Marx, holds that individual thought or agency could be so determined by social factors that there is no role for free, individual political agency in an account of political freedom. Hegel's organic account is supposed to provide the opposite result. One's being determined in one's thought and actions, to the degree that one is so determined, is a result of an overall rationality that is answerable to individuals, just because their reflective constituency is a requirement upon the rationality of the society in question.

Still, one must graft the concept of autonomy onto Hegel's political thought with great care. If one views autonomy as a species of self-governance or self-legislation, as it seems to be in contemporary Anglophone Hegelianism, much that is innovative about Hegel's thought is lost. Hegel is concerned that values be objects with which one can 'identify' and, whatever gloss one gives to the term 'identify', values are objects with which one can identify precisely because they are *self-given*. Self-legislation is one form of self-givenness, and autonomy a further specification of that. But it is wrong, Hegel would suggest, to think of self-*legislation* or self-*governance* as the proper philosophical characterization of the source for the political responsiveness of humans to their values, let alone their normative force. The problem with this way of putting things is not that the idea of self-legislation requires reflection to have a role in ethical and political life. Values of course can be, and in some situations should be, objects of reflection. Reflection on values can perform all manner of important critical and pedagogical service. Reflection can destroy moral knowledge, as Bernard Williams has argued, but it needn't.

But there are at least two things wrong with the idea of self-giving as law-giving to the self. First, the idea that one gives oneself a *law* mischaracterizes what it is that makes a value authoritative. It has been one of the great misfortunes of the history of philosophy that values have been thought to have true normative force only if they are analogs of something like natural laws. Values look to be poor candidates for this sort of treatment, and Hegel's historicism helps one to see why. It is true that Hegel cheats his own historicism when he interprets history autotelically, but few will embrace that part of Hegel's thought now. The only argument that I can see in favor of the claim that the normative force of ethical and political values should be put in terms of universalistic laws requires the corollary, namely that the only real source for normativity is strict law. But that just begs the question in favor of universalism. There is nothing incoherent at all in the idea that values are binding even though they are ultimately contingent, historical products.[26] The second way in which interpreting self-giving as self-legislation is misleading has to do with the quality of critical reflective distance it requires of ethical and political agents. The self-legislation model requires one to see ethical or political value as being *produced* in decisional judgment. According to that model, a value has normative force because it can be prescribed according to whatever test is relevant. While a value may be a proper object of reflection, it is not acquired as a value in that way. It is easy to see why this sort of distancing from values might be thought to undercut value-identification since it requires the agent to treat the value as alien. Self-legislation requires much more than critical distance; it mandates treating values as specimens that *then* are valued because they are brought under a law of which they are instances. Some values – ones designated by 'thick' ethical and political concepts like 'piety', 'patriotism' or 'shame' – may be such that no account at all can be given of their content under these conditions.

German thinkers prior to Hegel – most notably Herder, Friedrich Schlegel, and Friedrich Schleiermacher – thought that autonomy had its place, but as one good among others. There is much to be said, they thought, on behalf of the ability to distance oneself from one's given social life and its values in order to compare or criticize those values with others. Herder and Schlegel favored an approach where autonomy and social cohesiveness were unified or balanced in tension, Herder favoring the unity and Schlegel the tension. Hegel believed that he could demonstrate that humankind had progressed ethically and politically to the point where the balance no longer had to be effected.[27] This was not because the ancients were correct and social belonging, as they understood it, was by itself essential to ethical and political life; nor was it because the moderns were correct that individual autonomy was sufficient for ethical well-being. It was rather that human reflective rationality had come to produce social structures that express reflective rationality to such a high degree that a sense of *rational belonging* can ensue without the value-depleting explicit decisional relation to the values that constitute such structures.

III

Present-day attempts to extract from Hegel a non-metaphysical yet universalistic political theory that reserves a place in it for something like Kantian autonomy are not unprecedented. The so-called 'Young Hegelians' initiated just such a movement in the mid-1830s to mid-1840s. The immediate aftermath of Hegel's philosophy is an extremely complex subject that has lately received detailed and able scholarly attention.[28] The impetus for early Hegelianism was only secondarily political. Most of the debates in immediate post-Hegelianism concerned the issue of the continued pertinence of religious belief and practice. This question divided even the lesser-known first wave of 'Old' or 'Right' Hegelians – e.g. Eduard Gans, Leopold Henning, Heinrich Leo – into conservative and liberal wings. The political content of Hegel's philosophy comes into the debate prominently with what one might call the second wave of post-Hegelianism.[29] Right and Left Hegelians retained Hegel's view that political and ethical freedom should be understood primarily in social terms that move away from Kantian-Christian versions of ethical Idealism. In the crucial period of 1835–41, David Friedrich Strauss, Bruno Bauer, Ludwig Feuerbach and Max Stirner all formulated reactions to the Hegelian concept of *Geist* that incrementally stripped it of its residual religious and supernatural elements and reinterpreted it as a natural, social whole.

Strauss and Feuerbach are the better-known figures – the former on account of his excoriation at Nietzsche's hands in the first of the *Unzeitgemäße Betrachtungen* and the latter as an important precursor of Marx – but, in many ways, it is Bauer who is pivotal. Strauss inaugurated the move away from Idealism with his demand that the divine collectivity of human community be understood mythologically and not as a corporeal manifestation of the Christian Holy Spirit,[30] but it was Bauer who objected that myth was just another idealizing apparatus. Bauer argued that only a fully secularized idea of human culture could correspond to Hegel's idea of collective agency. Recanting his earlier attempts to partially accommodate traditional religion within the Hegelian framework, Bauer called for a dismantling of received ideas of political structure and agency, citing their covert religious roots.[31] This was to be replaced by a new conception of community based in empirical human being or 'ego' (*das Ich*).[32] Feuerbach's self-proclaimed closing role in the anti-Idealist reaction was to demand a deeper account of culture rooted in nature and in natural human responses to it. Feuerbach's central concern is that Hegel's dialectical categories correctly track more basic anthropological ones, displaying human progress in coming to terms with its secular humanity.

The liberal credentials of the Young Hegelians cannot be seriously doubted. They all made room within Hegelian political theory for the concept of autonomy as self-determination. In practice, the Left Hegelians were centrist-Republican almost to a person, with the possible exception of Stirner – if indeed, he can be classed as 'Hegelian' at all. Left Hegelian reassessment of the standard Hegelian categories is particularly instructive because, even while purging the metaphysical remnants, it did not draw the conclusion that autonomous, rule-governed judgment and duty no longer had a featured role to play in social and political thought. While some of the Left Hegelians were willing to admit 'rights' as a bromide, Marx was decidedly less sanguine. His insistence that such concepts are pertinent only relative to a background of a superseded ethical theory and to a particular social and economic point in history is therefore innovative. Marx was drawing the conclusion from a line of thought that had already rendered extremely problematic the standard conceptual arsenal of modern liberal political thought but that, nevertheless, was unable to bite the bullet and question liberalism as a view on democracy.

IV

The claim that philosophical theories are themselves products of more general cultural forces is not really debatable. What is subject to dispute is the extent to which philosophical claims in various areas of investigation can rise above their cultural specificity in order to claim the sort of objectivity that involves being true regardless of their cultural origin. We tend to think that the physical sciences, also cultural products, state claims that, if true, are true regardless of the cultural context in which they are stated, indeed perhaps claims that are true (or claims that state truths) regardless of whether there are human claimants at all. That the dinosaurs existed in the Jurassic, that a water molecule is composed of two atoms of hydrogen joined with one of oxygen, etc. are certainly treated as true come what may, and there are very good reasons, philosophical and otherwise, to believe them to be so. This is not to say that the cultural conditions of the production of such knowledge are unimportant, nor it is to deny that the way such facts figure in worldviews cannot differ very substantially (if such facts are included at all). Matters are less clear with the objects of social science and, thus, in philosophy. While some questions in epistemology and the philosophy of language may benefit by analogy to the physical sciences (perhaps because they deal with conceptual components of those sciences), other philosophical questions may not seem amenable to that analogy. Many philosophers, although not all of course, have thought that moral and political philosophy fall on that side of the ledger. The truth and objectivity of values – the objects of such theories – can seem quite distinct from the truth and objectivity of propositions that concern physical objects.

The notion of a self can seem to straddle the fence here. In analytic philosophy of mind and epistemology it is a much litigated question whether selves or subjects are properly thought of more on the order of physical objects with basic causal properties that extend throughout the realm of 'the mental' or not. In ethics and political theory the self has not tempted physicalism and this is in some measure because there is a good bit more to the idea that ethical and political theories are culture-bound. Ethical theories that prioritize individual assent to values according to rational principles that require those individuals to absent themselves from their concrete ways of life appear on the scene at about the same time as the emergence of the modern middle-class as the main vehicle of economic and political expression. It is no surprise of course that theories that emerge from such cultures take the predominant and most powerful actors in the culture as their objects. Such actors want to understand themselves in terms that justify, and indeed ramify, the sort of power that make them primary actors in society. Philosophical theories of moral and political value of a liberal sort are not immune from this truth.

Saying this out loud won't get you arrested anymore, but that's not because the judgment has become accepted as routinely true. It is rather because the thought is tolerated as being quaintly false. The idea of course is not new. Post-1845, Marx made such observations and applied them to liberal political theories, which, in his estimation, had to deploy concepts such as 'right', 'duty', 'fairness' and 'justice', 'autonomy', all with their basis in a very culturally specific idea of what it is to be a human subject. Marx also thought, less famously, that philosophy *as such* was so indebted to this structure that one had to stop doing philosophy in order to articulate and practice a form of life that better expresses human freedom. The idea of 'articulation' here is *not* that of theoretical articulation (although theories will have their place). One of Marx's main complaints was that theory *by itself* could not change anything and, indeed, that the idea that it could was in service of maintaining the liberal fantasy of self-interested, capitalist freedom. The first recipients of Marx's scorn on this issue were the Young Hegelians. For all their whittling away at the religious underpinnings of Hegelianism, they left in place the idea that theory was not, to put it in Marx's idiom, 'labor'. Theoretical activity is not autonomous, if what its being autonomous means is that theoretical practice operates unconstrained by cultural imperatives. One can deploy a concept of an autonomous self that pays lip-service to the idea that selves are social; one might even hold that the idea of individuality may have to be reformulated fairly substantially in light of the sociality of individual agency, but such a theory can still lack a crucial element. It still does not take seriously enough the idea that the activity of theorizing cannot be wholly antecedent to its source in society. Theories that do not take into account their emergent nature attempt to dictate terms of correct social evaluation in abstraction from culture. If this line of argument is more or less correct and if liberalism is such an abstracting theoretical exercise, then the liberal political and social theorist is left with a dilemma. Human beings are both (A) products of social forces and (B) rational agents, whose agency is engaged critically only when they are not such products. Marx thought this an insoluble antinomy for liberalism and, to my mind, it is likely that he was right. Modern reassessments of Hegel along Kantian lines cannot provide a way out of the impasse and not merely because they cannot construct a theory with sufficient generality or more consistent doctrine. The liberal way of looking at what theories are supposed to do and how they properly arise is the deeper problem. Having the wrong 'theory theory', so to speak, is what ends one up in antinomy.

V

But what might be ways out of it? It might seem that one way out is to turn our back on theory altogether. There is a tradition of this way of thinking; the most prominent instance is Heidegger. For several reasons that I cannot go into here, I do not think this is a very inviting path. There are presently two main alternatives that are live options. These approaches share a basic structure but develop it in quite different ways. The first of these one might call 'monistic particularism' and finds its most trenchant statement in MacIntyre's work. Monistic particularism takes seriously the idea that any theory that does not actually account for itself in terms of its emergence from ethical practices replicates in its structure what Hegel and Marx call 'abstraction'. The abstractness in question is not a matter of the generality of the theory. A theory is 'abstract' in the relevant sense if it views neutralizing distance between itself and its cultural origins as a precondition for its normative force and, as a result, runs the risk of prejudging the society in question in terms that distort the meaning of its values and thus their cohesive potential.[33] This abstract practice of theory is a modern invention, MacIntyre holds, and one that fosters the disintegration of the culture that produced it. One prime result of such theoretical activity is the unintelligibility of the sources for social value.[34] Monistic particularists argue for a reunification of social life and for a reinterpretation of what it is to be a social subject in terms of one main set of highly systematically unified precepts.

The second alternative also starts from the idea that theories must emerge from concrete ethical and political practice if they are not to distort certain core experiences by the wrong sort of explanation of them. This second view, however, accepts that there is a tremendous diversity of goods in the world, as well as much disagreement about how those goods rank or whether some of what seem to be goods for some people are goods for others. One might call this view 'pluralistic particularism'.[35] This view shares the idea so crucial for MacIntyre of 'internal goods' but denies that the search for one set of goods to bind a culture under the flag of 'social cohesion' is the be-all and end-all of thick human ethical practices. Pluralistic particularists might indeed charge their monistic counterparts with just the sort of antecedent ethical gerrymandering that particularists in general should abjure.

This alternative seems much more promising. In pursuing it one would likely investigate ethical and political life in a way that emphasizes precisely what autonomy/self-legislation theory rejects, i.e. ideas of heteronomy, would develop Marx's insight in ways that would have offended his sense of the base unity of 'species being' (although it can be argued that this idea still leaves quite underdetermined actual forms of free ethical and political life). According to this approach, ethical and political life, including the rational discourse within it, is characterized by contrasting and sometimes conflicting views on what is valuable. This state of affairs should be seen as constitutive of ethical and political life and not as something inimical to it. If one takes this perspective one might find a paradigm for how to both identify with certain values and yet discuss others in their own terms from certain ideas about the nature of art criticism. To argue ethically on this model would be analogous to bringing someone to see the salience of an element in an artwork by, for example, pointing out aspects of the work and how they work internal to it. In the same way ethical engagement with a claim would see it from the 'inside out', namely see how the claim figures against the more general form of ethical life from which it issues. It is more akin to bringing someone to see an aesthetic property – e.g. the delicate balance of a painting or the subtlety of a line of hexameter – than understanding an event in terms of physical law. Ethical argument would be an invitation to do a certain kind of fieldwork, to avert to a different, social scientific image. Of course one needn't accept a claim just because one engaged in this practice. Nor would such engagement be 'neutral' – power, desire, etc. would still be present in even the more sensitive of such engagements. But one would have a very detailed view of the commitments in terms of which the claim is rational. Such an activity requires ethical *imagination* and will not treat rule-rationality as an exclusive moral basis.

This approach would develop an aspect of Hegel's thought present in Marx – the idea of internal criticism – in ways that are both somewhat non-Hegelian and non-Marxian. Part of the problem with the 'sociality of reason' thesis that one often finds trumpeted by Hegelians is that it seems so superficial. Because the contemporary project of the reclamation of Hegel's political theory in the States and Britain takes some form of liberalism for granted and begins from there, the way Hegel re-enters the debate is precisely through the sort of antecedent theory-peddling of which particularists are rightly suspicious. No concrete specification of what 'sociality of reason' might mean can be provided just because the theory is produced in the wrong sort of way – out of the wrong social conditions. To the uninitiated non-Hegelian the thesis is bound to seem either trivial or empty. We have grown a culture that seems as a general matter to allow for these sorts of abstracting theories to emerge from it in ways that divorce the theories from the values of their objects. Philosophy on its own cannot do anything about this; it is part of the problem.[36]

Notes

1 See Strawson's *Individuals* (London: Routledge & Kegan Paul, 1959); see *The Bounds of Sense* (London: Methuen, 1966) for a more focused discussion of Kant and transcendental idealism.

2 Cambridge: Cambridge University Press, 1975. For Hegelian themes in Taylor's freestanding work in the philosophy of language and social science, see *Explanation of Behaviour* (London: Routledge & Kegan Paul, 1964) and the essays collected in his *Human Agency and Language*, vol. 1 of *Philosophical Papers* (Cambridge: Cambridge University Press, 1985).

3 John McDowell, *Mind and World* (Cambridge, Mass.: Harvard University Press, 1994), pp. 43–45, 83; Robert Brandom, *Making It Explicit: Reasoning, Representing and Discursive Commitment* (Cambridge, Mass.: Harvard University Press, 1994), pp. 85 ff. and *Tales of the Mighty Dead: Historical Essays in the Metaphysics of Intentionality* (Cambridge, Mass.: Harvard University Press, 2002), chs. 6–7. The *éminence grise* here is, of course, Wilfred Sellars.

4 See Danto's *Transfiguration of the Commonplace* (Cambridge, Mass.: Harvard University Press, 1982) and *The Philosophical Disenfranchisement of Art* (New York: Columbia University Press, 1985). Croce, Collingwood and Dewey are the main representatives of Hegelianism in aesthetics prior to Danto, but they do not figure much in the development of Danto's views. For the most succinct version of Croce's aesthetic Hegelianism see his 'Breviario di estetica', in *Nuovi saggi di estetica*, vol. 5 of *Saggi filosofici* (Bari: Laterza & Figli, 1919). For Collingwood's Hegelianism, see his *Speculum Mentis* (Oxford: Clarendon, 1924). For Dewey see his *Art and Experience* (New York: Putnam, 1934).

5 Cf. Christine Korsgaard, *Creating the Kingdom of Ends* (Cambridge & New York: Cambridge University Press, 1993), pp. 188–221; *The Sources of Normativity* (Cambridge & New York: Cambridge University Press, 1996) and, even more explicitly, the essays in Andrews Reath, *Agency and Autonomy in Kant's Moral Theory* (Oxford: Oxford University Press, 2006).

6 Hegel deploys the term 'autonomy' (*Autonomie*) in a marginal annotation to § 123 of the *Philosophy of Right*, in E. Moldenhauer & K.M. Michel (ed.), *Werke in zwanzig Bänden* (Frankfurt/M: Suhrkamp, 1971), vol. 7: 231 [hereafter HW], where he understands it as 'formal self-determination' (*formelles Selbstbestimmen*) and treats it as a core feature of Kant's ethics. There are several references to the concept of this sort in other versions of his lectures.

7 Allen Wood, *Hegel's Ethical Thought* (Cambridge: Cambridge University Press, 1990), pp. 39 f.

8 I am calling Hegel's own view of ethical life 'Hegelian *Sittlichkeit*' because Hegel also uses the word *sittlich* and its substantivizations to refer to Greek ethical life in the 5th–4th centuries B.C. Kantian morality is a great advance over the Greek form, although Hegel wants to mine elements of the Greek form for his own view that he thinks modern moral theory has incorrectly left to the side.

9 Of course, as Frederick Beiser notes, much depends on what one means by 'metaphysical' here – on some understandings of the term Hegel is clearly non-metaphysical but on others he may be just as clearly so. See 'Hegel and the Problem of Metaphysics', in F. Beiser (ed.), *The Cambridge Companion to Hegel* (Cambridge & New York: Cambridge University Press, 1993), pp. 1–24. Klaus Hartmann introduced the distinction between the 'metaphysical' and 'non-metaphysical' Hegel ('Hegel: A Non-Metaphysical View', in A. MacIntyre (ed.), *Hegel: A Collection of Critical Essays* (New York: Doubleday, 1972), pp. 101–24). There were, however, already by that time non-metaphysical interpretations of Hegel in the literature. See, e.g., J.N. Findlay, *Hegel: A Re-examination* (New York: MacMillan, 1958). Terry Pinkard's *Hegel's Phenomenology: The Sociality of Reason* (Cambridge & New York: Cambridge University Press, 1994) is perhaps the most resolutely non-metaphysical study of Hegel's thought. But Michael Quante's *Hegels Begriff der Handlung* (Stuttgart: Frommann-Holzboog, 1993) and Paul Redding's *Hegel's Hermeneutics* (Ithaca, N.Y.: Cornell University Press, 1996) also provide non-metaphysical interpretations of Hegel that owe much to Pippin. Wood, op. cit. allows that Hegel's own views are often metaphysical but argues that those views can be isolated from more interesting non-metaphysical aspects of his thought. Michael Rosen, 'From Vorstellung to Thought: Is a Non-Metaphysical View of Hegel Possible?', in D. Henrich and R.-P. Horstmann (eds), *Metaphysik nach Kant*, (Stuttgart: Klett-Cotta, 1987), pp. 248–62 is a percep-

tive counterargument for retaining a metaphysical view of Hegel's enterprise. For arguments that even Hegel's early political engagements were metaphysical, see Joachim Ritter, *Hegel und die französische Revolution* (Frankfurt/M: Suhrkamp, 1965).

10 This interest has come and gone and come around again, in a much more historically-informed literature. See Paul Franks, *All or Nothing: Systematicity, Transcendental Arguments, and Skepticism in German Idealism* (Cambridge, Mass.: Harvard University Press, 2005); Mark Sacks, *Objectivity and Insight* (Oxford: Oxford University Press, 2000); and Robert Stern, *Transcendental Arguments and Scepticism: Answering the Question of Justification* (Oxford: Oxford University Press, 2000). A particularly good representation of the current state of play are the essays collected in *Transcendental Arguments: Problems and Prospects*, R. Stern (ed.) (Oxford: Oxford University Press, 1999).

11 Excellent on this is Michael Forster, *Hegel and Skepticism* (Cambridge, Mass.: Harvard University Press, 1989).

12 Hegel's account of self-determination is situated in the broader context of his doctrine of 'self-realization' (*Selbstverwirklichung*). I cannot go into that connection here, but a couple of remarks are pertinent. Liberal reconstructions of Hegel have to contend with the great difference between Hegel's rather romantic idea of what a self is and the more substantivized understanding of that concept. It is crucial to mark two components of the concept of self-realization. The modifier 'self' in the hyphenated word must be understood as both (A) a reflexive prefix that indicates that the determination or realization in question involves being in a relation with oneself (in Hegel's case, of becoming aware of a property that one has) and (B) a noun that indicates that what is realized or determined is a 'self'. Putting (B) in this way can suggest that Hegel holds that the self is a pre-existent substance that undergoes a process of modification, i.e. of 'determination' or 'realization'. But the self that Hegel is concerned with here is emphatically not an entity that pre-exists its actualization – i.e. as though actualization were a process of extruding from an indeterminate, but in some sense still well-formed, self more determinate iterations according to a developmental algorithm. For Hegel the self is nothing but the process of actualization, so that the self is never what it is in advance of its development. Hegel thought that this process could be complete. The entire progression as a whole is its end and it is in this rather special sense that Hegel's theory is teleological – it is what one might call 'procedurally autotelic'. Although the idea that this process can be completed is not acceptable today, the idea of a 'dynamic' or 'procedural' self has had historical influence outside of Hegelianism, e.g. in Sartre.

13 Robert Pippin, *Idealism as Modernism: Hegelian Variations* (Cambridge & New York: Cambridge University Press, 1997), p. 97.

14 Ibid., pp. 26–27; Robert Pippin, *The Persistence of Subjectivity: On the Kantian Aftermath* (Cambridge & New York: Cambridge University Press, 2005), pp. 52–53. The appeal to 'history' by itself decides next to nothing on the metaphysical/non-metaphysical issue. Partisans of the metaphysical interpretation can turn to ringing statements of Hegel's – even in the *Phenomenology* which serve many as the non-metaphysical Hegelian text – that history is Geist 'emptied out into time [*an die Zeit entäußerte Geist*]'. HW 3: 590. The standard English translation of this text inserts the New Testament term *kenosis* ['drain', 'empty out', 'make place for', 'divest']. Miller is marking the clear theological connotations of the German 'Entäußerung', a term Hegel repeats in the passage. It is the standard word used to refer to the Christian incarnation, where place is made for the finite in the infinite. Hegel must have been aware of the many theological disputes, in both Catholicism and Protestantism concerning this doctrine. The German word is also used by Fichte in more secular terms. See *Gesammelte*

Werke, I.H. Fichte (ed.) (Berlin: de Gruyter, 1971), vol. 1: 165. Marx follows Fichte's usage.

15 *Persistence of Subjectivity*, p. 48.

16 This is the approach of Dieter Henrich, *Hegel im Kontext* (Frankfurt/M: Suhrkamp, 1971) and *Between Kant and Hegel: Lectures on German Idealism*, D. Pacini (ed.) (Cambridge, Mass.: Harvard University Press, 2003) and of Rolf-Peter Horstmann, *Wahrheit aus dem Begriff* (Frankfurt/M: Hain, 1984) and *Die Grenzen der Vernunft* (Frankfurt/M: Hain, 1991), ch. V, among others. The non-theological metaphysical approach takes its basic orientation from post-Kantian Spinozistic conceptions of substance.

17 Gerald Dworkin, *The Theory and Practice of Autonomy* (Cambridge: Cambridge University Press, 1988), p. 6 sets out several senses of 'autonomy' relevant to ethical and political philosophy.

18 See Isaiah Berlin, *Four Essays on Liberty* (Oxford: Oxford University Press, 1969), pp. 118ff.

19 *Kants gesammelte Schriften*, Königlich Preußischen Akademie der Wissenschaften (Berlin: de Gruyter, 1902), IV: 432.

20 Ibid., VIII: 366.

21 See J.B. Schreewind, *The Invention of Autonomy: A History of Modern Moral Philosophy* (Cambridge & New York: Cambridge University Press, 1998).

22 Hegel's decisive departure from Fichte is to reinterpret the structure of mutual recognition in terms of mutual conflict or struggle. Hegel's early work puts extraordinary systematic emphasis on recognition, whereas this structure becomes indicative in the *Phenomenology of Spirit* of one stage in Spirit's development. Kojève's very influential Marxist interpretation of Hegel argues for the primacy of the struggle of recognition over other elements in Hegel's thought. See his *Introduction à la lecture de Hegel* (Paris: Gallimard, 1947). Cf. Axel Honneth, *Kampf um Anerkennung* (Frankfurt/M: Suhrkamp, 1992), which is, in essence, an attempt to rehabilitate Hegel back to his earlier views.

23 By 'functional' and 'functional role' I do not mean anything having to do with functionalism in the social sciences, which would count as a competitor to Hegel's teleological views and not as a way to explain them.

24 *Foundations of Hegel's Social Theory: Actualizing Freedom* (Cambridge, Mass.: Harvard University Press, 2000), pp. 122–23. Neuhouser's is the best treatment of the influence of Rousseau on Hegel. It seems to me that discussion of this topic might benefit from closer attention to Rousseau's late work, especially the discussion of love in *Confessions* (pt. I, 1782, pt. II, 1789) and, particularly, in *Les rêveries du promeneur solitaire* (1782). Among other things, this might be an interesting avenue of investigation because it would consider the influence of Rousseau on Hegel in terms of a concept, 'love', that Hegel had already incorporated into his account of intersubjectivity from his friend Hölderlin. See A. Philonenko, 'Rousseau et Hegel: droit et histoire', in H.F Fulda and R.-P. Horstmann (eds), *Rousseau, die Revolution und der junge Hegel* (Stuttgart: Klett Cotta, 1991), pp. 23–40 for Rousseau and the young Hegel.

25 This does not mean that agents must know themselves to be free in Hegelian terms (or in terms of some highly philosophical substitute for Hegel's theory, if there is such). Such explicitly philosophical reflection is only required by Hegel at the level of what he calls 'Absolute Spirit'. The form of self-knowledge of one's ethical and political freedom operates at the lower level of 'Objective Spirit'.

26 By 'contingent' here I do not mean merely epistemically so, and so do not mean to invite Kripkean conventions that some feature of the world might be necessary (or universal) and yet our cognitive access to it might be *a posteriori*.

27 Hegel, in effect, denies that such a balancing act can be brought off – one is either a universalist or a particularist, one cannot be parts of both. For a contemporary view

very much like Hegel's on this point, see Alasdair MacIntyre, *After Virtue* (Notre Dame: University of Notre Dame Press, 1981), p. 32.

28 E.g. J.E. Toews, *Hegelianism: The Path Toward Dialectical Humanism, 1805–1841* (Cambridge: Cambridge University Press, 1980) and W. Breckmann, *Marx, the Young Hegelians, and the Origins of Radical Social Theory* (Cambridge & New York: Cambridge University Press, 1999). See Karl Löwith, *Von Hegel zu Nietzsche. Die revolutionäre Bruch im Denken des neunzehnten Jahrhunderts*, 9th ed. (Hamburg: Meiner, 1986), pt. II, § III.2 and § IV.2 for an influential alternative account.

29 Often Left Hegelianism on issues of religion goes hand in hand with political Left Hegelianism. That is, those who would claim, as did Feuerbach, both that (1) Hegel's form of constitutional republicanism is not the form of political organization that answers to the imperative of the time and (2) that standard, church-going religiosity no longer has a substantial role to play in an enlightened understanding of the relation of humans to the world. But this equivalence of liberality on both political and religious fronts was not a requirement. There were political Right Hegelians who were Left on issues of religion, e.g. David Friedrich Strauss, as well as political Left Hegelians who were Right on religion, e.g. August von Cieszkowski (a Polish Catholic). Toews, *Path Toward Dialectical Humanism* nicely separates out these various strands, which Lenin's very influential account runs together. For a particularly good statement of Lenin's views, see his 'Conspectus of the Book *The Holy Family* by Marx and Engels', in *Collected Works*, S. Smith (ed.) and C. Dutt (trans.), Moscow: Progress, 1961, 38: 19–51 [original 1895].

30 David Friedrich Strauss, *Das Leben Jesu* (Tübingen: Osiander, 1835–6).

31 Bauer's intervention in the 'Jewish Question' bears the mark of his overwhelming conviction that atheism was a prerequisite to political reform. Bauer finally came out against expanded civil rights for German Jews because of the religiosity of the Jews. In Bauer's view expanded civil rights for all was a requirement, but not for Jews *as Jews*. This doctrinaire embarrassment was, of course, criticized by Marx, who held that political emancipation (within capitalism) was fully compatible with the retention of strong religious ties. What Marx denied, and what makes his 'Zur Judenfrage' so historically important, is that political emancipation (under capitalism, or 'hucksterism', as he was then calling it) was the same thing as *human* emancipation.

32 Bauer, *Die Posaune des jüngsten Gerichts über Hegel, den Atheisten und Antichristen* (Leipzig: Wigand, 1841). Breckmann, *Marx, the Young Hegelians, and the Origins of Radical Social Theory* writes that 'Bauer had come to share as much with the monistic subjective Idealism of J.G. Fichte as with Hegel' (p. 249). Breckmann does not specify which of the many iterations of Fichte's enterprise he means to compare Bauer to, but if by 'monistic subjective idealism' one means the Fichte of the period of 1794–99, the claim is debatable. Bauer's ego has to do with *empirical* consciousness and agency, subjects about which Fichte has little to say. The fit with Nietzsche is much closer, although there are differences there as well. See Toews, *Path Toward Dialectical Humanism*, pp. 323–24 for a corrective.

33 This, I take it, is one of the main points of the eleventh thesis against Feuerbach. *Marx-Engels Werke* (Berlin: Dietz, 1958 ff.), III: 7.

34 MacIntyre, *After Virtue*.

35 I am unsure how comfortable they would be to be grouped together under this heading, but the views of Alain Badiou, Raymond Geuss, Richard Rorty, Charles Taylor and Bernard Williams are, in different ways, illustrative.

36 Many thanks to Karl Ameriks for very helpful comments on a prior version of this essay.

5

HABERMAS AND THE KANT-HEGEL CONTRAST

Espen Hammer

Hegel's influence on the thinkers associated with the early Frankfurt School has been vast. The notion of immanent critique, which Max Horkheimer, Theodor W. Adorno and Herbert Marcuse appropriated and used in their reflections on contemporary society, was in large part generated from their reading of Hegel, and so was their commitment to offering a philosophical account of the nature and aspirations of modernity. Their insistence on interpreting cultural and social phenomena dialectically had Hegel's method of self-reflection in the *Phenomenology of Spirit* as its most immediate forerunner, and they have all in some defining sense subscribed to an essentially Hegelian notion of *critique*.[1] In particular, what has united their efforts and given Critical Theory a sense of identity has been the project of trying to unravel what they have seen as the contradictions of late modernity between its actual practices and its ideals, and then, on the basis of that unraveling, perform an immanent social critique aimed at indicating how those contradictions might be overcome. Hegel, they have argued, offers a view of social reality that is not fixated on social facts as such, as though these exist on a par with those of the natural world, but on the way in which such facts are constituted and generated in processes that themselves, though not exclusively, involve claims and commitments that the critical theorist can turn to in order to obtain normative resources for conducting critique.[2] Most of the early proponents of Critical Theory, including Horkheimer, Adorno and Marcuse, followed the early Marx, however, in criticizing Hegel for having developed what they saw as an excessive form of idealism.[3] Hegel, they argued, ultimately succumbed to the idealist temptation to provide final, and in the ultimate instance indefensible, groundings for his philosophy.

More recently, Jürgen Habermas has sought to reconceptualize the nature of Critical Theory by turning more directly to Kant. In a crucial move, which in the early 1970s led him to embark on the long path of developing a formal-pragmatic theory of rational communication, Habermas claimed that *critique*, the central term, obviously, of any *critical theory*, involves not only, as he had initially argued, self-reflection (or immanent critique) but also, in a more Kantian vein, rational reconstruction of necessary presuppositions of rational action and judgment.[4] In contrast to the earlier representatives of Critical Theory, for whom reification and positivism (or, in Hegelian jargon, dogmatism) emerged as the fundamental issues to be confronted, Habermas's turn to Kant was in large part motivated by a growing desire to refute contextualism and relativism.

Echoing tendencies in thinkers such as Robert Brandom, Richard Rorty, Hilary Putnam, Stanley Cavell and Donald Davidson, what we might think of as the Hegelian side of Habermas is less interested in questions of representation (at least if conceived in strong realist terms, and with reference to an individual subject's experience independently of a community of speakers) than in how speakers, while belonging to a linguistic community, rationally go about understanding, communicating and justifying their claims to one another. Yet while reason's embodiment in language, practice and historical forms of life has become a dominant theme in contemporary post-analytical philosophy, the Kantian side of Habermas has called for the reconstruction of formal-pragmatic presuppositions of speech that can provide an account of how unconditional and context-transcending claims to universal validity are possible.[5] The claims a speaker makes, Habermas argues, do not simply reflect facts about this person's own position; they inevitably aim to be valid for all rational speakers.

This paper will be exploring Habermas's negotiation of the Kant-Hegel legacy. I will suggest that Habermas fails to appreciate the exact nature of some of the defining features of the idealist project, in particular its account of spontaneity and self-determination, which profoundly shaped Hegel's thinking. I will criticize, therefore, Habermas's claim that Hegel, despite being a protagonist of 'detranscendentalization', ultimately reverted to a 'mentalist' theory of absolute subjectivity. I will claim, moreover, that when read as a self-reflective criticism of positivity, Hegel's project can be shown to represent a challenge to Habermas's formal-pragmatic approach. In the final section, I will argue that Habermas's failure to adequately define the nature of Hegel's thinking may suggest the need for a retrieval of earlier and more manifestly Hegelian accounts of Critical Theory. At this point I will briefly invoke the work of Adorno.

Habermas's Critique of Hegel

The development of the early Hegel's thinking was profoundly shaped by his considerations of the Enlightenment, and of European modernity as such. As Habermas observes in *The Philosophical Discourse of Modernity*, the fundamental problem faced by Hegel was whether or in what sense modernity could be said to possess the conceptual and cultural resources requisite for reconciling individual aspirations to self-authorization and self-determination with objective institutional frameworks of various kinds.[6] How, indeed, is it possible to criticize and eventually overcome positivity – the arbitrary and, for Hegel, dogmatic and potentially authoritarian enforcement of normative claims and ideals, whether in religion, art, science, philosophy, or politics? In the name of what kind of criteria or aspirations can positivity even be located and diagnosed?

In his earliest phase of serious intellectual engagement, in Tübingen, Bern and Frankfurt in the 1790s, Hegel appeared as a strong critic of the Enlightenment project, arguing that it promotes an instrumental, fragmenting, and ultimately distorted vision of rationality.[7] The Enlightenment had celebrated understanding [*Verstand*] or reflection at the expense of reason [*Vernunft*]. Thus, rather than seeking to articulate some form of absolute unity by reference to which the various dualisms of modernity – faith versus reason, theory versus practice, morality versus ethical life, the finite versus the infinite, and so on – could be overcome, the proponents of the Enlightenment merely accepted or affirmed them, thereby elevating finite, arbitrary determinations to the status of something absolute. Moreover, the main adversary of the Enlightenment, protestant orthodoxy, fared no better. By failing to transform the historical-critical activity of biblical exegesis into a living element of ethical life that could motivate moral action in accordance with reason's commands, it left the individual believer without any means to identify with religious doctrine.

Like some of his contemporaries, such as Schiller, Schelling, Hölderlin, and, a few years later, the Jena Romantics, Hegel, despite his enthusiasm for the French Revolution and for Luther's revitalization of Christianity, found modern life essentially cold and alienating; and, following the lead of Rousseau's *Second Discourse*, advocated a reconsideration of moral and cultural ideals, mainly Hellenic and Christian, borrowed from bygone epochs of human history. Unlike many intellectuals of his own generation, however, Hegel was never nostalgic about these ideals, and when searching for ways to reactualize them, he always did so within the parameters set by what he understood to be the most sophisticated manifestations of modern thought.

In his early theological writings, in which he criticizes the positivity of Christianity, Hegel turns to Kant's moral philosophy. However, from framing his account of the teachings of Jesus, in 'The Positivity of the Christian Religion', in such a way as to make Jesus be a proponent of Kant's notion of self-resolved duty, Hegel soon started to view Kantian morality as aligned with the Enlightenment trend towards greater alienation.[8] The moral law, though self-imposed, requires unconditional obedience, independently of empirical motivation and nature; yet by dividing the subject along the familiar opposition of reason and sensibility (including the capacity for passionate attachment, or what Hegel calls 'love'), it came to epitomize the fateful dialectic of externalization which, in Hegel's view, seemed to be the hallmark of Enlightenment rationalization.

Around the turn of the century, Hegel became more focused on Kant's theoretical philosophy, arguing that it was caught up in the arbitrary dogmatism of Enlightenment thinking as well. The privileging of the understanding, which offered cognitive assurance at the cost of being, as he saw it, formal, finite, and ultimately psychologistic, over reason, the capacity to unify and reconcile the sundered 'whole', seemed unacceptable and called for a very different approach. Rather than following Kant, Hegel began developing a new systematic approach to the human mind and its relation to the social whole. Now this is the point at which Habermas starts to make his strongest claims.

Habermas's approach to the early Jena years is that '[Hegel] gambled away what, from hindsight at least, appear to be his original gains'.[9] There is, he claims, on the one hand, the 'good' Hegel of the Jena *Philosophy of Mind* and *Systementwürfe*, who was working his way toward a communicative and intersubjectivist theory of the formation of the human mind.[10] On this 'good' account, Hegel's 'spirit', operating in the media of language and labor, is nothing but the socially instituted structures of mutual recognition that provide grounds for identity-formation, and the categories according to which the objective world is cognitively processed emerge as functions or by-products of that process. For Habermas, however, there is, also the 'bad' Hegel of the *Phenomenology of Spirit* and beyond. Habermas claims that this 'bad' Hegel replaced the detranscendentalized (or situated, finite) subject of the earlier writings with a theory of absolute subjectivity, involving a single macrosubject allegedly capable of overcoming the opposition between subjective certainty and objective sociality by reference to some form of totalizing, otherness-absorbing self-conscious 'whole'.[11] While the earlier, 'good' Hegel set the stage for thinkers such as Humboldt, Peirce, Dilthey, Dewey, Cassirer, Heidegger, and Wittgenstein, all of whom are said to have 'put the transcendental subject back into context and [situated] reason in social space and historical time',[12] the later, 'bad' Hegel returned, albeit in a grandiose and ultimately absurd fashion, philosophy to the 'mentalist' position that the earlier Hegel had found in Kant but rejected. Hegel should have remained faithful to his early view that the subject-subject model characteristic of communicative action is more fundamental than the subject-object model on which the account of alienation is predicated. He would then have been able to articulate the promises of modernity in terms of the account he provides of rational dialogue and intersubjective understanding. Instead, what he did was to reclaim the notion of free, self-reflective subjectivity, yet this time not as a finite, psychologistic entity, but as embodying the capacity for absolute freedom and hence the ability to overcome every contingency or otherness by seeing it as the product of its own self-positing.

These are large claims, and in this crude sketch I have so far said nothing about why Habermas holds them to be true. Whatever one thinks of their cogency, however, it is hard not to appreciate how well they fit in with his own rejection of 'mentalism'. As in many of his readings of other thinkers in the Western tradition, there is here a promise that has been rejected, forgotten or repressed; thus by offering his dual interpretation, Habermas can place himself at the end of a history of failures and tell his audience exactly what went wrong.

For the moment, I will neither deal with Habermas's own theory of communicative rationality, nor with the corresponding, though rudimentary, intersubjectivist account he claims to have found in Hegel's Jena *Systementwürfe*. What interests me, rather, are the views he brings to bear on the notion of spirit and the role this entity is supposed to play in Hegel's version of the 'self-grounding of modernity'. Is it plausible that Hegel's theory of freely self-determining spirit, as it is developed and articulated in the *Phenomenology of Spirit*, should be viewed as a form of mentalism?

By 'mentalism', Habermas refers to any philosophical theory that, following the lead of Descartes's epistemology, takes *the* crucial challenge of philosophy to consist in the problem of accounting for the possibility of objective representation. A mentalist is someone who believes that objective representation (if at all possible given the skeptical doubts which, in Descartes, were epitomized in the construction of the famous dream-argument) takes place through some sort of ideational 'mirroring', and that such mirroring – available through introspection – can only occur for a self-conscious epistemic subject. As opposed to the, at best, indirect access one may have to mind-external or mind-independent reality, epistemic access to one's own private mental content is on the mentalist view understood to be immediate and incorrigible. Moreover, since there is no immediate access to a mind-independent reality, truth and objectivity become functions of the quality or mode with which ideas (or representational content in general) are presented to the mind. On the assumption that the mind actually is able to 'mirror' reality, Descartes famously introduced the criteria of clarity and distinctness in order to distinguish veridical from non-veridical representations. In acts of self-reflection, the subject assesses the degree of objectivity of its own ideas.

One difficulty which arises when assessing Habermas's lumping of both Kant and (the 'bad') Hegel with Descartes and mentalism is that it seems to do little justice to the specific form of idealism which emerges in Germany with the publication of the *Critique of Pure Reason*, and which, though in a radically reshaped fashion, is being continued in Hegel's *Phenomenology*.[13] The Cartesian (mentalist) view presupposes a robust realism according to which the world to be correctly represented is the world as it is independently of a subject's conceptual determination of it. Given a non-inferentially warranted mental state, the mentalist asks, how can we prove whether it corresponds to a mind-independent reality? Yet neither Kant nor Hegel believe a) that there is such a thing as a world *in itself* to be represented at all, or b) that the most promising way to reconstruct the conditions under which knowledge is possible is to try to identify an immediately given mental state and then inquire into its possible correspondence with a mind-independent object. Central to both Kant's and Hegel's projects is that non-inferentially warranted states cannot have an epistemic value because in order to take a mental state to possess any kind of determinacy (and it must have determinacy, be of something in particular, in order to represent something), it is necessary to take it to have a specific content, and one can only do so by making a judgment about it that involves the use of concepts. There is, on Kant's and Hegel's views, no intuitive knowledge of anything; all knowledge requires the mediation of concepts deployed in judgments. Rather than taking the mind's epistemic role to consist in passively representing the world, where the truth-claim of a given representation is assessed in terms of specific epistemic qualities, both Kant and Hegel argue that the mind is fundamentally active in that, in getting to know how things stand, it determines what is given to it by relating judgmentally (and hence apperceptively) to the given. To make judgments, then, and thereby to experience mind-independent objects, is for Kant and Hegel to submit oneself to the specific norms that govern their formation.[14] It is only when we actively process what is given by placing it judgmentally in normatively structured relations that questions of objectivity, and therefore of truth and falsehood, can emerge.

For Kant, such considerations achieve further elaboration when reflecting upon what it means to take representations to be representing an object. I am able to view myself as apperceptively self-aware of my representations *qua* representations of an object insofar as I take them to be combined and determined in certain ways that correspond to the possible forms of judgment. Whatever one's views are concerning Kant's influence on Hegel, the Hegel of the *Phenomenology* accepts that judging, or making a claim to knowledge, is an activity that presupposes a pre-given commitment to specific norms that determine what counts as authoritative or objective for the kind of self-conscious experience of objects that the idealists take to be required for there being a genuinely cognitive relation to the world. Yet on his account there is no fixed and transhistorical set of 'forms of judgment' such as Kant's categories that govern all possible judging; rather, the *Phenomenology* is a progressive testing of successive candidates for successful notional determination of judgment. For each putative experience, Hegel presents a test-case which will show whether the notional determination is adequate for the self-conscious experience of objects that is being promised. If it is not adequate (which it is bound to be, given Hegel's desire to recount a developmental story that will gradually lead to greater insight into the subject's own free responsibility for the notional determinations it applies), offering conflict, incoherence and paradox rather than self-conscious experience of objects, then a new notional determination is introduced which resolves the problems and disappointments of the former. In the final instance, the author of the *Phenomenology* will be arguing that the ultimate basis for epistemic authority is a community of agents – an aspect of what Hegel calls 'spirit' [*Geist*] – in which every member is recognized by the others as free and equal, and in which the members take their self-reflective form of life to be the absolute vantage-point from which any question of epistemic authority can be raised.[15] At no point, then, is Hegel venturing beyond the level of consciousness's own dialectical self-reflection in order to assess its norms with reference to the object as it is in itself. The only mentalism at stake in the *Phenomenology* is the one which Hegel himself introduces in the initial chapter on 'consciousness' only to discard it by showing that its claims about what counts as knowledge generate inconsistencies and paradoxes.[16]

In a recent essay on Kant's and Hegel's epistemologies, 'From Kant to Hegel and Back Again: The Move toward Detranscendentalization', Habermas recognizes the need to distinguish, within the group of positions which he characterizes as mentalist, between Cartesian realism and the transcendental turn in Kant and subsequent idealists.[17] The transcendental turn involves, he writes, 'the idea that the knowing subject determines the conditions under which it can be affected by sensory input'.[18] Yet the way in which Kant's project is subsequently described reveals why he continues to think of it as wedded to mentalism. Kant, he claims, 'wishes to solve a problem that he inherits from the mentalist paradigm, one that establishes the contrast between a representing subject and a world of objects offered for representation. At the same time, he also inherits those unanalyzed notions of subjectivity and self-reflection that are constitutive for the mentalist framework'.[19] This interpretation, however, is misleading. By understanding the central problem of Kantian epistemology to reside in the quest for correct representation of 'a world of objects offered for representation', Habermas fails to realize that the crucial issue in Kant is not representation but the uncovering of the *conditions* our representations must conform to in order for human agents to be able to take them as representing objects in the first place. The second claim, about subjectivity and self-reflection, is not easy to understand. However, what Habermas seems to get at is that Kant's conception of the transcendental apperception involves what he calls 'a self-reflection that operates as a representation of my own representings'.[20] Again, this is unpromising as an account of Kant's position. If self-consciousness (or self-reflection) were thought to be some sort of second-order representation, then that would require yet another level of self-awareness again, and so on ad infinitum. We would, as Dieter Henrich has argued, be faced with an infinite regress.[21] However, as I have already indicated, Kant is not committed to such a view. Very roughly, for him the transcendental unity of apperception is the capacity to take oneself as the author of one's experience, and therefore of the judgments made in relation to it. The subject's identity is a function of the capacity to ascribe experiences to one and the same self over time, which ultimately is made possible by the way in which the same subject is able to create a synthetic unity among its experiences.

Habermas's recent ascription of mentalism to Hegel is more complex. He does acknowledge that the specific form of self-reflection being practiced in the *Phenomenology* does not fall immediately under the mentalist paradigm. In clear opposition to Kant's transcendental epistemology, it involves:

a) a learning process whereby the subject comes to realize that its self-reflectively accepted notion of what counts as knowledge is ultimately dependent on standards that are upheld in and through communal practices of mutual recognition; and

b) that the orientation of the reconstructive philosopher therefore needs to change from that of being preoccupied with the spontaneity of a solitary transcendental subject to what eventually, when the Hegelian narrative reaches the level of 'Spirit', turns into an account of the intersubjective constitution of the objective world.

One might add to this that the *Phenomenology* can be read as one continuous battle with Cartesian realism. Starting, in the first chapter, with the experience of an individual consciousness embodying strong realist claims about knowledge, Hegel gradually undermines this picture by showing how experience is mediated – first, through conceptual determinations as such, and second, through communal recognition of the experiencing subject's conceptual determinations.

Why, then, can Hegel continue to be accused of mentalism? Habermas's argument is this. The intersubjectivist reading of spirit, while attractive in that it overcomes the 'methodological solipsism' of the Descartes–Kant–Fichte tradition, is 'deficient by Hegel's own standards'.[22] It is deficient because the intersubjectivist reading fails to bridge the gap between claims to knowledge that satisfy intersubjective criteria of validation and what is objectively true. It is simply not the case that idealized intersubjective validation implies objective truth. Thus, even if a contestable view has turned out to be acceptable 'for us', it has still not been established that it is true of the world as it is independently of the intersubjectively established framework. On Habermas's account, Hegel would see the intersubjectivist reading of spirit as involving a form of arbitrariness with regard to the norms which govern the community's reason-giving activities.

According to Habermas's *own* thinking, such arbitrariness must be accepted. It is simply another way of characterizing the postmetaphysical fact that the most authoritative source of knowledge in modern societies, namely science, can only develop in a spirit of inevitable fallibility. Scientific research is finite: it must humbly accept that what today counts as a rationally acceptable theory may tomorrow be overthrown by one of its competitors. However, in what Kuhnian philosophy of science has taught us, it is required that the scientist is open not only to piece-meal revisions, but also to anomalies that, if impossible to integrate into the adopted framework, may ultimately lead to a change of paradigm. This is another aspect of the inevitable arbitrariness characterizing all knowledge. It should be noted, though, that Habermas at this point is conflating two different claims. It is one thing to say that those who engage in scientific research must be open to the possibility of critique, revision and falsification, and that that involves the acceptance of a certain form of arbitrariness; it is quite a different thing, however, to say that the framework within which such research takes place – the normatively structured relationships of inference that must be in place for data to be interpreted and theories to be established and corroborated – is arbitrary. For us to be able to think of it as arbitrary it would be necessary to envision alternatives that would be equally well grounded in the learning process of a given culture, yet such alternatives are precisely not available for the simple reason that we could not make sense of them within our own life-form. It also suggests, along with the metaphysical realism which Habermas elsewhere wants to reject, that there is such a thing as the world as it is in itself, and that cultural standards must be arbitrary because they do not present us with an absolute view-point. Yet one of the central lessons of Hegel's thinking is precisely that the very idea of the world as it is in itself is incoherent: there is no objecthood independently of the conceptual scheme we employ. Only if we saw the conceptual scheme as imposed upon a world that somehow were epistemically constituted outside of our concepts would it make sense to ask whether it accurately matches or represents the world. However, the Hegelian view is that no such imposition takes place. Our rules for determining objects stretch out all the way to the object; thus discovering empirically what the world is like will not cast any light whatsoever on the constitutive or transcendental relation between thought and world.[23] Only the examination, as in the *Phenomenology*, of the different ways we can *take* the world to be determinate will reveal this relation.

Regardless of how Habermas would go about defending this particular version of contextualism (which certainly does suggest, along the lines of the mentalist paradigm, that there is a gap between our cognitive practices and the world as it is in itself), the view he attributes to Hegel is that the intersubjectivist understanding of objective spirit is insufficient to ground objectivity in the way Hegel (on this construal) would seem to want it to do. Instead, what is required (according to Habermas's Hegel) is an account of *absolute* spirit in which an 'absolute subject' is posited as the basis from which the history of consciousness emerges: 'This subject is thought of as the One and All, as the totality that "can have nothing outside itself".'[24]

The account Habermas invokes here is a version of Platonism whereby spirit, or the absolute subject, is considered to be a metaphysical entity – or, more correctly, a noumenal reality – that actualizes itself teleologically by progressively overcoming its own self-alienations. In analogy with Fichte's *Tathandlung* (or self-positing ego) yet expanded beyond finite consciousness, spirit becomes a 'self-reflection writ large'[25] that permeates the human mind, world history, and external nature. While this represents Hegel's solution to the arbitrariness-problem in that noumenal reality is now accessible for a philosophy of spirit, it can at the same time be interpreted as mentalism taken to its utmost extreme: for in contrast to the more modest conceptions of subjectivity that we find in Descartes or Kant, the Hegelian absolute subject expands to cosmic dimensions and becomes the source of all reality. Knowing the way it determines itself throughout its formative processes becomes equivalent with possessing the kind of absolute knowledge which Hegel's mature system promises.

Habermas's interpretation of Hegel may sound excessive. However, as Frederick Beiser points out, not only has it been pervasive in much scholarship on

German idealism but, insofar as Hegel is considered to represent the culmination of the Cartesian tradition, enjoys a certain inherent plausibility.[26] If the Cartesian (or mentalist) is committed to the view that the subject has immediate knowledge only of its own ideas, and therefore that it has no direct recourse to that which is beyond its circle of awareness, then the German objective idealists attempt to avoid the skeptical conclusion arising from this paradigm by widening consciousness to embrace everything: thus knowing the expanded mind's own ideas, which amounts to self-knowledge, becomes equivalent with having metaphysical knowledge that extends into the noumenal realm. By combining this idea with Kant's alleged notion of the world-creative powers of the subject, one could reach the kind of position that Habermas attributes to Hegel.

According to Beiser, however, this story has little or no truth to it:

> the absolute subject, the infinite ego, or universal spirit, *understood as a metaphysical principle or noumenal reality*, never had much of a role to play in German idealism. If it appeared at all, it was only very briefly, confined to a very short phase of Schelling's philosophical project, the few months he adhered to the doctrines espoused in his early *Vom Ich als Prinzip der Philosophie* (1796); and Schelling quickly moved away from this position, and even during this period he equivocated whether he meant to commit himself to the existence of the absolute subject.[27]

Beiser's own account, however, is different from the one I already outlined with regard to Hegel. According to Beiser, the German idealists, including Hölderlin, Schlegel, Novalis, Schelling, and Hegel, instead turned to 'something impersonal, neutral, or indifferent, whether it be pure being, life, or the indifference point; to construe it as the ego is to hypostatize and anthropomorphize it, dragging it down into the realm of finite experience'.[28]

I do not intend to discuss Beiser's positive account but will simply note that if Habermas's interpretive hypothesis were correct, then the question would arise of how finite humans may have epistemic access to the realm of absolute or infinite spirit.[29] Hegel would then fall behind Kant's critique of rationalism and introduce a version of transcendental realism that would be indefensible on the basis of the conceptual resources on offer in the *Phenomenology*, let alone on independent grounds. Habermas's claim that the adoption of an extremely ambitious metaphysical theory of absolute spirit would make it easier for Hegel to defend the unconditional objectivity of what is rationally acceptable 'for us' falters in that it so blatantly disregards that so much of the philosophical labor being performed in the *Phenomenology* is geared towards undermining the very possibility of, and rationale for, asking whether our conceptual schemas, or what rational beings can accept as authoritative, actually corresponds in some 'deep' sense to what is 'really' out there. If Habermas's reading were right, then Hegel, rather than succeeding in establishing transcendental conditions for objective judging, would commit himself to a view that would generate a radical form of skepticism.

Habermas's Kantianism

Much of Habermas's effort to establish a theory of rationality that, when added to his account of 'systemic intervention in the lifeworld',[30] can provide a more balanced understanding of modernity than those of both Hegel and most of the European thinkers who responded to his work over the next 120 years or so is predicated on a return to motives found in Kant.[31] We have seen that Habermas (wrongly in my view) believes to have located problems in Kant's theoretical philosophy that are inherited from the Cartesian or mentalist tradition; thus, returning to Kant must involve finding an alternative Kant who is *not* committed to, or in any sense dependent on, a mentalist framework. In Habermas's formulation of the task, it is necessary to look for 'paradigm-neutral types of self-reflection' in Kant's writings. Thus, in the important formulation of what he calls a formal pragmatics, he seeks to reconstruct the pragmatic presuppositions speakers allegedly must make when engaging in 'action oriented towards understanding' [*verständigungsorientertes Handeln*].[32] According to this theory, speakers understand and interpret each other in light of the reasons being offered for their respective claims, and when being oriented exclusively towards reasons they will inevitably have to take each other to be free and equal in senses Habermas spells out in great detail. In particular, Habermas introduces the notion of a specific set of idealizations that are said to underlie everyday speech and make up necessary and universal commitments that every rational speaker must undertake when communicating and discussing. Such idealizations, or 'discourse rules', stipulate for example that participants in discourse must have the same chance to put forward or call into question claims that are being raised, and that the discussion is free from distorting influences, whether their source is open domination, conscious strategic behavior, or the more subtle barriers to communication deriving from self-deception. Drawing on some of the deepest ideals of the German idealist tradition, what this means is that linguistic activity commits us to the assumption that other participants in the linguistic community are to be understood as fellow subjects, not manipulable objects, and so in all cases as potentially rational subjects, freely capable of advancing or rejecting various claims being made by subjects on each other. In his discourse ethics, Habermas even attempts to derive a moral principle from these rules, arguing that every serious speaker is committed to this principle when engaging in moral debate over disputed social norms.[33]

Yet what is the exact theoretical status of these rules? According to Habermas's close associate over many years, Karl-Otto Apel, the discourse rules – which, as outlining an indefinite community of mutually recognizing speakers, for him anticipate an ideal form of life – are of a transcendental nature: they articulate the apodictical requirements that every speaker must accept as binding.[34] They pretend, we might say, to be universally valid in roughly the same sense as Kant's categories are meant to be so. For Habermas, however, the formulation of the rules is itself hypothetical, the result of a collaboration between the empirical efforts of social and linguistic sciences, and the philosophical efforts of rational reconstruction.[35] One problem with this weaker account, though, is that it is not clear what would count as an empirically based disclaimer of the formulation. Is not a person who formulates an alternative set also committed to the discourse rules, and how can she then present her revision without presupposing that which she is about to criticize? Moreover, if the discourse rules really just have an empirical status, then how can Habermas draw on them in order to formulate a view of rationality that, as he wants, can withstand relativist skepticism? It is not enough to suggest that no one can engage, say, in rational debate without accepting the idealizations that the discourse rules stipulate if other cultures turn out to possess different language games for adjudicating controversial claims and proposals.[36] In short, if the discourse rules can be supported or objected to in light of empirical considerations, then they cannot ground what Habermas wants them to establish, namely a form of strong universalism. Habermas cannot have both: a strong universalism *and* an empirically based reconstruction of rules of discourse.

Another and possibly more interesting problem is that discourses may seem to satisfy the ideal requirements which Habermas outlines and still not deserve to be called rational. In evaluating the rationality of specific discourses, there will always be a need for context-sensitive and historically specific judgment. Why, one may for example ask, is it always rational to grant every participant in a rational debate the same right to intervene and raise objections, etc. when it seems widely, if not universally, accepted, both in theoretical and practical contexts, that some people will always be more competent, experienced, and insightful than others? To say that their competence, experience and insight will have to be proven in the discourse is a non-starter: if so, then very few serious discussions, whether in science or philosophy, would ever get started. No rational discourse can proceed without exclusions, yet how, when and the degree to which such exclusions should be carried out will necessarily be a matter of judgment. Needless to say, discourses take place in real life – that is, in unruly and singular situations that require decisions of various kinds.

At this point it may be useful to remind oneself of Hegel's critique of positivity. After all, one of the central claims that Hegel makes in this regard is that the idea of 'first philosophy' that informs a Kantian transcendental critique (and, by implication, Habermas's formal pragmatics, even though he seeks to soften it by introducing empirical constraints) is deeply problematic. There is always something prior and historically given on which reflection depends, hence the constitution of epistemic norms cannot be construed as an absolute origin but must itself be the outcome of historically mediated processes of self-reflection and immanent critique. However, by contrast to the position Habermas has been defending since the mid-1970s, which seeks to combine empirical and transcendental reflection in an external relation, Hegel can agree that claims concerning fundamental structures of rationality are themselves of a historical nature *without* accepting that they therefore must be possible to criticize by reference to empirical considerations. Habermas concedes this point in his 1968 discussion of Hegel in *Knowledge and Human Interests* but ignores it as soon as he starts developing his formal pragmatics.[37] The necessities which each formation of consciousness in the *Phenomenology* take as given are necessities – necessary epistemic norms – in the sense that they stake out what a particular formation of consciousness takes to be determinative for itself. They are so fundamental that it would make no sense either to support or disclaim them empirically. The claim that knowledge, as in the model of 'sense certainty' with which Hegel sparks off his dialectic, is equivalent with whatever presents itself immediately to consciousness, cannot be touched by empirical considerations: it can neither be supported nor falsified by such claims. The only procedure that can offer a rational testing of such a claim is the one which Hegel himself proposes, namely an immanent critique that seeks to verify whether the claim (or norm) *on its own terms* offers the kind of epistemic achievement that it promises. Does the immediacy of whatever is presented to consciousness really qualify as knowledge in the sense outlined by this formation of consciousness as it starts its process of self-reflection? As it turns out, it will experience failure: there can be no claim to knowledge unless the content of the claim has some form of determinacy, and Hegel will show that such determinacy is only possible insofar as concepts are being used to individuate and discriminate the given.[38]

I am not proposing that Hegel's *Phenomenology of Spirit* and its critique of positivity can be directly reclaimed as an account of rationality today. Hegel's ambition, for example, of showing that there is a necessary relation between each formation of consciousness, such that given the properties of formation X, a specific and unique formation Y will necessarily follow, introduces external demands (in Hegel's case the logical-dialectical entailment-relations explored in *The Science of Logic*) on the process of self-reflection that are at odds with the claim to autonomy ascribed to each formation.[39] If such autonomy is granted, then the outcome of the dialectical self-reflection may simply be whatever determination there is that resolves the epistemic quandaries of the original formation. If formation Y follows from formation X, then it is not because it is the *only* formation that satisfies the requirements arising from the breakdown of formation X, but simply because it satisfies them. Y is therefore a possible but not necessary consequence of X.[40]

Immanent critique takes the existence of language games and human practices as given and, without any attempt to establish foundations or presuppositionless beginnings, engages in critical self-reflection with a view to showing whether they offer what they purport to offer according to their criteria and conceptual determinations. Since the criteria (of what counts as something in particular, or of whether something is valid or right) and conceptual determinations make up the historical framework within which human speech and activity can appear as intelligible, they do not have an empirical status, nor can empirical considerations be appealed to in the process of reflecting upon them.

In *Knowledge and Human Interests* Habermas formulates a similar view.[41] Drawing on Fichte's critique of dogmatism, Habermas argues that there exists a form of self-reflection which is characterized precisely by the desire to achieve mature autonomy through the overcoming of false hypostatizations. As in Fichte, reason is not, he argues, a theoretical faculty, a faculty of contemplation, so much as it is the unification of theoretical and practical interest in the search for one's own autonomy; and Habermas's goal in this book is to reinstate this model as essential to the very endeavor of critical social theory in the Frankfurt School tradition:

> For reflection destroys, along with a false view of things, the dogmatic attitudes of a habitual form of life. . . . In false consciousness, knowing and willing are still joined. . . . The reversal of consciousness means the dissolution of identifications, the breaking of fixations, and the destruction of projections.[42]

In the 'Postscript' to *Knowledge and Human Interests*, however, Habermas, as already mentioned, starts to distance himself from this notion of *critique*. In particular, he finds that it harbors an equivocation between two very different notions, namely 'immanent critique' as already outlined and 'rational reconstruction' in the Kantian sense.[43] Of course, detecting such an equivocation in the historical use of a term does nothing to show that there actually exist philosophical *reasons* to add a program of rational reconstruction to the initially conceived program of immanent critique, and it certainly does not license the gradual abandonment of the latter in favor of the former. Perhaps the most weighty reason for differentiating between the two forms of critique and developing a theory of formal pragmatics and rationality was that, on Habermas's later view, it no longer seemed clear that the unmasking of ideological hypostatizations and world views had any intersubjectively valid standard to appeal to in characterizing perceptions and theories as distorted or false. Having abandoned what he thought of as Hegel's notion of absolute truth or the absolute subject (as articulated, ultimately, in *The Science of Logic*), it seemed to him that no alternative existed but to construct a theory that would account for the discursive commitments necessary in order to raise claims to intersubjective validity. Such claims are then meant to be redeemed in discourses that are rational according to the stipulations of the theory.

An earlier account of critical theory

We have seen that not only are there reasons to doubt the validity of Habermas's interpretation of Hegel, but arguments drawn from Hegel may well be used in order to question Habermas's own position. I will now complicate this picture considerably (and possibly too much) by introducing the thought that resources for obtaining a more refined conception of what immanent critique involves may perhaps exist not only in the early Habermas (who, as I said, quickly abandoned this procedure, or at least downplayed its theoretical role), but in earlier versions of Critical Theory, in particular those that are more directly influenced by Hegel than Habermas has been. One such early version is found in Adorno's negative dialectics. Like Habermas, Adorno does launch a high-pitched critique of Hegel, accusing him of adopting a pre-critical metaphysics of the absolute subject along the lines already explored. According to Adorno, Hegel's system falsely reduces everything to identity; it is, he writes, the 'belly turned mind', an extreme idealism that is incapable of respecting any theory- or mind-independent evidence.[44] Yet while making these accusations, however dubitable, Adorno nevertheless positions himself as a distinctly Hegelian theorist. He does so, I will claim, by conceiving of philosophy as a form of radical self-reflection capable of challenging the prevailing, more instrumentalist forms of reason in modernity.

The notion of instrumental reason – essentially end-indifferent, procedural and technocratic reasoning – is central to the early Frankfurt School's assessment of modernity but gets dramatized by Adorno to become the driving motor of human history as such. In his most philosophical writings, Adorno sees instrumental reason and the forms of domination on which its exercise is based as totalitarian and deeply damaging of both interhuman relations as well as the relation between man and nature.

It has occasionally been claimed, not least by Habermas himself, that Adorno's dark account of instrumental reason and its pervasiveness in late modernity undermines his program of self-reflection and critique.[45] If reason is instrumental and only capable of assessing the best means to given and therefore, from the standpoint of reason, arbitrary ends, then the critical theorist is sawing off the branch on which he sits: his practice of critique is then performatively at odds with his theory of rationality, and he will have to accept that he does not dispose of any normative resources on which to base his critique. Now Habermas's point would certainly be well-taken if it were indeed true that Adorno *needs* an independent theory of rationality to back up his claims. However, he would only need that if he accepted Habermas's anti-Hegelian premise, namely that a critique of life-forms and forms of rationality must be supported by a quasi-transcendental, universalist theory of rationality. The position we find in Adorno is rather that critique must proceed on an immanent basis. Although a theorist must always be open to the possibility of radical conceptual revision, there is no coherent standpoint beyond the practices that already exist. In his *Negative Dialectics*, Adorno tries to develop this point by arguing that the task of philosophically and socially motivated critique is to criticize the failure of specific norms or criteria to deliver the epistemic results they promise. On Adorno's account, the most pressing example of such a critique is one that focuses on 'identity', a notion which is best and most fruitfully interpreted in terms of Hegel's theme of positivity. This, at least, is how I read passages such as the following:

> The name of dialectics says no more, to begin with, than that objects do not go into their concepts without leaving a remainder, that they come to contradict the traditional norm of adequacy. . . . It indicates the untruth of identity, the fact that the concept does not exhaust the thing conceived. Aware that the conceptual totality is mere appearance, I have no way but to break immanently, in its own measure, through the appearance of total identity.[46]

What Adorno claims here is that knowledge of objects is made possible by norms, concepts or rules – that is, the criteria we dispose of for knowing the object in its objecthood. When they fail to yield such knowledge, an immanent process of conceptual revision is set in motion.

It would have served his purpose better had Adorno made it clear that the target of his critique is *false* identity and not identity per se. False identity, for Adorno, arises when epistemic norms or criteria are naturalized and viewed as expressions of an immutable order of things in themselves, beyond the contingencies of history. Such naturalized norms or criteria are thus claimed to provide an 'absolute identity' between knowledge and its object, or, in Adorno's Hegelian jargon, between subject and object. On Adorno's Weberian view of rationalization, the norms and criteria we possess as modern agents tend increasingly to provide some kind of higher-order abstraction in accordance with which the object of knowledge is supposed to be understood. Natural science, for example, typically presents its claims in terms of some formal mathematical procedure, and knowing the world becomes a matter of knowing it in those terms.[47] Likewise, the phenomenon which Adorno, following Marx, calls 'commodification' (and which can be traced back to Hegel's preoccupation with dogmatism) involves a reduction or transformation of the object (the commodified entity) to the terms and conditions provided by a capitalist system of exchange. In both cases – the Galilean ontology of natural science and the system of commodities in a modern market economy – one may argue that norms or criteria of what counts as knowing something can appear to call for further reflection. Adorno is not simply proposing that there is something inherently flawed in the way science and the economy operate; rather, he is inviting the critical theorist to consider whether what we take ourselves to know about certain objects – the physical world, the world of merchandise – really is fully coherent. Does science *on its own terms* offer the kind of knowledge it promises, or is perhaps quantification somehow at odds with the ambition, say, to also understand singular (and hence non-repeatable) processes and events? Does the notion of the commodity, of things being defined in terms of their exchange value, exhaust what objects are for us?

We do not need to accept what I have called Adorno's Weberian presuppositions in order to see that the notion of immanent critique can form the basis for an ambitious program of philosophical self-reflection.[48] On Adorno's view, philosophy is a particular form of self-reflexive critique that ultimately aims to place the individual – the subject – in a position from which normative commitments can rightfully be viewed as a rationally self-chosen result of processes of reflection. At the same time, however, Adorno is deeply skeptical about the very possibility of achieving such a position. On his account, which radicalizes Hegel's understanding of positivity, modernity, with its dominance of formal and instrumentalized modes of reasoning, offers very few spaces in which to exercise such a capacity. Moreover, to the extent that they do exist – in philosophy, but also in certain types of responses to the advanced modernist arts – he worries that the exercise of reflection, if taken to be capable of arriving at a reconciliation between the criteria of knowledge and the claims to it, could lapse into an unjustified affirmation of the given. Dialectical thinking should mainly keep the possibility of resolution and reconciliation open. It should focus on the incompatibility of claim and criterion, or, as Hegel puts it, subjective certainty and truth, yet avoid thinking that the progressive move towards a new formation that will reconcile specific claims to knowledge with their epistemic presuppositions can be performed in abstraction from its accompanying social conditions.[49] For Adorno, critique and social change go together: there cannot be an immanent critique that is not at the same time demanding social change.

We should now be able to see that despite Adorno's commitment to immanent critique in a roughly Hegelian sense, there are some crucial differences between his and Hegel's understanding of dialectics. Adorno avails himself of dialectical self-reflection in a much more provisional manner than Hegel. He is constantly concerned to avoid the temptations of systematicity and completeness. However, the claim to inherit the Hegelian project for the purpose of articulating a critical theory of modernity does carry considerable force and should be seen as offering a worthy competitor to Habermas's neo-Kantianism.

Notes

1 For a useful introduction to what such a Hegelian notion of critique involves, see Garbis Kortian, *Métacritique* (Paris: Les Editions de Minuit, 1979), pp. 24–38.

2 Perhaps the most programmatic and influential statement of this position within the history of the Frankfurt School is Max Horkheimer's 1937 essay 'Traditional and Critical Theory', in *Critical Theory*, trans. M.J.O. O'Connell *et al.* (New York: Herder & Herder, 1972), pp. 188–214. For another and equally important attempt to articulate the 'logic' of immanent critique, see Herbert Marcuse, *Reason and Revolution:*

Hegel and the Rise of Social Theory (London: Routledge, 1968), esp. pp. 16–29. In addition to Hegel, the 'classical' exercise of this type of critique is Marx's analysis and exposition of the internal contradictions of political economy. When the implications of categories such as labor and value are thought through to the end, they turn out to have a meaning which is incompatible with what they have when being applied in everyday, pre-theoretical practice.

3 By 'the early Marx' I mean in particular the author of the 'Introduction' to the 1844 *Contribution to the Critique of Hegel's Philosophy of Right* and the *Economico-Philosophical Manuscripts* of the same year. Both are printed in *The Portable Karl Marx*, ed. Eugene Kamenka (London/New York: Penguin, 1983), pp. 115–25 and pp. 131–52.

4 Jürgen Habermas, *Knowledge and Human Interests*, trans. Jeremy Shapiro (Cambridge: Polity Press, 1987), pp. 379 ff.

5 For a particularly succinct discussion of the difference between Habermas's Hegelian and Kantian side when it comes to issues of rationality, see Richard Rorty's review of Habermas's *Truth and Justification*, trans. Barbara Fultner (Cambridge, Mass.: The MIT Press, 2003) in *Notre Dame Philosophical Reviews* (12 August 2003).

6 Jürgen Habermas, *The Philosophical Discourse of Modernity*, trans. Frederick Lawrence (Cambridge, Mass.: The MIT Press, 1987), p. 25: 'As it seemed to the young Hegel, a *positivity of ethical life* was the signature of the age'. Habermas (p. 27) adds that 'In these years around 1800, Hegel made a case for the verdict that both – religion and state – had degenerated into sheer mechanisms, into a clockwork, into a machine'. The relevant texts by Hegel are *The Difference between Fichte's and Schelling's System of Philosophy*, trans. H.S. Harris and W. Cerf (Albany, N.Y.: SUNY Press, 1977); *Faith and Knowledge*, trans. H.S. Harris and W. Cerf (Albany, N.Y.: SUNY Press, 1977); and *Early Theological Writings*, trans. T.M. Knox and R. Kroner (Chicago, Ill.: University of Chicago Press, 1948).

7 For a good overview of Hegel's development in this period, see H.S. Harris, 'Hegel's Development to 1807', in Frederick C. Beiser (ed.), *The Cambridge Companion to Hegel* (Cambridge: Cambridge University Press, 1993), pp. 25–51. See also Terry Pinkard, *Hegel: A Biography* (Cambridge: Cambridge University Press, 2000), pp. 19–117.

8 Hegel, *Early Theological Writings*, pp. 67–181. In 'The Spirit of Christianity and Its Fate' (ibid., pp. 182–301), Hegel is much more critical of Kantian morality, arguing that it collapses into sheer legality – that is, into something alien.

9 Jürgen Habermas, 'From Kant to Hegel and Back Again: The Move toward Detranscendentalization', in *Truth and Justification*, trans. Barbara Fultner (Cambridge, Mass.: The MIT Press, 2003) p. 176. Habermas's works contain numerous discussions of, and references to, Hegel. The account offered in *Truth and Justification* can be read as a slightly revised restatement of claims made in the following three, previously published, texts: 'Labor and Interaction: Remarks on Hegel's Jena *Philosophy of Mind*', in *Theory and Practice*, trans. John Viertel (Boston: Beacon Press, 1973), pp. 142–69; *Knowledge and Human Interests*, trans. Jeremy Shapiro (Boston: Beacon Press, 1971), pp. 3–24; *The Philosophical Discourse of Modernity*, pp. 23–44.

10 Habermas is here drawing on Hegel, *Jenaer Systementwürfe* I-III (Hamburg: Felix Meiner, 1986).

11 For alternative interpretations of Hegel's development in Jena, see Rolf-Peter Horstmann, 'Probleme der Wandlung in Hegels Jenaer Systemkonzeption', *Philosophischer Rundschau* 19 (1972), pp. 87–118; Heinz Kimmerle, *Das Problem der Abgeschlossenheit des Denkens. Hegels System der Philosophie in den Jahren 1800–04* (Bonn: Bouvier, 1970); H.S. Harris, *Hegel's Development: Night Thoughts* (Oxford: Clarendon Press, 1983); Klaus Düsing, *Das Problem der Subjektivität in Hegels Logik* (Bonn: Bouver, 1976); Otto Pöggeler, 'Hegels Jenaer Systemkonzeption', in *Hegels Idee einer Phänomenologie des Geistes* (Freiburg: Verlag Karl Alber, 1973); and Robert Pippin,

Hegel's Idealism: The Satisfactions of Self-Consciousness (Cambridge: Cambridge University Press, 1989).

12 Habermas, *Truth and Justification*, p. 175.

13 For a succinct statement to the effect that Descartes, Kant and Hegel were united in such a common cause, see Habermas's discussion of 'prima philosophia as philosophy of consciousness' in *Postmetaphysical Thinking*, trans. William Mark Hohengarten (Cambridge, Mass.: The MIT Press, 1992), p. 31:

> Self-consciousness, the relationship of the knowing subject to itself, has since Descartes offered the key to the inner and absolutely certain sphere of the representations we have of objects. Thus, in German Idealism metaphysical thinking could take the form of theories of subjectivity. Either self-consciousness is put into a foundational position as the spontaneous source of transcendental accomplishments, or as spirit it is itself elevated to the position of the absolute. The ideal essences are transformed into the categorial determinations of a productive reason, so that in a peculiarly reflexive turn everything is now related to the one of a generative subjectivity. Whether reason is now approached in *foundationalist* terms as a subjectivity that makes possible the world as a whole, or whether it is conceived *dialectically* as a spirit that recovers itself in a procession through nature and history, in either case reason is active as a simultaneously totalizing and self-referential reflection.

What I say about the lumping of Descartes, Kant and Hegel together is indebted to Robert Pippin's *Hegel's Idealism*, pp. 3–41, and to his important article 'Hegel, Modernity, and Habermas', in *Idealism as Modernism: Hegelian Variations* (Cambridge/New York: Cambridge University Press, 1997), esp. pp. 161–63.

14 This is a dominating claim in Kant's first Critique. See for example *Critique of Pure Reason*, trans. Norman Kemp Smith (London: MacMillan, 1986), B102:

> Transcendental logic (. . .) has lying before it a manifold of *a priori* sensibility, presented by transcendental aesthetic, as material for the concepts of pure understanding. (. . .) But if this manifold is to be known, the spontaneity of our thought requires that it be gone through in a certain way, taken up, and connected. This act I name *synthesis*.

In Hegel's *Phenomenology of Spirit*, trans. A.V. Miller (Oxford: Oxford University Press, 1977), this idea enters explicitly at the end of the dialectic of consciousness – that is, at the end of the first chapter.

15 When I say that the notion of a self-reflective, rational community is an 'aspect' of what Hegel means by *Geist*, I mean to hold the door open to the view that *Geist also*, for Hegel, has a divine status. Without being able to show this here, I believe that Hegel predominantly held the view that *Geist* could be both the self-reflective rational community *and* God. For some useful reflections on this issue, see Jean Hyppolite, *Genesis and Structure of Hegel's Phenomenology of Spirit*, trans. Samuel Cherniak and John Heckman (Evanston: Northwestern University Press, 1974), pp. 29–31.

16 Hegel, *Phenomenology of Spirit*, pp. 58–103.

17 Habermas, *Truth and Justification*, ch. 4.

18 Ibid., p. 179.

19 Ibid., p. 180.

20 Ibid.

21 Dieter Henrich, 'Fichte's Original Insight', trans. David R. Lachtermann, in Darrel E. Christiansen *et al.*, *Contemporary German Philosophy*, vol. 1 (University Park: Pennsylvania State University Press, 1982).
22 Habermas, *Truth and Justification*, p. 201.
23 I am here alluding to John McDowell's proposition in *Mind and World* (Harvard: Harvard University Press, 1994), p. 67 that, for the absolute idealist, 'capacities of spontaneity' are 'in play all the way out to the ultimate grounds of empirical judgements'.
24 Habermas, *Truth and Justification*, p. 204.
25 Ibid., p. 203.
26 Frederick C. Beiser, *German Idealism: The Struggle Against Subjectivism, 1781–1801* (Cambridge, Mass.: Harvard University Press, 2002), pp. 1–2. Recent representatives of this view include Robert Solomon, *Continental Philosophy since 1750: The Rise and Fall of the Self* (Oxford: Oxford University Press, 1988) and Karl Ameriks, *Kant and the Fate of Autonomy* (Cambridge: Cambridge University Press, 2000).
27 Beiser, *German Idealism*, p. 5.
28 Ibid.
29 For my attempt to respond to Beiser's study, see Espen Hammer, 'The Legacy of German Idealism', *British Journal for the History of Philosophy* 11:4 (2003), pp. 521–35.
30 The theory of systemic intervention or 'colonization' of the life-world, which should be understood as Habermas's take on Hegel's positivity-thesis, is developed in great detail in the second volume of *The Theory of Communicative Action*, trans. Thomas McCarthy (London: Heinemann, 1984).
31 See Kenneth Baynes, *The Normative Grounds for Social Criticism* (Albany N.Y.: SUNY Press, 1992) for an excellent discussion of Habermas's Kantianism.
32 The development of formal pragmatics, or what he sometimes calls universal pragmatics, has a long and intricate history in Habermas's work. For the most important stations along the way, see 'Wahrheitstheorien' in *Vorstudien und Ergänzungen zur Theorie des kommunikativen Handelns* (Frankfurt: Suhrkamp, 1984), pp. 127–83; *The Theory of Communicative Action*, trans. Thomas McCarthy (Boston: Beacon Press, 1987), vol. 1, pp. 273–337; and all the collected essays in *On the Pragmatics of Communication*, trans. Maeve Cooke (Cambridge, Mass.: MIT Press, 1998).
33 For the theory of discourse ethics, see the essays in Habermas, *Moral Consciousness and Communicative Action*, trans. Christian Lenhardt and Shierry Weber Nicholsen (Cambridge, Mass.: MIT Press, 1990).
34 For representative statements of Apel's position, see 'Das Apriori der Kommunikationsgesellschaft und die Grundlagen der Ethik', in *Transformation der Philosophie* (Frankfurt: Suhrkamp, 1973), pp. 358–436; and "Sprechakttheorie und transzendentale Sprachpragmatik: Zur Frage ethischer Normen', in *Sprachpragmatik und Philosophie* (Frankfurt: Suhrkamp, 1976), pp. 10–173.
35 Habermas refers to 'a complementary relation' between philosophy and empirical theory. See his *Moral Consciousness and Communicative Action*, p. 39: 'The empirical theory presupposes the validity of the normative theory it uses. Yet the validity of the normative theory is cast into doubt if the philosophical reconstructions prove to be unusable in the context of application within the empirical theory'.
36 In order to demonstrate that the rules of discourse are 'inescapable presuppositions', Habermas introduces the notion of performative contradictions. A performative contradiction occurs when a particular speech act *k (p)* rests on noncontingent presuppositions whose propositional content contradicts the asserted proposition *p*. In one of Habermas's examples, the assertion 'Using lies, I finally convinced H that *p*' is said to be nonsensical and 'revisable' to 'Using lies, I finally talked H into believing that *p*.' (Habermas, *Moral Consciousness and Communicative Action*, p. 90). The point here is that convincing someone of something requires the offering of

justifications. If H lies, then he does not permit his proponent to form a rational conviction based on the consideration of reasons. He has talked H into something but not 'convinced' him. In my view, this simple analysis is not persuasive, and it hardly demonstrates that participants in argumentation *must* assume that rational persuasion cannot occur on the basis of lies. When Colin Powell presented evidence to the General Assembly of the United Nations to the effect that Iraq had weapons of mass destruction, he succeeded perfectly well in rationally convincing most of its members that this was true. I see no problem in saying that the evidence he presented (his 'good reasons') led to a reasoned agreement about the threat Iraq represented. Colin Powell and his associates knew, however, that what they did was precisely to 'use lies to convince H that *p*'. Without being able to demonstrate this claim here, I think similar problems beset all the rules of discourse. The more general lesson might be that speech acts are not governed in any strict sense by rules. Whether they make sense and achieve their illocutionary and perlocutionary aims depend ultimately on the concrete relation between speaker and hearer, and on the specific rhetorical and semantic context in which they are being made.

37 See the opening remarks on Hegel in Habermas, *Knowledge and Human Interests*, pp. 24–28.

38 Hegel, *Phenomenology of Spirit*, p. 66. Hegel's dialectic involves several different steps but here is a passage that captures the gist of the critique:

> They speak of the existence of *external* objects, which can be more precisely defined as *actual*, absolutely *singular*, *wholly personal*, *individual* things, each of them absolutely unlike anything else; this existence, they say, has absolute certainty and truth. They *mean* "this" bit of paper on which I am writing – or rather have written – "this"; but what they mean is not what they say. If they actually wanted to *say* "this" bit of paper which they mean, if they wanted to *say* it, then this is impossible, because the sensuous This that is meant *cannot be reached* by language, which belongs to consciousness, i.e. to that which is inherently universal. In the actual attempt to say it, it would therefore crumble away; those who started to describe it would not be able to complete the description, but would be compelled to leave it to others, who would themselves finally have to admit to speaking about something which *is not*.

39 Robert Pippin discusses some of them in 'You Can't Get There from Here', in Beiser (ed.), *The Cambridge Companion to Hegel*, pp. 52–85. For a defense of the priority of the *Science of Logic* in Hegel, including the *Phenomenology*, see Stanley Rosen, *G. W. F. Hegel: An Introduction to the Science of Wisdom* (New Haven: Yale University Press, 1974).

40 See Robert Pippin, *Hegel's Idealism: The Satisfactions of Self-Consciousness*, p. 108.

41 Habermas has a long story to tell about how the 'critical sciences' – Marxian critique of ideology and Freudian psychoanalysis in particular – by virtue of the very rationality they display, embody an interest in emancipation. He also, I think much more problematically, tries to show that the interest in emancipation is grounded in more deep-seated anthropological facts about the reproduction and self-formation of the human species.

42 Habermas, *Knowledge and Human Interests*, pp. 17–18.

43 Ibid., pp. 379–80.

> The studies I published in *Knowledge and Human Interests* suffer from the lack of a precise distinction . . . between reconstruction and "self-reflection" in a critical sense. It occurred to me only after completing the book that the tradi-

tional use of the term "reflection," which goes back to German Idealism, covers (and confuses) two things: on the one hand, it denotes reflection upon the conditions of the capacities of a knowing, speaking and acting subject as such; on the other hand, it denotes reflection upon unconsciously produced constraints to which a determinate subject (or a determinate group of subjects, or a determinate species subject) succumbs to in its process of self-formation. In Kant and his successors, the first type of reflection took the form of a search for the transcendental ground of possible theoretical knowledge (and moral conduct). . . . In the meantime, this mode of reflection has also taken the shape of a rational reconstruction of generative rules and cognitive schemata. Particularly the paradigm of language has led to a reframing of the transcendental model.

44 Theodor W. Adorno, *Negative Dialectics*, trans. E.B. Ashton (New York: Continuum, 1973), p. 23. 'Idealism – most explicitly Fichte – gives unconscious sway to the ideology that the not-I, *l'autrui*, and finally all that reminds us of nature is inferior, so the unity of the self-preserving thought may devour it without misgivings'.

45 Habermas makes this claim most explicitly in *The Theory of Communicative Action*, vol. 1, pp. 366–91, esp., p. 387: 'The critique of instrumental reason conceptualized as negative dialectics renounces its theoretical claim while operating with the means of theory'.

46 Adorno, *Negative Dialectics*, p. 5.

47 This, of course, is hardly an original claim. For a classical but essentially affirmative expression of the same point, see Ernst Cassirer, *Substanzbegriff und Funktionsbegriff: Untersuchungen über die Grundfragen der Erkenntniskritik* (Berlin: Bruno Cassirer, 1910).

48 It should be mentioned that Adorno does make gestures that point beyond the model of immanent critique. In 'Cultural Criticism and Society', in *Prisms*, trans. Samuel and Shierry Weber (Cambridge, Mass.: The MIT Press, 1997), p. 20, he claims that immanent critique 'remains imprisoned within the orbit of that against which it struggles'. There must be a certain freedom in regard to culture, for (p. 29) 'without consciousness transcending the immanence of culture, immanent criticism would be inconceivable'. Adorno remains, however, skeptical of the idea that critique can ever take place from a purely transcendent standpoint. It will always have to refer to the epistemic criteria that mark a specific object or object-domain. In a recently edited letter to his friend Gershom Scholem, Adorno (as quoted in Mauro Bozzetti, 'Hegel on Trial: Adorno's Critique of Philosophical Systems', in Nigel Gibson and Andrew Rubin (eds), *Adorno: A Critical Reader* (Oxford: Blackwell, 2002), p. 296) writes that 'I remain true to the *Phenomenology of Spirit* in my view that the movement of the concept, of the matter at hand, is simultaneously the explicitly thinking movement of the reflecting subject'.

49 Readers familiar with Adorno's thinking will hopefully recognize in this an appeal to the *Bildverbot* – the prohibition of graven images – which operates as a principle in this philosophy.

Part III

Brandom and Hegel

6

HEGEL AND BRANDOM ON NORMS, CONCEPTS AND LOGICAL CATEGORIES

Stephen Houlgate

Robert Brandom is unusual among philosophers schooled in the analytic tradition in acknowledging a far-reaching debt to Hegel. What especially attracts Brandom to Hegel is the latter's understanding of concepts.

According to Brandom, Kant taught that we are distinguished from other animals above all by our use of concepts. He also showed that concepts are not mental pictures of things, but rather rules or norms that determine the correct way to understand things. The concept 'dog', for Kant, is not an image in my mind's eye of a hairy, barking animal, but a *rule* that lays down what properties something must have to count as a dog rather than a cat.[1] Hegel is a particular hero of Brandom's because he recognized that concepts are not 'fixed or static items' but the *changing* products of social and historical practices. In particular, Brandom explains, Hegel understood the content of concepts to emerge gradually through the practice of applying and then revising them. Indeed, Brandom's Hegel is a pragmatist who believes that concepts have no content apart from that conferred on them by their application and use.[2]

Brandom's reading of Hegel is original and thought provoking. My aim in this essay, however, is to suggest one way in which, for all its merits, Brandom's interpretation seems to me to miss something significant in Hegel's thought.

Brandom's pragmatist conception of norms

Before I turn to Hegel directly, I need to give a sketch of Brandom's own pragmatist and inferentialist account of norms and concepts. This sketch will be simplified, but not, I hope, too distorting.

According to Brandom, what makes human beings distinctive is that we are subject not just to the laws of nature but also to certain *norms* that govern our actions and beliefs. These norms need not always take the form of explicit rules and principles. Sometimes they can take this form; but Brandom argues that all norms that are explicit in the form of rules presuppose norms that are *implicit* in our practices of judging and inferring.[3]

Brandom points out, however, that the norms implicit in a society's practices cannot be discerned simply by observing how the members of that society regularly behave. Regularities of behaviour show only what people actually do; they do not by themselves reveal what people deem it *appropriate* to do. To discern what is deemed appropriate or inappropriate in a society, we must consider not just the regular patterns of behaviour exhibited by its members but rather the normative *sanctions* that are applied in it. That is to say, we must examine what actions lead to the granting or withholding of permissions and entitlements in that society. If a person's failure to display a particular kind of leaf before entering a hut leads directly to his or her being prohibited from attending the weekly festival, then the requirement that the leaf be displayed is clearly a practical norm in that society.[4] Norms, for Brandom, are thus not just the *regularities* exhibited by our practice but the *proprieties* that are implicit in that practice.[5]

These proprieties are instituted, according to Brandom, by the practical attitudes of members of a society. That is to say, they are established by being *taken* or *deemed* in practice to be proprieties. Norms do not exist 'out there' in the way in which natural objects do. They arise only in being recognized and acknowledged and so constitute what Brandom calls '*social* achievements'.[6] The laws of nature constrain us whether we acknowledge them or not. Norms, by contrast, exercise an authority over us only insofar as we endorse and acknowledge that authority. In this sense, Brandom argues, 'what *makes* [norms] binding is that one *takes* them to be binding'.[7] Such acknowledgement, as we have seen, need not take the form of an explicit declaration of principles. Our acknowledgement of norms is *implicit* in the practical assessments we make of our own behaviour and that of our fellows.

The fact that norms are established by being *taken* to be norms does not mean, however, that we always fully understand what those norms require of us. Indeed, Brandom notes, the norms that we ourselves institute through our implicit, practical acknowledgement will frequently 'outrun' our own understanding of them.[8] Why should this be? Because the norms and proprieties that are implicit in our practice comprise not only what we *do* in fact acknowledge, but also what we *should* acknowledge, given what we do acknowledge; yet we often fail to grasp these normative consequences of the proprieties we recognize. We may, for example, acknowledge through our practice that the environment should be protected; yet we may not understand that that requires us to take recycling much more seriously than we do.

So who is to determine what norms and obligations follow from the proprieties we implicitly acknowledge in our practice? Brandom credits Hegel with the following answer to this question:

> the determinacy of the content of what you have committed yourself to – the part that is *not* up to you in the way that *whether* you commit

> yourself to it is up to you – is secured by the attitudes of *others*, to whom one has at least implicitly granted that authority.

Brandom continues:

> As Hegel puts it, I have a certain *independence* in which commitments [and norms] I embrace. Apart from my acknowledgement, they have no normative force over me. But in exercising that very independence, I am at the same time *dependent* on the attitudes of others, who attribute and hold me to the commitment, and thereby administer its content.[9]

The process of instituting norms and proprieties is thus a complex one. On the one hand, we ourselves institute norms – in the sense of giving them authority over us – by our practical acknowledgement of them. On the other hand, our acceptance of certain norms commits us in the eyes of others to further norms and proprieties that may exceed our immediate understanding. For Brandom (and for Brandom's Hegel), the norms and proprieties that are implicit in our practices comprise *both* ones we acknowledge *and* ones that are attributed to us by others on the basis of those we acknowledge. We are thus not in a position purely by ourselves to determine what norms are in fact implicit in our own practice. Rather, the precise content of those implicit norms is determined through 'a process of *negotiation*' involving ourselves *and* those who attribute further norms to us. We implicitly acknowledge certain norms in our judgements and actions; others then attribute further norms to us on the basis of what we acknowledge; and, in the ensuing conversation between ourselves and those who assess what we do, determinate ideas emerge of what is in fact implicit in our practice. This process, which goes on both *within* and *between* societies and which Brandom identifies with what Hegel calls 'experience',[10] continues indefinitely and reaches no final conclusion. 'There is never any final answer as to what is correct', Brandom writes; 'everything . . . is itself a subject for conversation and further assessment, challenge, defense, and correction'.[11]

Brandom's inferentialist conception of concepts

What I have sketched so far is the pragmatist conception of norms that Brandom believes he shares with Hegel: the idea that norms are instituted by being *taken* to be authoritative, that is, by being *acknowledged* in our practice and *attributed* to us by others. I now want to look at the inferentialist conception of concepts that Brandom also claims to share with Hegel.

Concepts, for Brandom, are norms that are applied in *judgements*.[12] When we judge that 'this car is red', we employ the two concepts 'car' and 'red'. These concepts are not, however, to be thought of as abstract pictures of objects or of properties of objects. They constitute norms that lay down what is to count as a 'car' or as something 'red'. That is, they determine what something *should* be understood to be, if it is considered to fall under one or other concept.

The judgements or assertions in which concepts are applied are taken by Brandom to express certain beliefs or *commitments* by which we stand.[13] The concepts involved in the judgements can thus be understood to specify exactly what it is that we have committed ourselves to in making the judgements. If we judge that the red object is a car, then we have committed ourselves to understanding it one way, but if we judge that the red object is an apple, then we have committed ourselves to understanding it another way. Grasping a concept, therefore, does not involve forming a mental picture of the thing being conceived, but entails 'knowing ... what else one would be committing oneself to by applying the concept, what would entitle one to do so, and what would preclude such entitlement'.[14] Indeed, the concepts we employ require us to undertake a whole chain of commitments whenever we make a judgement. They serve as norms determining 'the *correctness* of various moves' from one commitment to another, and so lay down how we should go on to understand something, given the judgements we have made.[15]

It should be noted that, for Brandom, content is actually conferred on our concepts *by* the commitments we acknowledge (and are deemed by others to have undertaken) in our practice. It is *because* we take the commitment expressed in a judgement to entail further specific commitments that we understand the concepts employed in that judgement to have a certain content. This is what Brandom has in mind when he claims that 'concepts can have no content apart from that conferred on them by their use' (or, rather, by the *proprieties* of their use).[16] Nonetheless, once concepts have been established (even if only temporarily), they then determine what we commit ourselves to when we make a judgement. In this way, they come to serve as norms governing our actions and beliefs.

As we saw above, Brandom holds that we do not control or decide completely by ourselves the *content* of the norms we acknowledge. The same is true of the concepts that determine the nature of our commitments. Thus, even though we freely acknowledge a certain commitment in making a judgement, we do not control precisely what we have thereby committed ourselves to. Our commitment will entail other commitments as its consequences, whether or not we recognize that fact. What specific commitments follow from the one we acknowledge is determined by the specific concepts that we employ. So, if we judge that it is a car we see, we are committed (whether we like it or not) to its being inedible (or at least not very nutritious), and if we judge that it is an apple that we see, we are committed (whether we like it or not) to its being extremely difficult to drive.

Our commitments (and the judgements in which they are expressed) thus stand in what Brandom calls 'inferential' relations to one another: one commitment necessarily provides the premise from which others can then be inferred. The specific inferences implicit in a given commitment are determined by the *concepts* that are employed in the judgement in which the commitment is expressed. Concepts are thus norms determining that certain inferences should be drawn from the judgements and assertions that contain those concepts. Indeed, Brandom argues that the content of a concept consists principally in the inferential connections in which it stands to other concepts.[17] The content of a concept is partly determined by the circumstances of its correct application; but it is determined primarily by the other concepts which it makes necessary (or which it excludes from itself). Concepts, as Brandom puts it, are thus 'inferentially articulated'.[18]

The content of a particular concept is not, however, simply something given. It consists in the inferential connections that it is *taken* to have by those who use it. That content can never finally be decided, but is determined through a process of negotiation. As we saw above, this process of negotiation takes place between those who assume in their practice that a concept licenses one inference, and others who judge that it licenses different inferences. It is in this social and historical conversation between interlocutors, therefore, that the precise contents of the concepts we employ are worked out.

Brandom understands Hegel to share this broadly inferential conception of concepts. The idea that the content of concepts consists in their inferential connections to other concepts appears in Hegel as the idea that concepts are 'mediated' by one another.[19] Hegel is also said to share Brandom's view that the inferential connections between concepts that constitute the core of our discursive practice are *material*, rather than purely *logical* in character.

Material inferences, for Brandom, depend on and articulate the non-logical *content* of the concepts involved.[20] They are taken to be good inferences not because they have a particular logical form, but because there is a material connection between the contents of the concepts that are incorporated into their premises and conclusions. In *Articulating Reasons* Brandom explains such inferences as follows:

> Consider the inference from 'Pittsburgh is to the west of Princeton' to 'Princeton is to the east of Pittsburgh', and that from 'Lightning is seen now' to 'Thunder will be heard soon'. It is the contents of the concepts *west* and *east* that make the first a good inference, and the contents of the concepts *lightning* and *thunder*, as well as the temporal concepts, that make the second appropriate. Endorsing these inferences is part of grasping or mastering those concepts, quite apart from any specifically *logical* competence.[21]

This last phrase is particularly important. Endorsing a material inference requires mastery of the relevant empirical (and spatio-temporal) concepts, but it demands no 'specifically logical competence'. To know whether a material inference is good, we thus do not need an explicit or implicit understanding of logical relations or of the rules of deductive inference. We simply need to understand what further concepts and judgements we commit ourselves to – or are deemed to commit ourselves to – when we use concepts with a particular empirical content.

For Brandom, therefore, neither explicit nor implicit mastery of logical vocabulary is required in order to count as rational. So what role does logical vocabulary play when we do learn to use it? Brandom maintains that it plays an 'expressive' role, 'namely, making explicit the inferences whose goodness is implicit in the conceptual contents of nonlogical concepts'.[22] In everyday discourse, we implicitly endorse all manner of material inferences through our behaviour and judgements. For example, we avoid stepping out in front of buses for fear of being run over, or we put up our umbrella when it rains in order to stay dry. Many of the inferences we implicitly draw are good ones, but some are not. In order to assess whether they are good or not – that is, to make them available for proper public scrutiny – we need to make their particular *inferential* structure plain for all to see. Logical vocabulary enables us to do this by putting an implicit inference in the explicit form of 'if p, then q'. Logical vocabulary thus allows us to present the inferences we implicitly endorse in a form that makes them subjects of rational debate and argument. It facilitates rational discussion of those inferences; but it is not needed in order to understand and endorse the inferences in everyday practice.[23]

For Brandom, therefore, being rational means understanding what we are committed to by the material – empirical and spatio-temporal – *content* of the concepts we use. It does not require that we have an explicit or implicit grasp of *formal*, logical relations (such as that between antecedent and consequent, or between particular and universal). It is especially important to note that for Brandom our ability to understand material inferences does not require any *implicit* grasp of logical relations.[24] Understanding in practice what follows from its being a rainy day does not require an implicit grasp of the conditional or of the rules of deductive inference; it simply requires a grasp of what follows from its being *a rainy day*. The role of logical vocabulary is not, therefore, to render explicit any implicit *logical* understanding on our part. Logical vocabulary, such as the conditional, enables us rather to state explicitly the *material inferences* we implicitly endorse in our practice. Such vocabulary allows us to formulate such implicit material inferences as explicit claims. It thereby lets us '*say* (explicitly) what otherwise one can only *do* (implicitly)'.[25]

Brandom maintains that Hegel shares his conception of everyday, 'material-inferential' rationality. He insists, therefore, that for Hegel *logical* categories and vocabulary are not constitutive conditions of everyday rationality itself but play a purely secondary, explicitating role. As Brandom puts it in *Tales of the Mighty Dead*, 'one of the overarching methodological commitments that guides my reading of Hegel is that the *point* of developing an adequate understanding of these categorical [or logical] concepts is so that they can then be used to make explicit how ordinary empirical concepts work'.[26] A later footnote in this book further clarifies the role of Hegelian logical categories. Whereas formal logical vocabulary allows us to express material inferences (and incompatibilities) as explicit claims, Hegel's logical categories allow us to 'make explicit the process by which the system of determinate concepts and judgments' – that is, the system of *empirical* concepts – 'progresses and develops'.[27] Such categories thus enable us to tell the story of – or at least *a* story about – the emergence of determinate, empirical concepts, but they do not constitute the implicit preconditions of the employment of empirical concepts themselves. In what follows I offer a different account of Hegel's view of logical categories.[28]

Hegel on logical categories

On my reading, Hegel does not believe that logical categories merely enable us to render explicit 'how ordinary empirical concepts work' and how they are developed. He believes that these categories constitute the *precondition* of employing empirical concepts in the first place. Consequently, they are also the precondition of the material inferences that depend on and articulate the content of our empirical concepts. Indeed, for Hegel, a grasp of logical categories is the essential condition of all human consciousness and cognition. This is the case because an understanding of logical categories is built into the very fact that we use concepts and words at all. Hegel makes this clear in the preface to the second edition of the *Science of Logic*:

> The forms of thought [*Denkformen*] are, in the first instance, displayed and stored in human *language*. ... Into all that becomes something inward for man, ... into all that he makes his own, language has penetrated, and everything that he has transformed into language and expresses in it contains a category [*Kategorie*] – concealed, mixed with other forms or clearly determined as such, so much is logic his natural element, indeed his own peculiar *nature*.[29]

Like Kant, therefore – though for different reasons – Hegel maintains that not only empirical concepts but also *logical* categories are essential to ordinary, everyday discourse and understanding. This does not mean that Hegel is a 'regulist' in Brandom's sense. He does not maintain that we always need an *explicit* understanding of logical relations and categories, or training in formal logic, in order to appreciate why it is not appropriate to jump in front of a bus if one wants to stay alive. Hegel mocks precisely this kind of regulism when he takes to task those who want an explicit grasp of the rules governing cognition before setting out to know things or who feel they need a full and detailed knowledge of how to swim before they venture into the water.[30]

Yet Hegel insists equally that we cannot employ empirical concepts, make judgements or undertake intentional actions without an *implicit* grasp of categories and logical relations. Such logical categories include, amongst others, 'reality', 'negation', 'something', 'other', 'identity', 'difference', 'actuality', 'possibility', 'necessity', 'cause' and 'object'. To understand a material inference, such as the one from 'Lightning is seen now' to 'Thunder will be heard soon', we must thus understand not only the concepts of 'lightning' and 'thunder', as well as 'now' and 'soon', but also the highly general concepts or categories of 'something', 'something else' and 'necessity'. For we must have an implicit grasp of what it means for something simply to be what it is and be different from something else, as well as an understanding of one thing's *having* to follow another. Without a grasp of those general concepts, we could not think of thunder as being *something* that *necessarily* follows *something else*. Similarly, without an implicit grasp of the way in which particulars and their universals are related, one could not recognize that the judgement 'That's scarlet' commits one to the judgement 'That's red'. An implicit understanding of logical categories and relations is thus, for Hegel, the indispensable precondition of even the simplest everyday inferences.

This should not be taken to imply that Hegel denies the existence of material inference in something like Brandom's (or Sellars') sense. Hegel need not disagree with Brandom's claim that most of the inferences we make in our everyday lives articulate the contents of the empirical concepts we employ. Hegel's insight is simply that no material inference can be *purely* material, since our practical grasp of the propriety of every such inference is informed by our implicit understanding not only of the empirical concepts involved but also of logical categories, such as something, other, identity, difference and necessity. To put it another way, there are no purely material inferences because all our understanding of the *matter* of the world is shot through with an implicit understanding of the general *form* of things and of their general ontological relations. In this sense, Hegel is closer than Brandom is prepared to acknowledge to the great, grey father of us all, Plato.

Hegel's claim that logical categories are built into the fabric of thought (and language), and so are implicit in everything we think and say, is more than a mere assertion. In the *Science of Logic*, he endeavours to support his claim by *proving* that such categories are immanent in thought as such. Hegel starts out in his *Logic* from what he thinks is the least that thought can be – the thought of simple, indeterminate being – and shows that this indeterminate thought transforms itself dialectically into a series of progressively more determinate categories. In this way, he claims, we discover that a whole array of logical categories is made necessary by and so inherent in thought itself.

According to Brandom, Hegel's *Logic lacks* necessity in two important senses. First, it offers merely a 'rationally reconstructed trajectory by which [logical concepts] *might* have developed' in history. Second, the task of reconstructing this trajectory is not itself one that it is necessary for philosophy to undertake: we would be better off simply using those logical categories to render explicit the way that ordinary, empirical concepts are produced.[31] In Hegel's own view, by contrast, the *Logic* attempts to provide an a priori derivation of the logical categories of thought that follows a strictly necessary path. Furthermore, the task of providing that a priori derivation is itself a necessary one, for without it we are left in the same uncritical position as Kant, namely that of just *assuming* without proper warrant that these categories, rather than those, are intrinsic to thought.

The role of Hegel's logic

This is not the place to provide an extensive discussion of Hegel's *Logic*, but I do wish to clarify a few things.[32] The *Logic* shows that certain categories are made *logically* necessary by thought. This does not mean, however, that every human society in every period of history will have a fully explicit understanding of these categories. Nor, indeed, does it mean that every society will have an *implicit* grasp of *all* the basic logical categories. Most categories will be implicit in the thinking of most societies, but some – such as the categories of 'causality' or 'chemism' – may be absent.

This discrepancy between what is logically necessary and what is found in actual historical societies is to be explained partly by the presence of irreducible contingencies in history that do not affect the logical development set out in Hegel's *Logic*. It is also to be explained by the fact that different historical societies inevitably embody different levels of understanding and so fall more or less short of what the logical necessity inherent in thought demands.

Even where an understanding of all the basic logical categories does implicitly suffuse given societies, Hegel claims that they will not always be understood in precisely the same way.[33] Indeed, some societies (or some of the individuals within a given society) may well display in their practice a profound *misunderstanding* of the categories. In this respect, therefore, the logical derivation of the categories undertaken by Hegel plays a corrective or normative role: it discloses how the categories implicit in our understanding and practice *should* in fact be conceived. As Hegel writes,

> at first [the categories] enter consciousness separately and so are variable and mutually confusing; consequently they afford to mind only a fragmentary and uncertain actuality; the loftier business of logic therefore is to clarify [*reinigen*] these categories and in them to raise mind to freedom and truth.[34]

What Hegel's *Logic* shows in particular is that logical categories – like empirical concepts – are (to use Brandom's phrase) 'inferentially articulated'. That is to say, they are connected through their own logical structure or 'content' to other logical categories. These connections, Hegel argues, are not merely historically contingent but are logically necessary. Hegel's *Logic* shows, therefore, that judgements we make that implicitly involve one logical category necessarily commit us to further judgements involving other categories. Let us briefly consider an example.

In his *Logic* Hegel argues that the category 'something' is intrinsically connected to the category 'other'. Every something must thus be understood to be other than something else. Furthermore, every something necessarily has a character or 'determination' of its own – its *Bestimmung* – which it asserts in its relations to other things. It also necessarily has a 'constitution' (*Beschaffenheit*) which is intrinsically vulnerable to being altered by the other things to which it relates. Finally, every something has a qualitative limit which renders it finite and so subject to ultimate destruction.[35] These logical connections between categories are built into the logical structure or content of the categories themselves and so commit us – whether we like it or not – to certain inferences concerning anything we judge to be 'something'. Such inferences can be regarded as 'material inferences' insofar as they are made necessary by nothing but the *content* of the categories; but they are logical-material, rather than empirically material, inferences.

So, when we judge that the car is scarlet, we not only commit ourselves to the further empirical judgement that the car is red, we also commit ourselves to the judgement that the car is vulnerable to damage caused by other things and subject to eventual decay. (And we also commit ourselves to the judgements that the car has a size, form, mechanical structure, and so on). These further judgements are made necessary not by the empirical content of the concepts 'car' or 'scarlet' but rather by the logical content of the category of 'something'. The category of 'something' thus serves (in Brandom's terms) as a norm that determines what inferences we commit ourselves to whenever we make a judgement about 'something' in the world.

Note that my account of Hegel's understanding of logical categories does not conflict with Brandom's inferentialist interpretation of Hegel. It is at odds, however, with the thorough-going pragmatism that Brandom endorses and attributes to Hegel. I shall not contest here Brandom's claim that Hegel has a pragmatist understanding of *empirical* concepts. We would need to look more closely at Hegel's account of the role of reason in history in order to determine fully how he understands our empirical cognition to develop; but the claim that Hegel understands empirical concepts to gain determinacy through a broadly pragmatic process of 'negotiation' strikes me as worthy of consideration. The process whereby our *actual* understanding of *logical* categories has changed in history might also be conceived – with some qualification – as one of pragmatic negotiation. In Hegel's view, however, the process through which we are finally to discover – in the science of speculative logic – how logical categories *should* be conceived is clearly not one of pragmatic negotiation, but rather one of a priori derivation. This process will turn out to be dialectical, but it is not conceived as being intrinsically dialogical.

This is not to say that the philosophical process of deriving the logical categories is an esoteric activity intelligible only to a few. Hegel regarded philosophy as an exoteric discipline to which 'all self-conscious reason', not just a handful of initiates, may contribute.[36] His point, however, is a methodological one: namely, that the way to determine the proper content of the categories is not through open-ended discussion and debate, but rather through seeking to unfold a priori what is logically inherent in thought as such. Only in this way, he thinks, can we discover the categorial norms to which we as rational beings are subject as a matter of logical necessity rather than historical contingency – the norms that *should* logically govern our lives. Any rational being may participate in this project; but they are all required to do the same thing: focus on the minimal character of thought and render explicit what is implicit in it.

This method of deriving the logical categories is privileged, in Hegel's view, precisely because it seeks to unfold what is in truth *immanent* in thought, rather than merely what has been held to be the content of the categories by philosophers and logicians of the past. Whether Hegel succeeds in providing a truly immanent derivation of the categories is a matter for debate. For Hegel, however, it is only by attempting to provide such an a priori immanent derivation that we will be able to determine the categories or norms that should *of necessity* govern our actions and beliefs.

The way to secure immanence, Hegel tells us, is to suspend all our inherited assumptions about thought and its categories and focus on thought at its most minimal. The science of logic, in other words, should be radically *presuppositionless*.[37] This claim has been subject to serious misunderstanding ever since Hegel's own day, so it is worth briefly explaining what it does and does not entail.

Hegel does not deny that what he calls 'speculative logic' presupposes the ability to use language and the ability to hold in mind abstract and often highly complex concepts. Such logic also presupposes a certain familiarity with the basic concepts of thought on the part of the philosopher or student: for if we lacked this familiarity, we could not recognize that the concepts developed in the *Logic* are in fact revised and 'clarified' versions of the concepts we use in everyday life. In these respects, therefore, speculative logic is clearly *not* presuppositionless.[38]

In two other respects, however, such logic is to be presuppositionless. First, we should not assume at the outset of logic that the categories of thought are to be understood in a specific way, or indeed that thought entails any particular categories at all. We should keep in the back of our minds the familiar, ordinary senses of the categories, but in the science of logic itself we should start from scratch by considering the sheer 'simplicity of thinking' as such and wait to discover which categories, if any, are inherent in such simplicity and how they are to be conceived. As new categories are derived in the course of speculative logic, we can compare them with the categories with which we are familiar and so determine to what extent our everyday understanding of the categories is adequate. That familiar, everyday understanding should not, however, play any role in the logical derivation of the categories themselves. In speculative logic itself the categories must be derived purely immanently – without presuppositions – from the sheer 'simplicity' of thought.[39]

Note that we may not, therefore, presuppose that the categories have a specific logical-material inferential structure or, indeed, that they have any *inferential* structure at all. We must rather wait to discover within the science of logic whether they are inferentially articulated and, if so, how. Hegel demonstrates in the course of the science of logic that the categories do entail one another and so are, in Brandom's terms, 'inferentially articulated', but he may not, and does not, assume from the start that this will be the case (just as he may not assume from the start that concepts are predicates of possible judgements).[40]

Second, we may not take for granted at the outset any specific rules or laws of thought. We may not presuppose that thought should abide by the rules of deductive inference or that it should be governed by the law of non-contradiction, and so may not find thought wanting if it fails to respect these rules and laws. Nor, indeed, may we presuppose from the outset that thought should be 'dialectical' (and certainly not that it should develop according to the pattern of 'thesis-antithesis-synthesis'). We may not presuppose such rules or laws because it is part of the task of speculative logic itself to discover *whether* any rules or laws are actually made necessary by the 'simplicity' of thought. Until this discovery has been made, their validity cannot be presupposed.[41]

How then is the speculative logician to proceed? Is there any *method* that such a logician must follow? Yes, indeed. The method we must follow is simply to *let* the 'simplicity' of thought unfold and determine itself before our very eyes according to whatever principles prove to be immanent in it. Heidegger is the philosopher with whom the idea of 'letting be' is usually associated.[42] Many years before Heidegger, however, Hegel argued that 'letting be' lies at the heart of genuinely free, modern philosophizing. 'When I think', Hegel explains, 'I give up my subjective particularity, sink myself in the matter, let thought follow its own course [*lasse das Denken für sich gewähren*]; and I think badly whenever I add something of my own'. My role as philosopher is thus not to pass judgement on this or that proposition or argument according to certain presupposed rules or proprieties of inference, but simply to 'let the inherently living determinations [of thought] take their own course [*für sich gewähren lassen*]'.[43] If one does this, Hegel claims, one will discover what thought proves logically to be *of its own accord*.

Our role as philosophers, therefore, is predominantly passive: we simply look on as the categories emerge immanently from the very 'simplicity' of thought. Yet we are not completely passive observers of this process. First of all, *we* are the ones who think through thought's immanent development: that development does not occur outside of us, like a film or a play, but takes place *in our thinking of it*. Second, although each category is made necessary by the one that precedes it and does not owe its emergence simply to our own astute insight, *we* nonetheless have to render explicit the categories that are implicit in thought at any particular point in its logical development. The deduction of the categories, Hegel maintains, involves nothing more than the '*positing*

[*Setzen*] of what is already contained in a concept';[44] but *we* are the ones who actually have to carry out this act of 'positing' or rendering-explicit.

As speculative logicians who *let* thought determine itself, we are thus both passive and active: we both allow our own thinking to be guided and determined by what is immanent in thought itself *and* play an active role in bringing what is immanent in thought out into the open. Indeed, Hegel notes, there is a degree of activity in our very passivity itself: for we can allow our thought to be guided by the matter at hand only if we actively focus on that matter and hold our own bright ideas at bay. Hegel makes this point in these important lines:

> Philosophical thinking proceeds analytically in that it simply takes up its object, the Idea, and lets it go its own way [*dieselbe gewähren läßt*], while it simply watches, so to speak, the movement and development of it. To this extent philosophizing is wholly passive [*passiv*]. [. . .] But this requires the effort to beware of our own inventions and particular opinions which are forever wanting to push themselves forward.[45]

One might be forgiven for suspecting that Hegel's method of simply 'letting' thought determine itself is a recipe for vague and undisciplined thinking. This, however, is far from the truth. Hegel's method demands 'that each thought should be grasped in its full precision [*Präzision*] and that nothing should remain vague and indeterminate'.[46] It also demands that one pay close and subtle attention to the logical structure of categories and render explicit only what is implicit in each category. As those who have studied Hegel's *Logic* know only too well, Hegel's method requires considerable mental discipline. It also requires mental flexibility, for speculative philosophers have not only to achieve a high degree of precision in their understanding of categories but also to allow those categories to mutate into new ones before their very eyes as they render their necessary implications explicit.

Logic and being

Like Brandom, Hegel understands the project of philosophy to consist in 'making it explicit'. In particular, it consists in making explicit the implicit conceptual *norms* that govern our lives.[47] For Brandom, all such norms are social and historical achievements. For Hegel, by contrast, empirical conceptual norms may be to a large degree social achievements, but the fundamental categorial norms to which we are – or should be – subject are rooted in the very nature of thought itself. They do not have any transcendent or supernatural ground; but nor are they simply the product of social and historical 'negotiation'. They are made necessary by the inherently dialectical character of thought itself. (As far as logical categories are concerned, therefore, it is not the case – *pace* Brandom – that for Hegel 'transcendental constitution' is nothing but 'social institution'.)[48]

Logical categories are also made necessary, in Hegel's view, by the inherently dialectical character of *being*. Commentators on Hegel, such as Terry Pinkard and Robert Pippin have in recent years popularized the so-called 'non-metaphysical' interpretation of Hegel's thought. Pippin, for example, takes Hegel's *Logic* to disclose the logical conditions under which alone objects can be determinate objects of *thought*, but he does not see it as laying bare the categories that are constitutive of being as such.[49] In my view, however, this 'non-metaphysical' reading of Hegel tells only half the story: for Hegel makes it clear that the categories set out in his logic are both the necessary concepts of thought *and* the intrinsic determinations of being itself. Hegel's logic, by his own admission, is both a logic and a metaphysics or ontology.[50]

The categories laid out in Hegel's *Logic* – such as 'negation' and 'opposition' – are thus both norms governing how we should think, if we are to be fully rational, *and* constitutive features of being itself. Hegel thus finds the categories governing our lives not just in human thought but also out there in the world. This, of course, means that in one sense he derives the 'ought' from the 'is'. At the end of his *Logic* Hegel argues that being proves to be not just being or substance or self-determining reason – the 'Idea' (*Idee*) – but *nature* – the realm of space, time and matter.[51] The categorial norms that Hegel sets out in the *Logic* are thus derived not from a realm of being beyond nature, but from being that proves logically to be nothing less than nature itself. It is nature, therefore, as much as human thought, that requires us to think in terms of dialectical categories such as 'something', 'limit' and 'finitude'. Accordingly, it is nature that commits us to inferences such as the one from the judgement 'this is a tree' to the further judgement 'this tree is something limited and finite'.

So can Hegel be considered a naturalist about categorial norms? In a sense, yes, since he understands those norms to be grounded in being that proves to be nature itself. His claim, however, is not just that the empirical contingencies of nature require us to think about nature in a certain way. Hegel's claim is that the inherent *logic* of nature – the rational dialectic or 'Idea' at the heart of nature – determines how we should think about it, at least in general terms. Hegel is thus ultimately a *rationalist* about categorial norms, rather than a conventional naturalist. He believes that reason alone determines the logical categories in terms of which we should think; but he thinks that reason is inherent both in our own thought and in the nature that surrounds us.

Brandom is right, in my view, to point out that we alone do not decide the content of the norms whose authority we acknowledge. Others can justifiably hold us to further norms that are implicit in the ones we endorse, even though we do not acknowledge those further norms ourselves. Brandom maintains that the content of the norms to which we are subject is determined solely through a process of social and historical negotiation involving both ourselves and others. Hegel, by contrast, maintains that the proper content of the *logical* categories implicit in all our ordinary judgements is determined by something more fundamental. Their content is ultimately determined by the rationality or dialectical logic that is immanent in thought as such, as well as in being or nature. *Pace* Brandom, Hegel is thus at most only partly a pragmatist, for he is also an a priori rationalist and metaphysician. Indeed, the genius of Hegel is to show precisely how – after Kant – it is possible to be such a rationalist metaphysician.

Notes

1 Robert B. Brandom, *Making It Explicit. Reasoning, Representing, and Discursive Commitment* (Cambridge, Mass.: Harvard University Press, 1994), p. 8; Robert B. Brandom, *Articulating Reasons. An Introduction to Inferentialism* (Cambridge, Mass.: Harvard University Press, 2000), pp. 80, 163–64, and Immanuel Kant, *Critique of Pure Reason*, trans. and ed. Paul Guyer and Allen W. Wood (Cambridge: Cambridge University Press, 1997), pp. 231–32, 273 [A 105, A 141].
2 Robert B. Brandom, *Tales of the Mighty Dead. Historical Essays in the Metaphysics of Intentionality* (Cambridge, Mass.: Harvard University Press, 2002), pp. 210, 215.
3 Brandom, *Making It Explicit*, p. 20.
4 Brandom, *Making It Explicit*, pp. 28, 43.
5 Brandom, *Making It Explicit*, p. 16: 'mastering of the public proprieties governing the use of linguistic expressions'.
6 Brandom, *Tales of the Mighty Dead*, p. 216.
7 Brandom, *Tales of the Mighty Dead*, p. 219.
8 Brandom, *Making It Explicit*, pp. 627, 631.
9 Brandom, *Tales of the Mighty Dead*, pp. 220–21.
10 Brandom, *Tales of the Mighty Dead*, p. 221.
11 Brandom, *Making It Explicit*, p. 647.
12 Brandom, *Tales of the Mighty Dead*, p. 212, and *Making It Explicit*, pp. 79–80, 624.
13 Brandom, *Articulating Reasons*, p. 80.
14 Brandom, *Articulating Reasons*, p. 11.
15 Brandom, *Articulating Reasons*, p. 29.
16 Brandom, *Tales of the Mighty Dead*, pp. 52, 210, 220, and *Articulating Reasons*, p. 196.
17 Brandom, *Articulating Reasons*, pp. 15–16.
18 Brandom, *Making It Explicit*, p. 622.
19 Brandom, *Tales of the Mighty Dead*, pp. 180–81.
20 Brandom, *Tales of the Mighty Dead*, pp. 95, 390, and *Articulating Reasons*, p. 37.
21 Brandom, *Articulating Reasons*, p. 52; see also *Making It Explicit*, p. 98.
22 Brandom, *Making It Explicit*, p. 109.
23 See Brandom, *Articulating Reasons*, p. 60.
24 Brandom, *Making It Explicit*, pp. 98–99.
25 Brandom, *Making It Explicit*, p. 108, my emphasis.
26 Brandom, *Tales of the Mighty Dead*, p. 211.
27 Brandom, *Tales of the Mighty Dead*, p. 387; see also pp. 393–94.
28 It should be noted, by the way, that Brandom understands Hegel's 'Concept' (*Begriff*) to be the system of determinate, *empirical* concepts; see *Tales of the Mighty Dead*, pp. 211, 387. In my view, by contrast, Hegel's 'Concept' – or, rather, his 'Idea' – is actually the system of *logical* categories. See G.W.F. Hegel, *The Encyclopaedia Logic. Part 1 of the Encyclopaedia of Philosophical Sciences with the Zusätze*, trans. T.F. Geraets, W.A. Suchting and H.S. Harris (Indianapolis: Hackett Publishing, 1991) (hereafter *EL*), p. 304 [§ 237 Addition]. For the German text, see G.W.F. Hegel, *Werke in zwanzig Bänden*, eds E. Moldenhauer and K.M. Michel, 20 vols and Index (Frankfurt am Main: Suhrkamp Verlag, 1969 onward) (hereafter *Werke*), 8: 389.

29 *Hegel's Science of Logic*, trans. A.V. Miller (Amherst, N.Y.: Humanity Books, 1999) (hereafter *SL*), p. 31; *Werke*, 5: 20.
30 Hegel, *EL*, p. 82 [§ 41 Addition 1]; *Werke*, 8: 114.
31 Brandom, *Tales of the Mighty Dead*, pp. 211, 393–94, my emphasis.
32 For a detailed discussion of the project, method and opening arguments of Hegel's *Science of Logic*, see S. Houlgate, *The Opening of Hegel's Logic. From Being to Infinity* (West Lafayette, Ind.: Purdue University Press, 2006).
33 *Hegel's Philosophy of Nature. Being Part Two of the Encyclopaedia of the Philosophical Sciences (1830)*, trans. A.V. Miller (Oxford: Clarendon Press, 1970), p. 11 [§ 246 Addition]; *Werke*, 9: 20–21.
34 Hegel, *SL*, p. 37; *Werke*, 5: 27.
35 See Hegel, *SL*, pp. 114–31; *Werke*, 5: 122–42.
36 G.W.F. Hegel, *Phenomenology of Spirit*, trans. A.V. Miller (Oxford: Oxford University Press, 1977), p. 43; Werke, 3: 65.
37 Hegel, *SL*, p. 70; *Werke*, 5: 68–69.
38 See Hegel, *EL*, p. 24 [§ 1]; *Werke*, 8: 41.
39 Hegel, *SL*, p. 31; *Werke*, 5: 19, and *EL*, p. 124 [§ 78 Remark]; *Werke*, 8: 168: 'die Einfachheit des Denkens'.
40 For Hegel's criticism of the assumption that thought is essentially judgement, see *EL*, pp. 66, 69 [§§ 28 Remark and 31 Remark]; *Werke*, 8: 94, 98. For Brandom's views on the priority of judgement, see *Articulating Reasons*, pp. 13, 159–60.
41 Hegel, *SL*, p. 43; *Werke*, 5: 35.
42 See, for example, M. Heidegger, *Being and Time*, trans. J. Macquarrie and E. Robinson (Oxford: Blackwell, 1962), p. 405.
43 Hegel, *EL*, pp. 58–59 [§ 24 Addition 2]; *Werke*, 8: 84–85.
44 Hegel, *EL*, p. 141 [§ 88 Remark]; *Werke*, 8: 188.
45 Hegel, *EL*, p. 305 [§ 238 Addition]; *Werke*, 8: 390–91.
46 Hegel, *EL*, p. 128 [§ 80 Addition]; *Werke*, 8: 171. See also J. Burbidge, *On Hegel's Logic. Fragments of a Commentary* (Atlantic Highlands, N.J.: Humanities Press, 1981), p. 42.
47 A fuller study of the relation between Brandom and Hegel would have to consider in detail whether Hegel does, indeed, understand concepts to be 'norms' in Brandom's precise sense. For the purposes of this essay, however, I assume that Hegel can be taken to regard concepts as norms in so far as he understands them to be capable of being employed *appropriately* and *inappropriately*.
48 Brandom, *Tales of the Mighty Dead*, p. 48.
49 R. Pippin, *Hegel's Idealism. The Satisfactions of Self-Consciousness* (Cambridge: Cambridge University Press, 1989), pp. 176, 188, 248, 250. See also Houlgate, *The Opening of Hegel's Logic*, pp. 137–43.
50 See, for example, Hegel, *EL*, p. 56 [§ 24]; *Werke*, 8: 81.
51 Hegel, *SL*, p. 843; *Werke*, 6: 573.

7

BRANDOM'S HEGEL

Robert B. Pippin

Bob Brandom's marvelous *Tales of the Mighty Dead* is an essay in "reconstructive metaphysics," especially the metaphysics of intentionality. Not surprisingly, he is drawn to early, implicit manifestations of his own account of the essential elements of a successful explanation of intentionality: that it be functionalist, inferentialist, holist, normative, social pragmatist, and, we now see more clearly, historically inflected. Brandom himself wants to claim that intentionality is not the primordial phenomenon in human mindedness; it is derivative, depends on normativity, the achievement of socially recognized normative statuses constituted by normative attitudes, and in such a context, Brandom's Hegel has to qualify as the most promising Brandomian, *avant la lettre*. "Making it explicit" is as important to Hegel as it is to Brandom; Hegel's notions of being-for-self and being-for-others, and their inseparability; the contrast between certainty and truth; the attack on any logical or empiricist atomism; the insistence on holism; the rejection of any Cartesian dualism between body and mind in favor of a compatible and systematically connected distinction between the factual and the normative;[1] the achievement of socially recognitive statuses as essential to the possibility of intelligibility and understanding; all this and much more, all have strong roles to play in Brandom's theory too.

I want to raise a number of questions about Brandom's Hegel, but I should admit at the outset that the relevance of those questions will depend on just what Brandom means by the "de re" method of interpretation he defends at the beginning of TMD.[2] I note that on the one hand, Brandom admits that his methodology involves "selection, supplementation and approximation," "selection" being the source of potential controversy since it is easy to imagine it functioning as a Get Out of Jail Free Card whenever questions about textual fidelity arise.[3] This "selection" issue is especially critical because, as Brandom of course knows, Hegel's theory of normativity in his *Phenomenology* is much, much broader in scope than the issues in Hegel about which Brandom has, up to this point at least, commented. Hegel's theory ranges over religion, art, burial practices, the Crusades, slavery, phrenology, hedonism, morality and forgiveness. Indeed, Hegel's version of the theory seems to do, in effect, exactly what Chomsky worried about when criticizing Davidson (past winner of the international "Hegel Prize"). When Chomsky accused Davidson of "erasing the boundary between knowing a language and knowing our way around the world generally" and complained that this would push a study of language (conceived in either a Davidsonean or a Brandomian/Hegelian, holist way) into a "theory of everything," Hegel would simply nod and agree and wait for what he would recognize as some sort of criticism to appear.[4] "*Das Wahre ist das Ganze*," after all. While it is of course possible to "select out" most of Hegel's account in order to concentrate on "*what in Hegel's idealist, pragmatist, historicist holism might be relevant to a theory of conceptual content*," that possibility at least raises the question of whether those elements in Hegel's thought are isolatable in this way, whether, seen in the light of Hegel's full *theory of normativity and especially normative change* (in effect what Hegel understood as his philosophical "theory of everything"),[5] even the role of such notions in an account of conceptual content will have to look different.

So there is some danger that the somewhat broader questions I want to raise could look irrelevant to the specific purpose to which Brandom wants to put Hegel's "objective idealism," or that they can be treated as topics for further study, once the nature of conceptuality is clear. But I don't think that the tasks can be divided like this and I take my bearings on the issue from Brandom's own self-imposed requirements, as when he asks questions like: "Do the notions of objective idealism and conceptual determinations that result from the two Hegel chapters [in TMD] fit well with other things Hegel says?"[6] This is just the question I want to pose,[7] especially because I am not sure that Brandom can get what he wants out of Hegel without something like Hegelian, comprehensive "theory of everything" questions inevitably arising. (I have also not found it possible to deal with Brandom's Hegel without importing a good deal of Brandom's Brandom, in MIE.[8])

There are several examples of how that problem arises. I only have time to discuss four well-known Hegelian claims and Brandom's take on them (or the absence of a take), and, as is common in these encounters, no time at all to describe how much I have learned from these extraordinary and inspiring essays.

(I) Hegel's philosophy is an idealism.

(II) This idealism is a holism.

(III) Rational norms must be understood as *socially* instituted over time. This means that their binding force comes from our having subjected ourselves to them (they are "self-legislated") and that later norms can be understood as the *result* of various breakdowns and crises in earlier, prior institutions. Indeed in Hegel's account our being able to understand them as such responses is a crucial feature in the claim that later norms are more developed, more successful an actualization of the appeal to reason in human affairs and so that they make possible a greater realization of freedom. At the very least one important aspect of this development must involve, Hegel thinks, some sort of social "struggle for recognition," sometimes violent, resolvable at all only in a state of true mutuality.

(IV) Finally, philosophy is historical, fundamentally and always "of its time," where that means several controversial things. The most controversial was just mentioned: human history should be understood as the progressive realization of freedom and this because reason is more and more "actual" in human affairs and freedom is self-rule according to laws of reason.

In each of these four cases, not only are Hegel's broader ambitions curtailed by Brandom, but the absence of these broader goals means that questions have to arise for Brandom's project which cannot be answered with the resources developed by it.

I

The first issue is *idealism*, a term Hegel uses in a wide variety of ways.[9] But whatever else he means, he certainly also means to signal an attack on at least one dogma of empiricism. The first three chapters in the *Phenomenology of Spirit* are clearly out to argue that no story about the origin of concepts, and no use of such a story to defend the objectivity of concepts, can rely on appeal to any putatively immediately given or non-inferentially warranted content, sensory or otherwise, as foundational or as tribunal. The unavailability of *any* sort of directly intuited item, even in concept realism or rationalist theories of *noesis*, means that we will need a different sort of story to justify the normative constraints imposed on the origination and explanation of judgmental claims, where they can be justified. This does not mean that one of those constraints cannot be something like "what experience won't let us say about it," but the nature and workings of that constraint will have to be different from any appeal to immediacy, the given, etc.

This can fairly be called an idealism since it seems to make the possibility of experience, experiential knowledge, and explanatory success *dependent* on conceptual rules that are not themselves empirically derived, given that the possibility of empirical experience already depends on such discriminating capacities. Thus, it can be said that such required discriminatory capacities and processes are "contributed by us," and are contentful only by virtue of their role in our practices, not by virtue of some story that can be traced back to something directly available in experience.[10] Since many people for many years understood Kant's version of this claim to be saying that such a dependence meant we could not be said to be experiencing external objects in the normal sense but only mind-dependent entities, appearances, or *Erscheinungen*, and since whatever else he is saying, Hegel is clearly not saying *that*, at least in Hegel's case we will have to be careful about what such dependence amounts to.

Brandom proposes a helpful distinction at this point. He suggests that we should distinguish between Sense Dependence and Reference Dependence and that doing so helps us see there is no evidence that Hegel understood his own claim of dependence as anything but Sense Dependence; that is, that he did not believe all finite particulars were existentially dependent on concepts which could pick them out, or that such objects could only exist when and for as long as they were thought by a human or a divine mind. Rather, in the examples used by Brandom, "the concepts of singular term and object are reciprocally sense-dependent. One cannot understand either without at least implicitly understanding the other and the basic relations between them." Likewise with the concept "fact" and "what is assertable in a proposition"; likewise law and necessity on the one hand, and counterfactually robust inference on the other.[11] Reciprocal sense-dependence like this – essentially between modally robust material exclusions in reality and subjective processes for identifying such exclusions and trying to avoid incompatible commitments – thus helps one interpret some of the well known battle cries in Hegel's assertion of his idealism, such as, in his *Differenzschrift*, "[T]he principle of speculation is the identity of subject and object,"[12] i.e. the principle of speculative idealism is the reciprocal sense-dependence of subjective processes and meaningful claims about objects.[13]

This interpretation of "objective idealism," the claim that the intelligibility of the notion of an objective world is dependent on, is only intelligible in terms of, the subjective process of acknowledging error in experience, or rejecting incompatible commitments, is clearly a variation, albeit a weak variation, on Kant's radical Transcendental Turn, such that all "object talk" could amount to (the only determinate experiential content that could be given the notion) is rule-governed synthetic unity, that the object *is* just "that in the concept of which the manifold is united." But this Kantian heritage would also seem to raise inevitably the Kantian question of just how robust Brandom's version of this dependence is, what I called his weak Kantian variation.[14]

That is, when Kant claimed that there is a "sense-dependence" between a notion like "*event*" and "*capacity to distinguish a succession of representations from a representation of succession*," and that this discrimination must itself be possible because otherwise there could not be a unity of apperception, and that it *is* only possible on the condition that all elements intuited successively in a manifold follow from another (some other) according to a rule (with necessity), he was not making the rather anodyne observation that the meaning of any claim to discrimination and unity in our experience is dependent on what could count as discriminable to us, given whatever capacities to discriminate we possess, and so that whatever discriminatory capacities we do have constitute in some way what intelligible claims about discriminable objects could meaningfully amount to. *That* sort of observation only gets its bite in positions like psychologism, or the positivist notion of verificationism, or in Kant's transcendental "necessary conditions for the possibility of experience" project, with its accompanying need for a deduction, or Wittgenstein's *Tractatus* idealism in which the limits of language *are* the limits of the world, and I do not yet see where Brandom thinks his version gets its bite, is more than anodyne. Moreover, for Kant, because object-talk is sense-dependent on our epistemic conditions, Kant feels he has to raise the question: "Granted, this is the only way we could make experiential sense out of 'event,' but what of events in themselves, considered apart from *our* conditions for meaningful claims about events?" This sort of question may already be a mistake (and Hegel certainly thought it was) but it is not clear why or in what sense it is on Brandom's account. It is only the great generality of the claims about objects, facts and laws that makes such a question otiose for Brandom; that is, who could disagree with the claim that the way one *understands* facts is tied to what one *understands* by the content of assertions?[15]

This is important in a Hegelian context because Hegel believed in radical conceptual change, at what Kant would regard (in horror) as the categorical or constitutive, empirically unchallengeable level. This means that it must be possible that a kind of gap can seem to open up in some sense-making practice, the appearance of a gap between what Hegel calls (subjective) certainty and what he calls "truth," which for now we can just mark as the beginning of some sort of insufficiency in that heretofore smoothly running practice. This gap is *internal* to a practice; it is not an empirical insufficiency, or a skeptical doubt about objects as they would be in themselves, and, if we follow Brandom's reformulations this must be understood as a kind of "meaning breakdown." This all suggests that at the very least we should say that whatever subjective capacity or process we *try* to identify as "all that an object or objective structure or value claim or obligation claim *could* mean for us" will have to be *provisional* and that some account of the nature of this provisionality is called for. Emphasizing Hegel's interest in basic historical change in constitutive normative commitments is not necessarily inconsistent with Brandom's take on Hegel, but I take it as significant that Hegel wants to make this point by discussing the relationship between "the This" and sense certainty, "the thing and many properties" and perception, "force" and the understanding, "life" and self-consciousness, reason and itself, and so on, and does not make a case for a general dependence between discriminable and discriminating capacity. That is, there is a determinate account of what this sense dependence could actually amount to and what these co-variations could look like, and it is especially significant that he tells the story of these putative dependencies and the "experience" of their insufficiency in a kind of idealized *narrative*. And in order eventually to get real historical development into Hegel's story of objective idealism, the constitutive (and socially instituted) dependence at issue will have to start out with more substantial claims just so that various specific historical failures (especially failures not due to empirical discovery) can be accounted for.

This issue of normative change will return a couple of more times. For now, we can note simply that for all that Brandom has helped us see how Kant changed the subject – from the character and quality of our grip on concepts to the question of the concepts' normative hold or grip on us – we also need to see how Hegel refocused the issue *yet again*, how he emphasized as of the greatest importance how a concept can come to lose that normative grip. In typical Hegelian fashion, it is only by understanding *that* that we understand what such a grip amounts to in the first place.[16]

The point is also important when we are talking about thick normative concepts and the sort of binding force they can be said to have in Hegel's account. For the basic ethical notions Hegel is interested in also function as instituted (made more than found) and constitutive. One becomes a citizen by being taken to be one, recognized as one; there *are* citizens only in so far as there *are* these rules applied in discriminating social roles. Yet it is still possible for such a practice to begin to fail in some way not at all tied to something essential in citizenship-in-itself that a former practice had simply "missed" (as, for example, in Hegel's account of the failures of Roman or Jacobin citizenship), nor (to anticipate again) tied simply to what a later community in fact "re-constituted" as citizen. Of course, since Brandom sides with Quine against Carnap, he is happy enough to admit even radical meaning change "within" experience and he has his own common-law analogy to explain it and its progressive character. More on that in the last section of this chapter.

II

Brandom's holism has already been manifest. It is paradigmatically what it is by virtue of its "material exclusions": excluded are any strict concept-intuition, or conceptual scheme vs. content dualism or any conceptual content atomism. He gives us several formulations of the position, many quite illuminating about historical changes in the modern notion of representation. (As in the dawning realization that "The vertical relations between thoughts and things depend crucially on the horizontal relations between thoughts and thoughts."[17]) This theme in Hegel brings us to the heart of Brandom's own theory of inferentialist rationality, his account of double book deontic scorekeeping, and his rich account of the variety of material inferential relations.[18] There is no way to do any justice to the details of what he takes to be manifestations of that theory in Hegel, or how extraordinarily illuminating much of that discussion is. I need to concentrate on the main potential problem Brandom detects in Hegel's version of holism.[19]

It is this. Brandom distinguishes between "weak individuational holism," and "strong individuational holism." The former holds that a necessary condition for the possibility of the determinate contentfulness of concepts is "articulation by relations of material incompatibility" (where, given his dependence claim, he means by such relations both those for properties and states of affairs, and for propositions and predicates). Strong holism claims that articulations by material incompatibility are *sufficient* for determinateness.[20] Since Hegel does not seem to start off with an antecedent set of possibilities, such that knowing what a concept excludes helps establish something like the location in logical space for such a concept (as in a disjunctive syllogism, say) and holds that immediacy as immediacy (such as direct receptive immediacy) is indeterminate (and this is the notion Brandom will want to "supplement" or alter), Hegel can seem to understand determinacy as *wholly* a matter of these relations of material exclusion, or what Brandom calls "symmetric relative individuation." But if *everything* is determined by relations of material exclusion then "the relata are in a sense dissolved into the relations between them," and we have the obvious problem: "relations between *what?*"[21] (This is actually an old problem in discussions of Hegel. The earlier and very important manifestation of Hegel as a strong individuational holist was the British "internal relations" monist version of Hegel's metaphysics.)

However, there is an assumption in this question that seems to me unHegelian, a kind of misleading either/or exclusive disjunction. It seems plausible to assume that, in coming to understand more and more about a concept's content, in the course either of empirical discovery or changing normative practices, we can just make do with some provisional, fixed designation of the relata, either a provisional definition or paradigm-case locator, which itself is subject to change in the light of broader inferential articulation, perhaps even very extensive alteration. We could even isolate and treat as privileged a small set of clear inferential articulations, holding in place what we are treating as relata so that we can explore various other inferential articulations (of *it*, that relatum, so loosely but effectively defined). We could do this just pragmatically, without any commitment to essentialism or analyticity or there really *being* a privileged set of inferential relations. For example, ultimately the notion of human subjectivity, marked originally by simple consciousness – in Hegel the possibility of a subject having a take on an object – comes to have over the course of the *Phenomenology* a "content" that is a function of very many various reflective and social and ethical capacities that Hegel (*mirabile dictu*) argues are ultimately necessary conditions even for the possibility of a simple take on an object. I see no reason to think that in order to present a theory like this, that, once we understand this array of capabilities, Hegel also owes us an answer to the question: yes, but what is the relatum here, what is *that which* has these capacities or contains these inferential possibilities? There are always provisional ways of picking out designata in order to introduce a more extensive capability, but only a grammatical illusion (a "paralogism" as Kant put it in this particular case) created by this "that which" locution would lead us to think we need a fixed relatum all the way through. (Even Kant's own "Merkmale" theory of concept determinacy allows *great* flexibility in the settling of concept determinacy.[22])

I suspect that Brandom introduces this question and tries to solve it because he is worried about making Hegelian objective idealism compatible with some sort of direct constraint by the sensible world (a way to fix the relata in inferential relations in a way that does not involve representing, claim-making or content, but which ties our concept application to a deliverance of sensibility), because he wants to preserve in some strongly intuitive way a strict co-variation between subjective processes and objective facts and objects (relations with no fixed relata is obviously counter-intuitive in this regard) and because he is thinking of what he takes to be a Sellarsian picture of how that happens. What Brandom often refers to as "the Harman" point is supposed to help at this point, a distinction between inferential *relations* and inferential *processes*.[23] As he puts it: "Inference is a process; implication is a relation."[24] This distinction will allow us to be more careful in understanding what we mean when we link conceptual content to "relations" of material exclusion. In Hegel's account that means that we should not be trapped into seeing material exclusion everywhere as relata simply *standing* in relations (or as, *per impossibile*, standing in nothing but relations). Objective relations of incompatibility can only be made sense of, in Brandom's sense-dependence claim, as processes of resolving and avoiding subjective incompatibilities of commitment, and fixed concept determinacy must be explicable under these "objective idealist" conditions. Once we understand that the relations in question count as implication relations just by constraining rational belief change, as playing that role in an on-going inferential process, and we understand how that process works, our earlier worry about Hegel's strong holism will not look so suspicious.

For, according to Brandom, we always, in our discursive practices, have to start with some sort of *antecedently* differentiated datum – he suggests *signs* like proposition letters. (This is supposed to satisfy our intuitions on the "object side.") This analogy trades on "orthodox mathematical abstraction by the formation of equivalence classes." His point is clearer, I think, in his summary of Hegel on perception.

In his Hegelian example of property determinacy, Brandom tries to make more concrete this model of holistic role abstraction by going over the supposed "stages" in Hegel's account, where properties are first thought of atomistically, determinate apart from any relation to another, and then, given the indeterminacy of these results, thought of wholly in terms of excluding incompatible material relations, a stage that according to Brandom threatens the dissolution of relata mentioned before. *These* relations among roles can now be thought of as consisting wholly in relations because "immediacy," marking as a kind of sign the content of experience responded to differentially, has already made it possible to track a class or set of such markers, even though on their own they remain a *je ne sais quoi*. The key is (and it is impossible to stress it too much) that this immediacy is not *representational*, a sign of something else. Our ability simply to respond differentially and non-inferentially is making a contribution to the process of determination of content (to that which is in relation) but initially only in our differential responsiveness and by such items expressing *potentially* a higher order inferential discrimination implicit in the discriminability of the item but not directly apprehendable as such. *We* must do that work of determination in this process. "(O)ne must build the holistic roles in stages, starting with something construed as immediate, and then investigating the mediation implicit in taking it to be determinate."[25]

This view of the relation between immediacy and mediation (and the insistence that immediacy play some sort of role like this in experience) strikes me as quite Sellarsian (at least as Brandom interprets him) and suggests the same problem one finds in (Brandom's) Sellars. The problem is the unHegelian language of "stages" rather than "moments," and this way of linking us to the sensible world by merely causally elicited "responses." Brandom's Sellars chapter is called "The Centrality of Sellars' Two-Ply Account of Observation," and the "twoness" involved is similar to what was just summarized. The first ply is what results from a "reliable differential responsive disposition" (or RDRD). We share with non-human animals, some machines and even some normal objects the ability to respond differentially and reliably to distinct environmental stimuli. But these responses, even if they involve the uttering of a word, are not representational, do not yet have content, and this primarily for Sellars because no *commitment* to anything has been established. That happens only with concept application and attribution of commitment by others. (There are several ambiguous formulations about this issue. In the second Hegel chapter, Brandom says, with respect to immediately elicited responses, that in these cases particulars exercise an "authority over the universals or concepts that apply to them."[26] But since these responses are merely elicited, or "wrung" from us, the question of authority should not arise. According to Brandom authority, or a normative claim in general, is something *granted*, not elicited.)

The greater problem comes when one tries to establish a connection between these two dimensions, since the first is a matter of what is simply causally elicited and the second involves a normative commitment not presumably simply provoked, caused or directly elicited by the RDRDs. These responses thus do not seem to be doing any "guiding," and when considered *just* as RDRDs to be normatively inert with respect to what I end up committed to.[27] If even perception is "normative all the way down" (and "reliable" already indicates that) then these causal episodes of elicited responses look like window-dressing designed to comfort a potential reliabilist or externalist or cognitivist. Brandom claims that while some of that might be true, there could not be a *global* independence of observational response from concept use, and he notes that "purely theoretical concepts do not form an autonomous language game, a game one could play though one played no other."[28] But the reason he immediately gives is that "one must be able to respond conceptually to the utterance of others to be talking at all."[29] But this almost concedes that what counts as *reliable* responsiveness (something that must be established for there to be any relation between these two "plys") is itself mediated by the social normativity Brandom is elsewhere eager to stress. If others in the discursive community administer such things as the "reliability" ascription, something of the content of such a norm will eventually begin functioning for individuals as norms, internal to the discrimination process itself, as a constituent of the sensible uptake itself. Brandom thus concedes that our very dispositions can be said to change as a result of systematic sources of error.[30] And Brandom himself also concedes that for thick moral concepts it is hard to imagine two such separate strands, such that one could differentially respond to instances of courage or cruelty, in a way that was just causally elicited.[31] Since whatever else it is, Hegel's philosophy is systematic, it is hard to imagine that the inapplicability to this case of the "build in stages" picture of the immediacy–mediation relation that Brandom proposes would not mean that something is wrong with the core picture.

The moral here seems to me to redound back to Brandom's account of Hegel on immediacy. Rather than having there be "stages," all in some way or other modeled after the Sellarsian two-ply, reliable-responder/normatively-committing observer, Hegel's position seems to me to be a more thoroughly "processual" holism. His position on the mediate character of even direct sensory experience is not poised to collapse everything into a "strong individuational holism," nor to adopt Brandom's building stages model, but to deny the separability of immediate and mediate elements, even while insisting on the contribution of both. In Hegel's account, I am suggesting, and in full Brandomese: the failure of atomistically conceived property determinacy is not meant to signal that our immediately elicited perceptual responses should therefore be construed as non-representational, sign-like discriminable items that will form something like the basis of an abstraction to roles that *are* inferentially articulated, but that a fuller, more adequate picture of this one-ply, but complexly and inseparably structured dimension of experience is required.[32] To be sure, this will seem to give us a much less robust picture of answerability to the world and a more important role for answerability to each other, but, since on Brandom's account, any immediate element in experience does not cause or on its own constrain concept application, he has that problem anyway. In the Sellars chapter, after noting the very basic theme of his inferentialism, that "grasping any concept requires grasping many concepts," he also has to ask a question that is not helped by his elaborate account of holistic role abstraction. The question is: "*how* good must one be at discriminating . . . in order to count as grasping the concept," and he answers that that is a matter wholly of how one is treated by the other members of the linguistic community, a matter of having achieved a "social status" by having been recognized as having achieved it. This seems to me both to undermine the real role any appeal to our immediate responsiveness to the world plays in discursive practices, and re-raises the problem of an inferential positivism. Our common sense and somewhat realist intuitions still require *some* response here: *what* is the community relying on when such a status is granted? Merely what future communities might, probably, decide? What constrains the granting of such status?[33] Isn't the basic question just pushed back a stage? Hegel has an answer to this but it involves that ambitious theory of the realization of freedom and "meaning breakdowns" noted earlier and about to arise again.

III

This last issue – our collective responsibility for our norms – obviously raises the question of the nature of the "Brandomian socialism," what he calls the semantic pragmatism, crucial to his theory of normativity and therewith of possible conceptual content, and the way he accounts for the historicity of norms and normative change. In neither case, I want to argue, is there "enough" of a Hegelian notion of sociality or historicity at work. Here is a summary formulation of the sociality of norms claim.

> What is needed is one of the most basic Hegelian emendations to Kant's normative rationalism: an understanding of normative statuses such as commitment, responsibility, and authority as social achievements. Hegel construes having bound oneself by applying a concept as occupying a certain sort of social position, having a certain sort of social standing.[34]

All of this seems to me quite right and a substantial and extremely valuable reformulation of the Kant–Hegel relation. However it is when Brandom goes on to discuss the nature of this social status that his account seems to me not so much wrong as critically incomplete. In Brandom's account (as well as in his account of Hegel's position), what commitments you undertake are up to you but the content of those commitments, just *what* you are committing yourself to by committing yourself to claim P, is not; that is "administered" by others. ("I commit myself, but then *they* hold me to it."[35]) These other score-keepers also resolve questions about what commitments you are in fact *entitled* to make, independently of what you claim to be entitled to. As we saw earlier, what it is to have achieved the social status of a competent concept applier is and is only a matter of being recognized as such by other score-keepers.

Brandom's language of normative commitment being a matter of "having bound oneself" is quite true to the deeply Kantian position on normativity, as necessarily self-legislated, which Hegel took up and vastly expanded, himself following many of Fichte's crucial emendations of the notion. I could not agree more that this is the heart of the heartland, what distinguishes the rationalism of the Kantian and post-Kantian German tradition from its rationalist predecessors.[36] Kant's notion that we are only bound to what we bind ourselves to shows up everywhere in what we call German Idealism, reappearing in Fichte's notion of self-positing and clearly manifest in Hegel's otherwise mysterious claims that Geist is a "product of itself," or that the Concept "gives itself its own actuality." It is however a *highly* metaphorical notion in all three thinkers; there is no original moment of self-obligation, any more than there is a Fichtean I which initiates experience *de novo* by positing a not-I. The metaphor is also very hard to interpret discursively; it can seem, as McDowell has put it, that Brandom is committed to a position "that brings norms into existence out of a normative void."[37]

However, because Hegel formulates the claim in the first-person plural, and as something that occurs over time, any worry about a transition from a normless to a normative situation is much less relevant to him. There is no original normless situation, only an on-going, continuous historical process of initiation or socialization into a community's normative practices, demanding allegiance in all sorts of practical, engaged and largely implicit ways and receiving it in an equally various number of practices of consent, affirmation, sustenance, in a variety of modalities of self-legislation and self-obligation.[38] Hegel thinks that art, for example, is one of these modalities. As noted above though, if the "autonomy thesis" is "[w]hat makes them [norms] binding is that one takes them to be binding,"[39] it is *extremely hard* to present a non-metaphorical notion of this self-imposition. As soon as we move beyond explicit assertoric judgments ("That metal is molybdenum"[40]) and explicit performatives ("I promise to drive you to the airport tomorrow morning"[41]), more practical and implicit modes of "commitment" are much more difficult to discern, both for an individual and for any potential score-keeper. (We can tell *something* by what a person does and what else he is willing to say or has said, but the situation gets immediately very complicated once we venture beyond assertions about molybdenum or promises about driving.) Moreover, equally important, just because such practices are rarely explicit or well-defined with respect to their scope, there is also an on-going unavoidable *contestation* about the claims made on behalf of such rules over historical time, about attribution and entitlement claims and denials, as the context of application changes and strains the original understanding. The issue Hegel is most interested in is one we would now call the basic difference (if there is one) between the *matter-of-historical-fact normalizing practices of the score-keeping police* and some sort of *progressive normative development*. And this still leaves a lot that is metaphorical since, in the phrase of Haugeland's that Brandom borrows and makes use of – "transcendental constitution" is always "social institution"[42] – there is no clear non-metaphorical reading of just *how* "societies" can be said to "institute" anything (or, especially, try and yet fail to do so, end up with mere coercive enforcement of some against many or many against some, rather than something that can be understood as a self-obligation to a self-legislated rule). But there is at least no reason to think this occurs at something like a constitutional convention of original, basic rule making and pledges of allegiance, and there is plenty of reason to think it is a problem that requires some answer if we are talking about genuinely normative social engagements, and not just "carrots and sticks" success at socialization.

Indeed Hegel believes that a kind of systematic sense can be made of the continuities and crises in attempts at institution and maintenance of allegiance; "wholesale" not just "retail" to invoke a Brandomean turn of phrase, and that without this systematic story we are left with no way to distinguish later normative improvements from later reconfigurations of social power in enforcing a new regime.[43] Without this more ambitious enterprise, a social pragmatist inferentialist holism like Brandom's is indistinguishable from a kind of "inferentialist positivism." I mean by this that while Brandom can avoid what he calls regularism or can justify attributing an original intentionality to a community and not just note regularities in behavior, (that is, he can justify the claim that its participants are playing the normative game of giving and asking for reasons and therewith both undertaking as well as attributing and assessing commitments of others), this does not yet explain *how* either an external interpreter or internal participant can properly challenge the authority of the norms on the basis of which the attributions and assessments are made, or how those norms can fail to meet those challenges. Brandom can describe *what happens* when such a challenge occurs but he wants to stay out of the question of the putative merits of challenges in general. That is for the participants to thrash out, and his (Brandom's) own account remains "phenomenalist."[44] Without that further account, though, we remain mere historical sociologists (or underlaboring explicit-makers); to be sure, makers explicit of what participants count as the *distinctly normative*, and of its history, but resigned to *recording* the sorts of challenges and defenses "they" would regard as appropriate then and there; or we can score them on our current scorecard, but without an account of how "they" got to be "us." While illegitimate claims to normative authority, in other words, are clearly still putative norms, and while, when they are invoked, the game of giving and asking for reasons has begun, unless we can go on to ground the difference between merely putative and genuine claims to authority, the distinction between manipulated or coerced behavior and norm-responsive conduct will be empty. Threatening you offers you in *some* sense a reason to obey me, and you would be obeying in *some* sense in a way responsive to a reason, your interest in your well-being. But it is hard to see how one could describe that as your being responsive to a claim for a distinctively normative authority.[45] ("Positivism" is an apt word for this not only because Brandom's take on idealism can sound a bit like verificationism,[46] but because in normative terms, from his first writings on Christianity and the early Christian community until his last writings on politics, Hegel's self-identified, chief problem was what he called "positivity." He meant by this the successful administration of what appear to be norms, but which, even with actual acknowledgement and the attitudinal support of individuals, still must count as missing some crucial element which would distinguish alienated from a truly affirmative (self-imposed) relation to the law.)

I do not at all want to give the impression that Brandom is committed to what he calls an "I–We" conception of sociality.[47] He makes crystal clear in Chapters One and Eight of MIE that he does not; that his sociality is of the "I–you" variety. By the "score-keeping police" I mean here whatever, for most score-keepers, when each distinguishes the difference between what another *takes* to be "what ought to be done," say, and "what ought to be done," will end up *determining* how they make that distinction in a way that is shared and so "which determines how the attitudes of those who keep score on each other are answerable to the facts."[48] Again, as just noted, Brandom does not want to go there, go any farther than this, thinks the conditions for the success of his theory are satisfied when he explains *what* "objectivity" *will amount to* in his inferentialist semantics (it amounts to being able to make this distinction between normative status (objectively correct) and normative attitude (taken to be correct)); all else is part of the messy contestation that philosophy cannot judge.[49] We need to stop with this understanding of objectivity as "a structural aspect of the social-perspectival *form* of conceptual contents."[50] We should be philosophically satisfied with the claim that "the permanent possibility of a distinction between how things are and how they are taken to be by some interlocutor is built into the social articulation of concepts."[51] This formalism is the most profoundly unHegelian aspect of his theory. From Hegel's point of view, we will not really know what being able to make this distinction amounts to (as distinct from, say, what individual perspectival score-keepers have in various times and places *taken* the distinction to amount to) unless we track the distinction as "realized" concretely and come up with some way to understand if we are getting any better at making it. (If we don't do this, we've got what I called inferentialist positivism.[52]) Put in a formula: Brandom believes that meaning or conceptual content is a matter of use, inferential articulations within a social game of giving and asking for reasons. He is right that Hegel agrees with this, but Hegel also claims that the question of the authority of the articulations scored in certain ways at certain times is also indispensable to the question of such content, and that we cannot understand that dimension except in so far as the possible articulations are, as he says everywhere, "actualized," verwirklicht. (For example, in Hegel's account, understanding why the basic norms of ancient Greek ethical life failed as they did, began to lose their grip, tells us something we need to know and could have come to know in no other way, about the difference between the purported authority of an appeal to a norm, and actual authority.[53]) As we shall see in a minute, this ties Hegel's notion of philosophy *much* more closely to history than Brandom does.

The claim is that from Hegel's perspective, the problem with Brandom's version is not so much a problem as a gap, a lacuna that Brandom obviously feels comfortable leaving unfilled (cf. the earlier discussion here of the "selection" of only some Hegelian themes), but which seems to me indispensable. This might seem a bit unfair. After all, Brandom has roped Hegel into an extraordinary, impressive project that has accomplished a very great deal in itself and as an illumination of Hegel: a way of understanding score-keeping practices sufficient to confer various sorts of conceptual content. These include nonlogical propositional content, contents associated with predicates and singular terms, pronouns, demonstratives and proper names, and even the logically expressive content of conditionals, negation, quantifiers and so on. And this is not to mention the ingenuity of the demonstration of how anaphoric chains work in communicative success, how one can secure both co-reference and token repeatability "across the different repertoires of commitments that correspond to different interlocutors."[54] Nevertheless, however ungrateful it sounds, there is something crucial to Hegel's project that does not appear in Brandom or Brandom's Hegel. The issue is most obvious in cases where the main problem Brandom tracks – the problem of conceptual determinacy, conceptual content – intersects with the question of conceptual authority; cases where everyone understands what the concept is about, purports to be about (the putative content is determinate), but where serious disagreement has arisen about whether that clear purport is *fulfilled*, justified, legitimate, whether the concept *really* picks out anything. (Since any application of a concept is a normative claim, a claim not that this is what has been thought to belong together, but this is what ought or even must be thought together, these two dimensions of the problem are obviously inseparable.) This distinction most interests Hegel when the issue is change or a partial breakdown with respect to fundamental, paradigmatic normative principles, *what scorekeepers rely on* when they distinguish between what another takes himself to be authorized to do and what he is really authorized (or forbidden or simply ought) to do. Cases like divine and human law, the claims of faith and of Enlightenment, the claims of natural right, moral freedom, revolutionary political authority, or moral purity. (When score-keepers cut up the normative world in a certain way, such as distinguishing between "the law of the heart" and "the frenzy of self-conceit," their scores *already* mean something, carry material normative implications, neither accessible to the parties in play, often directly contrary to their own intentions, and not dependent simply on how future score-keepers will as a matter of historical fact extend and supplement and alter the implications of their commitments.) It is a limitation of Brandom's account, and a mark of his differences with Hegel, that his theory of "meaning normativity" is reductionist in this way, reduces to the attitudinal states of individuals.[55]

The most intuitively clear manifestation of this limitation and the positivism that results from it occurs in Chapter Three of Part One in MIE, the "queen's shilling" example. Brandom calls to mind the eighteenth century practice wherein merely accepting the offer of such a shilling was counted as having enlisted in the queen's navy. The practice was intended to allow a public sign of acceptance for those illiterates who could not sign a contract, but was widely used by recruiters who essentially tricked drunken victims in taverns into such acceptance. According to Brandom, "Those who accepted found out the significance of what they had done – the commitment *they had undertaken*, and so the alteration of their status – only upon awakening from the resulting stupor."[56] I think most of us would say intuitively that the fact that others attributed such a commitment to an individual did not mean that that individual was, in normative fact, truly so committed, that the practice counted something as a commitment illegitimately, that it does not qualify as a commitment.

But for Brandom, to undertake a commitment is *just* for an individual to do something that makes it appropriate for others to attribute a commitment to that individual, where "appropriate" is a matter of a standing actual practice. Brandom's account will allow a distinction between what seemed a commitment but was really not (the recruiter mistakenly used the wrong coin), but not between what others count as a change in status and what really amounts to a change in status. *All* that the latter involves for Brandom is a change in the attitudinal states of others, and this position will not even allow the problem that bothered Hegel his entire career to arise: that problem of "positivity," subjection by others, according to appropriate, public practices, to a status of "undertaken commitments" not recognized as such by the individual. What Hegel takes as deeply problematic is counted by Brandom as a wholly unproblematic example of attributing commitments. (In this regard, the fact that Brandom concedes that "the whole community" may end up wrong in the way they score, even "by their own lights," is an idle concession. As his own theory would have it, unless we know what that concession includes and excludes, how it might actually be used in cases like this one, it is a concession *without content*. Brandom's own willingness to agree that our poor drunken sailor *is* in fact *normatively* committed to service in the queen's navy – that *he* actually *undertook* this commitment – is not encouraging about what such a content might be.[57]) While Brandom sometimes gives the impression that the position defended in MIE or the position attributed to Hegel just leaves open questions about genuine versus illusory claims to normative authority, I would say that it is quite clear that he has already taken positions on normativity, commitment, entitlement and obligation; the positions apparent in this passage.

What the issue comes down to is how, or to what extent, one can make a certain dimension of human sociality – the institution, sustenance, sanctioning, and administering of normative commitments – essential to one's semantics without offering anything like a much fuller social theory, a comprehensive view of the social bond *or* a full blown normative theory, a theory of what counts as the distinction between "exercise of normative authority" and "exercise of coercive power."[58] To be sure, Brandom considers that he has provided a general account of normativity and a sufficient view of sociality. For the former he often invokes "Kant's distinction between the realm of nature, and the realm of freedom, whose denizens are bound rather by their conception of rules – that is by rules that bind them only in virtue of their own acknowledgement of them as binding."[59] As noted, this does not help us much in trying to understand what *counts* as doing this ("acknowledging *authority*") and what settles the question of the scope and content of just what I have bound myself to.[60] When Brandom notes that the latter is a matter to be administered by others, it is easy enough to imagine cases where that appeal settles nothing and only invites further controversy (as when actions are taken in my name by a supposedly representative assembly, where commitments are attributed to me by others on the basis of what, given the institutional rules of elections and representation, I can be said to have bound myself to).

Moreover, it is precisely this *indeterminacy* that is important to Hegel. His theory of, especially, practical rationality is such a radically historical boot-strapping theory that essential elements will go missing (such as this unavoidable conflict) if we stay at Brandom's notion of "negotiation" between "those who attribute the commitment and the one who acknowledges it."[61] In a footnote, Brandom makes clear that he is well aware of this problem.

> Talk of negotiation is bound to sound too irenic a rendering for the sort of strife and confrontation of inconsistent demands Hegel depicts. But, though the issue cannot be pursued here, I think there are good reasons to treat the martial, uncompromising language Hegel is fond of as misleading on this point. Nothing is absolutely other, nor are any claims or concepts simply inconsistent for him. It is always material incompatibilities of content (rather than formal inconsistencies) whose mutual confrontation obliges an alteration of commitments.[62]

This passage has an odd ring to it. As Brandom clearly suspects, it *does* have a "Can't we all just get along" meliorism or irenecism that does not at all fit the *Phenomenology*. And it comes close to saying: if Hegel had understood Brandomian inferentialist semantics better (the resources for which are already implicit in other aspects of Hegel's project), and so had not sometimes confused negotiable material incompatibilities with formal inconsistencies or the clash of brute otherness, he would not have indulged such "martial" tendencies. But there is no evidence that I know of, and none provided by Brandom, that Hegel's emphasis on the "violence" that consciousness suffers at its own hands is just a result of such a view about brute otherness or formal inconsistencies. There is plenty of room for what Hegel often treats as tragic conflict if those two points are conceded.[63]

Moreover, Hegel's "slaughter bench of history" formulations are not the result of commitments in a philosophical anthropology (wherein, supposedly, a violent struggle for prestige and ultimately recognition as essential aspects of human nature are invoked as explicans for social and normative change). There is another reason why Hegel is so concerned in any account of the social mediation needed for communicative success, political stability or ethical life[64] that one never abstract from or in any way ignore that there are never simply human agents or subjects at play, that any such subject must always first be considered either subject to the will of another or able to subject others to his will, bondsman (*Knecht*) or lord (*Herr*). This is because the status of a person or free agent, someone capable of leading one's own life, of seeing oneself in one's deeds, is indeed, as Brandom rightly notes, not an ontological category for Hegel but a historical and social achievement. That achievement however has as its central task the problem of distinguishing between what we identified previously here as the difference between the administration of social power (perhaps complete with the "willing" submission of docile subjects) and the achievement of a form of life in which the freedom of one depends on the freedom of all. The whole ball game in Hegel comes down to the question of whether he has in fact discovered a historical, developmental way of making the case that this distinction *can* be made (without any form of moral realism or Kantian "moral law" universalism), of saying what institutional form of life actually achieves this desiderata, and his being able to show that it is the unfinished and still unfolding achievement of modernity to have begun to do all this. Hegel's claim to philosophical immortality rests on this novel attempt to make this distinction between putative claims to normative legitimacy that are in reality exercises of coercive power for the sake of unequal advantage (non-reciprocal recognitive statuses), and successful claims to normative legitimacy, to do so by beginning with an image of a situation regulated exclusively by exercises of power, and to show that the ultimate unsustainability of such a relation can be demonstrated "experientially," or "internally," that ultimate achievement of agent status requires a recognitive social status that cannot be achieved by exercises of power alone.[65] The nerve of this internally self-negating developmental process will ultimately amount to Hegel's theory of freedom, both required for successful normative self-regulation, but impeded or denied by just those forms of institutional practice that implicitly require that very status (of free subjects).

This turns out to be a long story, and I realize that Brandom thinks his version accommodates most of it. Indeed, in another essay on Hegel not included here, he has developed a rich and challenging reading of Hegel's claims that recognitive relations can be said to "develop" out of erotic ones, that reflexive self-relations depend on being able to attribute normative attitudes towards others, and ultimately that I can be a subject that things can be *for* only by recognizing those who recognize me, by being recognized by all those whom I recognize, and by recognizing all those whom those whom I recognize recognize (including, ingeniously, me). This is the story for him of how one crosses "the crucial boundary between the merely natural and the incipiently normative."[66] But here again, the crucial move occurs in attributing to others commitments or normative attitudes in the satisfaction of desire. I take the other to be a subject who *takes* this object to be suitable to satisfy his desire, not a being who merely differentially responds in a reliable way to what elicits such a response. And that again means attributing a possible difference for this other subject between what is taken to be an appropriate satisfier of hunger, say, and "what *is*." And, again, this not only *introduces* us to the basic condition necessary for the attitude to be a normative one (between what is taken to be K and what is K) by appealing to what unproblematically turns out to be empirically unsatisfying (a human cannot eat rocks), this simple empirical disconfirmation remains the only clear example we have of how this distinction can be cashed out. The absence of any such unproblematic "claim-settler" in any more complex human claim to appropriateness or propriety is why, I am claiming, Hegel's interests turn so quickly to the issue of a *Kampf*, a fight or struggle for recognition, again an issue that Brandom leaves out.[67] It is also why, in Brandom's account, the problem with the Master's assertion of mastery is simply a matter of the Master "overgeneralizing" the human capacity to self-constitution by being insufficiently sensitive to the importance of the distinction between how I take things and how they are.[68] But the Master in Hegel's drama has not simply *made an error*. He represents an immediate option in the unavoidable struggle to determine how we shall make that distinction, once we move beyond the edible and the inedible and the like.

This Hegelian contestation also does not seem to me captured by the notion of ongoing negotiations between individuals and score-keepers. For one thing, there is no reason to expect that there is available a "neutral" notion of what counts as proper negotiation available to both parties. The relevant distinction therefore, to use Kantian and Sellarsean phrasing, is not so much between the space of causes and the space of reasons, between subsumption under law and acknowledgement of the concept of a law, but between the illusory appeal to legitimacy and authority, and a justifiable appeal, between, as it were, the fact of power and the fact of reason. The absence of such a common measure in what counts as negotiating is one of the reasons why the question of the *proper* distinction between the fact of power and the fact of reason constantly arises and why it forms the narrative core of Hegel's *Phenomenology*. (I should also note that Brandom is certainly aware of this issue and raises such a "Foucault" problem in his response to Habermas. But here again he just notes that playing the game of giving and asking for reasons *is* categorically different from doing things with words like exercising power, without telling us *how* to make that distinction, and as if the latter could not go on well disguised as the former, which, according to the early Foucault, it always does.[69])

IV

Brandom's view on what he needs to say about human sociality to satisfy the requirements of his theory of conceptual content is certainly not one that leaves no room for the "challenges" that initiate "negotiation."[70] And he has provided a way to think about the developmental process that results from such challenges and responses. I have already expressed skepticism that the "negotiation" model will get us very far along on Hegelian tracks, but this image requires an independent hearing. There are two premises we need to examine first.

Brandom interprets Hegel's striking remark that the "I," the self-conscious subject of experience *is* the concept, *der Begriff*, as that concept "has come into existence,"[71] as affirming that, just as one becomes a contentful self only in recognitive relations with others, so concepts are contentful only in the social game of giving and asking for reasons, in the double bookkeeping game of undertaking and attributing/assessing. Spirit as a whole is modeled on being a self, and that means that it is "the recognitive community of all those who have such normative statuses, and all their normatively significant activities."[72] This interpretation is then linked to a fundamental Brandomian theme.

> All there is to institute conceptual norms, to determine what we have committed ourselves to by applying a concept, is other applications of the concept in question ... Thus the applications of the concept ... that have already been made already have a certain sort of authority over candidate future applications of the concept[73]

But also:

> The authority of the past applications, which instituted the conceptual norm, is administered on its behalf by future applications, which include assessments of past ones.

The model is common law applications of case law, where each judge inherits a tradition of past decisions about cases and must rely on, can *only* rely on, those past cases to decide about new, sometimes radically new cases. The authority of the tradition "consists in the fact that the *only reasons* the judge can appeal to in justifying his decisions are procedural."[74] Brandom takes this to be a good model for the Hegelian dialectical claims for both continuity and change in a normative tradition, for the fact that normative developments are in some sense "found," in another "made." The model also fits Brandom's theory well, and aspects of Hegel's, because it is crucial to both that the normative significance of some move or commitment I make almost always "outruns" what I may consciously be taking myself to be committed to and "catching up," being able to make those further aspects more explicit, can look very much like Hegelian development or *Bildung*.[75]

This model is also said to have the additional benefit of explaining what Brandom thinks would otherwise be inexplicable: how Hegel can talk of the human community, Spirit as a whole, as a "self," but yet insist on the irreducibly social character of that self. Who, in this sense, could be said to hold *Spirit as a whole* responsible to itself, since there is no other social subject outside of Spirit, in recognitive relations with it? These different *time slices* are said to answer that problem. "[T]he present acknowledges the authority of the past, and exercises an authority over it in turn, with the negotiation of their conflicts administered by the future."[76]

However, Brandom is out to solve a problem that Hegel does not have (any more than Brandom does), and the solution, the common law analogy, while revealing in many respects, does not go far enough in capturing what Hegel means by tying "normative life" to historical time. The problem again is that Hegel's position is far more substantive, far less formal, than that attributed to him by Brandom. This is because one of the aspects of what has been made explicit across historical time is not just a set of particular normative commitments (which are administered, altered, perhaps substantially revised by a successor ethical community) *but the nature of normative authority itself*, the "truth" that such authority is socially instituted, tied to claims of reason which are cashed out in terms of social roles embodied in institutions, institutions the basic structures of which have begun to develop in ways finally consistent with, rather than in underlying tension with, the true nature of normative authority. Mutuality of recognitive status (the true source of normative authority), is, Hegel argues, embodied in several modern institutions (the rights-protecting, representative modern state, the modern nuclear family founded on both romantic and parental love, the modern property-owning market economy and civil society, as well as late Protestant religion and theology and lyric romanticism, the final culmination of art). These are not counted by Hegel as *just* proposals for future administration and alteration. Brandom's common law model works well when we consider how one might "update" Hegel's substantive institutional story and extend the application of such a civil and ethical status to women and propertyless citizens, but not for the claims Hegel wants to make about the authority of these basic roles and functions themselves.[77] Their authority stems from the developmental justification Hegel has provided for his distinct account of the nature and authority of freedom ("the worthiest and most sacred possession of man"[78]). This is all parallel to the way in which Brandom's own account of conceptual content is itself a normative claim, a claim that the matter ought to be rendered explicit in this way, as a matter of inferential articulation, instituted social statuses and so forth, and not itself the carrying-forward of a tradition (one among many other philosophical traditions), itself subject later to the "authority of the future." It (Brandom's account) presumably has its own authority, assuming that it is meant as itself a philosophical claim, not just the interpretation and application of other claims.[79]

For the same reason, the common law analogy is too weak to capture Hegel's account of conceptual change. As noted before, Hegel is trying to introduce into a distinct kind of historical explanation an account of the way normative notions can begin to lose their grip, are experienced with weakening authority, and that explanation counts crises like incompatible commitments or tragic dilemmas as arising from *within* the community's own experiences, and not because a new case has contingently arisen. It is possible that some of these crises arise from trying to apply a familiar norm to a new, problematic case, but in almost all the significant cases in his *Phenomenology*, that is not so and the account of the underlying crisis points to the developmental account of the relation between freedom and authority that makes up the basic "plot" of that book. Contemporary concept-appliers are not, in other words, guided only by past cases, constrained too by being subject to future judges. For the most part the nature of normative authority itself is up for grabs, and the Burkean,

Whiggish claim at any point that such authority is best understood as transmitted by history, exercising authority over the present, would have to count as an *episode* in that contestation, and could not count as the general *form* of any such contestation.

Notes

1 Brandom is, I think, profoundly right to say that for Hegel the realm of the geistig, the spiritual, is "the normative order." Robert Brandom, "Reason, Expression and the Philosophic Enterprise," in C.P. Ragland and Sarah Heidt (eds), *What Is Philosophy?* (New Haven, Conn.: Yale University Press, 2001), pp. 74–95, p. 94. See also Robert Pippin, "Naturalness and Mindedness: Hegel's Compatibilism," *The European Journal of Philosophy*, 1999, vol. 7, pp. 194–212; Robert Brandom, *Making It Explicit: Reasoning, Representing and Discursive Commitment* (Cambridge, Mass.: Harvard University Press, 1994), pp. 30 ff. and 624 ff.

2 Robert Brandom, *Tales of the Mighty Dead: Historical Essays in the Metaphysics of Intentionality* (Cambridge, Mass.: Harvard University Press, 2002), hereafter referred to in the text as TMD. Brandom understands philosophical texts in a way consistent with his way of understanding understanding: the meaning of these texts is a matter of inferentially articulated commitments; we understand what a concept in a particular text means by seeing how it is used by an author, what moves it licenses and what it prescribes, and how it would be understood (used) in the community at the time. Or, in a different approach, we can try to understand how an original concept would be used in a later context, such as ours. In this latter case, one is concerned not with what the author took to follow from her premises, but with what really *does* follow. One can focus on what the conceptual content is *about*; what the author must be committed to if truth is to be preserved, given what one now knows, or given what logical expressive resources one now has. This is roughly what Brandom means by the difference between interpretations or "specifications of conceptual content," or "discursive scorekeeping," *de dicto* and *de re*, and his importation here of his own semantic arsenal, with its core distinction between undertaking and attributing commitments, serves his hermeneutical purposes very well. As the magisterial Chapter Eight of *Making It Explicit* argues, these two specifications are not ascriptions of different beliefs, beliefs with different contents. They "specify the single conceptual content of a single belief in two different ways, from two different perspectives, in two different contexts of auxiliary commitments." Cf. R. Brandom, *Tales of the Mighty Dead*, p. 102.

3 R. Brandom, *Tales of the Mighty Dead*, p. 111.

4 Noam Chomsky, *New Horizons in the Study of Language and Mind* (Cambridge: Cambridge University Press, 2000), p. 146. See also Richard Rorty's very valuable (non-Hegelian) response to such worries in R. Rorty, "The Brain as Hardware, Culture as Software," *Inquiry*, 2004, vol. 47, pp. 219–35.

5 Chomsky of course means that holist, conceptual-role linguists would have to be committed to a natural scientific theory of everything, that their version of language would not leave a discrete research program for modern neuro-linguists.

6 R. Brandom, *Tales of the Mighty Dead*, p. 114.

7 This question of "responsibility" to the text is a tricky problem to raise since however one raises it, one can seem to be insisting on some kind of *priority* for *de dicto* interpretation, and that is not, I think, what Brandom means. This assumption would take us back to thinking of original or core meaning as locked up inside a text, instead of in the process-like, inferential way proposed by Brandom. *De re*

interpretation is something *else*, something different, and equally respectable philosophically. Once Strawson, say, has discarded the problem of the justification of synthetic a priori judgments and Kant's idealist claim that we only know appearances, there is not much in his *de re* reconstruction that Kant could have acknowledged as a commitment. But there is *something* of Kant left after the "selection" and "supplementation," something of what *Kant* really looks like in the new context of Strawsonean descriptive metaphysics. What is left is the distinction between concepts and intuitions, the discursivity of the human intellect, and the idea of there being "bounds" to any experience we could make sense of. *De re* interpretation is a process, a way of navigating in *our* territory, but guided by *some* insight of an historical author. So even within interpretation understood this way, there must *be* this guidance, this responsiveness to, say, *Hegel's* understanding of conceptual content, even when expressed throughout in a non-Hegelian, new "logical expressive" vocabulary. (This is already a version of a common and very sweeping intuitive reaction to Brandom's inferentialism: that understanding the content of a concept cannot be exclusively understanding its inferential articulations since those material implications and incompatibilities must themselves be already guided by (are legitimated by appeal to) a grasp of something which directs such inferential processes. He has several ways of responding to this and the issue will come up frequently below.)

8 R. Brandom, *Making It Explicit*, hereafter referred to in the text as MIE.

9 Sometimes idealism is simply another word for philosophy, sometimes (it is claimed) it is invoked to attack any ontological commitment to finite particulars (cf. G.W.F. Hegel, *Hegel's Science of Logic*, trans. A.V. Miller (New York: Humanities Press, 1969), pp. 154–55; G.W.F. Hegel, *Wissenschaft der Logik*, vols I and II (Hamburg: Felix Meiner, 1969), p. 145); sometimes (it is claimed) it means a Platonic claim that all of reality is actually a manifestation of "the Absolute Idea."

10 In Hegel's radical language, concepts are "self-determining." He is forever saying that the Concept gives itself its own content. See R. Pippin, "Die Begriffslogik als die Logik der Freiheit," in Anton Koch, Alecander Overauer and Konrad Utz (eds), *Der Begriff als die Wahrheit: Zum Anspruch der Hegelschen Logik* (Paderborn/München: Ferdinand Schöningh, 2003), pp. 223–37.

11 For a much fuller defense of such views, especially with regard to the role of singular terms, see Chapter Six of Brandom, *Making It Explicit*. The great advantage of Brandom's way of formulating the issue of idealism is that it demystifies the notion of a normative fact. See Brandom, *Making It Explicit*, p. 625, and especially Jürgen Habermas, "From Kant to Hegel: On Robert Brandom's Pragmatic Philosophy of Language," *European Journal of Philosophy*, 2000, vol. 8, 322–46 and Brandom's reply in R. Brandom, "Facts, Norms, and Normative Facts: A Reply to Habermas," *European Journal of Philosophy*, 2000, vol. 8, 356–68.

12 G.W.F. Hegel, *The Difference Between Fichte's and Schelling's Systems of Philosophy*, trans. H. Harris and W. Cerf (Albany, N.Y.: State University of New York Press, 1977), p. 80; G.W.F. Hegel, *Differenz des Fichte'schen und Schelling'schen Systems der Philosophie*, in Rheinisch-Westfaelischen Akademie der Wissenschaften (ed.), *Gesammelte Werke*, vol. IV (Hamburg: Felix Meiner, 1968), p. 6.

13 There is a form of reference dependence in Brandom's fuller account, but it is, as he says, "asymmetrical." There could not be concept-wielding, judging subjects unless reality were conceptually articulated in the way Brandom proposes; but not vice versa.

14 These terms are all relative. Brandom's version is much stronger than Kant's in another sense, since he understands the inferential practices on which object talk (symmetrically) depends to be social in nature, to involve commitments undertaken and attributed to one by others. That is how he interprets Hegel's sweeping remarks

linking the structure of the subject with the structure of *der Begriff*. Cf. R. Brandom, *Tales of the Mighty Dead*, pp. 216 ff.

15 Put in a strictly Kantian way, on Brandom's account it would seem that we could get by with an "empirical deduction" (indeed a somewhat historically open-ended account, without a firm distinction between pure and empirical concepts), and not require a "transcendental deduction." And when Hegel calls the *Phenomenology* a "deduction" of the standpoint of philosophical science he seems to have more in mind than this general dependence claim.

16 G.W.F. Hegel, *The Phenomenology of Spirit*, trans. A.V. Miller (Oxford: The Clarendon Press, 1977), p. 51; G.W.F. Hegel, *Die Phänomenologie des Geistes* (Hamburg: Felix Meiner, 1999), p. 57.

17 R. Brandom, *Tales of the Mighty Dead*, p. 26.

18 See his introductory chapter in TMD: "Five Conceptions of Rationality," for a lapidary summary, as well as R. Brandom, *Articulating Reasons: An Introduction to Inferentialism* (Cambridge, Mass.: Harvard University Press, 2000).

19 A qualification here that introduces an issue too large for this context. Many times what Hegel means by "Das Wahre ist das Ganze" is not holism in Brandom's sense but completeness, what the German literature discusses as the "Abgeschlossenheit" of Hegel's system. This involves the claim that for a kind of concept (let us say, whatever sort is the subject of the *Science of Logic)*, full determinacy (and we can never be satisfied with anything else) requires understanding the *complete* inferential articulations of any concept in a system that is itself complete or closed. (See Hegel, *Wissenschaft der Logik*, vol. II, p. 486; Hegel, *Hegel's Science of Logic*, p. 826.) Brandom has (wisely, I think) relaxed that requirement, but as noted at the outset, there is still some sense in which Hegel ties a theory of linguistic meaning to a "theory of everything."

20 R. Brandom, *Tales of the Mighty Dead*, p. 183.

21 Ibid., p. 187.

22 See the discussion of empirical concepts in the second half of Chapter Four of R. Pippin, *Kant's Theory of Form: An Essay on the "Critique of Pure Reason"* (New Haven: Yale University Press, 1982). See also John McDowell's criticism of Brandom on concept determinacy in J. McDowell, "Comment on Robert Brandom's 'Some Pragmatist Themes in Hegel's Idealism'," *European Journal of Philosophy*, 1999, vol. 7, 90–93.

23 That is, to use Brandom's illustration: Modus ponens does not instruct you that from "If *p*, then *q*; and *p*;" you should conclude *q*. You might have better reasons for not concluding *q*. Modus ponens only expresses a logical relation that constrains what we should do (never: all of *p*; if *p*, then *q*; and ~*q*).

24 R. Brandom, *Tales of the Mighty Dead*, p. 192.

25 Ibid., p. 206. "Construed as immediate" already begins to give the game away.

26 Ibid., p. 224.

27 There is such an account in Sellars but it depends on two notions – picturing and analogy – that are best worked out in Wilfred Sellars, *Science and Metaphysics: Variations on Kantian Themes* (New York: Humanities Press, 1968).

28 R. Brandom, *Tales of the Mighty Dead*, p. 366.

29 Ibid.

30 Ibid., pp. 366–67.

31 Ibid., p. 367.

32 Cf. Hegel's remark: "die Kantischen Formen der Anschauung und die Formen des Denkens gar nicht als besondere isolirte Vermögen auseinander liegen, wie man es sich gewöhnlich vorstellt. Eine und eben diesselbe synthetische Einheit . . . ist das Princip des Anschauens und des Verstandes" (Hegel, *Wissenschaft der Logik*, vol. II, p. 327). An obvious concession here: this – "a fuller, more adequate picture, etc." – is easy to say, harder to do. Brandom has made clearer than anyone has just how

tricky and complicated are the issues in perceptual knowledge, singular reference, and modality that have to be faced in an inferentialist, rationalist, social pragmatist position, whether it be Hegel's or Brandom's.

33 This is roughly the kind of issue that arises in the exchanges between Brandom and John McDowell. McDowell typically challenges the notion of self-legislation by claiming, "The sense in which the source of the norms is in us is just that the norms are constitutive of the practice of thinking, and the practice of thinking is not optional for us" (John McDowell, "Autonomous Subjectivity and External Constraint," manuscript, p. 16, presented at a conference in Münster, Germany). But the complaint that any "legislator" is guided by the very norms of rationality that supposedly first have to be "conferred," can arise from any number of directions. Thus Habermas, "From Kant to Hegel," p. 24. I do not believe that Hegel is subject to this charge of paradox. See the reference in the following endnote.

34 R. Brandom, *Tales of the Mighty Dead*, p. 32.

35 Ibid., p. 220.

36 I have defended this interpretation of post-Kantian philosophy in several papers since the later 1990s, especially in the Dotterer lecture at Penn State, "On Giving Oneself the Law." That paper has appeared in German as Pippin, "Über Selbstgesetzgebung," *Deutsche Zeitschrift für Philosophie*, 2003, Bd. 6, 905–26. See also R. Pippin, "Fichte's Alleged One-Sided, Subjective, Psychological Idealism," in Sally Sedgwick (ed.), *The Reception of Kant's Critical Philosophy. Fichte, Schelling and Hegel* (Cambridge: Cambridge University Press, 2000); R. Pippin, "The Realization of Freedom: Hegel's Practical Philosophy," in Karl Ameriks (ed.), *The Cambridge Companion to German Idealism* (Cambridge: Cambridge University Press, 2000); and most recently in Pippin, "Die Begriffslogik als die Logik der Freiheit." These are all preliminary chapters in a forthcoming book, *Hegel's Practical Philosophy: Rational Agency as Ethical Life*. See also R. Pinkard, *German Philosophy: 1760–1860. The Legacy of Idealism* (Cambridge: Cambridge University Press, 2002) for a narrative of German philosophy that tracks developments in and responses to such an issue.

37 Nicholas Smith (ed.), *Reading McDowell: Essays on Mind and World* (New York and London: Routledge, 2002), p. 277. I have a more detailed response to McDowell's worries in R. Pippin, "Postscript: On McDowell's Response to 'Leaving Nature Behind'," in R. Pippin, *The Persistence of Subjectivity: On the Kantian Aftermath* (Cambridge: Cambridge University Press, 2005).

38 This is one reason why Brandom's invocation of Pufendorf and the strong "imposition" metaphor, like a "cloak thrown over its [the natural world's] nakedness," is, from a Hegelian point of view misleadingly subjectivist. Cf. R. Brandom, *Making It Explicit*, p. 48.

39 R. Brandom, *Tales of the Mighty Dead*, p. 219.

40 Ibid., p. 221.

41 Ibid.

42 John Haugeland, "Heidegger on Being a Person," *Noûs*, 1982, vol. 16, 15–26.

43 Hegel, that is, believes that participants in historical communities can come to suffer in some distinct way from unreason, what Brandom calls incompatible commitments, and that this sort of suffering can explain the most important conceptual-normative change and can explain it as progressive (where it can). He thinks that appeals to reason have a social power that needs to be distinguished from the mere exercise of social power parading as adequate reason, even if philosophers can only do so retrospectively.

44 For Brandom intentionality is derivative of, it depends for its explanation on, normativity. This normativity is understood as a deontic matter, of normative statuses instituted by deontic attitudes. The dependence of norms on institution or imposition resulting *from such attitudes* is normative phenomenalism. This much – that

normative statuses such as commitments are products of social practical attitudes – is not being disputed. The claim is that they cannot *just* be such products, full stop. For the content of the attitudes also needs to be explained, and for Hegel that will lead to a claim about the priority of "objective spirit" over "subjective spirit," or the priority of "institutions of meaning." Something counts as a gift not just because of the attitudes of the participants sustaining the institution of gift-giving, since those attitudes already reflect the institutional rules for the practice into which individuals have been socialized.

45 It is open to Brandom to concede freely that score-keeping practices can break down, change, etc. But if that is all we have to say about it this looks like something that happened *to* the participants, rather than something they did; did to themselves and for an end. The former may be all we can finally say, but the latter is Hegel's narrative ambition.

46 For Brandom's differentiation of himself from verificationism, see Brandom, *Making It Explicit*, pp. 121 ff. Making use of Dummett's distinction, Brandom claims that they, the verificationists, are right to tie meaning to circumstances under which a term can be employed but they neglect that the appropriate consequences of its use are also as relevant.

47 This is another book length theme with respect to Brandom's Hegel interpretation. Hegel does speak of "an I that has become a we," but he does not mean by that that what a "community" as a matter of fact takes to be true or right or obligatory is thereby the criterion of truth or right or obligatory or good for any individual "I," which is what Brandom is worried about in "I–We" talk.

48 R. Brandom, *Making It Explicit*, p. 632.

49 Ibid., p. 601. See also G. Rosen, "Who Makes the Rules Around Here?" *Philosophy and Phenomenological Research*, 1997, vol. LVII, 163–71; and Brandom's response in R. Brandom, "Replies," *Philosophy and Phenomenological Research*, 1997, vol. LVII, 189–204.

50 R. Brandom, *Making It Explicit*, p. 597.

51 Ibid.

52 Again, I hope it is clear that this does not accuse Brandom of what he has called "regularism," the reduction of norms to mere regularities in a practice. We can understand the difference between appeals to norms and summarizing "how we mostly go on" (for example, the latter can only in very odd circumstances be *offered* to someone as a reason and, in Brandom's language, commitments must be understood as instituted by proprieties of scorekeeping, not by actual scorekeeping), all while still remaining confused about how to differentiate appealing to an authoritative norm, and merely seeming to.

53 There are various ways of cashing out this notion of actualization. One would be the more traditional pragmatist emphasis on a kind of "coping successfully with reality" test, where, armed with various cognitive claims, one fails to achieve practical ends; this is the paradigm case for an empirical learning experience. See Habermas, "From Kant to Hegel," p. 330. There are a lot of false positives in this approach but in general it is closer to Hegel's approach than Brandom's, as in Hegel's Jena writings on labor, the account of desire in the *Phenomenology*, and the required transition between observing and practical reason in the Reason chapter there.

54 R. Brandom, *Making It Explicit*, p. 588.

55 Many of Hegel's arguments for the priority of sociality are familiar by now. Participation in a certain form of social life is *transformative* as well as instrumentally useful, and so there is too great a contrast between what an individual becomes by such participation, and what he would have been without it, for the pre-institution individual to serve as a standard for the rationality and authority of the institution.

Such social institutions are also originally *formative* of individual identities, and so would be conditions for the possible development even of rational egoists and rational egoist "culture" and so cannot be viewed as the product, even ideally, of such individuals. And the institutions necessary instrumentally to protect and guarantee individual egoism or conscience-following cannot *themselves* be sustained effectively without relations of trust and solidarity that cannot be supported on considerations of individualist interest or individual conscience. Cf. Rousseau, *Social Contract*, I.8, and R. Pippin, "Hegel on Institutional Rationality," *The Southern Journal of Philosophy*, 2001, vol. XXXIX, Supplement, "The Contemporary Relevance of Hegel's Philosophy of Right."

56 R. Brandom, *Making It Explicit*, p. 163, my emphasis.

57 See Brandom on Dummett on *Boche*, Brandom, *Making It Explicit*, pp. 126 ff. Brandom is right that the explicative task of philosophy can help make clear that the consequences implied by the use of a term (like *Boche*) betray materially bad inferences (that all Germans are unusually aggressive and war like), but he appeals here to an inference that everyone (or most everyone) would agree is simply empirically false. By and large that is not what is "discovered" or what is relevant in a claim that the status of a lord, or the nature of honor, or the private ownership of capital, all involve materially bad inferences, as if the badness of the inference can be discovered in this empirical sense. Even with *Boche*, it is highly unlikely that the use of the term became inappropriate when its empirical falsity was finally displayed.

58 There is a parallel here to a remark Brandom makes in *Articulating Reasons*, that "I have managed to say a lot about conceptual content in this essay, without talking at all about what is represented by such contents." Cf. R. Brandom, *Articulating Reasons*, p. 77. One might say that Brandom has managed to say a lot about the social administration of norms without telling us much about what a norm is (what it materially excludes) or what a society or social administration is.

59 R. Brandom, *Tales of the Mighty Dead*, p. 219.

60 There are also passages in TMD that give one pause for thought about the firmness of the distinction between nature and norm, fact and ought. In the essay on Sellars, he suggests that responsiveness to norms can be assimilated into, are just another manifestation of, reliable differential responsive dispositions, causally elicited, not the acknowledgement of what there is reason to say. See p. 360 of TMD:

> Besides these language entry moves, the language learner must also master the inferential moves in the vicinity of 'green': that the move to 'colored' is OK, and the move to 'red' is not, and so on. Training in these basic language-language moves consists in acquiring more RDRDs, only now the stimuli, as well as the responses, are utterances.

This sounds like Quine at his most behaviorist, not anything to do with Kant or Hegel. But see the bottom of p. 626 of MIE on irreducible normativity. Does a trained-up language-language move that is essentially triggered by an utterance-stimulus count as a normative commitment?

61 R. Brandom, *Tales of the Mighty Dead*, p. 221.

62 Ibid., p. 388.

63 Antigone and Creon both agree that there is a divine law and a human law and that each should stick to its proper place. Their disagreement is both "material" and not one of brute otherness, but it is nonetheless tragic. They are both right, as Hegel reads it.

64 The Fred Astaire–Ginger Rogers "dance" of sociality, with entwined, shared commitments, while allowing each his or her own different moves, the particularity of each, is the image Brandom sometimes evokes. See the exchange with Habermas.

65 Brandom is certainly willing to state that the entire community may be wrong about what commitments they are entitled to, and that if so, this can only be wrong "by their own lights," "wrong given how they have committed themselves to its being proper to settle such questions and assess the answers." This is in footnote 29 to Chapter Three of MIE, on p. 674. But Hegel does not treat this as something discoverable by an outside interpreter. He (Hegel) wants to understand what goes wrong *in* the actual game of giving and asking for reasons when things begin to "go wrong by their own lights," how that "going wrong" experience plays a role in the establishment of what going rightly would be.

66 R. Brandom, "Selbstbewusstsein und Selbst-Konstitution," in Christoph Halbig, Michael Quante and Ludwig Siep (eds), *Hegels Erbe* (Frankfurt am Main: Suhrkamp Verlag, 2004), pp. 46–77.

67 He does, in "Selbstbewusstsein und Selbst-Konstitution" note that a commitment, especially a basic, or identity-constituting commitment, is the sort of thing one will have to make sacrifices for, but he treats the story of a risk of life as a "metonymy" for this sacrifice.

68 It is not clear to me why, on Brandom's premises, he feels entitled to this flat-out claim about "overgeneralization." Suppose as a matter of empirical fact that all the other score-keepers *agree* that the Master is fully entitled to constitute himself as he will. What justifies Brandom's claim to "overgeneralization"?

69 Brandom, "Facts, Norms, and Normative Facts: A Reply to Habermas," p. 360.

70 R. Brandom, *Making It Explicit*, p. 178.

71 R. Brandom, *Tales of the Mighty Dead*, p. 226.

72 Ibid., p. 227.

73 Ibid., p. 229.

74 Ibid., p. 231.

75 Brandom calls this aspect of his project "semantic externalism." See R. Brandom, "From a Critique of Cognitive Internalism to a Conception of Objective Spirit: Reflections on Descombes's Anthropological Holism," *Inquiry*, 2004, vol. 47, 236–53, p. 250, for an interesting application of the notion.

76 R. Brandom, *Tales of the Mighty Dead*, p. 234.

77 Moreover, the common law practice is under-described here. By some accounts, what a contemporary judge is trying to do in applying precedent to a new sort of case is to keep faith with an underlying moral principle, the same one animating the earlier decisions, presumably. By other accounts, when the question is what a decider of the earlier case "would now find rational," the model of rationality is something like "insuring that everyone will be better off, in an economic sense." In other cases, one tries very hard simply to imagine what a constitution framer or earlier judge would himself (that real person) actually decide now.

78 Hegel, *The Phenomenology of Spirit*, para. 215.

79 I assume it is obvious that Brandom's anti-realist, rationalist, constructivist account of norms in general will, if believed or "actualized" (*verwirklicht*), have all sorts of implications in the real world, from daily social practices to the law (where his position again sounds like legal positivism).

Part IV

Recognition and Agency

8

RECOGNITION AND EMBODIMENT

(Fichte's Materialism)

J.M. Bernstein

Recognizing the human

In his *Foundations of Natural Right*, J.G. Fichte offers the first interpretation of rights as modes of recognition. One possesses a right insofar as one is accorded a certain status – that of an individual – through the manner in which one is treated, acted upon, by others. What makes rights forms of recognition is that one has a certain status and standing in the world, for oneself and for others, only through how some of those others or the collective body representing them act toward you. Rights are not possessed; they are given, bestowed, granted by others – albeit for reasons. The giving, bestowing, granting of a status is how one is recognized. Because rights are items bestowed, then they are only concretely had when formalized into laws backed by the coercive powers of a political state. Rights, then, demarcate the series of modes of action and entitlement one must possess in order to have a certain status, and being recognized as having a certain status, e.g. as a citizen, is how one acquires access to those modes of action and entitlement. Political right is interpreted in this manner by Fichte because he regards being recognized as a free and rational being by others who one in turn recognizes as free and rational beings as a necessary condition for one becoming a self-determining agent in the world. One achieves the status of being a full-fledged human being only through being recognized, and hence being recognized as a self-conscious agent is at least in part constitutive of what it is to be a self-conscious agent. Rights are recognitions because they secure one's standing as a self-determining subject, where being a self-determining subject is itself a product of being recognized and recognizing in turn. In brief, that is the structure of Fichte's argument.

What distinguishes Fichte's theory of right from competing recognitive theories is that it aims at an integration of the recognitive and the bodily material. The opening arguments of *Foundations* forward two central theses: first, a "finite rational being cannot ascribe to itself a free efficacy in the sensible world without also ascribing such efficacy to others, and thus without also presupposing the existence of other finite rational beings outside of itself" (p. 29)[1] – think of this as the commencement of Fichte's transcendental dissolution of the problem of other minds.[2] Second is the thesis that a rational being cannot posit itself as an individual – the object of the first thesis – without ascribing to itself a material body, where to so ascribe a body to itself requires simultaneously positing it as "standing under the influence of a person outside him" (p. 58). The first thesis presupposes the second: to posit oneself as one among others presupposes being an embodied being among other embodied beings who can mutually influence one another causally and intentionally. Self-consciousness is thus just as much inter-bodily as intersubjectively constituted. While there are curiosities galore in Fichte's defense of both theses, because in obvious and, I shall argue, unobvious ways he is seeking to materialize idealism, to provide an account of recognition and rights that fully acknowledges the material conditions of everyday life, his project is worth further detailing. That Fichte, who is often regarded as the arch subjective idealist without concern for the human body, should be forwarding a radically social and material conception of human experience should, at the very least, suggest that our conception of his philosophy wildly betrays its actuality.

After providing a brief discussion of what Fichte intends by providing a transcendental conception of right, I will examine each of his two core theses in turn.

Rights, proto-rights, norms

In a letter to Reinhold in August, 1795, Fichte argues that in order to consider myself a finite a subject, I must not only think of myself as determining a sphere of things regulated by mechanical laws of cause and effect, but must also think of myself "as *determined* in a realm of rational beings outside of myself ... There can be no individual unless there are at least two of them. *The conditions which make individuality possible* are called '*rights*.'"[3] Fichte is here beginning to explore the thought that actual self-consciousness, one's *empirical* awareness of oneself as a self-determining subject, is only possible if one is brought to self-consciousness – one must, in some constitutive sense, be determined by other individuals to become an individual. Persons are made, not born. Fichte calls the act by which I am determined by the other, by which I am called to freedom by the other, the "summons." Toward the end of §3 in which he has been discussing the summons of the other in quite abstract and formal terms, he suddenly baldly states that "The summons to engage in free self-activity is what we call up-bringing [*Erziehung*; education]. All individuals must be brought up to be human beings, otherwise they would not be human beings" (p. 38). Hence, what first appears as an abstract empirical condition of individuality is given empirical specificity: the summons, and the connecting of freedom to embodiment are products of childhood development.

How Fichte means to connect his transcendental conception of right with ordinary political rights is deeply problematic.[4] However, it is evident that throughout the early paragraphs of *Foundations* Fichte interprets the necessary conditions for the possibility of self-consciousness as involving some form of genetic analysis. That the analysis requires a genetic dimension follows from the role of the summons: an individual can ascribe self-consciousness to itself only by having its individuality recognized – summoned – by other beings whom the recognized subject in turn recognizes to be free. Demonstrating the necessary conditions for free agency thus involves demonstrating what conditions must be realized for free agency to be actual, that is, what conditions *must come to be* in order for free agency to manifest itself. The best evidence for this claim is that the human infant is born pre-maturely and becomes a person. Fichte assumes that evidence in his analysis (p. 76). We should take Fichte at his word here, interpreting and reconstructing the transcendental portion of his argument as sketching out an ideal process of socialization that is targeted on the child acquiring a minimum conception of individuality, a conception that could be understood as indifferent to the actual ideals and values of different societies while nonetheless being sufficient to underwrite the normative structures necessary to preserve the minimum core of individuality in any conceivable society.[5] Let us call such norms "proto-rights."

Proto-rights are obviously not political rights or explicit moral norms or actual values, although they may overlap with any of these; rather, they are the normative scaffolding that emerges in developmental sequences terminating in individuals capable of acting in the world and interacting with other individuals.[6] Behind the notion of proto-rights lies the thought that the structures of right through which individuals are recognized as individuals track the functional imperatives necessary in order for infants to become individuals. In this respect, one might say that transcendental necessity tracks functional necessity. But to say that transcendental necessity tracks the functional imperatives of an ideal process of socialization is not to reduce norms to functional demands. On the contrary, and this is patently Fichte's quasi-naturalist thought, his way of connecting idealism and materialism, norms (actual structures of right, however implicit or explicit) are the way in which functional imperatives become satisfied for free and rational beings whose modes of interaction with the world, with things and other rational beings, are not governed by instinct but by rule-governed, purposive actions. Proto-rights are value-contoured modes of other-regarding attitudes (sufficient for guiding action) and practical norms that condense the series of conditions necessary for becoming a self-moving, independent being capable of interaction with others and objects in a manner sufficient to meet survival imperatives. Proto-rights as the normative grid that must be satisfied by any actual society capable of reproducing itself, that is, capable of reproducing the life of self-determining individuals, can thus be understood as the transcendental outline of the recognitive structures making human life possible. I take it, this is what Fichte intends when he reprises his defense of right thus:

> it has been shown that a certain concept [X] . . . is necessary for the rational being as such . . . This X must be operative wherever human

> beings live together, and it must be expressed and have some designation in their language. It is operative on its own, without any help from the philosopher, who deduces this X with difficulty (pp. 49–50)

As this passage makes evident, Fichte intends transcendental right to be something that is uncovered or discovered as necessarily underlying all actual viable social worlds. Hence, its deduction should demonstrate why proto-rights have the role they do, and not why they ought to be adopted or obeyed or valued.

In claiming that proto-rights are a transcendental grid representing the minimum necessary conditions for individuality empirically and normatively for any possible society, I am simultaneously claiming that Fichte's actual way of connecting transcendental right and political right is insufficient. His theory of political right would need to become the demonstration that the rights of the liberal state are the fullest expression and the most adequate means "for the realization and flourishing"[7] of the minimum conception of individuality developed in the transcendental portion of his argument. It is doubtful that his concrete conception of the liberal state can stand up to that claim; but that is an argument for another occasion.

Individuality (I): the socialconstitution of freedom

The object of §§ 1–7 of *Foundations* is the transcendental elaboration of the minimum necessary conditions for individuality – and not moral autonomy or self-realization or self-perfection. Individuality is a more modest concept of the subject compared to these others. Let us, then, genetically examine some of the central steps in the becoming of the individual. In order to be a free and rational being one must be a self-determining being; hence, the self is defined by its activity. To be an agent is, minimally, to carry out doings in accordance with ideas in mind, imprinting on a world that is independent of one those ideas through intended actions. Agency and world are internally correlative: the infant learns what its powers are as it learns how objects can and cannot be altered.

Fichte contends that coming to awareness of one's agency through awareness of one's ability to bring about changes in the external world, while certainly an awareness of individual powers, is not yet awareness of oneself as self-determining. In the exchange between efficacious willing and object "the subject's free activity is posited as constrained" (p. 31), i.e. efficacious willing presumes only knowledge of what one is able to do or not able to do. There is nothing in this account of awareness of the self as a powerful agent that might not be ascribed to the learning sequences of higher non-human mammals. Fichte supposes that no elaboration of agency in the sense already established can bootstrap the individual into self-consciousness of its freedom. Self-consciousness cannot be transcendentally deduced or causally produced; it is transferred from one individual to another. The presumption here is that in order for an individual to be fully self-aware, it must become an object of its own awareness. To be self-aware *as object* requires that an individual first actually be the object of another's attention. But it must be the object of another's attention as a self-active subject. That, so to speak, is the puzzle: how can an object of awareness be simultaneously, as object, subject? The scene of this transforming transference in which the "thread of self-consciousness" is passed from one to another is a "summons [*Aufforderung*]." Because Fichte intends the summons to displace Kant's fact of reason, then it must be that through which the neophyte becomes aware of its freedom. And this is just how Fichte conceives the scene of instruction occurring: the beginner experiences a sensation coming from without:

> The object is not comprehended, and cannot be other than as a bare summons calling upon the subject to act. Thus as surely as the subject comprehends the object, so too does it possess the concept of its own freedom and self-activity, and indeed as a concept given to it from the outside. It acquires the concept of its own free efficacy, not as something that *exists* in the present moment ... but rather as something that *ought* to exist in the future. (p. 32)

Recall that what is here presented as a single episode is in reality a process, the education of a human to its humanity. As an episode, it condenses the complex set of eventualities that the process of socialization involves. In the first instance, the summons is conceived as a "bare" summons; Fichte strips the summons of complexity in order to focus its status as summons, and not conceivably a determinate object.[8] The summons is an act of another. It is an act whose purpose is to elicit an action from the infant. But if the only purpose of the summons was to elicit a response, it would fall short of its task, namely, awakening the child to its own freedom and self-activity. So it is insufficient to say, for example, that mother smiles for the sake of having the infant smile in return since that exchange could be conceived as a movement from stimulus to response; and, in fact, mimetic activity, however truly intersubjective, does begin through automatic reflex actions that, we now think, begin in the first week of life. If actions inviting mimetic response are as "bare" as could be, then in thinking of the summons as bare, Fichte must be attempting to elicit a feature or structural aspect of agent-other interactions rather than a particular type of action. Indeed, as we shall see, Fichte comes to regard "every human interaction, not only the original one, [as having] the form of a summons, of reciprocal recognitions."[9] To think of the summons as a *form* belonging to all actual interactions (of a certain type) explains how it could come to displace Kantian morality in installing individuals into a normatively constituted sphere in which their standing as self-determining agents is inscribed.

What is missing from the smile begets smile scenario? The summons, Fichte contends, is essentially something which opens the possibility of refusal, of not acting, of saying "no," of negation (p. 33). In becoming aware that a summons may be responded to either by acceding to its requirements or by not acting and so demurring, the agent becomes aware that it is free to respond or not respond. But becoming aware of being free to respond or not respond is the beginning of the awareness that for such types of objects, summons-type objects, there is an indefinite number of different ways of responding, and hence there is no necessary way in which the action or non-action that will come to be must be. Awareness that one can say "yes" *or* "no" is the condition for awareness of the openness of the future; and the openness of the future is a condition of one's awareness that what one is to do, and hence how one is to be in relation to the one who summons, is all undetermined.

In order for an agent to be self-conscious it must find itself as object, but an active object; hence it must find itself determined to self-activity. The external check which determines the subject must nonetheless leave it in full possession of its freedom and elicit that freedom as object of awareness. An agent can be determined to exercise its efficacy only if it finds that efficacy is something it *could*, possibly, exercise in some future, or not. The summons, then, must open a field, the minimum structure of which is the yes/no choice of to act or not to act. A summons is a purposive action that determines but does not causally compel. Summonses involve the producing of a non-natural sign of some kind (linguistic or non-linguistic), a sign whose fundamental character is that it is intentionally produced in order that another respond intentionally to it, and the one to whom it is addressed respond on the basis of being invited to respond and to do so in a manner that enables the original summoner to understand that the response given is intended as a response to the original summons (pp. 36–37).[10] While mother's smile could be simply the trigger for generating a smile from the infant, in time it will come to be understood as an invitation to smile in return, and the return, be it a smile or (ironic) grimace or stone-faced refusal becomes an element in the bond connecting mother and child. It is because Fichte recognizes the complexity of this exchange that he reframes the scene of instruction into up-bringing, the becoming bound to community through the learning of non-natural modes of interaction.

Proto-rights: a first ppproach

How complex the material conditions are for non-causal modes of mutual influence we shall come to shortly. What is significant here is that Fichte deduces his concept of right directly from the conditions of mutual interaction, which is to say, again, that right is being proposed as the normative lining of that very process, its flip-side, what the sequence is as seen from a normative perspective. In order for mutual interactions to occur, the neophyte must assume that beside objects with causal powers there also exist rational beings, beings who summon it. And hence, for there to be human beings at all, "there must be more than one" (p. 37); all these are direct inferences from the existence of episodes of mutual interaction. In participating in such interactions, the neophyte must have a sense of its difference from the summoner, and further a sense of a space under its control within which it is free to choose – to say "yes" or "no." Originally, that sphere is that of the body as the material medium through which non-natural signs (words or gestures) are produced. Ignore the question of embodiment for the moment. The neophyte must come to recognize that in being summoned it is being given a "free space" in which to respond, and that to respond in kind it must likewise permit its other a free space.

What is meant by the neophyte comprehending the summons as the provision of a free space? It is the comprehension that another, non-summons type action was possible and not acted upon, and that a summons-type action was deliberately chosen. Instead of smiling or saying "smile," mother could, with teeth bared and hand raised in a preparation to strike, utter threateningly "Smile." This mode of action, while formally intentional and thus formally leaving open the possibility that the infant may not smile, does not presume that it is up to the infant as to whether it smiles or not; it must smile – or else. Even more forcibly, after threatening, mother might take the two corners of the infant's mouth and roughly lift them – "See, you know how to smile, don't you." A summons is not only something affirmative, a call to free activity; it is in part defined by not being the use of (causal) force. In the midst of a world in which its body is routinely having things done to it – fed, changed, carried, picked up, put down, etc. – summons-type activities emerge as a distinctive form of activity, ones that interact with the infant in a non-(merely)causal way, aiming to elicit a spontaneous response. So the infant becomes aware that it has the different kinds of powers (to change the world or summon another), and that which action it chooses is up to it.

Fichte states this as a double requirement: free actions toward the neophyte must be understood as done in relation to the always existing possibility of transgressing the neophyte's free space, and thus as a self-limiting of the will by the issuer of the summons (p. 41). Every summons, as the paradigm of free action, is self-limiting in that it involves the treatment of its object *as* a free, self-determining being, and the forgoing of the use of force (or its intentional equivalents: deceit or threat). Because every summons, as the form of every free human interaction, implies a use of force that has been forgone, that is, implies a choice has been made from within the sphere of one individual's freedom to take into consideration another's sphere of freedom by leaving a sphere of choice open to her, then every summons *qua* self-limiting action is a recognition of the other as a free and rational being. *To issue a summons is to accord the other a normative status* (to be treated as a rational being and not a thing), and therefore to act in ways consonant with the one summoned being given a status or standing as free, as if she had a right to such standing – "only the moderation of force by means of concepts is the unmistakable and exclusive criterion of reason and freedom" (p. 43).

Fichte contends that transcendental reflection as the recapitulation of the genetic sequence through which the beginner becomes self-conscious demonstrates that through the emergence of the difference between the two modes of interaction there emerges a structure of *normative expectations* connected to summons-type interactions (p. 43). What gives this structure of expectations its authority is that being acted upon by and acting on summons-type forms of interaction is the necessary condition for the coming to be of self-determining individuality, one the individual cannot initiate for herself, and one that she is utterly dependent upon her care-givers to provide. However, once summons-type interactions have been realized with respect to any individual, then the transgression of the implicit norms operative in an individual's standing as free and self-determining comes to be experienced as an injury, as the illicit crossing of a border or boundary, as coercion.

Roughly, then, Fichte is contending that processes sufficient to produce self-conscious agency must include socialization processes having summons-type structures. These processes, by the very way in which they solicit self-determination automatically, precipitate the emergence of what the neophyte experiences as boundaries or borders or limits concerning what is and what is not under her immediate control. All of which, as we shall see directly, entails that Fichte requires his notion of embodiment for his conception of right. One cannot have an awareness of the power to say "no" as a choice (and not simply as an immediate response) without having an awareness that one is, in some sense, entitled to say "no." Fichte's ascription of right to this structure, as proto-rights, is a way of flagging that the development of this structure of expectations is normative whilst not being explicitly moral. And this is why, again, Fichte feels entitled to claim that right, in the sense of a given structure of expectations that is realized by being approached through summons-type modes of action rather than narrowly causal modes of action, "must be operative wherever human beings live together" (p. 59).

Individuality (II): freedom as embodiment

If individuality is a "reciprocal concept," a concept that can be thought and applied only in a relation to another, a concept that thereby determines "community" (p. 45), then freedom must also be a reciprocal concept for Fichte. In claiming that summons-type actions are self-limiting, Fichte is not claiming, *pace* Hegel, that such actions are a "limitation of the true freedom of the individual";[11] rather he is stating that relations to the other are normatively constituted, those norms can be transgressed, and that acceding to them involves, beyond habit and passion, deliberation and choice. Freedom is, indeed, "enlarged" by community for Fichte in the obvious sense that self-conscious freedom, and hence true freedom, cannot exist outside community. Nonetheless, it might still be complained that Fichte's image of a *sphere* of freedom that is possessed and might be overstepped is, as yet, merely metaphorical; and hence, second, with the notion of sphere hazy, so are the ideas of transgressing and trespassing, on the one hand, and, conversely, self-limitation on the other.[12]

Fichte supposes that these queries can be silenced by the demonstration that individuality, as self-determining efficacy, presupposes the possession of a material body (§5), and that the possession of such a body necessarily involves being influenced by the body of another (§6), making embodiment too a "reciprocal concept."

Each of the theorems constituting Fichte's deduction of the body is a recapitulation of his original arguments for individuality, showing embodiment to be a condition of possibility for the efficacy and sociality of freedom. Fichte summarizes his argument for embodiment thus: "The material body we have derived is posited as the *sphere of all the person's possible free actions*, and nothing more. Its essence consists in this alone" (p. 56). In claiming that the body is "nothing more" than the sphere of a person's possible free actions, Fichte is transcendentally regimenting the meaning of the body to its role of being the pure means through which the will becomes efficacious in the world. How can a free will become efficacious in the world? At the very least, this presupposes that there must be something mediating the rational will with an idea in mind about the material world, and the material world. And one way of thinking of the body is as the mediating medium between will and world. But this cannot be right: if the body were only a mediating function between will (self-activity or the spontaneity of the intellect) and world, then the will would need a further mediator to attach it to the body, and so on. Hence, on pain of an infinite regress, the body cannot be merely an instrument or means through which willing achieves worldly efficacy. The notion of the body is, rather, what directly or immediately is at the behest of the will: "*Immediately* by means of his will, and without any other means, the person would have to bring forth in this body what he wills; something would have to take place within this body, *exactly* as the person willed it" (p. 56; italics mine). In opting for an immediate realization of the will in a bodily movement, Fichte is meaning to remove from action any idea of there being a mentalistic shadow world of "intendings" or "tryings" or "volitions" that are then realized in bodily actions. One raises one's arm – and nothing else.

Lucy O'Brien, in developing what can be taken as a neo-Fichtean theory of action, begins by reminding us that agents seem to be authoritative over their actions in a way they are not over others' actions, that our knowledge of our actions appears to be relatively spontaneous, given with the action itself, and that actions could not be what we suppose them to be unless they were relatively self-intimating.[13] Reconstructing a theory put forward some years ago by Arthur Danto in order to explain these features of action, O'Brien persuasively argues that there must be basic actions. Basic actions are those actions "that a subject can carry out directly without having to do anything else," that descriptions of basic actions will be "in terms of bodily movements" over which the subject is directly authoritative – actions like "raising my arm" or "lifting my foot." Without trying to document which actions are basic, O'Brien contends that we are justified in supposing that an agent "will have a non-conceptual grasp of the possible ways they can act, which are in this way basic."[14] Basic actions have a perfect Fichtean character: when an individual acts consciously, the actions she engages in are something she can control; the directness of her control over the action entails that she knows about the actions, knows what she is doing through the action, through participation, rather than through observation or reflection. Basic actions are instances of the I intuiting itself as active through or in some bodily movement. Basic actions require a demanding intimacy between will and body: the body is, from a transcendental perspective, the immediate expression of the will; hence basic actions provide an outline of the body – or what is the same, a schema of the will – as seen from the perspective of self-activity. Bodily movements that are the concrete descriptions of *basic actions give precision to the claim for the body being "nothing other than the sphere of the person's free actions*" (p. 56; italics mine).

Fichte would need to demur from O'Brien's account in only one respect: he does not believe there can be a definitive inventory of basic actions. His argument commences from the idea that there are an indefinite number of possible conceptually mediated, non-basic actions. Consider the complex actions that go along with highly elaborated bodily activities like dancing (doing a pirouette in ballet, or a shuffle hop in tap dancing); playing a musical instrument (the movement of the fingers involved in playing a piano versus playing a saxophone); using a tool (turning a screwdriver); performing surgery; playing a sport; not to speak of more mundane activities like cooking (slicing and dicing), writing, speaking, and singing. Assume, first, that there is no definitive end to the possibility of such complex activities, that new ones (X game sports, for example) are continually being invented. Second, for each complex action the body performs what is an independent, moving part of the body changes: for some actions one or more fingers move while the arm and shoulder remain steady, in others the whole arm moves while fingers and wrist are firm, while in still others the wrist and fingers move as the arm moves (say, in shooting a jump shot). The relation of the body to its parts is a whole/part relation, but one that continually changes relative to the complex action being performed. Finally, to say that the notion of part must be relativized to the complex action performed entails that while the precise range of basic motions a part performs is not infinite (there are severe physical/structural constraints), it is indefinite – the lifting, bending motion of the arm while flicking the wrist, the fingers waving forward, seems unimaginable apart from the activity of shooting a basketball. A body conforming to these three requirements is necessarily "articulated" (p. 58). A human body (*Leib*), then, is "a closed articulated whole ... within which we posit ourselves as a cause that acts immediately through our will" (p. 58).

Genetically, this is all to say that the infant acquires a consciousness of itself as efficacious in the world by having an idea in mind in virtue of having an awareness that it possesses a body that it discovers to be directly under its control, whose capacities are the condition through which it can realize its idea in the world. Making a rattle involves kicking the leg; hence necessary to discovering her will's freedom is discovering that she has a sphere of influence she directly controls, and without which she would be utterly disconnected from the world. She becomes herself, in part, through discovering the range of movements over which she has direct control and over which no one else has direct control. As basic actions become involved in more conceptually mediated actions, the range of possible movements she can perform becomes the mirror image of the objects existing outside her, their powers, and the nature of her power over them. The world as a system of objects is, in the first instance, the internal correlative of the active body. So being an individual requires positing the articulated body capable of basic actions as what makes free willing actual.

The intersubjective body

The body so understood is not a natural body, but rather, again, the body as understood from the transcendental perspective of making self-consciousness possible. This body is fully active. Hence, Fichte must now proceed to deduce the passive body, the body that is exposed to the influence of others, the body that has been summoned, giving both active and passive powers a transcendental denotation. Notoriously, this stretch of argument involves Fichte in distinguishing "higher" from "lower organs," and "subtle" from "coarse" matter. What is he supposing in proposing these distinctions? Only this: if a subject is summoned and so influenced by another, then unless we are to believe in telepathy or magic, the influence of one person upon another must be some form of material influence. There is no way in which another can effect my will except through my body; if not every influence upon my body is a direct causal restriction upon my powers of willing, that is, a way of either prohibiting or coercing certain bodily movements, then my body must have sensible organs that are not directly subject to the influence of solid matter, and there must be a kind of matter that can influence the body without causally restricting it. That, in a nutshell, is the argument.

Fichte was the first to admit that the details of his argument were less than adequate (p. 66n), but the underlying thesis looks persuasive. Fichte means to be replacing standard accounts of the interaction of mind and body with an account of two aspects of embodiment. In particular, he is attempting to understand how it is possible that my body can be "influenced" without being mechanically determined. Perceptual episodes are of this kind; in them there is a binding of my sensory apparatus that nonetheless leaves my higher sense free in its response:

> For example, if a shape in space is to be perceived by sight, then the feel of the object (i.e. the pressure that would have to be exerted in order to produce the shape by sculpting it) would have to be internally

> imitated . . .; but the impression in the eye, as the schema of such imitation, would be retained (p. 66)

Here there is a dialectic between the physical impression of the object on the eye and the imaginative taking up of that impression in a manner that could, but does not, become the active determination to produce a further like object. On this model, reception or (passive) understanding has the structure of an active repetition. And this should be familiar enough to us; for example, when one is learning to read one repeats the words out loud, saying them, only later learning, first, to inhibit speaking the words aloud, and then learning to inhibit one's mouth from moving until, finally, one simply reads. Fichte's thesis is that this represents a deep structure of understanding, with the movement from reception to active repetition to silencing the repetition happening at lightning speed in adults, but nonetheless happening still.

Equally, then, learning to hear understandingly (which is a component of learning to speak) initially involves hearing words said to one *by* saying them back; or grasping music by following the rhythm by moving a part of one's body in time or the melody by humming along. Fichte is hence giving to understanding as a learning process a bodily mimetic aspect as the necessary antecedent to purer processes of intellection. And while this passive-reception-becoming-active-repetition model probably works less well for visual perception – although Hogarth and Merleau-Ponty, among others, have argued that drawing an object is the closest approximation to capturing the process of visual understanding, and hence itself an active model for conceptual understanding generally[15] – what is being thought here is how material influence can incite activity rather than coerced motion or physical inhibition. Not surprisingly, Fichte takes the prime example of reciprocal interaction via moveable subtle matter to be speaking with one another (p. 71). What Fichte does here is make mimesis operate both as a feature of the relation between the subject and the world, and as part of the subject's self-relation, modeling the relation between the higher and lower senses after the mimetic exchanges between subject and subject, and subject and object. While there is obviously more than a mimetic relation between higher and lower organs, inner and outer senses, mimesis is crucial to learning, and hence pivotal in any genetic account of the development of self-consciousness.

By allowing there to be a dialectic between inner and outer sense, imaginative activity (as still sensible action) and outer bodily action, Fichte generates two forms through which the body is influenced and influences the world. Once these powers are in place, he can then rewrite the original scene of instruction in which the neophyte is awoken to self-consciousness of her freedom in appropriately material terms, each moment of the interaction now having a corresponding material character (pp. 64–65). The other will influence the beginner through material signs rather than physical force: smiling *as* an invitation to smile in return, or saying the physical sounds composing the word "smile."

For Fichte, words as composed of phonemes are a paradigm of sense-making. Making such sounds with the mouth gives the mouth its spiritual sense; just as directing those sounds to human hearing entails that the ears are material/spiritual organs. The mutual determination of the material and the meaningful is what Fichte means by an object having *Sinn*. What constitutes an individual as an individual is thus that it be able to effect the sensible world with movements whose medium has a density corresponding to the density of ordinary physical objects (in which case the body is an instrument of the will), and that it also can be approached through being an object of sense rather than a mere physical thing. The beginner must come to realize that in so being approached she could have been physically coerced rather than summoned, hence that she has capacity for summoning in turn (doing certain types of bodily movements: gesturing or speaking), and that the being that originally summoned and which is to be summoned in response has the same complex dual material character as she. Because reciprocal summons-type interactions deliberately forswear the use of physical force, then willing in this manner is self-limiting, and to act in a self-limiting manner is *a fortiori* to recognize the other as having the status of a rational being, where such recognition is equivalent to the other being accorded a right.

The details of Fichte's speculative psycho-physiology need not detain us. What is central is that the account permits him to satisfy both his desiderata: on the one hand, by insisting that the body's active and passive powers are intertwined (that the body is for itself both "instrument" and "sense [*Sinn*]"), he can reasonably argue that the human body is not just metaphorically but literally the minimum necessary "sphere" making freedom possible, that is, unless the neophyte is free to move her body through some large subset of the indefinite range of possibilities that its articulated character permits in response to need, desire, intention, and summons with respect to a culturally standard range of objects and persons she could not become self-conscious of herself as a self-determining individual. On the other hand, unless there were different aspects of embodiment, corresponding to the difference between solid and subtle matter, she could not be "influenced" by another in a manner that left her free to respond in the ways required by the summons. Hence, the recognition of another as a self-active subject is the recognition of a particular human body. Because the *human* body is in part constituted by its being treated as having sense, and has sense, finally, only in being so treated (summoned), then the human body is intersubjectively constituted, or what is the same, the human body is a reciprocal concept. Formally, this sounds very like the beginning of a solution to the problem of other minds, namely, the recognition of an other mind is the recognition of a certain kind of body. But this entails that the way in which the human body appears is the original bearer, the foundation of all human interconnectedness – or so Fichte contends.

The appearing body

To this juncture, Fichte's transcendental and genetic arguments lack a certain fit. From a transcendental perspective, he argues that:

> The presence of a body was inferred from the concepts of independence and freedom. But freedom exists only insofar as it is posited; and therefore, since what is grounded cannot extend beyond its ground, the body can exist only for one who posits it (p. 68)

The body cannot have the complex structures entailed by its dual character unless they are appropriately cognitively recognized – posited; only then does material difference take on normative significance. Conversely,

> I become a rational being – *actually*, not merely *potentially* – only by being *made* into one; if the other rational being's action did not occur, I would never have become rational. Thus my rationality depends on the free choice, on the good will, of another; it depends on chance, as does all rationality (p. 69)

I am a free being only by positing myself as one; I am a free being only by being made into one, which making is a matter of sheer contingency. Fichte's anxiety here is not that I have been made into a free being (the logic of the summons as the outline for an educative process is meant to answer the paradox of being made to be free), it is that the making itself is so utterly contingent that it undermines the claim for self-positing – each individual becomes merely the "accidental result" (p. 69) of another person's summons.

In order to avoid this result, Fichte must argue that there can be no misrecognition without recognition, however partial, and that recognition not be a matter of chance – there must be a ground for it. And this can be so "only by presupposing that the other was *compelled* already, in his original influence upon me, compelled as a rational being . . . to treat me as a rational being; and indeed he was compelled to do so by *me*" (p. 69), which would entail that even in the original scene there was at least something approximating reciprocal interaction. This sounds contradictory since Fichte is proposing that in the very scene in which I am made an individual by another, I am already summoning the other. Well, certainly not summoning her through anything I do, that is, not through engaging in summons-type activities for these as yet are unavailable to me. Against the background of the previous argument, we know where this is heading: since my independence and efficacy in the world are dependent upon my body, my body as the material inscription of my will making my individuality possible, then the appearing of my body on the scene is the manner in which I might exercise efficacy, "be active, without *me* exercising my efficacy through it" (p. 70).

In providing a deduction of the necessity of embodiment for self-consciousness, the body emerges as a series of active and passive powers and as a material object capable of a range of doings and undergoings, and thus as a being with sense. What is implausible is that on the basis of its powers this body should not have a distinctive form or appearance: there cannot be anything that satisfies those requirements that yet lacks sensible form. A living being capable of a certain range of activities must have a distinctive shape, a distinctive relation of whole and parts that enables it to carry out just those activities. From the opposing angle, we have already argued that the inventory of basic actions (that are to be read off from the expanding catalogue of complex actions) provides a schema of the human will – precisely, its *look*. So we have to imagine a being that can: speak, sing, eat, call, cry, scream, walk, run, jump, balance on one foot, make love (kiss, stroke, fondle), give birth, suckle its young, bow, do a triple Salchow, play the piano, dice onions, shoot an arrow, throw a boomerang, draw, write, knit, make funny faces, etc. The more fine-grained the list of actions, and hence basic actions, the more evident it is that the human body must have a specific shape, a particular organization of articulated whole and parts that enables it to perform this diverse range of activities. There may be another shape and organization of whole and parts made from another material that could do all this, but certainly till now nothing like it has ever been imagined. But if this is true, and the range of activities are the expression of the possession of a rational will, then the converse must hold as well: the human body's appearing just is the appearance of a rational being, that is, "this appearance of my body must be such that it cannot be understood or comprehended at all except under the presupposition that I am a rational being" (p. 71).

Above, in saying that the human body is the necessary appearance form of the human soul (freedom, the subject), I was functionally refashioning a dictum of Wittgenstein's; his original saying is the perfect complement to its derivative: "The human body is the best picture [*Bild*] of the human soul."[16] Form and function mutually entail one another, or, we might say, the transcendental specification of the material powers of the human body entail an aesthetic, a figuring of the human body. The human body with respect to both function and form is the *necessary image* of the human soul. Fichte's thesis presumes that what is specific about the human body is that its appearance form is intimately related to the actualization of its capacities for acting in the world, and hence to what it is as a worldly object. From this perspective, the aesthetics of the human body is not the relegation of the human to mere appearance, but the ever surprising shock that the mere appearing of the human body should demand an acknowledgement of this object in its rational, normative core.

What little detail Fichte provides here offers some indication of how his (transcendental) anthropology (p. 72) would work. The orienting premise of the argument is that the human is born prematurely, unlike the animal that is born "clothed," with the capacity for movement and provided with the instincts necessary for survival. Being born "naked" (p. 76) entails not just helplessness and absolute dependency on care-givers, but that the provisions for inhabiting the world that other animals have through their instincts, the human must acquire through processes that continue the detachment of the human from the determination of nature. Education is the process through which reason and culture compensate for what nature leaves absent; reason is thus a species-wide accomplishment that supplies the means for species reproduction as well as individual self-realization. All this I take to be standard fare.

The first functional/aesthetic upshot of prematurity is that the human animal does not possess a determinate set of (law-governed) action routines. Consequently, *the human body cannot be comprehended "through any determinate concept at all*"; while the animal body points to a determinate sphere of movements, the human must be capable of "all conceivable movements *ad infinitum* ... The articulation would ... [have] an infinite determinability ... the human being is only intimated and projected" (p. 74; italics mine). While these words certainly have an existentialist sound, they are meant to capture how the human body, when freed from a design dictated by narrow survival imperatives, must be open to realizing conceptualized possibilities of acting. But these possibilities are indefinitely open; hence, the body of the human must accommodate, enable, and express the open character of human self-understanding, the human capacity for self-making and self-fashioning, for being the vehicle and expression of the fact that human action is conceptually governed, and thereby indefinitely formable.

Fichte continues by analyzing the most perspicuous features of the human body: upright posture, arms and hands free from direct functional demands, the expressivity of the human face, especially eyes and mouth (pp. 77–78). What organizes and motivates these speculative constructions is the same principle that drove the preceding argument linking form and function: in each case the capacities of the human body to act in accordance with conceptual determinations entail a capacity for formability such that both conceptual content and the openness to re-formation are returned to the body as indelible features of its appearing. Indeed, it is precisely because the parts of the human body are necessarily freed from direct functional imperatives, that the body is an ongoing shifting of relations of whole and parts in relation to conceptually determined activities, that the shape of the body as a whole is completely material while not being determinate like other natural bodies. Isn't this just to say that, conversely, because in the specified sense it is not natural, not conceptually determinate, the human body *must* be conceived as the appearing of the human soul? What Fichte wants from his argument is, however partial, the acknowledgement that we cannot coherently describe or analyze the appearance of the human body without acknowledging these macro-aspects of its appearance: the broad range of activities that human beings do and how they do them must be visually manifest, however indefinitely, in the kind of object carrying out those activities.

Once this is acknowledged, however, then his normative conclusions follow directly. First, from the argument that the human is "originally nothing at all" (p. 74), but is a perpetual becoming through its formative and self-forming activities, it follows that "it is impossible to superimpose upon a human shape any concept other than that of oneself, [therefore] every human being is inwardly compelled to regard every other human being as his equal" (p. 74). If I understand Fichte aright, he is arguing from indeterminacy to equality. Indeterminacy follows from the human body being the vehicle for indefinite possibilities of action. Equality follows from there being no definite concept which is appropriate for the grasping of such a body; to encounter a human body is to encounter something that perpetually outruns one's capacity to make it conceptually determinate as the vehicle of human doings. If there is nothing determinate in the body of the other, if the other keeps escaping my power of determination, then my comprehension of her can only be connected to her likeness to me. In being conceptually indeterminate like me, she is my equal. It is just this feature of the appearing of the human body, its formability and indeterminacy, its readiness for unknown possibilities, which might lead one to engage such a body in a battle for recognition.

Second, deepening this thought, Fichte contends that taking into account the whole of the analysis of the appearing body, not considered element by element the way philosophers do, "but rather in their amazing, instantaneously grasped connection – *as given to the senses* – these are what compel everyone with a human countenance to recognize and respect the human shape everywhere . . . The human shape is necessarily sacred to the human being" (pp. 78–79; italics mine). Perhaps the word "respect" is more moralized than the argument can support, although it is now clear that Fichte means the appearance of the human body to be the ultimate fact of reason. What compels recognition in the first instance is the appearing body. Hence the human body in its appearing is what institutes the possibility of individuality and so self-consciousness, that is, through the manner in which the appearance of the human body compels visual attention individuals enter immediately into interaction with others, summoning through appearing the very recognition which will give back to them the standing necessary to be one who (actively) summons. The visual spectacle of the human body inscribes the kind of agency and rationality human beings possess, and therefore on its own initiates the communication between each self and its others whose floundering and flourishing compose the history of the race.

Fichte's claim here cannot be a discovery – it is too universalist in its scope for that. His transcendental anthropology must be functioning as a kind of reminder. The reminder can have the force it does because the argument for it is in reality a step-by-step dispelling of the illusions, repressions, and fantasies that have permitted us to daily forget what is there right before our eyes: the human body is the appearance of the human. Fichte accomplishes this by: closing the gap between (material) mind and body; making the (basic) doings of the body the necessary and direct expressions of the rational mind; while focusing its materiality, he detaches the body from determinate nature; reconfiguring the meaning of whole/part logic so that it is tailored to the diversity of human action; revealing how the various aspects of the body can be bearers of our humanity; making the experience of embodiment a source of dignity and standing in the world rather than something to be despised, overcome, repressed.

The appearing body, genetic conditions, and proto-rights

Fichte's deduction of the human body as the necessary material/visual condition of individuality is both structurally continuous with his generation of a conception of right as independent of morality, and a fundamental presupposition for that notion of right. By making intersubjectively mediated bodily performance the essential medium of self-conscious activity, Fichte literally gives to self-determination and normativity a radical materialist twist, fully inserting the self into a world of material objects and embodied others as the natural habitat of human existence.

Two final criticisms become pertinent here. First, by so radically figuring the body as a medium for action and interaction, Fichte over-idealizes the body, suppressing its natural and animal functions, above all making coercion the paradigm of wrong rather than physical injury. The Fichtean subject might well be finite, but it is not quite a suffering mortal; pain, often thought to be the criterion for sentience, makes no appearance in Fichte's *Foundations* anthropology. The second criticism, while not deeper, is more complex. As we have already noted, and as nearly all commentators agree, something goes wrong in the transition from original right to political right. One aspect of this that we have already acknowledged is that proto-rights, as actually universal through their connection to functional necessity, are necessarily thinner than liberal rights. The problem I have in mind is somewhat different: it is that the normative authority of original right fails to adequately inform the conception of empirical right.[17] Critics equally agree that this argumentative lapse undermines the architecture of *Foundations*, ruining the project as a whole. This criticism is just, but altogether too fast. The failure is different and simpler than usually supposed, and hence more remediable. In order to better focus the difficulty, let us briefly track Fichte's argument.

The orienting normative thesis that Fichte deduces from his account of embodiment is, again, that

> at the basis of all voluntarily chosen reciprocal interaction among free beings there lies an original and necessary reciprocal interaction among them, which is this: the free being, by his mere presence in the sensible world, compels every other free being, without qualification, to recognize him as a person. The one free being provides the particular appearance, the other the particular concept. Both are necessarily

> united, and freedom does not have the least amount of leeway here ... *Both recognize each other in their inner being, but they are as isolated as before.* (p. 79; italics mine)

What is surprising here is how Fichte moves seamlessly from the necessary unification of subjects through – compulsive – mutual recognition to, in that recognition, each being as isolated as before. It is this isolation that will lead Fichte to construct his state on the basis of a scenario that is logically closer to Locke and Hobbes than Rousseau and Hegel.

The crux of Fichte's isolation argument turns on the fact that while the norms of mutual recognition would be sufficient to compel rights-respecting behavior if no other options were available, in fact because each person is also a material object composed of coarse matter, then in each interaction between subjects they must choose whether to act on the basis of recognitive norms or through the use of (material) force. Because the employment of recognitive norms involves a self-limiting of the will, then while the recognition of another as a person, if followed out consistently, would compel rights-respecting treatment, nothing compels consistency and hence nothing obligates any individual to treat another in a rights-respecting manner. To do so would be a matter of free choice, say the free choice of a social contract. Hence, the situation collapses into one all but indistinguishable from classical individualist constructions of society and the state. All the recognitive connections among subjects that Fichte has worked so fervently to construct suddenly dissolve like the morning mist.

In response to both the naturalist objection and the isolation criticism I want to urge that the logical space that gives these objections purchase occurs because Fichte fails to adequately carry through his genetic analysis of the emergence of self-consciousness – so prominent in his account of the summons – when he introduces the body as the essential medium of human interaction and sociality. And this is a flaw since the whole point of the account of embodiment is to insist that it is the *original* locus of intersubjective communication, the implicit summons to humanity underlying all explicit summonses. Consider again the fact of prematurity. If the prematurity of the human infant is the indeterminate space that enables the institution of conceptualized rationality in place of mechanical instincts as the source of action, it must equally be the case that the process of socialization through which that occurs is what enables the human to satisfy the minimum conditions of animal life. On Fichte's own account, to be an animal is to have capacities for motility and action that enable it to satisfy survival needs: procure food, protect itself from harm, etc. The animal body is whole and complete because the action routines through which these ends are satisfied are themselves closed and determinate. Hence, the organic wholeness of the animal body represents the functional interconnection of its various parts so that it can satisfy survival needs in a manner sufficient for species reproduction. From here one might reasonably argue that the minimum necessary element that must be present in each socialization process is that the human body become whole in a manner sufficient for its animal needs, whole in a manner that is necessarily analogous to and approximates animal wholeness. The necessity here is obvious: the human is also an animal.

It is at just this juncture that Fichte's account misfires. Roughly, Fichte uses the fact of prematurity as an opening to altogether suppress or sublate to the point of disappearance the animal elements that are interwoven with and a substratum of the socialized body. After recording traditional thoughts about prematurity, he urges:

> If the human being is an animal, then he is an utterly incomplete animal, and for that very reason he is not an animal. It has often been thought that the free spirit existed for the sake of caring for animal nature. Such is not the case. Animal nature exists for the sake of bearing the free spirit in the sensible world and of binding it with the sensible world. (p. 76)

If to be an animal is to have a permanent and determinate structure of body and behavior, then the human is no animal. Reason is not an evolutionary device to compensate for and satisfy survival needs in place of instincts and mechanized routines, but a self-determined world of ideas, values, and norms that employ the body for acquiring sensible presence in the world.

One could argue that Fichte's idealist extremism here is a necessary consequence of his transcendental approach. But that claim is not compelling. Rather, the source of the extremism is Fichte posing the structural issue in sharply dualist terms, as the exclusive alternatives of *either* reason being for the sake of animal life *or* animal life for the sake of realizing an autonomous rationality. It is this false either/or that ruins Fichte's argument. There is an obvious third alternative, namely, that the very character of reason as providing non-mechanical means for satisfying survival imperatives simultaneously enables it to generate ends, norms, values, and ideas that outrun and even supplant the ends of individual survival and species reproduction; which is why the societal mechanisms that allow for species reproduction also enable the reproduction and expansion of rational culture more generally.

Once rational culture is viewed as an extension and development of the reasoned reproduction of species life, and species life is hence seen as a permanent ingredient within rational culture, then the genetic conditions for the emergence of individual self-consciousness must simultaneously facilitate the emergence of a being whose bodily powers are sufficient to secure the needs of its animal life. The preservation, continuation, and elaboration of animal life are a component of each human life. Because it is functionally necessary that each human individual acquire the bodily powers that make it a good animal, an animal capable of living, and because the acquisition of these powers is a matter of socializing the body, then there is a wholly non-optional, functional necessity to recognitive norms. Recognitive norms are *first* norms sufficient for animal life, and as sufficient for animal life thereby potentially sufficient for the indefinite cultural elaboration of human animal life that is a consequence of reason being the medium of survival.

Again, as argued above, it is the genetic location of the empirical and normative conditions of self-consciousness that gives them their prima facie authority. In failing to follow through his genetic approach when tracing out the role of embodiment, Fichte can construct a scenario in which each separate human encounter involves the participants in deciding in a groundless manner whether to treat the other as person or object. But the scenario itself is false. Summoning each infant to personhood involves each infant acquiring both the bodily powers for individuality and the norms integral to the possession of those powers, that is, awakening to the powers of self-consciousness is simultaneously to become awakened to their normative character. It is these normative presumptions that lie behind every child's demand to be allowed to do this or that activity on its own, to be allowed to express her powers of movement and action; that make all physical injury, not only that which is intentionally caused, to be experienced initially as a wrong that should not have occurred; and hence that construct the interwoven character of active powers and passive boundaries into a normative self-understanding of my body as 'mine' – fact and norm. These presumptions bear within themselves the normative necessity of those expressions for animal life. Inevitably, then, the culture educating a child must possess firm norms for its treatment, norms that make possible her development of the basic physical skills necessary to survival and social interaction, and that protect her both as an injurable animal and as active member of this family, clan, tribe, society. Coming to appreciate precisely how powers and norms are interwoven is what the education to self-consciousness involves; hence *the child cannot acquire the bodily powers for self-consciousness without acquiring the norms underpinning the ongoing expression of those powers as the prima facie norms governing social interaction generally.* (If there were space, I would want to argue that the first meaning of the taboo against incest is the protection of children from parents.) These normative expectations seem a fair match for original right, which recall are the "right to the continued existence of the absolute freedom and inviolability of the body" and the "right to the continued existence of our free influence in the entire sensible world" (p. 108). Because these rights must be interwoven with the ordinary expression of human powers in a setting sufficient to permit a child to develop into a self-conscious agent, then when facing another human body, a body whose appearance is itself a summons to respond to it in rights-respecting ways, there is not an abstract choice as to whether this being should be respected; there is a prima facie demand that respect be accorded.

My claim that norms expressing proto-rights must have prima facie authority is thus bound to their embeddedness in the routines through which new-comers are socialized and become agents. Embeddedness in the structures necessary for societal reproduction at the level of the individual removes even the hint that these norms might be cognized as optional for any being to whom they apply. Of course, the way culture comes to express those prima facie demands, as Fichte insists it must, does not deny the patent fact that most cultures are provincial, thriving on forms of repression and fear that lead to collective and individual blindness and prejudice. But that is only to say that the possibility of misrecognition is ever present, all but inevitable. Being ever present is not, however, the same as being legitimate: there is a flagrant irrationality in every denial of universality.

Fichte's account of the transition from proto-right into political right is flawed because it fails to find a natural, empirical locus for the actualization of proto-rights, and hence an empirical set of circumstances in which efforts of mutual recognition that already exist come to evolve into law and political right. The communal setting that enables the development of the infant into a socialized member of the community provides such a locus, a juncture in which the good of the bare life of the individual is taken up into the mechanisms through which the life of the society, and so the species, are transmitted across generations. What Fichte insists upon, as no else, is that all this transpires in and through the human body, making the vision of the human body itself the pulsing insistence of the dignity of human life generally.[18]

Notes

1 J.G. Fichte, *Foundations of Natural Right According to the Principles of the Wissenschaftslehre*, trans. Michael Bauer (Cambridge: Cambridge University Press, 2000). Henceforth, all references to this work will be given in parentheses in the body of the essay.

2 This beginning has been argued, beautifully, by Paul Franks, "The Discovery of the Other: Cavell, Fichte, and Skepticism," *Common Knowledge* 5–2 (1996), pp. 72–105.

3 J.G. Fichte, *Early Philosophical Writings*, trans. and ed. Daniel Breazeale (Ithaca: Cornell University Press, 1988), p. 409.

4 Frederick Neuhouser, in his introduction to J.G. Fichte, *Foundations of Natural Right According to the Principles of the Wissenschaftslehre*, p. xvii.

5 In *Hegel's Ethical Thought* (Cambridge: Cambridge University Press, 1990), Allen Wood connects Fichte's remark about the role of education with contemporary work into developmental psychology, and suggests that the most promising way to interpret Fichte's theory of recognition is "as an account of an ideal socialization process for individuals in a culture in which values such as individual freedom and autonomy hold an important place" (p. 83).

6 For an alternative account see Paul Franks, *All or Nothing: Systematicity, Transcendental Arguments, and Skepticism in German Idealism* (Cambridge, Mass.: Harvard University Press, 2005), pp. 321–25.

7 Frederick Neuhouser, "Fichte and the Relationship between Right and Morality," in Daniel Breazeale and Tom Rockmore (eds), *Fichte: Historical Contents / Contemporary Controversies* (Atlantic Highlands, NJ: Humanities Press, 1994), p. 176. Neuhouser's essay is a powerful defense of Fichte's separation of right from morality. I consider the argument of this paper as a further inflection of his defense of Fichte's non-moral conception of right.

8 I always imagine the Fichtean summons becoming, also, Laplanche's "enigmatic message," and thus also the origin of the unconscious. See Jean Laplanche, *Essays on Otherness* (London: Routledge, 1999).

9 Paul Franks, "The Discovery of the Other," p. 89.

10 Instead of the language of a non-natural sign, Fichte here uses the language of an exchange of cognitions that must be understood as cognitions and responded to in kind.

11 G.W.F. Hegel, *The Difference between Fichte's and Schelling's Systems of Philosophy*, trans. H.S. Harris (Albany, N.Y.: SUNY Press, 1977), p. 145.

12 These two objections are from Paul Franks, "The Discovery of the Other," p. 90.

13 Lucy O'Brien, "On Knowing One's Actions," in Johannes Roessle and Naomi Eilan (eds), *Agency and Self-Awareness: Issues in Philosophy and Psychology* (Oxford: Oxford University Press, 2003), p. 359.

14 Ibid., p. 363.

15 For a defense of mimesis along these lines see Tom Huhn, *Imitation and Society: The Persistence of Mimesis in the Aesthetics of Burke, Hogarth, and Kant* (University Park, Pa.: The Pennsylvania State University Press, 2004), Ch. 2.

16 Ludwig Wittgenstein, *Philosophical Investigations*, trans. G.E.M. Anscombe (New York: Macmillan, 1958), p. 178.

17 For a nice handling of this criticism, see Robert Williams, "The Displacement of Recognition by Coercion in Fichte's *Grundlage des Naturrechts*," in Daniel Breazeale and Tom Rockmore (eds), *New Essays on Fichte's Late Jena Wissenschaftslehre* (Evanston: Northwestern University Press, 2002), pp. 47–64.

18 Mark Sacks spent years try to convince me that it must be possible to provide a transcendental deduction of moral universalism; I doubted it. If I have succeeded here, he will have won that argument. For all the tea and whiskey and argument, I am dedicating this essay to him.

9

LIBERAL RIGHTS AND LIBERAL INDIVIDUALISM WITHOUT LIBERALISM: AGENCY AND RECOGNITION

Terry Pinkard

Kant begins his *Religion Within the Limits of Reason Alone* by distinguishing three components of the human condition. There is, first of all, our *animality*, that is, our natural, organic make-up. Second, there is what Kant characterizes as our *humanity*, that is, our social make-up, which Kant, in an overt reference to Rousseau, characterizes as "the inclination *to acquire worth in the opinions of others*," an inclination which, although it may start with a desire for equality, inevitably develops into a contest for social superiority, which in turn leads inevitably into "the unjustifiable craving to win [worth] for oneself over others."[1] Finally, there is *personality* (or what might be accurately called "moral personality"), which is Kant's own solution to Rousseau's problem of how *amour propre* (the desire for social superiority and esteem) is to be replaced by *amour de soi* (a kind of self-confidence or perhaps self-respect) – that is, how a concern with "independence" (which Rousseau locates in a mythical time of noble savages, each of whom is free from worry about how he is seen by others) is inevitably corrupted by the rise of culture and politics, which in turn make us increasingly dependent on the judgments of others, dependent in ways that become so deeply rooted in our lives that the dependence is no longer even noticed. Kant, like Rousseau, located the ability to achieve the requisite independence in our capacity to will universally, although for Kant this was, of course, not Rousseau's political "general will" but instead the "universal will" of individual autonomous agents, for whom "respect for the moral law is in itself a sufficient incentive of the will."[2]

Kant's threefold distinction certainly captures what is at work in a very general type of individualist (or what is often called "liberal") conception of agency: We are organic beings who begin our lives in complete dependency (and often end them in complete dependency), who, in becoming socialized, quite naturally (that is, inevitably, in the course of things) acquire a dependence on the views of others, but each of whom has a capacity to free himself from those dependencies, reflectively think for himself, endorse or reject maxims for action based on criteria that are not simply matters of social respectability or competition, and thus achieve at least in the sphere of morality the independence that Rousseau thought was the hallmark of true *amour de soi*. The way in which (moral) personality, as it were, rises above our "inclination to acquire worth in the opinion of others" and submits those inclinations to its commands, makes each of us, in the words of John Rawls (and Neo-Rawlsians such as Henry Richardson), self-originating sources of claims that no claim of social utility may override.[3]

Kant himself, of course, thought that the only way one could sustain this kind of distinction was by also distinguishing between the causality we must attribute to ourselves as deliberative agents and the causality that we find in the phenomenal world in which we live. And he thought that was sustainable only by adhering to the strictures of his critical philosophy, in particular, the distinction between the deterministic world of appearances and the unknowable realm of things in themselves. Kant's solution thus comes at a price; but the payoff seems so large and enticing that it has created a scholarly industry on its own with attempts to show how Kant's threefold distinction can be maintained without adhering to his distinctions between things in themselves and appearances, or by showing that the distinction is not as odd or indefensible as it has in fact seemed to be by so many people working in the wake of Kant's revolutionary philosophical work.

Indeed, one might phrase Kant's distinction between "humanity" and "personality" as the expression of an unvoiced antinomy in his work. As in the presentation of the antinomies in the first *Critique*, one can imagine this antinomy being laid out in two separate columns. The left-hand column would begin with the claim that we are always completely constituted by a mixture of animality and sociality and that our normative status is completely derivative from that; and the right-hand column would begin with the claim that we are free, self-originating sources of claims that no claim of social utility may override. One would imagine the left-hand column being filled out with arguments from anthropology, sociology, naturalist philosophy, and various post-modern genealogies; the right hand column would be filled out by various neo-Kantian arguments about how the idea of ourselves as self-originating sources of claims captures our moral intuitions about ourselves, how we must think of ourselves in practical terms as free, how we are always caught up in the normative space of reasons that cannot be reduced to the space of causes, and so forth. For an orthodox Kantian, the solution to this antinomy would no doubt look like the solution to the third antinomy (that, roughly, between freedom and nature) in the first *Critique*, that is, a solution in terms of a "positive" account of ourselves as part of the phenomenal world on one side and a "transcendental" account of us as possessing noumenal freedom on the other side.

There is, however, a crucial distinction between this and the third antinomy. Where the third antinomy takes as its central problem the threat that *nature* (as a deterministic system) poses to freedom, Rousseau's problem is different: It is concerned with the threat of a certain form of *social dependence*, especially one that "civilization" (i.e. modern life) makes to freedom. If the orthodox Kantian solution to the problem of nature's threat to freedom is jettisoned (that is, that we jettison the demand that we think of ourselves as capable of exercising a non-natural form of causality), then Rousseau's problem should send us back to the Kantian drawing board.

I

The antinomy seems to appear in many areas of contemporary thought, cross-cutting its way through communitarian critiques of liberalism to all the different versions of social-contractarian theory around nowadays. There is, however, another line of thought responding to this which has not been as well represented in contemporary Anglo-American theory, which finds its expressions both in Rousseau and in Hegel. To be sure, this has not been without its proponents; in particular, Robert Pippin and Frederick Neuhouser have each argued in their own way for a reconsideration of the Rousseau–Hegel alternative, and what I have to say draws heavily on their own work as a point of departure. In this view, to put it in a summary form that will require much unpacking, what is at stake is a claim to the effect that a certain form of sociality is essential for us to be liberal individuals at all; that this sociality is not just the relatively trivial claim that we must be socialized into being such liberal agents, but that I (or each of us) can be such an agent *only if others can be and are* such agents. Or, to put it in Hegel's preferred mode: I can be free only if others are free.

This of course is tied into Hegel's (and, implicitly, also Rousseau's) conception of *recognition* as fundamental to agency. The outlines of the position, to stay in generalities, look like this: To be an agent (or a subject) is to be *recognized*, that is, to be granted a normative status by others; for others to do that, they must have the authority to grant such a status, and that authority in turn requires that they in turn are recognized by others; that such mutual "bootstrapping" requires us to think of this authority as social and historical; that there is an internal teleology to all such social and historical attempts at recognition that in modern times has led to the realization that only a full "mutuality" of recognition can be successful; and that there is a dialectical element to this, such that the kind of independence aimed at is possible only within certain forms of dependency, such that what at first looks like contradiction or paradox is resolved by a richer comprehension of what is involved, in particular, how the conception of ourselves as self-originating sources of claims is, as it were, itself a precipitate out of a structure of mutual recognition.

Hegel's point is, moreover, not that recognition is simply a good which others may deny us, so that being deprived of such recognition would be the root of some kind of suffering on our part (which is also not to deny that in many cases recognition in fact can function as such a good). His point is different: unlike natural objects, which are what they are without being taken to be so in any particular way, subjects, or agents, must be *taken to be* agents if they are to be agents. This is not to deny any kind of natural basis for agency, nor is it to claim that everything about our agency is a cultural construct of some sort. We almost certainly come into the world wired for language acquisition, and there are many things to which we are naturally disposed and for which our brains and nervous systems are naturally organized to pay attention. The Hegelian point, though, is that our status as *subjects* of responsibilities and as beings capable of rational, intentional action is not itself a fully natural concept but something more like a normative status, that being an agent is more akin to something like a social status (such as engineer, professor, or lawyer) than it is to a natural kind.[4] To be held responsible is thus a way of *being taken* to be responsible by others, and, when those ways of taking are appropriately learned and internalized, it is also a way of *holding oneself* to be responsible, which involves locating oneself in a kind of social, normative space.[5]

II

If, however, Kant was the way into this problem, Kant might also be the way out. For Kant, the key idea in agency has to do with our ability to grasp reasons and to have them be effective in guiding our actions or in forming our beliefs, and there is a line of Kant interpretation which argues that, taken in that way, Kant's position does not really make a commitment (or may do without such a commitment) to two different realms of causality.[6] In practical deliberation about actions, we are doing something more like forming commitments, "binding ourselves to the practical law," as Kant puts it.[7] In deliberating on what to do, we have to look for justifications, not causes, and there is no way out of this deliberative standpoint; we are always, already within the "space" of what Kant called the *fact of reason*, and everything that seems like a door out of that space is really itself only an opening back into the same space (or, to put it differently, the way out is itself normative, that is, the difference between the normative and the non-normative is already itself a normatively established distinction).[8] Even the picture that itself provokes the idea of two realms of causality can itself be recast, not as struggle within ourselves between two independent sources of motivation as two different realms of causality – with inclinations pulling us in one way and ourselves as rational deliberators pushing us in another direction – but as a struggle within ourselves over what counts as a reason, a struggle over whether, for example, I am supposed to take my particular desires as a good reason for action or whether I am supposed to take some kind of universalizable maxim as a reason to act.[9]

The capacity to act in light of reasons crisscrosses with another, equally well known Kantian distinction between autonomy and heteronomy. In autonomous action, I am (somehow) dependent only on a law for which only *I* am responsible, of which *I* am the author, whereas in heteronomous action, so it seems, I am dependent on something *other* than that for which I am responsible, or in which I cede my responsibility to something else.

However, taken literally, this lands all such Kantian conceptions in a kind of bind I have elsewhere called "the Kantian paradox."[10] That is, in Kant's language, I can only be obligated by a law of which I can regard myself as the author, which in turn means that I have to have a law that is non-self-legislated to will the law, since an arbitrarily willed law would be non-binding, and any act of willing not bound by law is arbitrary; but that non-self-legislated law would itself therefore not be obligatory, since not self-legislated, and therefore the law willed on its basis would also not be obligatory.[11] This might seem to suggest only two equally unpleasant options for a Kantian: Either one rejects Kantian conceptions of autonomy altogether as just self-contradictory; or one has to opt for some kind of miraculous generation of normative space out of a non-normative one (or that one see oneself as magically moving from a state of not being obligated to one of being obligated just by virtue of authoring a law for oneself).[12]

Kant himself is, however, more careful in the way he sets his problem: I must be able, he says, to *regard* the law as having been authored by me, and that means *not* that I must create that law from scratch (as it were, pulling in the black-letter normative law from out of the non-normative blue), but that I must be able to understand what it is that I do as expressive of what I value most, which for an orthodox Kantian has to be something like "duty for duty's sake" or "treating all humanity as an end and never merely as a means"; or to put it in the terms notably put forth by Christine Korsgaard, Barbara Herman, Allen Wood and others, to express the conception of *value* at work in Kantian conceptions, namely, that of valuing humanity as capable of setting its ends.[13] In Korsgaard's formulation of this view, once one is working within such a conception of value, the action must express one's "practical identity," that is, those descriptions "under which you value yourself ... under which you find your life to be worth living and your actions to be worth undertaking."[14] When one's actions reflect one's commitments in *that* way, then those actions *may be regarded* as having been authored by oneself (that is, are "just as good as" having been authored by oneself).[15]

This gets Kant, so it seems, out of that bind, but it imports into the Kantian conception an *expressivist* conception of action (to give it the name Charles Taylor coined for it). This has the virtue of avoiding Kant's causal language altogether, putting the distinction instead as something like: I am free when *I* am fully *present* in the action, such that I may be said to be acting in a way in which I am not dependent on something other than myself (at least in the true sense of myself). What makes the action count as *mine* is that it reflects or expresses *my* commitments, that is reflects or expresses what I value most. But what makes a commitment *mine*? One can easily conjure up cases in which one is dependent on the other person in such a way as to be heteronomous (as when, as in one of Korsgaard's examples, one "allows oneself to be governed" by another person because one is afraid to think for oneself).[16] But the Rousseauian worries go deeper as to whether in many cases, one may very well reflectively decide on what to do and still be heteronomously guided by the opinions of others. T. S. Eliot's "hollow men" may indeed have their self-conceptions picked up and confirmed by others but their "practical identity" has nonetheless been shaped almost entirely by, in Kant's words, "the inclination *to acquire worth in the opinions of others*," where *that* "inclination" has never itself come under scrutiny. They are absorbed in their social roles, they fully identify with their practical identity, they have their identities recognized and confirmed by others, and yet they still are heteronomous, dependent in a negative way on others.

But Kant has an answer to that in his *Metaphysics of Morals*: The "my" in the idea of an action expressing my deepest commitments is not just a descriptive feature of the action but functions normatively as singling out some commitments as more basic, more "me" than others in the same way that the "my" in "my property" points out a normative fact about my relation to certain things which I am said to own.

On this amended Kantian conception, an end has value for me, or *matters* to me, only because of the *quality of the reasons* involved in setting that end; and an inclination is genuinely mine, that is, it expresses *my* commitments, only if I do or can "reflectively endorse" it, and the master principle behind this conception, the source of all value behind all my reflective endorsements is supposed to be the value of my "humanity," my capacity to rationally set ends.[17] Indeed, on this amended conception, such "reflective endorsement" is the real way in which *pure* reason becomes *pure practical* reason; it may be put to use to judge the permissibility or obligatoriness of contingent ends generated by various practical identities, but it is not itself tied down to any of those contingent identities. The idea is that the obligations that come with my practical identity cannot be binding unless I make them binding, unless I reflectively endorse them (or least am in the position of being able to reflectively endorse them). And, of course, this ideal of reflective endorsement can be at work in one's life only if it *matters* to oneself that one be able to reflectively endorse the various practical identities that one has; and on the Kantian conception of mattering, one does not merely submit oneself to rational standards but in some sense one is the *author* of those standards which are the basis of one's reflective endorsement, which in its expressivist version means that those standards express who one is in the sense of what ultimately, absolutely matters to oneself.

That aside, what keeps this as a *Kantian* position is its insistence on a conception of *pure* practical reason, even if that conception is rather thinned out after one has abstracted away from all the more particular commitments which are tied into our "practical identities." What is then left functions as the standard for "reflective endorsement," and it thus opens itself up to the familiar worry about how, once it is so thinned out, this thinned out conception of pure practical reason could justify anything at all or could possibly serve as a motivational basis for action.

However, it is the very abstractness of any conception of *pure* practical reason – the idea of what "any rational agent" would reflectively endorse in these circumstances – which led Hegel to conclude not that Kantian morality is therefore a chimera, but that it itself is possible only when embedded in a set of practices with a thicker social and historical shape; that the claims of morality make sense and have their basis only in a larger *embedding* of the agent within a set of institutions and practices of *Sittlichkeit*, "ethical life"; and that abstracted out of such embedding, this moral worldview leads to a predictable sets of tensions and blind alleys when one tries to make sense of what one is doing in moral commitment and assessment. The point is analogous to that argued by people as various as Nancy Sherman and Robert Pippin: Ultimately the *commitment* itself to being a moral agent has to be itself grasped as a constituent facet of a larger pattern of commitments, not all of which are themselves moral; or, to put it in very different terms, there simply is no such thing as *pure* practical reason; there is only practical reason *as embedded* in a set of historically and socially constituted practices and institutions (which brings up the characteristically audacious Hegelian thesis, which would require a whole other discussion, that not merely individuals but a whole "form of life" can fail, not because people are straying from the true morality or because they have become less pious with regard to its certainties, but because it itself can no longer maintain an allegiance to itself).[18]

However, rather than sounding like the direction in which a more refined Kantian position should go, this may just sound more like exactly the problem for which Kantianism is the answer. It has the ring of arguing that moral obligations are really just versions of "role obligations," and any idea that "my roles" are enough to obligate me is quickly brought up short by two ideas, both quite easy to formulate, that there can obviously be bad roles and reflectively endorsing role-bound obligations is not something that is itself a matter of just playing yet another social role.

III

That, however, brings us right back to the antinomy with which we began the discussion, namely, that between ourselves as self-originating sources of claims and ourselves as socially constituted.[19] It would be one-sided for any account to fill out, as it were, the left-hand side of the antinomy (dealing with our natural constitution) without making room for Kantian normativity on the right-hand side, however richly the left-hand side is illustrated. But, so goes the lesson of the amended Kantian conception, it would be equally one-sided to insist on Kantian normativity and autonomy without telling where it finds its home in our lives. One of the leading lines of thought nowadays is to do just that by mating Kantian conceptions with Aristotelian conceptions to make up the deficits on both sides. Going in that direction is, of course, already several steps down the road to Hegel's own attempted synthesis of the two lines of thought.[20]

The Hegelian emendation of the already amended Kantian conception turns on how we understand the way in which agency – that is, minded, "*geistige*," organisms – stands within the natural order. Much more needs to be said about this, but this all turns on Hegel's version of what we could call his disenchanted Aristotelian naturalism. For Hegel, on the one hand, the nature *we* moderns confront is the one described and explained by modern natural science, not the one described and explained by Aristotelian science; as Hegel famously says, "not only must philosophy agree with our experience of nature, but the unfolding and formation of philosophical science has empirical physics as its presupposition and condition," and for modern philosophy that means modern and not Aristotelian physics.[21] On the other hand, there is nonetheless room within such a disenchanted picture of nature for an understanding of organisms as *functional* wholes, that is, as embodying *purposes* that do not contradict any of the causal laws by which they are explained, but whose adequate comprehension requires an understanding of what it is that the organism itself is trying to accomplish in its activities. The functional structures of organisms carry a kind of normative force within them in doing what they are supposed to do (pump blood, admit oxygen, and so on). Seen in that way, organisms exhibit the Aristotelian view of them of aiming at their own good. To the extent that we view organic life in nature as having this kind of internal teleology – Hegel himself firmly rejected any external teleology to nature, that is, any sense that organisms or the natural world itself were designed by a creator – we can understand that there are *goods* in nature, where a good for an organism is what figures in the satisfactions of its functions, its purposes (which, as Hegel argues, for animals consists solely in the animal's reproductive success). Hegel's own illustration of this has to do with the concept of disease: A diseased organ is simply one that is not fulfilling its function within the life of the organism.

It is only with social, self-conscious beings that these reasons become articulated *as* reasons and are then linked with each other inferentially in such a way that reasons come to *favor* actions or beliefs. On the Hegelian "disenchanted Aristotelian conception" of nature, "normative force" in nature consists in organic structures simply functioning as they are supposed to function, whereas "normative force" for self-conscious agents is *true* normativity, in the sense of their normativity not just being a matter of functioning rightly but a matter of conveying truth and falsehood. Reasons, on the Hegelian account, thus enter the naturalist picture for us when there are goods that figure in the satisfactions of our goals and projects, where these goals and projects themselves go beyond what is necessary for our more limited organic functioning. It is crucial to human agency that these reasons become truly normative, go beyond matters of various mechanisms within the organism functioning as they are supposed to function; in becoming self-conscious agents, we begin to leave nature, as it were, behind.

We always already find ourselves in practices informed by norms, something which Hegel throughout his career sometimes called a "form of life" and sometimes a "shape" (or "form") of spirit.[22] Such "forms of life" are structured around a set of normative convictions which constitute the usually inarticulate background in terms of which one acts and which are at work in that background in an immediate, ready to hand fashion (what Hegel calls "self-certainty"). The skills necessary to navigate around in such a form of life shape the ways in which one copes with one's world and with others and resist any kind of formalization. They are part of the background grasp, rarely fully explicit, of a joint conception of both our *norms* and what features of the *world* make those norms *realizable*, what resists their realization, what tends to make their realization rare, and so on.[23] As a joint conception of norm and fact, a form of life provides the *orientation* for the participants in that form of life with regard to what it makes sense to strive for and what they have some kind of reasonable hope of achieving. This background understanding that animates this form of life thus provides the outlines of the ways in which people, individually and collectively, *imagine* how their lives, individually and collectively, *will* go, how things *ought* to go and how they *expect* them really to proceed.[24] This background understanding constitutes a kind of tacit knowledge – or, as Hegel himself illustrates the point, such knowledge involves a fluency which "consists in having the particular knowledge or kind of activities immediately to mind in any case that occurs, even, we may say, *immediate in our very limbs*, in an activity directed outwards."[25]

Part of Hegel's disenchanted Aristotelianism had to do with the way he attempted to rework the Aristotelian metaphysics of potentialities and their actualizations into a conception of practices as historically spread out with a historically situated realization of the meanings that are at work in the practices. Much more needs to be said about this, but Hegel's point there is in part pragmatist: The full *content* of what we have been doing only emerges after the fact, after we have worked out the meanings in practice, after we have seen what they lead to when the conditions for realizing the implicit aims of a practice are themselves finally put on view. Or, to put it another way, the content of a principle is not indifferent to its application, to how it is worked out in practice. This kind of realization of meaning, moreover, is carried out in a variety of ways, not all of which involve translating a propriety of practice into its appropriate propositional form; and even where it is a matter of rendering such tacit knowledge into propositional form, there are often intense contestations about how to state just what the norm really is, what it really means in concrete cases, what exactly is to count as falling under the norm, and how far the scope of certain entitlements goes; different ways of "making it explicit" rule in and rule out certain consequences, and the participants in a form of life are thus often at odds with themselves on how best to state, or make explicit, what it is that they are really doing, since making it explicit in one way rules some things in, rules some things out, and it is usually just those matters which are up for contestation.[26]

Now, part of the attractiveness of the Kantian conception has to do with the way in which it formulates the conditions under which the kind of independence which Rousseau worried about is itself to be understood; part of that attraction also has to do with the way in which it captures so well one of the most basic commitments of liberalism itself, indeed a commitment so basic that it could also be said to be almost constitutive of the liberal psychology itself. Classical liberalism operated with a picture of what it would mean to realize in practice the abstract idea of a "liberal individual," and without too much distortion, we could call this the picture of the "genuine adult" as distinguished from the "child." From Locke to Kant, the great psychological horror for classical liberals was the idea of an adult (almost always an adult man) being made or seduced into acting like a *dependent*, that is, a child. Indeed, we can say that with classical liberalism, the distinction between childhood and adulthood became not just a human developmental category but a *political* category of prime importance.[27] The diagnoses for what leads to this dependency were various – ranging from Kant's famous declaration that it was in fact a "self-incurred" tutelage which could be broken simply by an act of courage to think for oneself, all the way up to various conceptions of how it was the social structure of honors and orders of the *ancien régime* which had debased adult men into conditions of child-like dependency – but the idea of adults being made into dependents was the key evil to which classical liberalism responded with its cure: The exercise of rational self-rule, which would be underwritten or promoted by various doctrines of basic rights, civil society, and limited government. (It is important, but is a story for another time, as to how this also underwrote both the otherwise puzzling classical liberal disregard for women's rights and why so many classical liberals, Kant included, had what nowadays can at best be described as embarrassing views about the abilities of non-Europeans; those views also belong to the psychology of the deep fear of adult dependency that were coupled with their views about what kinds of adults – namely, for them, women and non-Europeans – would supposedly by virtue of their natural makeup *always* be dependents and what a horror it would thus be like to be *them*.)

The great liberal revulsion at the prospect of adult dependency underwrote liberalism's great critical potential in challenging the many modes tyranny has taken in the modern period, but it also blinded it to the ways in which such dependencies are written into the pattern of human agency. As *Don Quixote* long ago showed, it is at best comical for somebody to attempt to play out a social role for a context that no longer exists; one simply cannot be a knight-errant unless others recognize one as a knight-errant, and, in Quixote's world, the possibility for others recognizing Quixote as such a figure had long since passed away. Likewise, one can be a certain type of agent only if others can recognize you as being such an agent, and that ability for mutual recognition is dependent on a kind of social authority. The people of Quixote's day could not by fiat make him a knight-errant; and one cannot be a liberal individual without the requisite social authority behind that conception.

What the Hegelian dialectical model recommends is a shift away from regarding political and social life in terms of a picture, as it were, of individuals bringing certain interests to the bargaining table and then looking to see what kind of ideal negotiation would give rise to an ideal political society. Instead, the shift is to a concern with why certain things matter to the individuals in question, a concern with what things are "for them," with what matters to people from the "inside." Indeed, one of the key ideas is that of people *making sense of*, for example, the institutions in which they work and live, and "making sense" ultimately means that people have to look for reasons for what is happening (both for what they are doing, what the institution is doing, and what is happening to them). If indeed the goods at which an individual aims take on their character as goods for an agent by virtue of the quality of reasons that the agent has for claiming them to be goods, then even the goods of liberal individuality are themselves possible only in a social context in which those goods can be recognized. Or, to put it differently: I can be a free liberal individual only if others are also free liberal individuals; the recognition I receive as being an individual can only come from those authorized to bestow such recognition, and they can only be so authorized if, as it were, the form of life has already authorized them to be the kind of individuals who have the authority to do that. Or (to put it in the kind of paradoxical way Hegelians like to phrase their claims): The status of being a self-originating source of claims is itself a social status, and as a social status, it can be sustained only in a form of life that is structured around a certain set of practices and institutions (such as the traditional liberal lineup of limited constitutional government, some kind of market society with legal protection of property rights, independent judiciaries, equality before the law, lists of basic freedoms that either cannot be violated or which require some kind of extraordinary justification to do so, and so on). Or: I can be an *independent* liberal agent only by virtue of a determinate set of structured *dependencies*.

The kind of independence that is the hallmark of liberal individualism is thus, on this dialectical view, possible only under various structures of dependency (and not under just any structures of dependency). If we keep to the amended Kantian conception according to which an action is *genuinely* mine if it expresses *my* deepest commitments, then we are led to the more dialectical conclusion that prior to my own willing of this or that, I am *always already tied into* a non-chosen intersubjective background without which I could not have and could not have made these commitments at all.

Two aspects of this in particular interested Hegel. First, we should think of this kind of liberal individuality and the intersubjectively embedded commitments that make it what it is as itself a historical, normative *achievement*, not as something we have either naturally grown into nor as the natural end-point of human development (that is, as the endpoint to which humans would grow if they had not otherwise been interfered with by tyrants or been inflicted with other pathologies that would supposedly prevent the human organism from growing into its putatively natural status of being a modern individual). The "liberal individual" is itself a complex normative status, and what looks like its metaphysical ultimacy is really only its *practical unavoidability* within a certain historical context which itself emerges as practically unavoidable within a larger narration. Hegel's own narration of this, carried out first and paradigmatically in his 1807 *Phenomenology*, is far too complex to summarize, but certain key themes at least stand out. His account of the self-defeating character of individualist conceptions of agency as they twist and turn through various ways of arguing that the metaphysical constraints of individuality itself are sufficient to generate a workable social and political order; his account of the ancient Athenian version of social order, an object of intense nostalgia in Hegel's own day, and how it itself had generated within its own practices a conception of the individuality that was not only not compatible with those practices, but which in turn produced a form of *ethical* fanaticism which made it ultimately unviable; the equally self-defeating characteristics of modern moralism, which tend to veer off into moralistic beautiful souls (quick to condemn, glacially slow to act) and other forms of modern moralizing, which generates as its modern counterpart a kind of moral rigidity coupled with a quickness to find fault with those who do in fact act; and the way in which the very notion of subjective *commitment* itself emerges in the development of Christianity, such that an intense inward turn (what Hegel calls an *In-Sich-Gehen*) takes place in the historical development of subjectivity, a turn that ends up carving out a realm of individual conscience and a sense of humanity as having an inviolable dignity. None of this *had* to happen, even if it was the result of a kind of "logic" at work in history; and, being a fragile, historical achievement, it need not necessarily last. Shifting to a political theory based on recognition thus shifts our question to the one Hegel thought most pressing: Under what practical, social and institutional setup can something like the "liberal individual" be secured?

Second, Hegel was interested in the way such individualism easily slides into the fantasy of self-sufficiency which itself threatens to undermine the basis on which it is continually generated. That I must see the action as "my own" for it to count as free quite easily glides into the idea that for me to be genuinely self-determining, I must be able to do this *independently* of my relations to others, be able to will my own actions without the result necessarily being what others want of me or expect me to do or as the result of hidden social pressures. From there it is a short step to the idea that my relations to these others can be affectively rich but nonetheless must always be subject to a "reflective endorsement" that is in principle independent of my relations to any of them.[28] If, however, my own willing is always and already possible only by virtue of my relation to others – if my own subjectivity is possible only by virtue of intersubjective relations – then such a view is at best a partial and one-sided view of what agency is, and at worst a misguided fantasy of personal independence which, coupled with the liberal's psychology of horror at adult dependency, leads to its own form of moral fanaticism as a way of holding all threats to such dependency at bay.

The Kantian conjecture, as we might put it, is to see in Rousseau's anxiety about the loss of freedom in our "civilized" dependence on others a summons to carve out some area of personal independence, a zone of "reflective endorsement" or a sphere of *pure* practical reason in which such dependence can be overcome or mitigated; and to do that is to establish a sphere of self-sufficiency of a sort, which, *if taken in its social and historical context*, may indeed be part of what counts as living up to the moral point of view. However, the moral agent, standing back from all his other ties, consulting his conscience, asking himself what is the right thing for a human being to do in this situation, is not acting in a historical and institutional void but rather is acting within the standpoint of a thickly constituted historical and social set of practices that involve a commitment to more than the moral point of view and which embed the moral point of view within themselves.[29]

It is in that sense that the "liberal individual" is a historical achievement, not a transcendental condition of agency, and as such a historical achievement, it rests on pre-volitional relations to others which themselves make such moral volition possible in the first place. On this Hegelian picture, Kant is surely right to hold that the moral point of view is not itself a matter up for negotiation among rational individuals but instead forms the condition under which they can rationally negotiate; but he is wrong in thinking that this point of view is itself possible without the kinds of relations to others that precede and make possible the moral agency itself. In that light, something like Kant's universalization test is, to make a turn on one of Nancy Sherman's suggestions, best construed as the necessity to incorporate into our character an idealized picture of giving and asking for reasons from each other, a kind of idealized negotiation in the "kingdom of ends" that takes into account the newly established, very modern authority of individual end-setting and self-assertion in the kinds of modern forms of life that come with the institutions and practices celebrated by classical liberalism. It is the achievement of genuine, *wahrhaftig*, self-sufficiency in terms of what Hegel calls *realized freedom*. This is not a thesis about the absorption of the individual into the social – it is not recommending submersion into social conformity, the fear that obsessed people from Rousseau to Heidegger – nor does it posit the kind of absorption that so worried people from Kant to Rawls, namely, that, so construed, the individual must cease to be a source of claims (which, following Hegel, would mean that the difference between individuals would thus not be taken seriously[30]); to point out the immense achievement at stake in modern individualism and the extremes to which it could be taken (in all the various pathologies that stem from the fantasies of self-sufficiency that develop out of such individualism abstracted out of its sustaining social context) and to point out both the strength and the fragility of such an achievement is not to argue that the individual somehow vanish into, or be "absorbed" within, the social. It is a Hegelian attempt to gather up what was true in classical liberalism and provide the philosophical account for those truths without having to spin them out of classical liberalism itself. That it also moves us away from more traditional "problem oriented" philosophies into a view of philosophy as involved with the "logic" of "forms of life" (that is, as inherently interdisciplinary) is part of the Hegelian story, but is a story for another time.

Notes

1 Immanuel Kant, *Religion Within the Limits of Reason Alone*, trans. Theodore M. Greene and Hoyt H. Hudson (New York: Harper and Row, 1960), p. 22.

2 Ibid. p. 23.

3 See Henry Richardson, *Democratic Autonomy: Public Reasoning about the Ends of Policy* (New York: Oxford University Press, 2002).

4 To see what the Hegelian view is not, consider the claim that as subjects we are the loci of responsibilities. On a metaphysical and individualist model, we might try to locate the conditions for ascribing responsibility prior to any of our practices of holding each other responsible, and then evaluate those practices in terms of whether they track this. That is, we would look for the metaphysical facts about responsibility that are both prior to and independent of our practices of holding people responsible. One obvious candidate for such a view would be Kant's version of voluntarism in which we are held to be responsible only if we are capable of initiating a causal chain that is not itself the effect of any other causal chain; within that view, the paradigm for assessing responsibility holds that it is fair to attribute responsibility only to those cases in which one could have always done otherwise. In that view, my being the *subject* of responsibility is dependent on my being an *agent* of the voluntarist sort. The counter-claim in this case is that such metaphysical interpretations will always give us a distorted picture of what responsibility amounts to. In particular, it rests on two rather implausible claims. First, it makes it look as if our practices of holding people responsible involve both an incredible conception of causality and second that our practices are dependent on some metaphysical fact which would be what it is even if we *never* in practice held people responsible for anything. To be sure, assertions of implausibility do not themselves amount to anything like a knock-down argument against such a view. Instead, they should be taken as a suggestion that we shift the question away from, "Could I have done otherwise?" as the paradigm question about delimiting responsibility to something more like "When is it fair or reasonable to hold someone or oneself responsible?" On this point, see Jay Wallace, *Responsibility and the Moral Sentiments* (Cambridge, Mass.: Harvard University Press, 1996). Wallace ties this into a Strawsonian conception of the reactive emotions. Wallace argues that there is an essential connection between reactive attitudes and a distinctive form of evaluation which consists in holding a person to an expectation or demand, not in the sense of a probabilistic expectation, but instead in the "attitudinal" sense: "To hold someone to an expectation is essentially to be susceptible to a certain range of emotions in the case that the expectation is not fulfilled," the paradigms of which are resentment, indignation, and guilt (Wallace, p. 21). The difference between the Hegelian position and Wallace's is that between the more individualist account of moral agency which Wallace offers (despite his insistence on the priority of practices) and Hegelian, more fully social accounts. Wallace's position is, on his own account, a refinement of the Kantian position; the suggestion being offered here is that Wallace should have pushed this Kantianism to its next step, to a more *social* Hegelian account.

5 This might seem to suggest some kind of relativist line on being an agent and being responsible in the sense that it might seem that the fact of the matter as to whether one is responsible for something is equivalent to being taken to be responsible, which would be to say, of course, that there is no independent fact of the matter, but only our different ways of taking people to be responsible. There, so it seems, one confronts another "either/or": Either there is some metaphysical fact of the matter about responsibility, or there are just contingently different ways of ascribing responsibility relative to our interests. Part of Hegel's alternative is to avoid that particular "either/or" with regard to issues of responsibility.

6 The literature representing these two ways of reconstruing Kant is, of course, immense. However, for the line that "Kant is not really committed to this," see Henry Allison, *Kant's Transcendental Idealism: An Interpretation and Defense* (New Haven: Yale University Press, 1983); *Kant's Theory of Freedom* (Cambridge: Cambridge University Press, 1990); *Idealism and Freedom: Essays on Kant's Theoretical and Practical Philosophy* (Cambridge: Cambridge University Press, 1996). The most influential of those who take the line that "Kant need not be committed to this" is Christine Korsgaard, *Creating the Kingdom of Ends* (Cambridge: Cambridge University Press, 1996); *The Sources of Normativity* (Cambridge: Cambridge University Press, 1996).

7 Thus, the difference between the view of ourselves as subject to the deterministic laws of appearance and the view of ourselves as agents is not best assimilated to that of two independent realms of causality but perhaps to two different kinds of self-conception, something that might be better assimilated to what Wilfrid Sellars calls seeing ourselves within the "space of causes" and within the "space of reasons." See Sellars, "Philosophy and the Scientific Image of Man," in *Science, Perception, and Reality* (Atascasdero: Ridgeview Publishing Company, 1963).

8 The phrase, of course, comes from Robert Brandom: "Freedom and Constraint by Norms," *American Philosophical Quarterly*, April, 1977, pp. 187–96. This picture, though, goes further in suggesting a dialectical conception of reason than Brandom is willing to countenance; the fundamental distinction for such a conception is that between the normative (the realm of thought) and the non-normative (the sphere of "being"), where "thought" posits its difference from "being" as its having something to which thought answers.

9 As Kant puts it, "freedom of choice (*Willkür*) is of a wholly unique nature in that an incentive can determine choice to an action *only so far as the individual has incorporated (aufgenommen) it into his maxim* (has made it the general rule in accordance with which he will conduct himself); only thus can an incentive, whatever it may be, co-exist with the absolute spontaneity of choice (*Willkür*) (i.e. freedom)." Immanuel Kant, *Religion Within the Limits of Reason Alone*, trans. Theodore M. Greene and Hoyt Hudson (New York: Harper and Row, 1960), p. 19. (Translation altered by me.) This is famously characterized by Henry Allison as the "incorporation thesis." Henry Allison, *Kant's Theory of Freedom* (Cambridge: Cambridge University Press, 1990), p. 40.

10 Terry Pinkard, *German Philosophy 1760–1860: The Legacy of Idealism* (Cambridge: Cambridge University Press, 2002).

11 "The will is therefore not merely subject to the law, but is so subject that it must be considered as also *giving the law to itself* and precisely on this account as first of all subject to the law (of which it can regard itself as the author)." *Groundwork of the Metaphysics of Morals* (trans. H.J. Paton, New York: Harper and Row, 1964), p. 98 (AA 431, translation modified).

12 In fact, this temptation is so large that Charles Larmore has argued that it really only amounts to a contradiction, not a paradox. Larmore is led to that view because

he thinks that it is claiming what is surely only a fantasy, namely, that in such autonomous action, one is required to make an unjustified leap from the non-normative realm to the normative. Charles Larmore, *Les Pratiques de moi* (Paris: PUF, 2004). This, however, simply misunderstands, or at least misrepresents, the claims being put forward by Kantians (or Hegelians), who in fact never claimed any such thing, and whose systems are partly constructed out of the denial of that fantasy.

13 See Barbara Herman, *The Practice of Moral Judgment* (Cambridge, Mass.: Harvard University Press, 1993); Allen Wood, *Kant's Ethical Thought* (Cambridge: Cambridge University Press, 1999).

14 Korsgaard, *Sources of Normativity*, p. 101.

15 It is very unclear that this can really count as a Kantian conception, and, even if it does, if it can survive as an independent conception. See Robert Pippin, "Rigorism and 'the New Kant'," in *Kant und die Berliner Aufklärung: Akten des IXth Internationalen Kant-Kongresses*, V. Gerhardt, Rolf-Peter Horstmann and Ralph Schumacher (eds) (New York: de Gruyter, 2001), and "Über Selbstgesetzgebung," in *Deutsche Zeitschrift für Philosophie*, Bd. 6 (2003). Pippin rightfully (to my mind) is puzzled about several moves made in this interpretation of Kantian moral theory. They fall short in that they make Kant into a "value-theorist" concerned with promoting a basic, core value instead of deriving all moral content and moral worth from the pure demands of practical reason itself; and that some of the more procedural interpretations of the imperative do not, as they claim to do, definitively free Kant from the charge of "rigorism." On the first point: Pippin argues that it seems like a bit of a leap to argue from "I must value my humanity in myself as a condition of valuing everything else" to "I must value *your* humanity in you"; your capacity, for example, "to set the end" of becoming the greatest collector of Hummel figurines in the world is hardly the kind of thing that is likely to, or even should, inspire the unconditional awe that Kant thinks is supposed to accompany this value. Second, with regard to the "rigorism" charge (that is, the idea that acting from duty alone imposes such rigid restrictions on what can count as moral that it in effect rules out most of what otherwise – even in many of Kant's own examples – pass as moral and thus actually rules out moral worth instead of capturing what it is about), Pippin argues that what lands Kant in this predicament is his own way of conceiving the issue of responsibility in terms of our ultimate responsibility for all our actions as being based in our own causality (which initiates a causal chain without itself being the effect of any prior cause). But the idea that all we are testing for is some kind of "what we would have done if the other contingent, sensible inclinations had not been present" does not help us to get at what really constitutes the so-called duty to act only out of a sense of duty which would not itself be subject to the rigorism charge; this is so since such a counterfactual conception involves us in so many undecidable conditionals that it becomes, at least as a piece of *practical* philosophy, useless.

16 This is a conception of autonomy developed in Christine Korsgaard's writings; for example, in her recent Locke lectures (which she has posted on her website), she says with regard to a character (Harriet, taken from Jane Austen's novel, *Emma*) who "whenever she has to make any of the important decisions and choices of her life, the way that Harriet does that is to try to figure out what Emma thinks she should do, and then she does that." Korsgaard concludes,

> Harriet is heteronomous, not in the sense that her actions are caused by Emma rather than chosen by herself, but in the sense that she allows herself to be governed in her choices by a law outside of herself – by Emma's will. It even helps my case here that the original Harriet does this because she is afraid to think for herself. For as I have argued elsewhere, this is how Kant envisions the

operation of the principle of self-love. Kant does not envision the person who acts from self-love as actively reflecting on what he has reason to do and arriving at the conclusion that he ought to do what he wants. Instead, Kant envisions him as one who simply follows the lead of his inclinations, without sufficient reflection. He's heteronomous, and gets his law from nature, not in the sense that it causes his actions, but in the sense that he allows himself to be governed without much thought by its proposals – just as Harriet allows herself to be governed by Emma's.

p. 16, Lecture V. (http://www.people.fas.harvard.edu/~korsgaar/Korsgaard.LL5.pdf)

17 As Korsgaard argues in *The Sources of Normativity*, we *endorse* our impulses by determining whether they are consistent with the ways we identify ourselves, that is, with what our practical identities are. But, as she grants, most of our self-conceptions are contingent (p. 120). Thus, the reason for conforming to your particular practical identity is not a reason that springs from one of those particular identities; it springs instead from one's humanity, and it is thus a reason only if you treat your humanity *in that way* as a practical identity, which raises the question as to whether there is a non-question-begging way of arguing for the rationality of that practical identity (p. 121).

18 This is especially stressed in Pippin's writings. See his most recent collection, Robert Pippin, *The Persistence of Subjectivity* (Cambridge: Cambridge University Press, 2005). See also Nancy Sherman, *Making a Necessity Out of Virtue* (Cambridge: Cambridge University Press, 1997), where Sherman argues that Kantian morality must function as a component within a more Aristotelian style set of commitments.

19 This antinomy itself finds its mirror image in the well known feature of first person statements: On the one hand, in stating, say, a belief, I am not so much reporting on some area of psychological fact within myself (to which I supposedly have some kind of privileged access) as much as I am undertaking a commitment; believing something is committing myself, for example, to the truth of certain claims; but, knowing that I am a finite, fallible creature, I also acknowledge that my believing something is not equivalent to its being true. I acknowledge, that is, a potential gap between all my commitments and what is really true. Let us call this potential gap by the term Hegel gave it: Negativity. We should also note that such "negativity" also has a kind of proto-form of itself in nature, where there can be a gap between what an organ (such as a heart or lungs) is *supposed* to do (pump blood, gather oxygen for circulation) and what it might really do (if, for example, it is diseased and does not do what it is supposed to do); but the genuine shape of negativity has to do with the distinction between something not functioning as it is supposed to (as in the case of diseased organs) or an agent not performing as he is socially enjoined to (as in the case of somebody violating a social rule) and that of a claim being *false*, that is, with the distinction between something "functioning right" and our "getting it right." This basic and simple idea – that our thought answers to the way the world is, that there is a fundamental distinction between being and thought which is itself a normative distinction, something set by "thought" itself, such that this *absolute* distinction must be held within a *single* thought of "thought and the world" – is what lies behind the idea of the Hegelian "dialectical negativity."

20 Indeed, it can be said without too much exaggeration that to understand Hegel is to understand how it is that he wanted to unite three seemingly disparate influences: Kant, Aristotle, and Christianity. This is not to deny the obvious influence of other thinkers on Hegel, such as (obviously) Plato, Spinoza, Fichte, and Schelling (along with a host of others). It is to say, though, that Hegel's omnivorous appropriation of

these other thinkers is mostly structured by his synthesis of the big three (Kant, Aristotle, Christianity).

21 G.W.F. Hegel, *Enzyklopädie der philosophischen Wissenschaften*, § 246 in Hegel, *Werke in zwanzig Bänden* (ed. Eva Moldenhauer and Karl Markus Michel, Frankfurt a.M.: Suhrkamp Verlag, 1971), vol. 8.

22 In his early, pre-*Phenomenology* writings, Hegel often used "life" in contexts where he would later prefer the term, "spirit," and he would speak of a "shape of life" in a way that foreshadowed his later preference for a shape of spirit. In "The Spirit of Christianity and its Fate," he even (more or less) equated a "shape of life" with a "form of life" (*Lebensform*):

> und die Liebe mußte immer die Form der Liebe, des Glaubens an Gott behalten ohne lebendig zu werden und in *Gestalten des Lebens* sich darzustellen, weil jede Gestalt des Lebens entgegensetzbar vom Verstand als sein Objekt, als eine Wirklichkeit, gefaßt werden kann; und das Verhältnis gegen die Welt mußte zu einer Ängstlichkeit vor ihren Berührungen werden, eine Furcht vor jeder Lebensform, weil in jeder sich, da sie Gestalt hat und nur **eine** Seite ist, ihr Mangel aufzeigen läßt und dies Mangelnde ein Anteil an der Welt ist.
>
> *Werke*, I, p. 403. (Underlining refers to italicized words by me)

In the later 1820 *Philosophy of Right*, he instead employed only the phrase, "Gestalt des Lebens," to express the idea of a "form of life."

23 This is what Hegel in his own jargon called the *Idea*, the "unity of concept and reality," or "the unity of concept and objectivity."

24 Heinrich Heine reported that Hegel once casually remarked to him that "if one were to write down all the dreams that people in a particular period had, then there would arise out of a reading of these collected dreams a wholly accurate picture of the spirit of that period." Henrich Heine, *Lutetia*, Part 2, p. 376. (Vol. IV *Sämtliche Werke*) ["Mein großer Lehrer, der selige Hegel, sagte mir einst: 'Wenn man die Träume aufgeschrieben hätte, welche die Menschen während einer bestimmten Periode geträumt haben, so würde einem aus der Lektüre dieser gesammelten Träume ein ganz richtiges Bild vom Geiste jener Periode aufsteigen.'"]

25 Hegel, *Enzyklopädie*, § 66. (My italics.) This idea is also congruent with Wittgenstein's oft-cited conclusion: "If I have exhausted the justifications, I have reached bedrock, and my spade is turned. Then I am inclined to say: 'This is simply what I do.'" *Philosophical Investigations*, trans. G.E.M. Anscombe (New York: Macmillan, 1953), para. 217. In the passage cited, Hegel goes on to add, "In all these cases, immediacy of knowledge not only does not exclude mediation, but the two are so bound together that immediate knowledge is even the product and result of mediated knowledge."

26 This is one of the main reasons why Hegel opts for those cases where the "norm" is losing its grip on people in order to explain how it is that a norm ever has its grip in the first place. Understanding how an accepted norm breaks down is also the key to understanding how we can at first stand behind our actions only to come to a realization later that those reasons were not sufficient, or were not the reasons we told ourselves we had, such that our "fate" can be that we are not in fact exercising self-rule but (as we come to see) are being pushed around by inclinations that we could not in retrospect redeem with good reasons.

27 Curiously, this feature of classical liberalism has been little noted by philosophers; the sociologist-historian, Richard Sennett, on the other hand, has made it a focus of some of his accounts of the psychological problems of liberalism. See Richard Sennett, *Respect in a World of Inequality* (New York: W.W. Norton and Co., 2003).

28 This is the original Rousseauian worry, a fear that runs from Rousseau up through Heidegger. Such worries typically center around the fear that in our modern social world, we are regularly called on by something like the logic of our own institutions to do things that do not match up or congrue well with our own deepest commitments. The result of this distortion is that we somehow become so *absorbed* into the social order that we never even notice the conflict, and we thus face two choices: We become "one of them," what Heidegger describes as an individual unreflectively carrying out the practices of *das Man*; or we live the life of the internal exile, forever alienated from all that we are called on to do.

29 Or, as Hegel also puts it in *Grundlinien der Rechtsphilosophie*, para. 317 *Zusatz*: "The principle of the modern world demands that what each is supposed to recognize show itself to each as entitled to such recognition. In addition, each individual wants to have a voice and to be given a hearing." ["Das Prinzip der modernen Welt fordert, daß, was jeder anerkennen soll, sich ihm als ein Berechtigtes zeige. Außerdem aber will jeder noch mitgesprochen und geraten haben."] *Werke*, vol. 7. Nancy Sherman's modified proposal for understanding the place of the categorical imperative in ethical life is relevant here: She claims that the "Formula of Humanity" should be taken to play a different role from that of "didactically supplementing a universalizing procedure. I propose that in many cases in which we must deliberate about the morally right action, Kantian deliberation is not a matter of universalizing but, rather, a matter of reflecting on what respect for rational agency requires of us in the circumstances before us." Sherman, *Making a Necessity of Virtue*, p. 310.

30 John Findlay in his *Values and Intentions* (London: Allen and Unwin, 1961) claimed that the lessons of the Hegelian discussion of the Terror in the French Revolution consist in this: "The values of justice and injustice may be held to be the fruits of the *disjunction of persons*," which he also refers to as the "*exclusiveness of persons*" (p. 293). It was John Rawls, of course, who put it in the terms of not taking the differences among individuals seriously, and the inspiration for that seems to have come from Findlay.

10

HEGEL, FICHTE AND THE PRAGMATIC CONTEXTS OF MORAL JUDGEMENT

Paul Redding

Hegel's treatment of '*Moralität*' in both the *Phenomenology of Spirit* and the *Philosophy of Right* provides important clues as to how he conceives the recognitive dynamics of modern moral life. As 'spirit that is certain of itself', morality as comprehended in the *Phenomenology* is the final form of spirit [*Geist*], which, in Hegel's exposition, follows 'reason' which itself had followed 'consciousness' and 'self-consciousness'. Spirit had first been considered in its objective form as an 'in itself'. This was the 'true spirit' of the ethical world of antiquity. As something 'for itself', spirit had then been considered in its self-alienated form as 'culture' which had culminated in an analysis of modern politics – specifically the political project of 'absolute freedom', the French Revolution, and the terroristic consequences that had been so acutely linked to the modern rationalist political project by Schiller. But, as many have pointed out, if Rousseau was the theorist of the modern political struggle for autonomy, Kant had an equally revolutionary conception of moral autonomy, which, like Rousseau, put the idea of a self-legislating will at the centre of thought. Such an internalization of the self-legislating will, however, now reveals the proper object for judgement in terms of the evaluative polarity of good and bad – the will itself. This evaluation becomes the task of *conscience*.

In this paper, I examine Hegel's treatment of the role of conscience in moral judgement in the light of his relationship to Fichte, and interpret it in terms of a broadly conceived pragmatics of reason-giving in moral life implicit in his concept of intersubjective *recognition* [*Anerkennung*].

The dilemmas of Kantian morality: the 'moral worldview' and conscience

As the stance of 'morality', which is meant to combine the 'in itself' and 'for itself' dimensions of the earlier moments of spirit, Hegel examines the subjectivized version of practical reason more characteristic of the situation in Germany, in the period after the French Revolution, than in France, and traces it through a series of dialectically related forms. The first of these, 'the moral worldview [*moralische Weltanschauung*]', is identifiably Kantian and has clear connections to the Fichtean shape of self-consciousness. From within the moral worldview, a conscious moral agent takes rationally determined *duty*, that is, 'pure' duty as determined by the moral law, to be their absolute essence, the expression of their absolute freedom. But duty conceived in this way will be regarded as 'indifferent' to the natural world, which in turn will be regarded as 'indifferent' to it.[1] That is, the moral worldview so conceived arises at the same time as the modern scientific view of nature, with the normative law-governed realm of duty and the descriptive law governed realm of nature – the Kantian noumenal and phenomenal realms – thought of as somehow complete in themselves and unable to interact, and hence, as mutually 'indifferent'.

The general complexion of Hegel's criticisms of (what he regards as) the abstract 'formalism' and 'rigorism' of Kant's conception of morality are well known. Here Hegel's emphasis is on the moral outlook's response to what it learns of the indifference of the natural realm to the duty of which it is certain. Unable to harmonize morality and nature, the moral worldview resorts to the Kantian *postulates*, effectively utilizing the symbolic formal correspondence between prescriptive and descriptive laws. Grasping its own finitude and its inability to act on *pure* duty, the moral worldview construes the idea of pure duty, the determinate moral law, as the object of another, *divine*, consciousness. This all leads to the thought, however, that the world of morality exists *only* in thought, and this leads to the 'dissemblance and duplicity', combining the acknowledgement of morality by a subject forced to act in a world conceived as indifferent to it.

Hegel had been critical of the constitutive dichotomy at the heart of Kant's moral consciousness from at least the time of his early writings on religion. Like many (probably most) other interpreters of Kant, Hegel seems to have taken *as the whole* of Kant's moral philosophy what more liberal Kantians have come to take as *one part* of a fuller account – the deduction of the 'objective' conditions of the moral will, requiring the augmentation of a 'moral anthropology' setting out the conditions for the *application* of the moral law in action.[2] Reacting against those forms of philosophy in which practical reason was assimilated to theoretical cognition, Kant's project, from the time of the transcendental turn, had been most focussed on the 'objective' side of the larger project, and the exploration of the 'subjective' conditions concerning the application of reason had been confined to the margins. Nevertheless, Kant himself had signalled the need for the development of this applied side of ethics, and this need was felt even more strongly among his immediate followers such as Fichte.[3] It is Fichte's attempt to do just this that comes into focus in the next section of 'Morality' in the *Phenomenology of Spirit* in the context of Hegel's discussion of *conscience*.

After following the fate of the moral worldview into the antinomies that are expressed in 'duplicity', Hegel turns to a moral stance in which the Kantian approach had been given a particularly subjectivistic inflection in order to address the problem of the applicability of the formal moral law, the approach of 'conscience [*Gewissen*]'. The moral worldview had located the moral law, *qua* law with material content, in *another* consciousness, that of God as absolute moral authority, effectively re-enacting the attitude of the earlier 'unhappy consciousness'. The idea that this other consciousness is *nothing other* than its own thought, however, causes the moral worldview to relocate the source of this authority back within itself. It believes that *it itself* is 'in its contingency completely valid in its own sight, and knows its immediate singularity [*Einzelheit*] to be pure knowing and doing, to be the true reality and harmony'.[4]

One aspect of the disunity of theoretical and practical reason found in Kant that worried the post-Kantians was just that aspect of his moral theory about which Kant himself had been concerned – that of the subjective conditions for the application of the moral law. In short, one has to be able to identify both actions and worldly situations in morally salient terms that allow the *application* of the moral law in practice, but this presupposes some quasi-theoretical form of description of actions or situations in terms sensitive to their *intrinsic* normative status. This, however, is just what neither theoretical nor practical reason conceived on Kant's strictly transcendental model were able to deliver. Theoretical knowledge, as conceived within the 'Transcendental Analytic' of the *Critique of Pure Reason*, is more or less identified with the knowledge constitutive of modern science – that resulting from the operations of 'the Understanding' – and describes a world 'indifferent' to morality. Practical reason, on the other hand, was formal and, as even Kant himself had acknowledged,[5] in need of something akin to the 'schemata' of theoretical reason for application in concrete situations.

It was to address this issue of the applicability of the moral law that Fichte, in *The System of Ethics According to the Principles of the Wissenschaftslehre* (1798), had put forward a theory of conscience.[6] As Hegel portrays it in the *Phenomenology*, conscience is a quasi-aestheticized form of moral consciousness in that an immediately *felt* assurance is taken as criterial for the goodness or purity of the will. Indeed, for Fichte, the feeling involved in conscience testified to the purity of the will in a way analogous to the way that feeling testifies to the beauty of some presentation in aesthetic experience. It is just this *immediate certainty* [*Gewissheit*] that attaches to the judgements of *conscience* [*Gewissen*] that characterizes the moral stance of Hegel's 'beautiful soul'.[7] As has often been commented upon, with this notion Hegel alludes to moral positions expressed within literary works of his time, such as Goethe's *Werther* and Jacobi's *Woldemar*,[8] but the account of 'conscience' lying at the core of his account seems to be distinctly Fichtean.[9] The 'beautiful soul' may not represent a straight-forwardly Fichtean moral stance, but it would at least seem to represent what Hegel understood as a certain romantic variant of it.

Fichte discusses conscience in a number of places in *The System of Ethics* in ways which overlap with aspects of earlier approaches such as that of Rousseau, who had similarly established a link between sentiment and lawfulness with his notion of conscience as an 'infallible judge of good and bad' whose acts were not conscious judgements but rather innate sentiments.[10] In §11 of *The System of Ethics*, Fichte talks of conscience as a higher 'power' or 'faculty' of feeling [*Gefühlsvermögen*], through which we reproach ourselves or, alternatively, are at peace with ourselves when we reflect on our empirical will.[11] Negatively, feelings of disapproval of the self range from a type of annoyance at oneself to stronger forms of self-reproach and self-contempt. In its positive form, it is the feeling of self-respect – a respect for one's 'higher character' that gives courage and strength.[12]

In the discussion of conscience Fichte reprises the theme of absolute self-positing from his earlier *Wissenschaftslehre* of 1794–95.[13] Conscience is effectively a summons to self-determination, an *immediate* form of self-consciousness in which we are conscious of our 'higher nature and absolute freedom', that 'pure drive' in which we strive after freedom.[14] Unlike the lower faculty of desire, the pure drive for self-determination does not present itself as a simple feeling or affection of *being driven*, but as the intuition of *active striving*: it is expressed as an absolute demand for self-determination.[15] In conscience, in contrast to those feelings bound up with the satisfaction or frustration of natural drives, I am in immediate intuitive contact with my higher, essential, self. While the sensuous pleasure which accompanies the satisfaction of natural drives, 'tears me away from myself, alienates me from myself', in conscience I am led *back into myself*.[16] That the expressions of conscience provide that within which one recognizes one's true identity is an idea carried through in Hegel.

The types of non-sensory pleasures and displeasures of conscience suggest Kant's notion of 'disinterested' aesthetic pleasure, and Fichte explicitly compares the particular feelings involved in conscience with those of *aesthetic* experience so conceived. Acting morally involves the determination of what it is that constitutes one's duty in specific circumstance – the recognition of some envisaged path of action as being the one to be followed. The moral law alone cannot do this. It is purely formal and tells us simply to act according to the 'conviction of our duty', but, as such it is itself incapable of determining any material content *for* duty, that is, incapable of determining what our duty actually amounts to.[17] On the other hand, for its part, theoretical reason can represent and reason *about* actions, but cannot determine whether or not any particular action *is* required by duty.[18] It is just this gap between theoretical and practical reason that conscience is to bridge.

It is the distinctively *polar* nature of the judgements of conscience, the feelings of approval or disapproval we have when considering, say, possible courses of action, that is relevant in the task of applying the moral law. We can bring possible actions before ourselves in imagination, and reason about them by the use of the theoretical faculty, but this process needs some *non-inferential* judgement that plays a role parallel to that played by perception in theoretical inquiry. Judgement based on the immediate moral feelings of conscience is what performs this task. The feelings of approval and disapproval experienced here are unlike the pleasures and displeasures that accompany the satisfactions and frustrations of the 'lower' faculty of desire which would be relevant to the determination of a purely instrumental – prudential rather than moral – action. But these feelings belonging to conscience can be compared to the aesthetic feelings: 'All aesthetic feelings are similar to the feeling that we have described here in that they arise from the satisfaction of a drive in accordance with a determinate representation.'[19]

Not only are the moral sentiments of conscience like those of disinterested aesthetic judgement in their polarly opposed approvals and disapprovals, Fichte also appeals to the same faculty or 'power' of judgement for their employment. The 'faculty of the free imagination' involved in the search to determine one's duty is able to hover between and contemplate alternative possibilities in its attempt to find the right way of characterizing these alternatives.

> As soon as the power of judgment finds what was demanded, the fact that this is indeed what was demanded reveals itself through a feeling of harmony. The power of the imagination is now bound and compelled, as it is in the case of everything real. I cannot view this matter in any way other than in the way I do view it: constraint is present, as it is in the case of every feeling. This feeling provides cognition with *immediate certainty*, with which *calm* and satisfaction are connected.[20]

Crucially, like Rousseau, Fichte attests to the *infallibility* of the moral authority of conscience:

> Conscience never errs and cannot err, for it is the immediate consciousness of our pure, original I, over and above which there is no other kind of consciousness; it cannot be examined nor corrected by any other kind of consciousness. Conscience is itself the judge [*Richter*] of all convictions, and acknowledges [*anerkannt*] no higher judge above itself. It has final jurisdiction and is subject to no appeal.[21]

But the role of sentiment for Fichte is compatible with an essentially *cognitive* approach to the judgements of conscience as is clear in his treatment of what is entailed by *freedom of choice*.

Freedom of choice, Fichte points out, concerns the capacity to choose *among* alternative courses of action: for example, from the envisaged alternatives A, B or C, I might choose C, and the very idea of *freedom* in choice here implies, he claims, that there must be some *basis* or *reason* for this choice, otherwise the nomination of one of the alternatives would look random and a mere matter of chance.[22] This in turn implies that the choice must be mediated by *concepts*: in choosing C from the range of alternatives A, B, or C, there must be some property F belonging to C that renders it *preferable*. But this implies a rule –

what Kant had called a 'maxim' – and it is this maxim that is 'the object of most immediate consciousness'.[23] It would seem then that what is given in an immediately felt preference must be able to be displayed as something like the conclusion of a syllogism the major premise or 'rule' of which displays the *grounds* of the preference. It is this 'maxim' rather than the merely chosen action that is the 'immediate object' of moral evaluation, and this has to do with the fact that what is being judged in conscience is not action *per se* but the quality of the moral character expressed *in* it.[24]

Fichte remarks that the term 'maxim' is well chosen as the maxim is indeed the 'highest' or 'maximum' to be encountered in the pursuit of 'grounds'. In the 'Transcendental Dialectic' of the *Critique of Pure Reason*, Kant describes the pursuit of grounds or conditions as a matter of prosyllogistically *ascending* a formal structure that in its formal logical interpretation is a *descending* (episyllogistic) one.[25] As in theoretical reason this rule or maxim is then to be thought of as the 'major' premise of a syllogism. But whereas in theoretical reason the major premise can always be subordinated to a higher rule, here, as Fichte notes, we are dealing with the highest or 'maximum', and that it is this inner *ground* of the action that is judged in conscience links up with Kant's discussion of maxims in the opening paragraphs of *Religion within the Boundaries of Mere Reason*. It is the purported moral maxim that is adopted by a person as the subjective ground of their action that is what we refer to, Kant tells us, when we use terms like 'good' or 'evil' of them. 'We call a human being evil . . . not because he performs actions that are evil (contrary to law), but because these are so constituted that they allow the inference of evil maxims in him'.[26] The affirmation of this subjective ground must *itself* be considered to be 'an *Actus* of freedom (for otherwise the use or abuse of the human being's power of choice with respect to the moral law could not be imputed to him, nor could the good or evil in him be called "moral")'.[27] Kant makes the same point that Fichte alludes to in his comment on the appropriateness of the word 'maxim': while it may look as if it could generate an endless prosyllogism of grounds in seeking further grounds for the individual's chosen maxim,

> one cannot . . . go on asking what, in a human being, might be the subjective ground for the adoption of this rather than the opposite maxim [*der entgegengesetzen Maxime*]. . . . Whenever we therefore say, "The human being is by nature good", or "He is by nature evil", this only means that he holds within himself a first ground (to us inscrutable) for the adoption of good or evil (unlawful) maxims.[28]

From an Hegelian position we might anticipate where the problems afflicting conscience so conceived will lie. Inevitably for Hegel it will be the *givenness* and *finality* of the authority of a pure conscience untainted by finitude that will be found to be problematic, and equally inevitably it will be dealt with by being 'negated' but nevertheless 'preserved' within a further recognitive unity.

There is, of course, already an internal moment of '*Anerkennen*' present within conscience, as the quasi-judicial rulings of the 'voice' of the moral subject's conscience are recognized as definitive by it. Such a voice will itself have to be shown to be equally marked by the finitude that accompanies objectivity, and Hegel will follow the now well-established pattern initiated in the original treatment of recognition in chapter 4 of the *Phenomenology*. That is, he will split the *conscientious* self into independent and dependent agencies, the judging conscience (the pure I) and the judged (actual or anticipated) acting empirical self, and it will be the *non-reciprocal* nature of this relation that will bring this formally 'conscientious' self undone.

The lessons of the beautiful soul

The beautiful soul, who aspires to act on the purest of motives, comes to learn that others will not necessarily recognize its good intentions *in* the actual deed itself. Just as the nature of a force will be displayed in its effects, the essential nature of an action will be displayed in the effects it brings about in others. From this point of view, then, it is likely that an interpreter affected *by* the action of another is going to see the action in different terms to those operative in the agent's own self-understanding.

Hegel's discussion of action here broaches issues made explicit in twentieth-century analytic philosophy by Elizabeth Anscombe and Donald Davidson, who have stressed the significance of the description under which any action is attributed to an agent by others or herself.[29] While any 'deed' will be able to be described in a variety of ways, we only attribute to an agent as intentional an action described in ways such that the agent herself would recognize it as her doing. In the *Philosophy of Right* Hegel captures this idea by describing action as an 'expression of the subjective will', and by insisting on what he calls the agent's 'right of knowledge'.[30] The beautiful soul, then, having found that the act which he believed to be expressive of a good will could be interpreted by others as evil,[31] will resort to attesting to the act's underlying subjective grounds. That is, the agent now attests to the goodness of the *convictions* behind its potentially misreadable act. This move from the act itself to the subjective intention expressed in it underscores a difference that Fichte had insisted on with regard to practical reason. Where what is in question is primarily a matter of the rightness or otherwise of the intentional action performed, the matter is effectively a legal one, but where the issue is primarily about the quality of the maxim expressed in the action, the issue has become a properly moral one. Thus, now it is the agent's attested motivations, understood in their function of expressing something of the agent's moral character, that comes to exist 'for another'.[32] For Hegel this is a crucial move. In grasping the importance of justifying his intentions by placing them in the 'space of reasons', the beautiful soul has found a properly 'spiritual' environment for them. Now they are expressed to others who are capable of challenging the agent's self-interpretations from their own points of view. The beautiful soul has thus found the medium in which the felt convictions of his conscience are subject to a genuinely 'higher' judge – that of a promised intersubjectively achieved rational agreement.[33]

The 'aesthetic' theme within the story of the beautiful soul is underlined with Hegel's reference to 'the moral *genius* which knows the inner voice of what it immediately knows to be a divine voice'.[34] This idea might be regarded as pointing in two complementary directions. First, the Fichtean interpretation of conscience as the infallible supreme judge – 'who acknowledges no higher judge above it' and whose jurisdiction is 'subject to no appeal'[35] – equates the authority of conscience with that of a God who is entirely *within*. In the remark in the Heidelberg *Philosophy of Right* where Hegel links Fichteanism with the beautiful soul, he remarks that fear of the finitude that taints action means that beautiful souls 'remain enclosed within themselves, and revere their inner infinitude, all of which led them to make themselves, their ego, God'.[36] Added to this, the pantheistic twist given to Fichtean 'innerness' by the romantics could allow *feeling* to be interpreted as both natural and normative. In Kant's own aesthetic theory it was through the medium of genius that nature was said to 'prescribe the rule' to art.[37] This, however, had provided an open door for the more romantic of the post-Kantians to a kind of *aestheticized* and *naturalized* moral sense theory, and Hegel's allusion here to the inner 'divine voice' brings out the attendant divinizing of nature (as that which would 'prescribe the rule to' *morals* or life in general) implicit in such a move. The beautiful soul, then, would seem to be Hegel's characterization of just such a composite romanticized Fichtean moral position, and while it was not a position Hegel shared with those contemporaries, it was one whose anti-dualistic motivations he could appreciate, and it was one which he regarded as a distinct advance on the earlier 'Kantian' conception of the moral worldview.[38]

The *romantic* beautiful soul grasps itself and its community of like-minded souls as 'natural' and divinizes this nature by regarding it as the source of normativity. Thus 'this solitary divine worship is at the same time essentially the divine worship of a *community* [*Gemeinde*]'.[39] This fundamentally religious conception of community involved here is crucial for Hegel. But just as nature has to be *taken* as 'giving the rule' to our normative practices, so too can it be regarded as divine only *in so far as it has been divinized* by those who act according to rules. That is, for Hegel 'the divine' resides *not* in nature itself but rather in a particular normative practice within which 'natural' immediate feelings are afforded a particular but fallible normative role. And just as pantheism in general comes to grief on the problem of evil, so too does this form of pantheism. The romantic community so constituted has yet to come to terms with the consequences of the perspectival difference that had earlier expressed itself in the discovery that *well-meant* actions can be *taken for* 'evil'. The beautiful soul has yet to acknowledge the fact that such 'evil' potentially attributed by the other is *not* simply a function of the other's subjective *mis*recognition of the intention of an action, but is more deeply grounded: it inheres in the real antitheses between particularly embodied and individuated agents and the purported universality of the intentions upon which they claim to act.[40] The beautiful soul therefore has to get beyond such naïve innocence and be brought to the point where it acknowledges the 'evil' that is irreducibly attendant on its necessary moment of singularity and difference from others, an evil that Kant had captured in his doctrine of 'radical evil' and that had been expressed in the Christian doctrine of original sin.[41] And to achieve this, the beautiful soul must be brought before a harsh judge capable of unmasking the attested universality of its will.

We might think of this 'hard-hearted' judge as giving voice to just that infallible authority that Fichtean 'conscience' is supposed to possess. But throughout the *Phenomenology* Hegel has been intent to point out that such ultimate sources of authority *always* require mediation. Thus the discussion of recognition in chapter 4 had concluded with an account of the 'unhappy consciousness', a shape of self-consciousness which identified the divine law as its final authority but which required the mediation of the priest who represented God to the unhappy consciousness in the way that the lord represented the power of death to the bondsman. But lords, priests, and other representatives of authority are also themselves individual human beings, and so will be whoever it is that plays the role of harsh judge for the beautiful soul. Thus, despite their implicit claim to be representing the universality of moral law, the conscientious judge must have *his* actions and intentions, and hence *his* judgements, marked by the same isolating singularity. The hard-hearted judge in his very activity of judging must therefore be himself caught up in the dissembling that had marked the acts of the acting conscience when he claimed to be acting on purely universal principles. So too, in turn the judge must also 'confess' to the first confessor, similarly acknowledging the irreducibly evil aspect of his own intention, marked as it is by his own essential singularity. The 'reconciliation' which can emerge from this interaction of mutually confessing and forgiving moral agents is of profound importance for Hegel: it is *this*, not nature itself as pantheists would have it, that is the presence of the divine in the world. 'The word of reconciliation is the *objectively* existent Spirit, which beholds the pure knowledge of itself *qua* universal essence, in its opposite . . . a reciprocal recognition which is *absolute* Spirit'.[42] The speech act of mutual forgiveness, the 'reconciling *Yea*, in which the two 'I's let go their antithetical [*entgegensetzten*] *existence*', says Hegel,

> is the *existence* of the 'I' which has expanded into a duality, and therein remains identical with itself, and, in its complete externalization [*Entäusserung*] and opposite [*Gegenteile*], possesses the certainty [*Gewissheit*] of itself: it is God manifested in the midst of those who know themselves in the form of pure knowledge.[43]

Thus the source of normativity that transcends the instituting act of any individual, that which is grasped from the religious point of view as divine, is the dynamic process of reciprocal recognition itself that is inherent in a community of agents who deal with the *evil* consequences of their own ineliminable singularity by the mutual confessing and forgiving of such evil, in the context of holding each other to mutually acknowledged norms. In this form of recognition each is now *certain* of his or her singular self *not* as a perfect essence embedded in an imperfect individualized shell – a soul in a body or its Fichtean counterpart, an unlimited 'I' in an inessential finite particular context – but in such a way that their finite aspect is as equally essential as the infinite.

Morality in the *Philosophy of Right*

In a discussion of 'the moral standpoint' and conscience in 'Part 2' (headed 'Morality') of the *Philosophy of Right*, Hegel alludes to a distinction which can help us to understand the nature of the resolution of the dialectic of the beautiful soul. There he differentiates the same *formal* conscience that we see at work in the beautiful soul from true (or truthful, *wahrhaftige*) conscience. Formal conscience is, it would seem, a false or somehow inadequate or one-sided form of true conscience. In fact, (formal) conscience seems to be the *isolated* 'for-self' aspect of an orientation that is to be understood as it is 'in and for itself'. True conscience is described as a disposition or character [*Gesinnung*] that is itself 'contained in' *ethical* [*sittlichen*] character: it is the character 'to will what is good in and for itself'.[44] In contrast, (formal) conscience is the isolable 'for self' aspect of such a true conscience, the *certainty* that it is what it *claims* to be in its 'assertion [*Behauptung*] that what it knows is truly right and duty'.[45]

While in the *Phenomenology*, the topic of morality is followed by that of religion, in the *Philosophy of Right*, the discussion of conscience concludes in the transition to ethical life – *Sittlichkeit* – the immediate form of which is the family. In both places, then, the message seems to be that the *truth* of that authority which conscience *claims* to have, is to be found not 'within', but in the concrete conditions of social dependence. In both religion and the family, there is a reliance of the individual on external authority which contrasts with the inner authority claimed by conscience. But this is not to be understood as if Hegel is advocating some lapse back into the decidedly unfree state of taking one's moral authority from the external world in which one finds authority ready made. Both family and religion are only 'immediate' forms of spirit, and spirit *qua* substance in which an individual subject necessarily dwells is, as is claimed in the preface to the *Phenomenology*, also *subject*. Thus the 'romantic' community of beautiful souls would seem to prefigure a new type or region of *Sittlichkeit* which combines the authority of conscience with communally given norms of social life, a genuinely moral community in which conscience can appear in its *true* form and not in the distorted self-divinizing form from which it started. For its part, the objective ethical life from which conscience in the

Philosophy of Right must draw its substantive content necessarily incorporates the abstractly individualistic structures of civil society for the principle of subjectivity to penetrate through it.[46]

Hegel describes conscience as a distinctly *modern* phenomenon,[47] but also notes that this one-sided type of conscientious *claim*, the claim based on the assumption of having a source of infallible moral authority inside one, typically arises in epochs when subjects lose faith in the moral fabric of the society in which they live, mentioning the examples of Socrates and the Stoics.[48] Typical of all forms of 'self-certainty', the formally conscientious subject claims autonomy from all externally given sources of moral authority, the claims of which are to be struck down by appeal to its own infallible criterion. We might suppose, then, that the type of moral community providing the 'substance' for true conscientiousness must itself be a modern phenomenon, a little like the community of 'beautiful souls', but one in which the idea of conscience as *infallible* has been replaced by one marked by *fallibility*. Here, the individual rulings of the highest judge itself, *conscience*, can be called into question, opposed by their contraries, and asked for justification. Clearly, this could not mark a return to a more traditional form of *Sittlichkeit*. Perhaps Hegel here has in mind something like the form of sociality that Kant had called 'moral friendship' that entails 'the complete confidence of two persons in revealing their secret judgments and feelings to each other, as far as such disclosures are consistent with mutual respect'.[49] The important thing is that whatever this form of *Sittlichkeit* might take, it must be such that the subject could find in its interactions a form of individual identity that is both contentful (like the *immediate* identity gained in the family) but that preserves the 'singularity' that otherwise characterizes the *form* of modern subjectivity at the expense of content.

In one suggestive remark in the *Philosophy of Right*, the verb '*anerkennen*' – to recognize or acknowledge – is used twice in discussing conscience: conscience 'recognises the good *only* in what it knows', and '*is recognized* as . . . holy [*als ein Heiliges . . . anerkannt wird*]' by the individual whose conscience *it is*.[50] These two acts of recognition referred to here are described as operating within the internal dynamics of a single conscientious agent, but in the *Phenomenology of Spirit*, the resolution of the unbridgeable moments of the beautiful soul is, of course, achieved by the most developed form of recognition found in that work, the reciprocal recognition of mutual forgiveness that *is* '*absolute* Spirit'.[51] We might then see Hegel's treatment of the Fichtean concept of conscience as his answer to the problem set by Fichte's 1794–95 *Wissenschaftslehre*.

In Part III of that work Fichte had invoked the primacy of the *moral* subject in reconciling the difference between the I's essential freedom on the one hand and its limitedness by the not-I on the other, and in the *Foundations of Natural Right* of the following year had used the notion of recognition to show how, in a legal context, we might understand the limitation marking individual subjectivity as resulting from its own act of *self*-limitation in the face of the demands of another.[52] For Fichte, however, the notion of recognition is effectively restricted to the context of *legal* self-limitation, morality being handled in terms of the notion of the effectively solipsistic notion of conscience. But, as Robert Pippin has suggested, Hegel extended this approach by treating '*all* normative claims as claims of, attempts at, mutuality of recognition'.[53] It is not unexpected, then, that he treats the claims of *conscience* in this way as well.[54] But with this extension of Fichte's limited concept of recognition Hegel attempts to do justice to just those aspects of conscience thematized by Fichte himself – its profound connection to a dimension of identity that is distinctly modern. On the one hand the voice of conscience is to be grasped as expressing the core of one's moral identity in all its singularity, on the other, this voice must itself be grasped as mediated by that of some other moral agent, some 'moral friend' perhaps, to whom it is addressed.

Brandom's pragmatics and Hegel's 'expressivism'

Among the recent attempts to use the notion of 'recognition' to present Hegel's thought in a way that frees it from charges of a 'dogmatic' pre-critical metaphysical content, Robert Brandom's suggestion that we read Hegel as putting forward a pragmatic 'inferentialist' account of meaning provides one of the most suggestive ways of inserting Hegel into contemporary debates. In Brandom's pragmatics, however, exclusive focus is placed on the form of recognition in which the content of an agent's action is assessed in terms of that agent's 'entitlement'. Thus a theoretical action, an assertion, is a move in a language game to be 'scored' by an interlocutor who assesses the move *qua* change in the asserter's 'doxastic' commitments and entitlements.[55] *Practical* action, the traditional home of the notion of 'entitlement', is handled in a parallel way. In the action of assertion, an agent can be criticized for lacking justification for the content of their belief – entitlement to that which they *take* to be true; in practical action, the agent can be criticized for lacking entitlement to that desired *goal* – to that which they intend to *make* true. But, as we have seen, there is another, crucial, layer of recognition in Hegel's account of the conditions of self-consciousness, beyond that of the quasi-legal concept of 'entitlement'.

For Hegel, following and *extending* Fichte, the recognition involved in the *moral* realm has a different structure to that involved in legality, and what is at issue in the practice of the asking for and giving of reasons in the interchanges between the beautiful soul and his interlocutors differs from that which is at issue in the context of contested claims to *right*. The *moral* perspective I adopt with respect to my own action differs from a legal one in that the former grasps it in terms of what it *expresses*, by way of its purported 'maxim', about my moral character, while the latter grasps it in terms of the conformity of the action so described to some universally applicable law. Kantian morality is often discussed as if it amounts simply to something like an 'internalisation' of the external law governing the 'rights' of members of a polity, and Hegel himself often discusses Kantian morality in this way. But if we view Fichte's account of conscience as a development of that dimension of Kant's approach to morality which focuses on its *subjective* conditions, then we see a quite different conception of morality emerge, and with this, a quite different conception of its difference to legality. From this perspective, morality is not just 'internalized' legality: rather, morality is fundamentally concerned with one's being, we might say, *who* one *must* be, rather than one's *doing* what one *ought* to do. It is this approach which is behind the claims of the beautiful soul as to its *worth* or *value*, claims about the 'goodness' of its expressed will, and not simply to the 'rightness' of its acts.

Modern morality will be presented as categorical because of the way normative considerations have in modernity penetrated beyond the circle of *particularity* (their instantiation of a social role) to the individual considered in their utmost *singularity*, and hence in their radical differentiation from others, and it is this that is given expression in Fichte's conception of conscience through which Hegel wants to pass. Stanley Cavell has lucidly brought out this dimension of the categorical nature of morality in and after Kant. Pointing to the limits of the 'moves in a game' analogy in understanding action, Cavell claims that

> [w]hat you say you *must* do is not 'defined by a practice', for there is no such practice until you make it one, make it *yours*. We might say, such a declaration defines you, establishes your position. . . . This is the way an action Categorically Imperative feels. And though there is not The Categorical Imperative, there are actions which are for us categorically imperative, so far as we have *a* will. . .[56]

Brandom's legalistic approach to practical reasoning goes along with his scepticism towards what he calls the 'romantic expressivist' tradition from which he wants to isolate Hegel. Traditional romantic expressivism, he says, had taken 'as its paradigm something like the relationship between an inner *feeling* expressed by an outer *gesture*',[57] but Hegel gives 'pride of place to *reasoning* in understanding what it is to say or do something',[58] and with his '*rationalistic*, inferentialist' version of expressivism 'holds out the promise of . . . an alternative paradigm'.[59] This rationalistic version of expressivism looks much like what we might call the 'rule expressivism' that results from Sellars's reinterpretation of early twentieth-century 'emotivism'.[60] Like the emotivist, Sellars had claimed that we should indeed think of ethical judgements as *expressing* something about the judge, rather than saying something about the world being judged – in the case of ethics, expressing something about the action being judged. But what is *expressed* in the judgement is not some non-cognitive state, the type of brute feeling that the expressivist has in mind, but the *norm* or *rule* in terms of which the action can be justified. And like Brandom after him, Sellars here sees the issues in the 'legal' terms of conformity of an action to a law, rather than in the moral terms concerned with the agent's *character* that is being expressed in the action's maxim.

It is incontestable that at various points Hegel set himself at odds with those typically 'romantic' contemporaries like Schelling, Schleiermacher and Friedrich Schlegel, but does Hegel's opposition to romanticism warrant interpreting him in terms of Brandom's anti-romantic and 'rationalistic' expressivist alternative? The account of 'conscience' and 'the beautiful soul' given in the *Phenomenology of Spirit* suggests not.[61]

Notes

1 G.W.F. Hegel, *Phenomenology of Spirit*, trans. A.V. Miller (Oxford: Oxford University Press, 1977), § 599 [2.461]. Here and elsewhere, in referring to Hegel's texts the numbers in square brackets following the reference to the given translation refer to the corresponding volume and page numbers in G.W.F. Hegel, *Sämtliche Werke: Jubiläumsausgabe in zwanzig Bänden*, ed. H. Glockner (Stuttgart: Frommann, 1951).

2 As has been stressed, for example, by Robert B. Louden in *Kant's Impure Ethics* (Oxford: Oxford University Press, 2000).

3 Günter Zöller points out that Fichte was critical of the abstract and formalist nature of Kant's moral philosophy, and had brought the perspective of Kant's third *Critique* to bear in his own reinterpretation. G. Zöller, *Fichte's Transcendental Philosophy* (Cambridge: Cambridge University Press, 1998), pp. 63–65.

4 Hegel, *Phenomenology of Spirit*, § 632 [2.484].

5 According to Kant:

> [J]ust as a passage from the metaphysics of nature to physics is needed – a transition having its own special rules – something similar is rightly required from the metaphysics of morals: a transition which, by applying the pure principles of duty to cases of experience, would *schematize* these principles, as it were, and present them as ready for morally practical use.

Immanuel Kant, *The Metaphysics of Morals*, ed. and trans. Mary Gregor (Cambridge: Cambridge University Press, 1996), § 45 [6.468]. Here and elsewhere, in referring to Kant's texts, page numbers to the given translation will be followed, in square brackets, by volume and page numbers to Immanuel Kant, *Kants Gesammelte Schriften* (Berlin: Preussische Akademie der Wissenschaften, 1900–).

6 J.G. Fichte, *The System of Ethics According to the Principles of the Wissenschaftslehre*, ed. and trans. D. Brezeale and G. Zöller (Cambridge: Cambridge University Press, 2005). Here and elsewhere, in referring to Fichte's texts, page numbers to the given translation will be followed, in square brackets, by volume and page numbers from *Johann Gottlieb Fichtes sämmtliche Werke*, I.H. Fichte (ed.) (Berlin: Veit, 1854). The discussion of conscience occurs mostly in 'Part III, Systematic application of the principle of morality, or ethics in the narrower sense'.

Kant himself discusses conscience in Part II of *The Metaphysics of Morals*, 'Metaphysical First Principles of the Doctrine of Virtue', as forming, along with moral feeling, love of human beings, and respect, '*subjective* conditions of receptiveness to the concept of duty'. Kant, *Metaphysics of Morals*, pp. 159–62 [6.399–403]. The link to this quasi-aesthetic feeling (which conscience is said to 'affect by its act', p. 160 [6.400]) is not present in Kant's earlier discussion in *Religion in the Limits of Reason Alone* (in Immanuel Kant, *Religion and Rational Theology*, A.W. Wood and G. di Giovanni (eds) (Cambridge: Cambridge University Press, 1996)), where the issues of *conviction* and *certainty* are most prominent. Fichte refers to Kant's discussion in *Religion* (Fichte, *The System of Ethics*, p. 159 [4.168]) but not to that in the 'Metaphysical

First Principles of Virtue' which had appeared in August 1797, the year prior to the publication of *The System of Ethics*.

7 In the *Critique of Judgment*, Kant uses the phase 'beautiful soul' [*schöne Seele*] in reference to the person whose selfless appreciation of natural beauty suggests the possession of a 'good soul'. Immanuel Kant, *Critique of Judgment*, trans. W. S. Pluhar (Indianapolis: Hackett, 1987), pp. 165–67 [5.298–300].

8 In his *Lectures on Aesthetics*, Hegel himself associates the 'beautiful soul' with these works, most forcibly with Jacobi's *Woldemar*. *Hegel's Aesthetics: Lectures on Fine Art*, trans. T.M. Knox (Oxford: Clarendon Press, 1975), vol 1, pp. 241–42 [12.362].

9 In the discussion of conscience in the Heidelberg 'Lectures on Natural Right', Hegel explicitly links Fichte to the stance of the beautiful soul.

> The point we are now at is pure inner certainty. It is the concept of freedom in its negative relation to self, it is abstract activity, in which no action ensues. The universal element in subjectivity is the good. The Fichtean philosophy, which makes the ego the absolute principle, has in subjective form remained on one side; the objective side has always been given the side of negativity, but the identity [between the two sides] remained incomplete. Objectivity ought to be congruent with pure certainty of oneself, but has remained [self-] perpetuating. The highest standpoint of Fichte's philosophy is *striving*, *yearning*; the inner good has remained merely what ought to be, and what this philosophy amounts to is merely a yearning for what is supposedly good. Beautiful Souls, who have within themselves this infinite self-consciousness, this clarity, have held fast to this standpoint.

G.W.F. Hegel, *Lectures on Natural Right and Political Science: The First Philosophy of Right, Heidelberg 1817–1818, with additions from the lectures of 1818–1819*, as transcribed by Peter Wannenmann; ed. staff of the Hegel Archives; intro. O. Pöggeler, trans. J.M. Stewart and P.C. Hodgson (Berkeley: University of California Press, 1995), § 68 remark, p. 127. I am grateful to Jean-Philippe Deranty for pointing out this reference to me.

10 Jean-Jacques Rousseau, *Emile: or, On Education*, trans. A. Bloom (New York: Basic Books, 1979), pp. 290 and 285. Earlier, the role of individual conscience within life had, of course, been made central by Luther. On Luther's notion of conscience see Michael G. Baylor, *Action and Person: Conscience in Late Scholasticism and the Young Luther* (Leiden: Brill, 1977).

11 Fichte, *The System of Ethics*, pp. 139–40 [4.147].

12 Ibid., p. 139 [4.146]. Fichte takes pains to dissociate the pleasure [*Lust*] involved in positive self-assessment from any sensory enjoyment [*Genuss*], but then goes on to suggest that the 'repose' or 'peace' of a good conscience should not even be considered as a *pleasure* at all. Ibid. pp. 139–40 [4.146–47].

13 J.G. Fichte, *The Science of Knowledge with the First and Second Introductions*, ed. and trans. P. Heath and J. Lachs (Cambridge: Cambridge University Press, 1982).

14 Fichte, *The System of Ethics*, p. 137 [4.144].

15 Ibid., pp. 137–38 [4.144–45].

16 Ibid., p. 139 [4.146].

17 Ibid., pp. 171–72 [4.180–81].

18 Ibid., pp. 157–58 [4.166].

19 Ibid., p. 158 [4.167]. But, Fichte continues, 'aesthetic feelings are unlike the feeling that we are now discussing inasmuch as the drive underlying them does not absolutely *demand* satisfaction, but simply *expects* it, as a favor of nature'.

20 Ibid., p. 159 [4.167–68].

21 Ibid., p. 165 [4.174].
22 Here he seems to have in mind the idea that a 'choice' so experienced would be experienced more as something that *happens* to the chooser, rather than something that *they do*.
23 Ibid., p. 171 [4.180].
24 Michael Baylor also stresses the similarly *expressivist* significance that conscience had for Luther, who appealed to conscience to deflect evaluative focus from concrete particular actions to the *whole person* whose *faith in Christ* is to be expressed in their actions. Baylor, *Action and Person*, ch. 6.
25 Immanuel Kant, *Critique of Pure Reason*, ed. and trans. P. Guyer and A.W. Wood (Cambridge: Cambridge University Press, 1998), A330–31/B386–88.
26 Kant, *Religion and Rational Theology*, p. 70 [6.20].
27 Ibid., [6.21].
28 Ibid., p. 71 [6.21] translation modified. Kant goes on to clarify in a remark that the proposition 'The human being is (by nature) either morally good or morally evil' is truly *disjunctive* and that there is no 'middle position between the two extremes'.
29 For an excellent account of these issues in Hegel see Michael Quante's *Hegel's Theory of Action*, trans. D. Moyar (Cambridge: Cambridge University Press, 2004).
30 G.W.F. Hegel, *Elements of the Philosophy of Right*, ed. A.W. Wood, trans. H.B. Nisbet (Cambridge: Cambridge University Press, 1991), § 117.
31 Hegel, *Phenomenology of Spirit*, § 642 [2.491–92].
32 Ibid., §§ 650–56 [2.498–502].
33 C.f., Allen Speight, 'Hegel on Conscience and the History of Moral Philosophy', in K. Deligiorgi ed. *Hegel: New Directions* (Chesham: Acumen, 2006), pp. 28–29.
34 Hegel, *Phenomenology of Spirit*, § 655 [2.501], emphasis added, to which Hegel adds 'and since, in knowing this, it has an equally immediate knowledge of existence, it is the divine creative power which in its Notion possesses the spontaneity of life'. (Ibid.)
35 Fichte, *The System of Ethics*, p. 165 [4.174–75].
36 Hegel, *Lectures on Natural Right and Political Science* § 68. An addition to the Berlin lectures from the winter semester 1818–19 has Hegel describing conscience as 'the highest seat of judgment [*der höchste Richtestuhl*], the highest place of innerness [*Innerlichkeit*], something holy'. G.W.F. Hegel, *Die Philosophie des Rechts: Die Mistschriften Wannermann (Heidelberg 1817–18) und Homeyer (Berlin 1818–19)*, Herausgegeben, eingeleitet und erläutert von K.-H. Ilting (Stuttgart: Klett-Cotta, 1983), p. 246, § 70, addition.
37 Kant, *Critique of Judgment*, § 46 [5.308].
38 For Hegel, the reason that the beautiful soul marks an advance over Kantian moral self-consciousness has little to do with nature itself and much to do with the fact that the beautiful soul has learned to express its 'inner' states within a properly *spiritual* space – the discursive space of reasons and justifications – rather than in the 'natural' space of actions. In a certain sense Hegel thinks of feelings and their expression as natural, but it is the propensity for their expressions to be put into words and so raised to the level of conceptuality that makes them the most immediate form of something 'spiritual'.
39 Hegel, *Phenomenology of Spirit*, § 656 [2.501]. Hegel describes this community within which concrete moral consciousness subsists as marked by a type of collective narcissism:

> On account of this utterance in which the self is expressed and acknowledged as essential being, the validity of the act is acknowledged by others. The spirit and substance of their association are thus the mutual assurance of their conscientiousness, good intentions, the rejoicing over this mutual purity, and the

refreshing of themselves in the glory of knowing and uttering, of cherishing and fostering, such an excellent state of affairs (ibid. [2.502]).

Nevertheless, this is going to provide an immediate form of the developed moral community which he will identify as that which does allow an adequate moral intentionality.

40 Hegel notes that the antithesis into which conscience enters when it acts not only expresses itself internally (in the judgments of others) but is 'at the same time a disparity on its outer side in the element of existence, the disparity of its particular singularity against another singular [*die Ungleichheit seiner besonderen Einzelheit gegen anderes Einzelnes*]' ibid., § 660 [2.506].

41 Kant, *Religion and Rational Theology*, pp. 69–97 [6.18–53].

42 Hegel, *Phenomenology of Spirit*, § 670 [2.514].

43 Ibid., § 671 [2.516].

44 Hegel, *Elements of the Philosophy of Right*, § 137. Following Hegel I will simply refer to 'formal' conscience as conscience and the contrasting essential form as *true* conscience.

45 Ibid., § 137 remark.

46 Allen Speight stresses the parallels between conscience and private right in 'Hegel on Conscience and the History of Moral Philosophy', pp. 29–30.

47 Conscience 'represents an exalted point of view, a point of view of the modern world, which has for the first time attained this consciousness'. Hegel, *Elements of the Philosophy of Right*, § 136 addition.

48 Ibid., § 138 remark.

49 Kant, *The Metaphysics of Morals*, § 47 [6.471]. Such relationships as characterized by Kant are marked by *neither* the intimacy of familial ones (as the distance of *respect* balances the closeness of love (ibid., § 46 [6.470])) nor the pragmatic character of those mutually advantageous relationships of civil society.

50 Hegel, *Elements of the Philosophy of Right*, § 137 remark.

51 Hegel, *Phenomenology of Spirit*, § 670 [2.514].

52 J.G. Fichte, *Foundations of Natural Right*, F. Neuhouser (ed.) (Cambridge: Cambridge University Press, 2000).

53 Robert Pippin, 'What is the Question for which Hegel's Theory of Recognition is the Answer?', *European Journal of Philosophy*, 2000, vol. 8, 158, emphasis added.

54 Fichte's contrast to Hegel here attests to Zöller's claim that 'rather than constituting a social ontology outside of individual consciousness and its transcendental conditions', for Fichte 'interpersonality emerges *within* the confines of his transcendental theory of the subject'. Zöller, *Fichte's Transcendental Philosophy*, p. 7.

55 Brandom's most complete account of this approach is set out in Robert B. Brandom, *Making It Explicit* (Cambridge, Mass.: Harvard University Press, 1994).

56 Stanley Cavell, *The Claim of Reason: Wittgenstein, Skepticism, Morality, and Tragedy* (Oxford: Clarendon Press, 1979), p. 309. Allen Wood has stressed the way in which 'Fichte's theory strongly anticipates twentieth-century existential conceptions of a "situation ethics", except that it utterly rejects the metaethical noncognitivism and normative agent-relativism with which such views have typically been conjoined'. 'The '*I*' as Principle of Practical Philosophy', in Sally Sedgwick (ed.) *The Reception of Kant's Critical Philosophy: Fichte, Schelling, and Hegel* (Cambridge: Cambridge University Press, 2000), p. 106.

57 Robert B. Brandom, *Articulating Reasons* (Cambridge, Mass.: Harvard University Press, 2000), p. 16.

58 Ibid., p. 34.

59 Ibid.

60 See, for example, Wilfrid Sellars, "Language, Rules and Behavior," in Sidney Hook (ed.), *John Dewey: Philosopher of Science and Freedom* (New York: Dial Press, 1950), reprinted in Wilfrid Sellars, *Pure Pragmatics and Possible Worlds: The Early Essays of Wilfrid Sellars*, ed. and intro. J.F. Sicha (Atascadero: Ridgeview, 1980), p. 134.

61 I am very grateful to Jean-Philippe Deranty, Simon Lumsden, Robert Sinnerbrink, Nick Smith and, especially, Günter Zöller for very helpful feedback on an earlier version of this paper.

Part V

Autonomy and Nature

11

FREEDOM, SELF-LEGISLATION AND MORALITY IN KANT AND HEGEL: CONSTRUCTIVIST VS. REALIST ACCOUNTS

Robert Stern

Each wave in the revival of interest in Hegel, from his death in 1831 to today, has had its own distinctive set of issues and concerns, ranging from the focus on holism and monism in Britain in the late nineteenth century, to existentialist themes in France in the early twentieth century, to the work on alienation and dialectic in the Western Marxist tradition. If one considers the current wave of interest washing over contemporary Anglophone philosophy, the issue that perhaps stands out the most, and so may be said to characterise it as distinctive, is the focus on problems relating to *idealism and realism*. There is thus a preoccupation with questions such as: in what way does Hegel's idealism differ from Kant's (and Fichte's and Schelling's)? How does Hegel resolve the dualism between subject and object, mind and world, and what does that tell us about his idealism? Can Hegel provide an answer to scepticism that would be acceptable to the realist, or does it presuppose idealism in some form? Which way of reading Hegel is more or less metaphysically and epistemologically extravagant, and which makes the best sense of his historical context? Although not all the major Anglo-American interpreters of Hegel in recent years would identify themselves with one pole or the other, most may be placed on some sort of spectrum on this issue,[1] so that at present it appears to be central to current concerns.

While some of these debates have focussed on traditional questions concerning idealism and realism in metaphysics and epistemology, more recently they have begun to focus on questions in *ethics* and *social philosophy*, where crucially it is the Kantian notion of *autonomy* that has been made central to the idealist account of post-Kantian German philosophy: if we take Kant's claims about autonomy seriously, then does some form of constructivism or anti-realism in ethics have to follow, whereby norms and values are not taken to be 'out there' in the world, but the products of the self-legislating will?[2] In this paper, I want to explore whether this constructivist argument from autonomy to anti-realism can be traced through to Hegel, or whether, to the contrary, he may be read as showing that on a proper account of autonomy this argument is mistaken, so that for Hegel there is no incompatibility between realism in ethics on the one hand and freedom on the other.

Within the contemporary debate, one prominent place where this question is brought out is in the recent exchanges between Robert Pippin and John McDowell.[3] I will therefore begin by outlining that debate in section I, before exploring the argument from autonomy to anti-realism more generally in section II; and then in section III I will consider the implications of this argument for the interpretation of Hegel and what this tells us about his relation to Kant. I will suggest that despite Pippin's very strong case on behalf of the anti-realist, nothing shows autonomy and realism to be incompatible, and that Hegel should not be thought of as following this route into a constructivist conception of ethics.

I

In this section, I will consider Pippin's arguments for an anti-realist reading of Hegel's ethics, set against the background of his critique of McDowell.

As is well known, McDowell has identified himself with a broadly realist position in philosophy, and has credited Hegel with helping him see how one might adopt aspects of Kant's approach without succumbing to the kind of idealism that in the end characterises Kant's own view.[4] When it comes to McDowell's specifically *ethical* realism, while Aristotle is his most direct inspiration, it is still Hegel who he thinks can be used to 'modernise' aspects of the Aristotelian picture that may now appear problematic in the light of Kantian concerns.

Very briefly, McDowell's case for a certain form of naturalistic realism in ethics runs as follows. On the one hand, McDowell argues, realism is warranted as the 'default' position insofar as it is best able to do justice to the phenomenology of our ethical (and other) evaluations, namely 'that ordinary evaluative thought presents itself as a matter of sensitivity to aspects of the world',[5] just as our perceptual judgements do, so that for him both are equally receptive and open to the layout of reality. On the other hand, McDowell is aware that such moral realism can seem incoherent, if it is allowed (as he thinks it should be) that moral values are not part of the 'absolute conception of world', that is, not part of reality conceived of as accessible from outside any human perspective on it or human responses to it – from outside our 'form of life'. He argues, however, that only a misplaced scientism could lead us to feel a difficulty here, insofar as it is claimed that science can take us outside that perspective and give us access to reality 'as such'.[6] His response is not to argue that science cannot give us access to reality conceived of in this way, but to argue that there is no reason to think that this is all there is to reality, so that unless values can be taken in from some sort of Archimedean standpoint, they should not be viewed as 'real' but rather as subjective figments. After all, McDowell suggests,

Wittgenstein's rule-following considerations show that this point applies to cases like mathematics, where it is only from within the practice that the necessity of a particular step can be grasped or discerned, but where nothing in this needs to shake our mathematical realism.[7] So, McDowell asks, why shouldn't we think of reality itself as containing these features, even if they will only be evident from within a 'form of life', and thus not accessible from an Archimedean standpoint? Even if we recognise that these features cannot be made accessible from this standpoint, why does that make them any less 'worldly' or real? Now, McDowell argues, while scientistic naturalism, with its conception of reality as what is revealed from an Archimedean standpoint, might seem to block off this idea, Aristotelian naturalism does not, and in fact can be used to reinforce it: for, as McDowell understands it, a vital part of Aristotle's position in ethics is to suggest that ethical values may only be apparent to those who have been brought up the right way, and thus see the world from a certain ethical perspective;[8] but nothing in that upbringing is 'non-natural' or 'otherworldly' – rather, in fact, it constitutes a 'second nature' for us. Thus, there is no reason to think that the values we are then aware of by going through this socialisation are *not* part of the world independently of us, but are mere projections on it (as the 'bald' naturalist thinks) or somehow outside it (as the rampant Platonist thinks).

This, then, is the kind of position which Hegel shows us how to hold on to, according to McDowell, even in a post-Kantian context that may appear to put such Aristotelian doctrines under pressure. Thus, while that context means that he gives a role to concepts in shaping our experience, Hegel did not succumb to sceptical doubts about the possibly distorting effects of such conceptualisation; and while he was more aware than Aristotle of the variety in forms of ethical life, he did not succumb to relativism; and while he saw that the natural sciences have come to take a fully 'disenchanted' view of nature, he avoided both the reductionism of 'bald naturalism' as well as the dualism of Kant's phenomenal realm of nature and law on the one side, and noumenal realm of freedom and value on the other. On McDowell's account, therefore, there is a continuity between Aristotle's position and Hegel's, where Hegel's outlook is understood in fundamentally realist terms.

In his powerful responses to McDowell on this issue, however, Pippin has argued that McDowell is mistaken to view things this way, and that 'the Kantian and even Hegelian elements that [McDowell] has imported' are incompatible with his realist and Aristotelian talk of our being able 'to "see the reasons that are always there whether we notice them or not"'. For Pippin, therefore, 'those elements that McDowell would want to call "subjectivist," given the starting points common to McDowell and the Idealists, cast reasonable doubt, raise appropriate questions, about McDowell's position'.[9] This is particularly so in ethics, Pippin believes, because Hegel takes seriously the Kantian idea of *self-legislation*, where according to Pippin this renders untenable any naturalistic realism of the Aristotelian kind.

This Kantian notion of self-legislation is set out by Kant in the following well-known passage from the *Groundwork*:

> Hence the will is not merely subject to the law but subject to it in such a way that it must be viewed as also giving the law to itself [*als selbstgesetzgebend*] and just because of this as first subject to the law (of which it can regard itself as the author [*Urheber*]).[10]

Along with others such as Schneewind, Rawls and Korsgaard, Pippin takes this doctrine of self-legislation to constitute a vital constructivist and anti-realist turn in ethics: for the first time, it is argued, Kant clearly raises the idea that norms and values are not 'out there' in the world independently of our act of determination, while also arguing that this determination is based on the rational will and not on our contingently given desires and interests.[11] Kant's position is thus opposed both to realist intuitionism on the one hand, which holds that there is an order of value independent of us, and to Humean expressivism on the other, which rejects this realism but says that the creation of values is based on sources outside reason.[12] On this constructivist account, Kant's case against both is that each would mean that in respecting certain values or obeying the moral law, we would be acting heteronomously rather than autonomously: if realist intuitionism were right, we would be following a moral order that exists independently of our will, while if Humean expressivism were right, we would be obeying a moral order fixed by factors within us that are not sufficiently under our control or grounded in who we fundamentally are.[13]

Hegel, Pippin argues, was profoundly influenced by this Copernican revolution in ethics, in a way that undercuts McDowell's realism. Thus, while Pippin is prepared to allow that some element of receptivity may play a role in Hegel's thinking, he claims that it is embedded in a much more constructivist context, whereby if we can be said to 'see' and 'experience' moral reasons in the world, this can only be because we have put them there ourselves through a process of legislation; thus, according to Pippin, the difference between Kant and Hegel in this regard is not that the former is an idealist and the latter a realist, but that Kant makes this legislation a matter of the practical reason of each individual subject, whereas Hegel makes it a matter of a collective subject or *Geist*.[14] Once we drop this realist account of Hegel, Pippin claims, we can abandon McDowell's project of arguing for a 'partially re-enchanted nature' as a locus for values,[15] and his defence of experience as a source of moral knowledge,[16] as neither of these issues are relevant to the kind of constructivist position Hegel is said to pursue. Instead, on Pippin's reading, Hegel must be seen as trying to resolve the issue of how self-legislation can constitute a viable and coherent source of ethical values, and thus as a continuation of Kant's position and a response to its difficulties.[17]

In these respects, therefore, Pippin takes himself to have shown that Hegel cannot properly be assimilated to the kind of Aristotelian realism in ethics that

McDowell espouses, as Hegel's essential post-Kantianism makes such realism inherently alien to his thinking on these matters.

II

Having seen how Pippin argues for a constructivist account of Hegel's ethics based on the Kantian notion of self-legislation, I now want to explore what I take to be the central argument for such constructivism, which is the *argument from autonomy*:[18] unless something like the self-legislation picture holds, our ethical actions are rendered heteronomous in some way. On the other side, however, the realist will argue that unless some form of realism is accepted, self-legislation will not amount to autonomy but to mere licence or arbitrary choice; so that the constructivist is mistaken to think that a proper respect for autonomy within ethics is possible *without* realism. It is this debate that now needs to be explored.

Beginning with the first issue, this is put in a very general way by Rawls as follows:

> Another and deeper meaning of autonomy says that the order of moral and political values must be made, or itself constituted, by the principles and conceptions of practical reason. Let us refer to this as constitutive autonomy. In contrast with rational intuitionism, constitutive autonomy says that the so-called independent order of values does not constitute itself but is constituted by the activity, actual or ideal, of practical (human) reason itself. I believe this, or something like it, is Kant's view. His constructivism is deeper [than the constructivism of Rawls's political liberalism] and goes to the very existence and constitution of the order of values. This is part of his transcendental idealism. The intuitionist's independently given order of values is part of the transcendental realism Kant takes his transcendental idealism to oppose.[19]

However, if this is a statement of the general worry, it also needs some spelling out and motivating. For, while it is plain that *some* forms of realism in ethics pose a threat to our autonomy as moral agents, it is not immediately clear that *all* do. Thus, firstly, if autonomy means not being subject to the will of another, then this might plausibly be said to exclude certain forms of divine command theory, where (say) the rightness of an act consists in the fact that it involves obedience to the will of God.[20] Secondly, if autonomy means that agents should be able to judge for themselves whether or not what they are doing is right, then this would exclude a realism in ethics that made the right inscrutable or unfathomable in some way (again, as on some voluntarist versions of divine command theory, where God's grounds for willing the moral law are made inchoate to us as subjects). And thirdly, a realist moral theory might be said to be heteronomous because the only way it can explain how agents are determined to act by the right or the good is through their inclinations or needs (such as the desire for happiness or respect of others, or the fear of God's displeasure); but this not only means than in so doing, the moral agent is acting instrumentally and so following a hypothetical rather than a categorical imperative, but it also leaves the will of the moral agent conditioned by given desires and interests, and so less than fully free, so that in both these crucial and related respects the dignity of the moral agent is compromised by the realist, in a way that treats our moral behaviour as driven by psychological needs and laws, so that arguably this behaviour falls short of full autonomy.[21] On these three grounds, therefore, it certainly seems plausible to argue that *some* sorts of moral realism could put our status as autonomous agents under threat.

But what about a realism that appears to have none of these features, such as McDowell's, which holds that a moral agent can be aware that a particular act is required of her in some given situation, where (if she is right) that awareness will consist in an acknowledgement of a moral reason, and where the motivation is grounded in the perception of that reason, and so is not hypothetical or derived from externally given ends? It is not clear how, if she acts in the light of this awareness, the agent is being constrained by a will other than her own, as it is not yet clear that there is a role for a *will* within this realism at all, rather than just *reasons* of a moral kind. (Indeed, some might argue that a divine command theory is *not* a form of realism at all but a form of *voluntarism* on precisely these grounds, that is gives a role to the *will* of God, in a way that realism proper does not.)[22] And nor does it yet seem that this sort of moral realism would render judging the rightness of a moral action hard for agents in principle (though of course there may be difficult cases in practice), such that they could not really know what they were doing and why when they acted morally. On McDowell's picture, it seems, the agent can claim to see quite clearly what it is about the situation that makes it right, and so attain the kind of awareness and cognitive transparency required to make their action autonomous rather than unthinking and blind.[23] Finally, McDowell can claim that he can do full justice to the categorical force of moral reasons, where the reasons for doing or refraining which lie in the ethical features of the situation itself are what motivate the virtuous agent, and not any other determining object of the will (such as the desire for happiness or the fear of the Lord), which is what the Kantian thinks renders the action heteronomous.[24] On all these counts, therefore, there seems no route from McDowellian realism to the problem of heteronomy that the Kantian might identify in other forms of realism, so that we still need some further grounds for endorsing the argument from autonomy to constructivism in this case.[25]

It may be, however, that what would make even McDowellian realism seem problematic to the Kantian is a vital aspect of the Kantian's own conception of morality itself, which is that morality is a matter of *obligation*, and so to that extent is a matter of laws or principles that *bind* or *command* us – where it then seems to follow that laws require a *legislator*, so that morality can exist only as the result of some act of legislation that this legislator undertakes. Thus, as Korsgaard summarises the view of morality that Kant is working with here: 'Obligation must come from law, and law from the will of a legislating sovereign; morality only comes into the world when laws are made'.[26] But if we take this view, it may then appear that we are left with two options: either morality is legislated by *us*, or by some *other* sovereign authority (such as God). If we opt for the second alternative, the link with heteronomy becomes much clearer, because now it seems that in following the dictates of morality, we would be following the directions of another *will*, as the institutor of that moral law. Faced with that alternative, it may then appear that the Kantian is right, and the only way to preserve our autonomy is to go for the first alternative, and to make *us* the legislators of the moral law, in a way that takes us from autonomy to constructivism.

However, if this reveals more of the thinking behind the Kantian position, it also opens that position up to being challenged. One way to challenge it, is to question the terms in which the Kantian characterises the moral situation, as essentially involving commands, obligations and laws:[27] if the realist need not think of morality in these terms, might it be possible to abandon the law conception of ethics that seems to go with it, and thus do without a moral lawgiver altogether, in a way that would thereby avoid any threat to our autonomy as moral agents? It will remain to be seen, however, whether this approach can do justice to what appears distinctive in the moral 'ought'. Another response for the realist to make, therefore, is to accept the distinctive obligatoriness of this 'ought', but to claim that the obligatoriness the good person feels is not the result of a legislative act by us or by anyone else, but simply stems from the moral facts that obtain in this case: these moral facts are intrinsically or inherently obligatory, and no legislative will is required to make them so.[28] The Kantian may reply, however, by claiming that this is unsatisfactory: it just tells us that the right or good *is* obligatory, but not how it comes to be so, whereas the legislative model makes this clear – its obligatoriness comes from the fact that it has been *commanded*.[29] As with all claims about explanation, however, it may be hard to get the realist to see the argument here, unless he feels the explanatory gap in the first place.[30] One way to make this gap vivid is a naturalistic one: namely, to argue that unless the right and the good are commanded by a will, it is hard to see how the world could contain values that obligate us in the way that the moral realist claims. But then, of course, we have come full-circle: looking for a way to argue *from* autonomy *to* constructivism or anti-realism, we are now relying on an argument *from* anti-realism *to* self-legislation, by claiming that values cannot be aspects of the world but must be imposed on it as nothing in the world can have the required obligatoriness, where it is then argued that that obligatoriness requires an act of legislation by a law-maker, who must be us, if autonomy is to be preserved.

While this puts the parts of the constructivist picture together in a neat way, it does not seem likely to convince the realist, who has not yet been given an argument that uses premises he is inclined to accept.

Having explored the possible connection between autonomy and constructivism, let me now turn to the second question that I raised at the beginning of this section, namely whether the constructivist model of self-legislation is coherent, and whether it must collapse into some form of realism.

From a realist perspective, the central difficulty here is this:[31] if there is nothing prior to the act of legislation that is itself normative, how are any responsible or rational law-making decisions to be made? Unless the process of legislation is grounded in some reasons that obtain prior to the process, won't that leave the legislating will in a void, unable to take any legislative decisions at all – or at least, unable to take any rational ones, that are more than a mere motiveless plumping for one thing rather than another? Thus, as Charles Larmore puts it, in the course of an argument for realism:

> when we impose principles on ourselves, we do so for reasons: we suppose that it is fitting for us to adopt them, or that adopting them will advance our interests. Self-legislation is an activity that takes place against a background of reasons that we must antecedently recognize, whose authority we do not institute but rather find ourselves called upon to acknowledge.[32]

The realist's concern is that the Kantian gives the agent no way to act except through a kind of 'arbitrary self-launching',[33] and it is hard to see that as either an accurate picture of our agency, or as a promising account of the way in which normativity can be explained.[34] The anti-realist must therefore show how these difficulties can be avoided, if the constructivist account of self-legislation is to be maintained.

We have therefore considered in outline the central issues that can arise in the debate between the realist and the constructivist on these questions. Setting the debate between McDowell and Pippin against this context, we can now consider whether Pippin is right to see Hegel as developing his own form of constructivism, or whether McDowell is right to see him as fundamentally turning away from this sort of position, and back towards a form of realism, while also avoiding Kantian concerns about heteronomy.

III

In this section, I want to focus on the question of whether Pippin can put forward a constructivist account of Hegel's position that avoids the realist objections discussed in the previous section; and on the question of whether McDowell can put forward an account of Hegel as a realist that avoids the problem of autonomy raised by the constructivist.

Beginning now with the first question, we have seen that the realist will argue that the constructivist picture of self-legislation is not truly coherent, as the legislating will must always start with some prior set of reasons and norms on which to base its legislating. As McDowell himself puts this worry:

> Pippin is surely right that the central image in the German idealist tradition is one of legislating for ourselves. But the idea of subjectivity as source needs delicate handling if it is not to put at risk the fact that, as Pippin puts it, 'we cannot legislate arbitrarily.' The point of the image is that subjection to norms should not be an infringement on freedom; we are authentically subject only to norms whose authority we acknowledge. Thus the norms that bind us are our own dictates to ourselves, not alien impositions. But any intelligible case of agency legislative or any other, whether on the part of an individual or a group, must be responsive to reasons. It makes no sense to picture an act that brings norms into existence out of a normative void. So the insistence on freedom must cohere with the fact that we always find ourselves already subject to norms. Our freedom, which figures in the image as our legislative power, must include a moment of receptivity.[35]

McDowell is here urging the need for realism and receptivity, if we are to avoid leaving the legislative will spinning in a normative void: can the constructivist find a way out of this difficulty?

It may seem that we could perhaps give content to the self-legislating will on the one hand, while avoiding realism on the other, by determining the will in accordance with those laws and principles that enable it to realise its *freedom* as a will. By treating freedom as a goal or end for itself as a will, it can then determine what laws it should impose on itself, while in enabling the will to realise that end, those laws can be said to be 'internal' to it, in so far as they are in accord with its nature as a will, which is to act freely.

There is indeed something authentically Hegelian about this picture.[36] However, this does not yet seem adequate as a truly *constructivist* solution to the problem, and thus I think it would be rejected by Pippin on that score. For, while it treats the law as being grounded in the nature of the will because this is required for its full realisation, the value of what is realised, namely our freedom, is not given that value in any constructivist manner, as stemming from the process of self-legislation itself, but is rather given a normative status *prior* to that process, and used to guide it. Thus, a realist interpretation of Hegel (such as the one proposed by Allen Wood, for example)[37] could accept what has been said so far, without that realism being compromised in any way – as I think Pippin would acknowledge.[38]

Pippin holds instead, therefore, that an account of Hegel's position is needed, that follows Kant's own constructivism more closely. While Kantians themselves have made and continue to make attempts to show that constraints on self-legislation come from principles of practical reason, such as those concerning universalisability and non-contradiction,[39] Pippin offers what he takes to be a more Hegelian approach, and one which he thinks can be more successful, because it adds a social and developmental dimension to the account that is missing in Kant, whereby 'The formation of and self-subjection to such normative constraints is gradual, collective, and actually historical'. Thus, on Pippin's account, Hegel holds that 'we do not face normative claims as singular, unattached, noumenal beings, capable of acting as uncaused causes, but as subjects located in historical time (as modern subjects) in various non-detachable social and ethical relations to each other'.[40] What this means, Pippin argues, is that (contra the Kantian) 'the legislation of such a law does not consist in some paradoxical single moment of election', because the subject has no context for their legislating because everything must be fixed at once; rather, each individual finds themselves 'in medias res' (so to speak), with values and norms that belong to the community in which they are part.[41] However, (contra the realist) these values and norms are not things that the community can claim to have 'found' or 'discovered' in some realist manner, but are themselves the result of a collective and historical process of value creation, driven by the problems in previous attempts to take up values and norms of other kinds, which themselves have proved unstable. As Pippin puts it:

> On [Hegel's] account, the question of what comes to count as, in general, an authoritative explanation of objects and events, the decisive classificatory procedure, or evaluative criterion, can never itself be resolved by appeal to an ultimate explanatory principle, or general regulative ideal, or basic argument strategy. There are, finally, no rules to tell us which rules we ought to follow in regulating our discursive practices, no institutions certifying the axioms out of which such rules should be constructed, and no transcendental arguments for the necessary conditions for any experience. What we always require is a narrative account of why we have come to regard some set of rules or a practice as authoritative. In Hegel's "phenomenological" version, such an account must always appeal to a pre-discursive context or historical experience (sometimes simply called "life") as the origin of such authoritative procedures and rules (even while Hegel also maintains that such a context or experience is itself the "product" of a kind of prior reflective principle, now become implicit, taken for granted, in everyday social life). Our account of our basic sense-making practices is thus tied to an account of the *aporiai* "experienced in the life of Spirit," and so such a justification is everywhere, to use the famous word, "dialectical," and not "logical."[42]

On Pippin's account, therefore, Hegel completes the Kantian self-legislation project in a way that aims to avoid the worries raised by the realist, by introducing the characteristic Hegelian themes of sociality and historicity.[43] This, then, forms a central part of Pippin's response to McDowell, and the latter's concern (as Pippin puts it) 'that the self-legislation language I employ is extreme and seems to be committed to normless situations mysteriously becoming norm-governed and the norms being created out of the void'.[44]

There is, however, a worry I would like to raise about Pippin's approach, which is whether in the end it is itself stable. On the one hand, as critics like Larmore have argued,[45] if the anti-realist or constructivist approach is to prove compelling, it should presumably offer itself as an account of *all* reasons and norms, not just ethical ones, and so should argue not just that the norms about what we should do are constructed (in the light of which some things become reasons to act and some do not), but also the norms about what we should believe as well (in the light of which some things become reasons to believe and some do not); and Pippin would seem to accept this, by talking in constructivist terms not just about moral norms, but theoretical ones too.[46] On the other hand, Pippin claims that our ethical norms are not constructed 'in a void' because in constructing those norms we do so against the background of previous value systems that have proved aporetic in various ways; but that seems to mean viewing such aporiai as *reasons* for rejecting some set of norms and embracing others, where avoiding these aporiai must therefore act as precisely the sort of 'ultimate explanatory principle, or general regulative ideal, or basic argument strategy' that Pippin claims the self-legislation model is trying to eschew. It is hard to see, on Pippin's interpretation, what could entitle Hegel to hold that an aporia in a practice governed by certain norms gives those engaged in the practice a reason to overcome that aporia, in such a way that this reason has *itself* got its normative status from the prior aporia in previous practices;[47] rather, it looks as if this reason governs the way in which our practices are meant to be constructed, but is not itself constructed in the same manner. Ultimately, then, there is something unsatisfying here about Pippin's account, where the fundamental problems for constructivism still remain, and McDowell's objections have seemingly gone unanswered.

However, if Pippin's constructivist account of Hegel's position is rejected, and we move to a realist account of that position instead, can we avoid the worries on the Kantian's side, that any such realism will lead to heteronomy? If we interpret Hegel as holding that, there is (in Rawls's words) 'an independent order of values' which involves no legislation by us, does that threaten our autonomy as moral agents? Given Hegel's emphasis on freedom, this is clearly a pressing issue for any realist account: doesn't that emphasis mean that in the end, Pippin is right, and Hegel must be interpreted as some sort of constructivist?[48]

We saw in the previous section, however, that the argument from autonomy to constructivism is perhaps not as straightforward as it may at first appear, and that on some accounts of moral realism, there may not be any tension here at all. And the same is true when it comes to interpretations of Hegel. The key issue is how Hegel is seen to handle the apparent *obligatoriness* of morality. As we saw previously, this is what makes the question of autonomy pressing: if moral oughts *command* or *oblige* us, how can they do so except on a legislative model? But then how can they be legislated in a way that will preserve our autonomy unless they are legislated *by us*?

It is an important feature of Hegel's position, however, that he precisely wanted to put this legislative conception of morality into question, and challenge the Kantian assumptions behind it. Hegel may therefore be interpreted as being more radical than Kant on this issue: while Kant can be seen as wanting to move the source of the authority that morality has over us from God to the structure of our will, Hegel raised the more fundamental question of whether the relation between a good person and what he ought to do is a relation of being *commanded* or *bound* at all – any more than on Kant's own conception of the holy will, God himself is commanded or bound by the moral law, insofar as nothing in him stands against it.[49] We might therefore say of Hegel what he himself said of Jesus in his early and unpublished essay 'The Spirit of Christianity and Its Fate': 'To complete subjection under the law of an alien Lord, Jesus opposed not a particular subjection under a law of one's own, the self-coercion of Kantian virtue, but virtues without lordship and without submission, i.e. virtues as modifications of love'.[50] On this conception, as Hegel writes earlier in that essay:

> This spirit of Jesus, a spirit raised above morality, is visible, directly attacking laws, in the Sermon on the Mount, which is an attempt, elaborated in numerous examples, to strip the laws of legality, of their legal form. The Sermon does not teach reverence for the laws; on the contrary, it exhibits that which fulfils the law but annuls it as law and so is something higher than obedience to law and makes law superfluous.[51]

There are clear parallels here between what Hegel says of us, and what Kant says of the holy will – so if in one sense Kant's anthropocentrism represents the divinisation of the human in making us and not God the legislators of the moral law, Hegel may be said to take this a step further, in freeing us from subjection to any law at all, not by setting us outside the ethical, but by seeing us as fundamentally capable of aligning our desires and characters on the one hand and what it is right for us to do on the other, much as Kant sees the situation for God, and God alone.

While in his mature writings, Hegel speaks somewhat less of love and virtue,[52] it is still this fundamental contrast between Kant's legislative conception and his own that lies behind his central distinction between *Moralität* and *Sittlichkeit*: whereas in the sphere of *Moralität*, duty still has the feeling of a command imposed on the agent, in the sphere of *Sittlichkeit*, this is precisely what is lost. Thus, while in the *Philosophy of Right* Hegel does speak of the ethical laws in apparently more Kantian terms, as having 'an absolute authority and power',[53] he immediately qualifies this by saying:

> On the other hand, they are not something *alien* to the subject. On the contrary, the subject bears *spiritual witness* to them as to *its own essence*, in which it has its *self-awareness* [*Selbstgefühl*] and lives as in its element which is not distinct from itself – a relationship which is immediate and closer to identity than even [a relationship of] *faith* or *trust*.[54]

At first sight, this passage may seem to support the constructivist position, where it might seem to say that the 'alienness' of the ethical laws is taken away by the fact that *we* legislate them, so that in this sense they are our creation. However, this account cannot explain what Hegel means when he says that 'the subject bears *spiritual witness* to them as to *its own essence*'. This suggests, I would argue, the kind of structure that Hegel had argued for in 'The Spirit of Christianity and Its Fate': namely, a unification between the individual moral agent and his nature on the one hand, and the ethical laws on the other, whereby it no longer makes sense to think of these as external obligations at all, and so as alien in this sense.

In the *Philosophy of Right*, therefore, Hegel sets out to show that just as in the case of love, where we do not feel *bound* or *obliged* by the beloved when we act in this relationship, despite the fact that we may also not be acting in our immediate interest and would in some sense perhaps prefer to do something else (as when a parent takes their child to a party, or where one partner cares for another through a period of illness) – so the same can be true in the political and social world at large. Of course, given a narrow focus on our interests and an inability to enter properly into these relationships, we might come to feel them as involving some sort of burden or constraint, so that a sense of obligation may be all that can continue to move us when this occurs. But for Hegel, that just shows that the legalistic conception of obligation is a sort of *projection* of a more fundamental breakdown, rather than being intrinsic to the ethical domain itself, and so should not be thought of as requiring the kind of explanation the Kantian offers, when in fact it is an aspect of ethical life which can, in the right context, be made to drop away and appear (in the spirit of Jesus' Sermon on the Mount) 'superfluous'.

On the basis of this characterisation of Hegel's position, therefore, I think it can be argued that the tension that the constructivist feels between realism and autonomy is not one that has a place in Hegel's thought – but not because he himself is a constructivist, but because the legalistic conception of morality that generates this tension is not there in the first place. Thus, Pippin may be right when he says that for the Kantian: 'Laws, to be laws, require legislators, and once a divine legislator is excluded, "we" are the only candidates left';[55] however, we have seen that from the Hegelian perspective, the proper response is to challenge the law-like conception of ethics on which it is based, rather than follow the Kantian into a constructivist account of self-legislation, so that no real issue of heteronomy remains. The way is open, therefore, for McDowell to treat Hegel as an ally in his defence of realism in ethics, notwithstanding his commitment to freedom and the fundamental question that this raises both in Kant's moral system and his own.[56]

Notes

1 For a helpful outline of some of the complexities of the idealism/realism issue in Hegel, in a way that locates the views of several of the commentators concerned, cf. T.E. Wartenburg, 'Hegel's Idealism: The Logic of Conceptuality', in F.C. Beiser (ed.), *The Cambridge Companion to Hegel* (Cambridge: Cambridge University Press, 1993), pp. 102–29.

2 Of course, not all commentators even see Kant himself as a constructivist on these matters: see e.g. K. Ameriks, 'On Two Non-Realist Interpretations of Kant's Ethics', in his *Interpreting Kant's 'Critiques'* (Oxford: Oxford University Press, 2003), pp. 263–82. I do not have space to go into interpretative issues involving Kant here, and will assume the constructivist reading is correct for the sake of this discussion, as it is that reading that has had most bearing on the account of Hegel that I want to examine.

3 The exchange begins with Pippin's discussion of McDowell's *Mind and World* in R. B. Pippin, 'Leaving Nature Behind: Or Two Cheers for Subjectivism', originally published in N.H. Smith (ed.), *Reading McDowell: On Mind and World* (London: Routledge, 2002), pp. 58–75 (reprinted in R.B. Pippin, *The Persistence of Subjectivity: On the Kantian Aftermath* (Cambridge: Cambridge University Press, 2005), pp. 186–205, where subsequent references are to this version). McDowell replies to Pippin in his 'Responses' in Smith (ed.), *Reading McDowell*, pp. 274–77, to which Pippin reacted with his 'Postscript: On McDowell's Response to "Leaving Nature Behind"' in his *The Persistence of Subjectivity*, pp. 206–20. Since then, McDowell has also written a reply to Pippin's 'Postscript' and Pippin has written a response to that: both these pieces are forthcoming in the *European Journal of Philosophy*.

4 Cf. J. McDowell, *Mind and World* (Cambridge, Mass.: Harvard University Press, 1994), p. 111:

> In that recapitulation of something I said in my last lecture, I have described a philosophical project: to stand on the shoulders of the giant, Kant, and see our way to the supersession of traditional philosophy that he almost managed, though not quite. The philosopher whose achievement that description best fits is someone we take almost no notice of, in the philosophical tradition I was brought up in, although I have mentioned him a couple of times before: namely, Hegel.

5 J. McDowell, 'Value and Secondary Qualities', reprinted in his *Mind, Value, and Reality* (Cambridge, Mass.: Harvard University Press, 1998), p. 131. McDowell is in fact crediting J.L. Mackie with this view; but he also makes clear here that it is a view that he supports.

6 Cf. J. McDowell, 'Aesthetic Value, Objectivity, and the Fabric of the World', reprinted in his *Mind, Value, and Reality*, pp. 128–29.

7 Cf. J. McDowell, 'Non-Cognitivism and Rule-Following', reprinted in his *Mind, Value, and Reality*, pp. 198–218, pp. 208–9 (my emphasis):

> none of what I have said casts any doubt on the idea that the correctness of a move, in a mathematical case of going on doing the same thing, can be proved – so that it

> is compulsory to go on like that. *The point is that we should not misidentify the perspective from which this necessity is discernible.* What is wrong is to suppose that when we describe someone as following a rule in extending a series, we characterize the output of his mathematical competence as the inexorable workings of a machine: something that could be seen as operating from the platonist's standpoint, the standpoint independent of the activities and responses that make up our mathematical practice. The fact is that it is only because of our own involvement in our 'whirl of organism' that we can understand the form of words as conferring, on the judgement that some move is the correct one at a given point, the special compellingness possessed by the conclusion of a proof.

8 Cf. McDowell, *Mind and World*, p. 84.
9 Pippin, 'Leaving Nature Behind', p. 198.
10 I. Kant, *Groundwork of the Metaphysics of Morals*, Ak 4: 431; translated by M.J. Gregor, in *Immanuel Kant: Practical Philosophy*, translated and edited by M.J. Gregor (Cambridge: Cambridge University Press, 1996), p. 81.
11 See Schneewind's influential discussion of Kant in J. B. Schneewind, *The Invention of Autonomy: A History of Modern Moral Philosophy* (Cambridge: Cambridge University Press, 1998); and for Pippin's broadly similar take on these issues, see R.B. Pippin, *Modernism as a Philosophical Problem* (Oxford: Blackwell, 1991), pp. 12–15. Further relevant background to this view of Kant can also be found in S. Darwall, *The British Moralists and the Internal 'Ought' 1640–1740* (Cambridge: Cambridge University Press, 1995).
12 Rawls argues strongly that the former target is as important for Kant as the latter, notwithstanding the fact that Kant makes fewer explicit references to it. See J. Rawls, *Lectures on the History of Moral Philosophy*, edited by B. Herman (Cambridge, Mass.: Harvard University Press, 2000), pp. 226–30 and pp. 235–37.
13 Cf. Rawls, *Lectures on History of Moral Philosophy*, pp. 236–37.
14 Cf. Pippin, 'Postscript', p. 220:

> In [Hegel's] picture, it can be said that some sort of second-nature *Bildung* has made it possible to see a reason 'in the world' that exists as such a reason even if unacknowledged by many. Antigone's perception of what has happened to her brother and her awareness that he is her brother just thereby gives her a reason to act. But that it is a reason is because of what has in effect been collectively 'legislated' at a time (what would not be there had it not been so legislated), because of the role the family has been determined to play in Greek political life, a role that is cracking in effect under the pressure of the incompatible commitments created by the overall legislated (Hegel's word is often actualised, *verwirklicht*) results within this community.
>
> So here again, as in the cognitive case, we do have a kind of receptivity, but the kind of role it plays is a certain sort of result of free activity. And that will remain so in Hegel's account of the modern world. Someone's being a partner in a contract, a mother, a businessman, or a citizen just thereby gives him or her reasons to do or forebear from doing (if he or she has been properly socialized). But such 'reasons' do not and cannot play the particular role they play 'on their own,' as it were. They are results. Indeed, as Hegel says, a common human-mindedness, *Geist*, is essentially a 'result of itself.'

15 Cf. Pippin, 'Leaving Nature Behind', pp. 189–90:

Although the historical issues are too unwieldy to be treated here, the theme that I want to pursue amounts to one way of understanding the difference between Hegel on the one hand, and Schiller, Schelling, and even the Kant of the third *Critique* on the other, at a crucial period in modern philosophy. The last three all still felt the force of the question *What must nature be like* in order for meaning in nature – conceptually informed sensibility and practical reasons having a grip, for example, but also purposive life, organic wholes – to be possible? This is the question McDowell wants to avoid, as he sometimes puts it, with a 'reminder' about, or a pointing toward, a 'partially enchanted nature.' But ultimately, Hegel did not feel the force of this question. There is, of course, a *Philosophy of Nature* in his *Encyclopedia*, but as anyone who has slogged through it knows, there is a lot there that seems to turn no other wheels elsewhere in what Hegel says, and very little in the *Philosophy of Spirit* seems to depend on or refer back to it. Said very crudely, the developmental 'direction' of Hegel's system (a systematic account of forms of intelligibility, even better explanatory adequacy) is 'away' from nature and 'toward' 'spirit,' *Geist*; his 'logic' concerns more the inadequacy of *appeals* to nature as *explicans*. And so he rejects as misguided such 'how possible' questions, questions with which it seems to me that McDowell, despite 'quietism,' is still grappling (even if not answering) by appealing to the possibility of second nature. It is not that McDowell wants to reanimate a romantic or Schellingian philosophy of nature, but even his 'reminder' remains tied to the problem of nature, and I want to propose the nonmetaphysical character of the *Natur-Geist* distinction in Hegel as a better way of leaving first nature behind.

16 Cf. Pippin, *Modernism as a Philosophical Problem*, p. 76:

> Hegel too accepts the now widespread post-Kantian anti-empiricism: the 'world as such' does not come to us pre-categorized; at a sufficient level of generality, it should be conceded that it can be cut up and evaluated in all sorts of different ways, and so the relevant question is to account for what we end up collectively sanctioning as the decisive kinds of 'cuts,' the Notions.

17 Cf. also the recent work of Terry Pinkard, who makes the 'Kantian paradox' of self-legislation central to his account of post-Kantian German Idealism. See T. Pinkard, *German Philosophy 1760–1860: The Legacy of Idealism* (Cambridge: Cambridge University Press, 2002), and 'Subjects, Objects, and Normativity: What is it like to be an Agent?', *International Yearbook of German Idealism* 1, 2003, 201–18.

18 I am not of course claiming that this is the *only* one; for example, constructivism may be endorsed simply on the grounds of naturalism: that unless values are legislated by us, they are simply too 'queer' to have any reality at all, given what science tells us about the natural world. But this kind of argument is less interesting in relation to our concerns here, where first it is clear that McDowell would have taken himself to have already addressed this issue, and second it relies on a more contentious commitment to naturalism which many would be prepared to question – whereas autonomy represents a more neutral and intuitive starting point for an anti-realist argument.

19 J. Rawls, *Political Liberalism* (New York: Columbia University Press, 1993), pp. 99–100. For a more recent expression of this sort of view, cf. F. Rauscher, 'Kant's Moral Anti-Realism', *Journal of the History of Philosophy*, 40, 2002, pp. 477–99, esp. p. 497:

> If the distinctive feature of Kant's moral theory is autonomy and the avoidance of heteronomy, and if autonomy requires the dependence of moral principles

upon the human will, and if this dependence on the human will is idealist, then the distinctive feature of Kant's moral theory is its idealism.

20 Of course, not all forms of divine command theory need take this form. For a version of such a theory which explores its compatibility with autonomy, see J.E. Hare, *God's Call: Moral Realism, God's Commands, and Human Autonomy* (Grand Rapids: William B. Erdmans Publishing Company, 2001).

21 Cf. Kant, *Groundwork of the Metaphysics of Morals*, Ak 4: 433–45, especially 4: 444 (translation, p. 92):

> Whenever an object of the will has to be laid down as the basis of prescribing the rule that determines the will, there the rule is none other than heteronomy; the imperative is conditional, namely: *if* or *because* one wills this object, one ought to act in such and such a way; hence it can never command morally, that is, categorically . . . [In this case] because the impulse that the representation of an object possible through our powers is to exert on the will of the subject in accordance with his natural constitution belongs to the nature of the subject . . . it would, strictly speaking, be nature that gives the law; and this . . . is *always only heteronomy* of the will; the will would not give itself the law but a foreign impulse would give the law to it by means of the subject's nature, which is attuned to be receptive to it.

22 Cf. C.M. Korsgaard, *The Sources of Normativity* (Cambridge: Cambridge University Press, 1996), pp. 21–27.

23 The Kantian might argue, however, that even though McDowell thinks as a matter of fact we are capable of acquiring moral knowledge, for a realist there is always a *possible* gap between what is right and our grasp of it, so that heteronomy is possible here after all. (Rauscher, 'Kant's Moral Realism', p. 496 suggests this thought, but doesn't really explain it in any detail.) But, in response, the realist could accept that while this gap is indeed conceivable, in fact we have no reason to think this is our actual situation, so that in our current epistemic position, the reality of moral reasons does not put our autonomy under threat.

24 Cf. J. McDowell, 'Are Moral Requirements Hypothetical Imperatives?', reprinted in his *Mind, Value and Reality*, pp. 77–94, especially pp. 87–88:

> According to this position, then, a failure to see reason to act virtuously stems, not from the lack of a desire on which the rational influence of moral requirements is conditional, but from the lack of a distinctive way of seeing situations. If that perceptual capacity is possessed and exercised, it yields non-hypothetical reasons for acting.

25 For related reflections, see D.H. Regan, 'The Value of Rational Nature', *Ethics* 112, 2002, 267–91, especially pp. 290–91.

26 Korsgaard, *The Sources of Normativity*, p. 23. Cf. also G.E.M. Anscombe's discussion of the 'special moral sense' of 'ought' and its connection with the '*law* conception of ethics' in her 'Modern Moral Philosophy', in *The Collected Papers of G.E.M. Anscombe* (Oxford: Blackwell, 1981), vol. 3, pp. 26–42. Again, I will leave aside here any detailed discussion of whether this is the right conception of Kant's position, although the following passage may seem to put it into question, in suggesting that while lawgiving for Kant extends to putting us under obligations (e.g. when I get you to promise to visit your grandmother, and so put you under an obligation to do so), this in itself isn't the source of the rightness of what we are obliged to do

(e.g. visit your grandmother), so giving someone (or ourselves) the law in this sense is not the same as making or originating it:

> The lawgiver is not always simultaneously an originator of the law; he is only that if the laws are contingent. But if the laws are practically necessary, and he merely declares that they conform to his will, then he is a lawgiver. So nobody, not even the deity, is an originator of moral laws, since they have not arisen from choice, but are practically necessary; if they were not so, it might be the case that lying was a virtue. But moral laws can still be subject to a lawgiver; there may be a being who is omnipotent and has power to execute these laws, and to declare that this moral law is at the same time a law of His will and obliges everyone to act accordingly. Such a being is then a lawgiver, though not an originator; just as God is no originator of the fact that a triangle has three corners.

I. Kant, Ak 27: 282–83; translated by P. Heath in *Lectures on Ethics* (Cambridge: Cambridge University Press, 1997), p. 76.
I am grateful to John Skorupski for this reference, which is taken from Kant's lectures given in the winter semester 1784–85, and so from around the time when he was writing the *Groundwork*. Cf. also the discussion of this passage in Hare, *God's Call*, p. 94.

27 Cf. B. Williams, *Ethics and the Limits of Philosophy* (London: Fontana, 1985), where in chapter 10, Williams makes this the core of his attack on 'Morality' as 'the Peculiar Institution'.

28 Cf. S. Clarke, 'A Discourse of Natural Religion', in D.D. Raphael (ed.), *British Moralists 1650–1800*, vol. 1 (Oxford: Oxford University Press, 1969), pp. 189–225, p. 192:

> these eternal and necessary differences of things make it *fit and reasonable* for creatures so to act; they cause it to be their *duty*, or lay an *obligation* on them, so to do; even separate from the consideration of these rules being the *positive will or command of God*; and also antecedent to any . . . *particular private and personal advantage or disadvantage*, *reward or punishment*, either present or future.

And cf. also Roger Crisp's observation in relation to Anscombe's famous worries in 'Modern Moral Philosophy' about how the obligatoriness of morality can function in the absence of a divine law maker:

> Oddly, Anscombe appears never to consider the view that claims that we have such obligations might be self-standing, requiring no justification from elsewhere, though she does consider, as alternatives to divine legislation, the norms of society, self-legislation, the laws of nature, Hobbesian contractualism, and the virtues. Perhaps, like the early Greeks, she also felt that a *nomos* had to be *nomizetai* ('dispensed').

R. Crisp, 'Does Modern Moral Philosophy Rest on a Mistake?', in A. O'Hear (ed.), *Modern Moral Philosophy* (Cambridge: Cambridge University Press, 2004), pp. 75–94, p. 86 note 33.

29 Cf. Korsgaard, *The Sources of Normativity*, pp. 34–40, and C.M. Korsgaard, 'Kant's Analysis of Obligation: The Argument of *Groundwork I*', in her *Creating the Kingdom of Ends* (Cambridge: Cambridge University Press, 1996), pp. 43–76, p. 52: 'The rationalists saw that obligation is only possible in one way: the perception of the bindingness of the right action must be what moves us. But instead of explaining how this is possible, they simply insisted that it is'. Korsgaard raises similar objections

in her paper 'Realism and Constructivism in Twentieth-Century Moral Philosophy', APA Centennial Supplement to the *Journal of Philosophical Research*, 2003, pp. 99–122, especially pp. 110–12. Cf. also Andrews Reath, 'Autonomy of the Will as the Foundation of Morality', in his *Agency and Autonomy in Kant's Moral Theory* (Oxford: Oxford University Press, 2006), pp. 121–72, p. 166, note 22:

> Rational intuitionism might offer a simpler solution by assigning the function of practical laws to self-evident principles ... As standardly understood, if a principle is self-evident, any rational being on reflection can grasp its validity and authority, but no further justification for the principle can be given. But then its normative force is unexplained and it will appear to be rationally rejectable; one can coherently ask why one should follow it.

30 Cf. R. Jay Wallace, 'Normativity and the Will', in his *Normativity and the Will* (Oxford: Oxford University Press, 2006), pp. 71–81, pp. 75–76:

> The normativity or bindingness is built into the content of the [normative] principle, its standing as a principle that specifies what we have reason to do. The question whether we are obligated to comply with a given principle is already settled by whatever considerations establish it, in the first place, as an expression of the independent truth of the matter about what there is reason to do.

Cf. also D. Parfit, 'Normativity', in R. Shafer-Landau (ed.), *Oxford Studies in Metaethics*, vol. 1 (Oxford: Oxford University Press, 2006), pp. 325–80.

31 There are also other difficulties, which are less relevant here: for example, if a law is legislated by the agent, can it truly be said to bind him? And then there is the worry raised by Anscombe, and used to dismiss the Kantian approach: 'The concept of legislation requires superior power in the legislator', which is why it may have worked when *God* was the legislator, but can't work when it is *us*.

32 C. Larmore, 'Back to Kant? No Way', *Inquiry*, 46, 2003, 260–71, p. 269. Cf. also J.D. Velleman, *Self to Self: Selected Essays* (Cambridge: Cambridge University Press, 2006), pp. 293–96.

33 Regan, 'The Value of Rational Nature', p. 278.

34 Korsgaard herself raises this difficulty as follows:

> Since reasons are derived from principles, the free will must have a principle. But because the will is free, no law or principle can be imposed on it from outside. Kant concluded that the will must be autonomous: that is, it must have its *own* law or principle. And here again we arrive at the problem. For where is this law to come from? If it is imposed on the law from outside then the will is not free. So the will must make the law for itself. But until the will has a law or principle, there is nothing from which it can derive a reason. So how can it have any reason for making one law rather than another?

Korsgaard, *The Sources of Normativity*, p. 98. Similar sorts of issues are discussed by Iris Murdoch in *The Sovereignty of Good* (London: Routledge, 1970), where she comments that 'The ordinary person does not, unless corrupted by philosophy, believe that he creates values by his choices' (p. 97).

35 McDowell, 'Responses', p. 276. McDowell thus endorses only a modest interpretation of the notion of self-legislation:

> What the image comes down to is that we are subject to norms only in so far as we can freely acknowledge their authority, so that being subject to them is not being under the control of an alien force. But apart from special cases, their authority is not brought into being by acknowledgement.

'On Pippin's Postscript', unpublished manuscript, p. 17.

36 Cf. G.W.F. Hegel, *Philosophy of Right*, § 21 Addition trans. H.B. Nisbet (Cambridge: Cambridge University Press, 1991), p. 53: 'The will in its truth is such that what it wills, i.e. its content, is identical with the will itself, so that freedom is willed by freedom'. Cf. also ibid § 27.

37 Cf. A.W. Wood, *Hegel's Ethical Thought* (Cambridge: Cambridge University Press, 1990), pp. 30–35.

38 Cf. Pippin's contrast between what he sees as a properly Kantian conception of self-legislation and the interpretations (such as Paul Guyer's and Allen Wood's) that take freedom to be the value on which that legislation is based: see R. B. Pippin, 'A Mandatory Reading of Kant's Ethics?', *The Philosophical Quarterly*, 51, 2001, 386–93, and 'Kant's Theory of Value: On Allen Wood's *Kant's Ethical Thought*', *Inquiry*, 43, 2000, 239–66. Cf. also Pinkard's related criticism that this sort of account confuses Kant's position with that of a perfectionist realist like Christian Wolff:

> For Wolff, the laws of practical reason had their authority in being tied into the ways in which humans could seek their metaphysical perfection, and Wolff realised that those laws do not automatically lay hold of us; our freedom, as it were, consists in our having to take up those laws in some way, and I was not 'really free' unless I willed in accordance with those laws. Unfortunately [for readings like those we have discussed], it was *exactly this position* that Kant rejected.

T. Pinkard, 'Response to Stern and Snow', *Bulletin of the Hegel Society of Great Britain*, 49–50, 2004, 25–40, p. 26.

39 Korsgaard is a celebrated recent example: cf. *The Sources of Normativity*, pp. 236–37:

> In both Kant's version and mine the subject is unequivocally the author of the law, but autonomous lawmaking is not something you can do any way you like, any more than thinking is. It must be done universally.

For Pippin's own critique of Korsgaard's position, and an attempt to push it in a more Hegelian direction, see his 'Über Selbstgesetzgebung', in *Deutsche Zeitschrift für Philosophie*, 6, 2003, 905–26.

40 Robert B. Pippin, 'Hegel's Practical Philosophy: The Realization of Freedom', in K. Ameriks (ed.), *The Cambridge Companion to German Idealism* (Cambridge: Cambridge University Press, 2000), pp. 180–99, pp. 194–95.

41 Cf. Pippin, *Modernism as a Philosophical Problem*, pp. 72–73:

> Just as when we attempt to 'judge objectively' or 'determine the truth,' we inherit an extensive set of rule-governed, historically concrete practices, so when we attempt to 'act rightly,' and attempt to determine our action spontaneously, we must see ourselves as situated in a complex collective and historical setting, a dependence on setting very much like that implicitly asserted by the narrative form of the modern novel ... Thus it could be said that, in a way much like the classical ideal of freedom as 'realization within the whole,' Hegel

too tries to show how the attempt at self-determination requires (at least at some, often very implicit, level) an understanding of oneself as occupying a 'place' within a larger whole, except in his view that whole is not nature or the cosmos, but the history of a collectively self-determining subject.

42 Pippin, *Modernism as a Philosophical Problem*, pp. 69–70.

43 Similar themes are also emphasised by Pinkard: see e.g. *German Philosophy 1760–1860*, p. 280, and 'Subjects, Objects, and Normativity', p. 214.

44 Pippin, 'Postscript', p. 216.

45 See C. Larmore, *The Morals of Modernity* (Cambridge: Cambridge University Press, 1996), Chap. 5.

46 Cf. Pippin, *Modernism as a Philosophical Problem*, p. 14 (my emphasis):

> Such a 'spontaneous subjectivity,' *completely determining for itself what to accept as evidence about the nature of things*, and legislating to itself its proper course of action, is, if nothing else, the appropriate image of modernity's understanding of itself as revolutionary and 'self-grounding,' and so an invaluable focus of raising a number of questions.

47 One Hegelian-sounding thought might be that it is 'internal' to every practice that it must overcome incoherencies that develop within it: but that would still give the normative force of this 'must' a distinctive explanation, as not getting *its* force from the way in which it has resolved aporiai in previous systems of norms.

48 In this connection, Pippin is fond of quoting the following addition from the *Encyclopaedia Logic*, § 31: 'This pure being at home with ourselves [*Beisichsein*] belongs to free thought, that voyages in the open, where nothing is below us and nothing is above us, and we stand in solitude with ourselves alone', taking this to be Hegel's view of modernity, as finding ourselves in the position of needing to create our *own* values around us, where we cannot rely on anything being there already – this constitutes our solitude, and also our freedom (see e.g. Pippin, *Modernism as a Philosophical Problem*, p. 67). However, although it can be read in this way, the meaning of this text is not altogether clear. For, while Hegel is certainly contrasting our position to something like Scholastic metaphysics, which was not free because it 'adopted its content as something given, and indeed given by the Church', it is less clear that he is rejecting realism, in so far as he claims that the Greeks also 'thought freely', where it seems that all that is necessary for this is to avoid any such appeal to authorities in one's speculations:

> We must imagine the ancient philosophers as men who stand right in the middle of sensory intuition, and presuppose nothing except the heavens above and the earth beneath, since mythological representations have been thrown aside. In this simple factual environment, thought is free and withdrawn into itself, free of all [given] material, purely at home with itself.

49 Cf. e.g. Kant, *Groundwork* Ak 4:414 (translation p. 67), *Critique of Practical Reason* Ak 5:81–82 (translated by M.J. Gregor in Kant, *Practical Philosophy*, pp. 205–6).

50 G.W.F. Hegel, 'The Spirit of Christianity and Its Fate', in *Early Theological Writings*, trans. T.M. Knox (Philadelphia: University of Pennsylvania Press, 1971), p. 244 [G.W.F. Hegel, *Werke in zwanzig Bänden*, E. Moldenhauer and K.M. Michel (eds) (Frankfurt: Suhrkamp, 1970), vol. I, pp. 359–60]. Cf. also 'The Spirit of Christianity', p. 215, note [*Werke*, vol. I, p. 327], where Hegel writes in a cancelled passage:

> A command can express no more than an ought or a shall, because it is a universal, but it does not express an 'is'; and this at once makes plain its deficiency. Against such commands Jesus set virtue, i.e., a loving disposition, which makes the content of the command superfluous and destroys its form as a command, because that form implies an opposition between a commander and something resisting the command.

51 Hegel, 'The Spirit of Christianity', p. 212 [*Werke*, vol. I, p. 324].
52 But cf. G.W.F. Hegel, *The Encyclopaedia of the Philosophical Sciences*, § 516.
53 Hegel, *Philosophy of Right*, § 146 (translation p. 190).
54 Hegel, *Philosophy of Right*, § 147 (translation p. 191).
55 Pippin, 'Postscript', p. 219.
56 A previous version of this paper was presented at a conference in London of the AHRC funded 'Transcendental Philosophy and Naturalism' project, and I am grateful to the audience for comments on that occasion. I am also grateful for comments from Karl Ameriks, Robert Audi, Fabian Freyenhagen, Jimmy Lenman, David Owens, Robert Hopkins, Stephen Houlgate, John Skorupski, Sebastian Gardner and Yonatan Shemmer. I owe particular thanks to Robert Pippin and John McDowell, for sharing with me their unpublished work on this topic, and for providing invaluable comments on previous drafts of this paper.

12

FROM EPISTEMOLOGY TO AESTHETICS

Richard Eldridge

I

Richard Rorty once wrote that skepticism (especially skepticism about the external world and about other minds), the seventeenth-century theory of ideas, and roughly 1950s and 1960s ordinary language philosophy (the intimate antagonist of skepticism and the theory of ideas) are all "temporary, historically conditioned little frenzies."[1] Yes, it was a big wrench to haul the attentions and interest of educated Europeans away from natural theophysics and toward mathematical-experimental science, and talk of ideas and of skepticism may in fact have played a functional or at least propagandistic role in that wrenching of attentions and interest. But talk of ideas and rehearsals of skepticism – however temporarily useful as a kind of loosening up propaganda – did not, in fact, really do the work of justifying experimental science in foundational terms. Nothing did. Rather, physical science itself advanced in predictive power and the affordance of technological control over nature. In this way, it both displayed its interest on its own and made life better. "We philosophy professors," Rorty goes on, including himself, have too often misunderstood this and pretended that the construction and rehearsal of foundationalist arguments in epistemology itself has "moral worth"[2], that is, that grasping these arguments really will of itself help us to become better, more aptly curious people, able better to exercise their rational nature within a system of natures. This is a professional guiding myth. But in fact nobody really believes it, at least not anymore, according to Rorty. Many of "us philosophy professors" feel "shame . . . ever since we began to suspect that our introductory courses in epistemology merely kicked up a cloud of dust around our students, so that they might be grateful to us for leading them out of it into the light."[3]

> The only people who go all existential about the invisibility of the rest of the tomato are lecturers on philosophy who relieve the classroom tedium by hype. When such lecturers encounter an unstable freshman who actually does feel the tomato to have catastrophic implications, they hasten to join his more robust classmates in assuring him that it is all "just philosophy".[4]

Rorty concedes that there really are important existential questions: questions about how to find meaning in life, questions of the kind that Hegel and Tolstoy and Sartre addressed. His point is simply that these latter questions are neither raised nor answered by worries about the justificatory basis of ideas in mind. Epistemology – as least epistemology of the kind practiced by Berkeley, Descartes, Moore, and Price – is not romance.

In my own view, a great deal of this is either right or almost right. Rorty has certainly done us a great service in raising the questions of the moral worth and the place in human life of foundationalist, idea-based epistemology and, by implication at least, of its naturalist-causalist successors (such as Dretske's information-theoretic account of belief). I will, however, in the end disagree with Rorty's confidence that there is any resting place within either common sense or our provisional commitments, such that our practical and historical forms of life can, will, and should henceforth always be changed only via incremental ameliorations in relation to already formed commitments. Human life is, I think, more open to sharp reversals than Rorty quite sees, and rightly so. To quote Hegel on this point,

> Spirit in its formation matures slowly and quietly into its new shape, dissolving bit by bit the structure of its previous world, whose tottering state is only hinted at by isolated symptoms. The frivolity and boredom which unsettle the established order, the vague foreboding of something unknown – these are the heralds of approaching change. The gradual crumbling that left unaltered the face of the whole is cut short by a sunburst which, in one flash, illuminates the features of the new world.[5]

Hegel himself grows more reformist as his career develops, coming to argue in the 1820 *Philosophy of Right* that the work of history has been completed, so that now "*basically* . . . *everyone* [is] . . . able to satisfy [his or her] knowledge and volition . . . within the actuality of the [modern] state"[6] and its sub-institutions of family life and civil society. Whatever the charms of modern democracy and of reformist politics within its framework are (and they are many), it is by no means clear that modern democracy and its institutions will automatically enable us successfully to address problems of dramatic religious diversity, gender conflict, and economic inequality, among others. It may not be as easy as all that for all individuals in all situations to understand the worth of their way of life and to choose to continue it (to have their knowledge and volition satisfied). In this respect, Hegel's 1806 sense of the continuing agonistic character of historical development seems more plausible than his later reformism.

But how, then, are problems of understanding and commitment to be addressed, given that they are not always by-and-large already settled? As Rorty has also trenchantly remarked, the answer to this question that has largely been canonical for the discipline of philosophy and for its role in culture, especially in circles in which modern natural science is taken seriously, focuses on epistemology. The idea is that a region of cultural practice is at least legitimate if and only if the most basic knowledge claims (e.g. about the existence of God and how to honor him, or about the nature of the right, or about material reality, its causal ordering, and how to know it) are well founded or at the very least well-formed and possibly true. As Rorty puts it,

> Philosophy can be foundational in respect to the rest of culture because culture is the assemblage of claims to knowledge, and philosophy adjudicates such claims. It can do so because it understands the foundations of knowledge, and it finds these foundations in a study of man-as-knower, of the "mental processes" or the "activity of representation" which make knowledge possible. ... Philosophy's central concern is to be a general theory of representation, a theory which will divide culture up into the areas which represent reality well, those which represent it less well, and those which do not represent it at all (despite their pretense of doing so).[7]

Rorty, however, is suggesting that philosophy is (and always has been) unable to play such a foundational role for the rest of culture. What could the argument in favor of such a position possibly be? And if problems of cultural orientation and commitment are not by and large settled by the course of historical practice, then how can such problems be addressed at all, if not by foundationalist epistemology? Are we simply, always and inevitably, ultimately adrift in our commitments, insulated from recognition of this fact only by having, most of the time, enough of our fellows drifting along with us? And could we, for all we know, be bound for an abyss?

These are, I believe, the questions that are (or should be) most prominent in current thinking about knowledge, culture, and value. They *are* prominent in certain circles. Yet the contemporary arguments in favor of their importance are frequently neither very fully developed nor properly located against their relevant historical backgrounds, where both a commitment to the importance of these questions was better worked out and where ways of responding to them were more explicitly developed in systematic thinking than is often the case at present. The relevant background in question is significantly Kantian-Hegelian, combining Kant's emphases on the priority and ineliminability of judgmental structure in our conscious life with Hegel's emphasis on norms as cultural affordances. If these questions are genuinely to be established to be important, so that our attentions must be turned toward the formulation of a "successor discipline" to foundationalist epistemology, then it will help to review this Kantian-Hegelian background in order to find the relevant arguments, to show how (incomplete) versions of them figure in some contemporary thinking in the philosophies of mind and language, and finally to trace their implications for current ways of thinking critically about commitments.

II

Notoriously, Kant argued that a judgment consists of parts – typically an intuition or object-referring mental item plus a concept or object-sorting mental item – that are actively synthesized into a whole by a human subject. The occurrence of a judgment is not a simple natural-material happenstance. It is rather something that is actively brought about by a subject. As Kant puts it, a concept is "the unity of the *act* of bringing together various representations under one common representation";[8] more prosaically, concepts just are rules for classing together singular intuitions of objects or events as intuitions of the same kinds of things: sortal rules. These sortal rules are applied to intuitions of objects and events when and only when we so apply them to form a judgment.

That there are sortal rules available for combination either with intuitions or with other concepts (e.g. in a universal generalization) to form a judgment is the result of the work of the understanding, the faculty of concepts. This talk of a faculty may seem to raise a problem rather than solving one, for it amounts roughly to saying that we are able to form concepts (sortal rules) because we are able to form concepts. No explanation is given of how we have this ability, and in his "Open Letter on Fichte's *Wissenschaftslehre*" Kant makes clear his opposition to all efforts "to cull a real object out of logic,"[9] that is, to *explain* by reference to some given substance and *its* powers what gives us the cognitive abilities we have. Instead, it is just to be accepted that, as Kant puts it in the *Opus Postumum*, "we can know no objects, either in us or as lying outside us, except insofar as we insert in ourselves the *actus* of cognition, according to certain laws."[10]

Still, how could we do such a thing: insert in ourselves the *actus* of cognition? What does it even mean to claim that we do this? A key to grasping Kant's thought here is to appreciate his emphasis on our responsibility for what we do. What we do is, always, assessable according to norms, whether in the form of sortal rules for how it is correct to classify empirical objects and events or in the form of a moral principle that determines (given further supplementary specifications) what is permissible and what is obligatory in the way of actions within the material world. That is, we can and do raise for ourselves, and others can raise for us, the question whether we are correct either to act or to judge thus-and-so. It is no accident that Kant takes formal logic to have been successful in giving "an exhaustive exposition ... of the formal rules of thought."[11] Setting aside the claim to exhaustiveness, accepting any inference of the form "p, p $\rightarrow$ q; therefore q" is a paradigm act on the part of a free being who is responsive to norms. I do not accept such inferences because I am caused to do so, but rather because I have come to recognize that they are valid. As Onora O'Neill has cogently characterized the relevant line of argument, we are, according to Kant, always already "incipiently reasoning beings" who seek to achieve "an active grasp rather than a passive response to the manifold of life."[12] Achieving such an active grasp involves, first, doing something actively – classifying objects, or accepting or rejecting inferences, or acting on material objects – and, second, doing so successfully, that is, doing so in such a way that one can *recognize oneself* (and be recognized by others) *over time* as the one who *has actively done thus-and-so* (judged, inferred, acted) *for reasons* rather than being construable as a merely material object buffeted about by material forces.

While this line of thought is at least attractive in undertaking to describe what is distinctive about what we do in judging, inferring, and acting, it nonetheless remains unclear *how* we come to do these things, that is, *how* we "insert in ourselves the *actus*" of cognition, inference, or action itself. Puzzlement about exactly what we do freely and actively in judging and about how we do it can perhaps be reduced somewhat by using more modest twentieth-century terms to describe what we do. With Collingwood one might talk of *attending* to objects or events or with Ryle of *heeding* or *minding* them. Language of this kind is useful in showing just how typical and ordinary judging as bound up with "freely paying attention to" is. Such language does not quite fully locate, however, what is going on in metaphysical terms. What kind of a being is capable of this kind of free attention? How does free attention develop? Even if it is impossible to "ground and explain" in purely material terms what is going on, it would be helpful to know more, descriptively, about *what* is going on when we judge and about how our judgmental life develops.

Providing such a description, including a descriptive account of the metaphysics of judgment and personhood as not purely material phenomena, is a central aim of Hegel's project in philosophy. Hegel explicitly accepts Kant's claim that judgment and conception are the results of our free actions, of which we can become explicitly conscious and for which we are responsible. As Hegel puts the point, "materials [from sensuous sources] when *conceived* are expressly characterized as in me and therefore mine" just as "conceptions constituted by materials emanating from self-conscious thought, such as those of law, morality, religion, and even of thought itself" are also.[13] That is to say, conceptions (concepts) and judgments, which are necessarily composed at least in part of concepts (including relations), are my products, the results of my activity. They are not simply given or produced as a result of material processes alone. Though they are world-responsive, they are the results of *my* way of responding to objects and events, as a developing free and self-conscious being.

Though concepts and judgments are in this way mine as a free and self-conscious being, they are not simply and only mine. My concepts and judgments are both world-responsive and collectively formed, albeit that they are *also* centrally mine. In explaining how this is so, Hegel is setting himself against what he regards as Kantian mystery-mongering about faculties for doing thus-and-so that are simply fixed in individuals. Thinking, conceiving, inferring, and judging are, Hegel holds, only possible *for me* and *as my acts* when they are both world-responsive and common (or commonly explicable), rather than flights of subjective fancy. I cannot judge *that that is a third out in the seventh inning* without there being both an actual event there before me and a shared or sharable practice together with shared or sharable terms for assessing events within it. While this is an intuitive enough point for judging events within the social-artifactual setting of baseball, Hegel extends it quite explicitly to judgment, conception, and thought in general.

> To think is in fact *ipso facto* to be free, for thought as the action of the universal is an abstract relating of self to self, where, being at home with ourselves, and, as regards our subjectivity utterly blank, our consciousness is, in the matter of its contents, only *in* the fact and its characteristics. . . . For in point of contents, thought is only true in proportion as it sinks itself in the facts; and in point of form it is no private or particular state or act of the subject, but rather that attitude of consciousness where the abstract self, freed from all the special limitations to which its ordinary states or qualities are liable, restricts itself to that universal action in which it is identical with all individuals.[14]

It is not I, with my own idiosyncratic flights of fancy and feeling, who judges that 2 + 3 = 5, nor is it I who so judges independently of immersion in the content of numbers, addition, and identity, but it is nonetheless I who so judges – I *qua* rational agent in general who is immersed in the content.

It is important that concept formation and judgment are free acts of discernment of what is there, not passively and causally formed impresses from what is given. Concepts and judgments are formed, in Hegel's terminology, in reflection, and it is only by way of our free acts of reflection that the natures of things become evident to us. "It is thus only by means of an alteration that the true nature of the object comes to consciousness."[15] Though this claim sounds odd to contemporary ears, the thought is really quite intuitive. I am confronted say, with a lump of stuff before me. I receive sensory stimulations from it. To understand it as yellow or dense, however, I must already locate this object that provides sensory stimulations against a background of comparisons and contrasts that I deploy. When I further identify it as gold – perhaps by establishing its atomic weight; perhaps by carrying out tests with various acids – I actively do something in order to locate this stuff in the relevant matrix of kinds. *Its kind* – its goldness – does not simply *present itself* to me in passive sensation alone. I must actively identify it. Or as Hegel puts it, "the real nature of the object is brought to light in reflection, but it is no less true that this exertion of thought is my act."[16]

How do we become capable of carrying out the relevant tests and so of locating objects in relevant matrices of kinds? We do arrive at the conclusion that the relevant kinds are there in nature, at least independently of the perspective of any particular inquirer, and our identifications of objects as belonging to kinds must respect our best current ways of determining kind-memberships. Nonetheless that we have available a matrix of kinds in which to locate objects, together with tests for determining specific identifications, is a result of a history of our grooming our concepts (our terms for kind identification) to suit our situation and projects in nature. While this grooming must be world-responsive, both from the beginning and always, it is also free from complete control by the world. Again, the process of concept formation is active, not passive. And it is collective, not individual. Hence, "it is not *we* who frame the notions"; that is, we do not simply as individuals with psychological faculties "colligat[e] the points possessed in common by the objects."[17] Rather the relevant collective and free (but world-responsive) actions of concept-formation, concept-revision, and judgment are controlled ultimately by our efforts-in-the-world to find satisfaction in our self-identities and concrete ways of life.

Hegel's position thus amounts (as is often remarked) to a kind of dematerialized or inverted Spinozism. Like Spinoza, Hegel sets himself against the idea that anything Platonically abstract serves or can serve as a template for conceptualization and judgment. The development of concepts and judgments rather takes place immanently within our efforts to form stable and satisfying self-identities within material situations and (revisable) frameworks of concrete practice. Not correspondence with anything just given (either Platonically or in material nature alone), but satisfaction in how we concretely live is the aim of our formation and revision of concepts and judgments. (To be sure, getting wrong what things are like and how they can threaten us or how we can use them sets very significant constraints on our possibilities of satisfaction. Still, it is satisfaction that is the aim, not correspondence of thought with anything brutely given.) Unlike Spinoza, however, the aim is satisfaction in having a stable identity within a stable course of shared, worldly, concrete, active practice, rather than either individual calm or individual intellectual contemplation alone.

If we begin, against Hegel, from the thoughts that the material world is just given (it was, after all, there before we were) and that we exist in the strictest sense only as individual members of a biological species who are struggling to survive, then Hegel's picture will seem fantastically speculative and ungrounded. Thought, conception, and judgment will seem to be matters primarily of present individual world-representation (whether construed as material or as intellectual) that seeks correspondence with the material given. Against this thought, one might try to prop up Hegel's picture by showing genetically how we can and do construct for ourselves the aim of satisfaction in having a stable identity in a stable course of practice. Robert Brandom's recent writing on Hegel has moved in this direction, as he has attempted to show exactly *how* we construct and revise norms that govern our judgmental practice, without presupposing that that effort has any overarching aim from the beginning.[18] This strategy runs the risk, however, of covertly importing into the description of what we do *ab novo* the very aim that it would rather see us as constructing out of our efforts and our reflections on them alone. Alternatively one might try to argue that it is a presupposition of judgmental awareness of objects – part of its very structure, as distinct from mere animal sentient awareness – that we have this end. This is the core, neo-Kantian argumentative line of the *Phenomenology* that Robert Pippin has explored.[19] This line of argument develops by beginning from a simple description of the nature and structure of judgmental consciousness, exploring what that description really involves, and then arriving at the result that if consciousness really were like that (e.g. consisted in, at bottom, simple sensory awareness of given sensible particulars only), then consciousness could not be judgmental (its contents could not, for example, be assessable as true or false). Then the description of the nature of judgmental consciousness is enriched, until at last we find a characterization that is not self-contradictory. This final characterization then turns out to include the thought that we seek to form and sustain stable identities in stable courses of worldly practice, in quite specific, collectively structured ways, and, moreover, that we are by-and-large succeeding in this effort. As Pippin has noted, however, this line too faces the problem that when we "enrich" and improve on an incoherent conception of consciousness we may simply import or impute the end we are trying to argue that we possess.[20] Neither the genetic nor the presuppositionalist line of argument is, therefore, likely to satisfy someone who begins from an anti-Hegelian view of human existence in material nature.

Yet anti-Hegelian views face problems of their own. Either world-representing will be construed as an "inner" and "intellectual" activity of mind, in which case insuperable problems of mind-body interaction, mental causation, volition taking effect in the world, and the like will arise. Or world-representing will be conceived of as ultimately causally engendered and controlled, in which case it is unclear how and why representations can be normatively assessable as apt or inapt at all. Or talk of world-representing will be dismissed as an idiom that serves no serious purpose in natural science, in which case it is unclear how we can talk about science as getting anything right or wrong. None of these options is terribly attractive.

Hence, although there may be no good "foundational" argument in favor of Hegel's inverted Spinozist picture of human life, it is a picture that may at least be coherent and may enable us to make sense of many things we do. In the most general terms – terms that Hegel maps onto the Biblical story of fall and redemption:

> For the spirit it is a duty to be free, and to realize itself by its own act. Nature is for man only the starting-point which he has to transform. . . . The hour when man leaves the path of mere natural being marks the difference between him, a self-conscious agent, and the natural world. But this schism, though it forms a necessary element in the very notion of spirit, is not the final goal of man. It is to this state of inward breach that the whole finite action of thought and will belongs.[21]

Thought, self-consciousness, and voluntary action – and with them conceptualization and judgment – belong to the life of a being situated within nature who has it as a not-yet-realized aim to live "beyond nature" in achieving satisfaction in having a stable identity in a stable course of concrete, worldly practice. We are, that is to say, to achieve self-recognition in absolute otherness, or at-homeness in the world in and through our concrete practices and human relations. Having this end is what judgmental consciousness is "all about," and this picture of its nature has at least a fair claim to offer an illuminating and coherent account of who we, as agents and thinkers, are.

III

With this dramatic picture of human judgmental life in the background, we can now turn to a key text – a passage from Donald Davidson's "A Coherence Theory of Truth and Knowledge." The idea will be to see just how Hegelian certain contemporary ways of thinking about mindedness, thought, and representation are. In seeing this, we can see first how Hegel's thought can be more humbly appropriated and paraphrased and, second and perhaps more interesting, we can bring to the fore more clearly the Hegelian commitments and burdens that are undertaken in these contemporary ways of thinking. In this way, we can see more clearly just how these contemporary ways of thinking are caught up in the picture of human beings as seeking satisfaction, in ways of which their proponents may not always be aware.

The key text runs as follows:

> It will promote matters at this point to review very hastily some of the reasons for abandoning the search for a basis for knowledge outside the scope of our [already formed] beliefs. By 'basis' here I mean specifically an epistemological basis, a source of justification.
>
> The attempts worth taking seriously attempt to ground belief in one way or another on the testimony of the senses: sensation, perception, the given, experience, sense data, the passing show. All such theories must explain at least these two things: what, exactly is the relation between sensation and belief that allows the first to justify the second? and, why should we believe our sensations are reliable, that is, why should we trust our senses?
>
> The simplest idea is to identify certain beliefs with sensations. Thus Hume seems not to have distinguished between perceiving a green spot and perceiving that a spot is green. (An ambiguity in the word 'idea' was a great help here.) Other philosophers noted Hume's confusion, but tried to attain the same results by reducing the gap between perception and judgment to zero by attempting to formulate judgments that do not go beyond stating that the perception or sensation or presentation exists (whatever that may mean). Such theories

> do not justify beliefs on the basis of sensation, but try to justify certain beliefs by claiming that they have exactly the same epistemic content as a sensation. There are two difficulties with such a view: first, if the basic beliefs do not exceed in content the corresponding sensation they cannot support any inference to an objective world; and second, there are no such beliefs.[22]

This passage is a fine bit of drama, with the penny dropping at the end: there are no such things as beliefs that are either identical with or have exactly the same epistemic content as a sensation; even if there were such things, they would fulfill no justificatory role. Mostly I will want to play out the reasons for this conclusion, reasons which are not yet given in this passage alone. But it is worthwhile to linger for a moment on some of the earlier remarks in this passage.

The ambiguity in the word "idea" that Davidson has in mind is that between a) a simple awareness or having of a felt qualium, and b) a judgeable content of the kind that is expressed in a that-clause. That is, the idea of the sourness of a lemon might be construed as either a specific, felt, occurrent sourness, such that one can actually have it only (or usually) in experiencing a lemon, or it might be construed as the judgment that a lemon is sour. To conflate these two distinct senses would then be to run together the passive, causally induced occurrence of a sensory process, on the one hand, with the making of a judgment about how things are, on the other. And to do that would in turn be to deny – as Hume did deny – the activity of the mind in making even a perceptual judgment. Kant, and after him Hegel, corrected this error in emphasizing our active role in synthesizing judgments and their materials ("we insert in ourselves the *actus* of cognition"). Neither Kant nor Hegel, however, accepts any immediate regress blockers: there are no simply given intellectual intuitions and no in principle unchallengeable perceptual *arche*. And so the best we can do is to reflect critically, comparatively, and imaginatively on our judgmental commitments. We begin from making judgments, not just from "having" sensations. In assessing our judgments, we must then betake ourselves to what Kant calls critique and what Hegel calls logic, rather than reverting to fixed "foundations."

Let me now turn explicitly to the dramatic final claim that there are no perceptual beliefs that are identical in content with a corresponding sensation: no purely sensation-based regress-blockers. According to Davidson, why not? Here is what Davidson goes on to say:

> If the intermediaries [that is, purely perceptual judgments, with no epistemic content above the having of a sensation, which perceptual judgments stand "between" us and the things of the world] are merely causes, they don't justify the beliefs they cause, while if they deliver information, they may be lying. The moral is obvious. Since we can't swear intermediaries to truthfulness, we should allow no intermediaries

> between our beliefs and their objects in the world. Of course there are causal intermediaries. What we must guard against are epistemic intermediaries.[23]

"If they deliver information, they may be lying." This claim is crucial. Information is something that is, always, to be assessed. When a subject forms a belief, then the subject is actively responsible for having assessed the informational content and come to a conclusion, where the defending of this conclusion by reference to some suitable reasons *must* be in view (even if "absolute" reasons remain unavailable). To be sure, there are judgments that are formed by us directly and not as a result of inference: basic perceptual judgments, for example. But these judgments carry further commitments, and they are in principle open to challenge and defense, rather than being "just given" causally once and for all.

Perhaps Davidson has Husserl in mind as someone who saw us – incoherently, Davidson is claiming – as capable of making certain judgments whose content does not exceed what is given. There is a lot to explore in this passage from Davidson about why there are no Husserlian purely intellectual regress-blockers available to us. Is it just taken for granted that I lack, say, mathematical knowledge purely a priori? Or is it taken for granted that I am unable to judge with certainty at least that I am now in a state of F-awareness? Just why is it impossible to conceive of some givenness to which I am judgmentally responsive without any possibility of error, insofar as my judgmental commitment does not exceed what is "just given"? Here is where the Kantian-Hegelian-inverted Spinozist picture, together with its resistances to intellectual intuitions, perceptual *arche*, and responsibility-denying materialisms, is doing some covert work.

The underlying idea here is that a judgeable content (something that a subject forms) is something that stands in relations of implication to other judgeable contents. When a subject takes a judgeable content to be true – that is, forms a belief – then the subject is both undertaking commitments to offering at least minimal reasons, when queried, in favor of this judgeable content and to endorsing what is implied by it.

Robert Brandom has worked out this conception more fully with his language of commitment and entitlement. Brandom argues that "even . . . non-inferential reports [i.e. 'purely perceptual judgments' such as 'This is red'] must be inferentially articulated. Without that requirement, we cannot tell the difference between noninferential reporters and automatic machinery such as thermostats and photocells, which also have reliable dispositions to respond differentially to stimuli."[24] The central thought here is that:

> For a response to have *conceptual* content is just for it to play a role in the *inferential* game of making claims and giving and asking for reasons. To grasp or understand such a concept is to have practical mastery

> over the inferences it is involved in – to know, in the practical sense of being able to distinguish (a kind of know-*how*), what follows from the applicability of a concept, and what it follows from. The parrot does not treat "That's red" as incompatible with "That's green," nor as following from "That's scarlet" and entailing "That's colored." Insofar as the repeatable response is not, for the parrot, caught up in practical proprieties of inference and justification, and so of the making of further judgments, it is not a *conceptual* or a *cognitive* matter at all.[25]

We could spend a good deal of time on this passage, too. Jerrold Katz wrote a wonderful paper a few years ago, called "*The* Problem in Twentieth-Century Philosophy,"[26] in which he surveyed various strategies – Chomskyan-naturalist, Wittgenstein-conventionalist, and Platonic-Fregean – for accounting for the necessary truth of "Nothing is both red and green all over," himself urging that only the last strategy, the Platonic-Fregean, made sense in explaining how we can know this as a *truth* about how things are and must be. That, however, is not Brandom's stance. Note the important word "practical" in this passage from Brandom. Proprieties of inference and justification are laid down in human linguistic and discursive practice. They are neither housed in Platonic heaven nor built by God or nature into the conceptual structure of the pure Cartesian intellect nor somehow just materially given. As Brandom himself puts it,

> Understanding or grasping a propositional content is here presented not as the turning on of a Cartesian light, but as practical mastery of a certain kind of inferentially articulated doing: responding differentially according to the circumstances of proper application of a concept, and distinguishing the proper inferential consequences of such application. This is not an all-or-none affair; the metallurgist understands the concept *tellurium* better than I do, for *training* has made her master of the inferential intricacies of its employment in a way that I can only crudely approximate.[27]

According, then, to the roughly pragmatist stance that Brandom and Davidson share, understanding or grasping either propositional contents or concepts (central constituents of propositional contents) is an achievement – an exercise of an ability – that is brought off by embodied human beings with rational capacities who take up (and can modify) going social practices. This stance involves a Kantian view of the nature of concepts (unities of *acts* of subsumption). It involves a neo-Aristotelian appeal to the idea that human beings are bits of matter with a certain sort of organization, such that in virtue of that overall organization of their matter (and not in virtue of a sub-component of the brain alone) they have by nature rational capacities – second-order abilities to develop first order abilities to do things in rule-governed practices. And finally it involves a neo-Hegelian view of the conditions under which alone this development is possible – namely, through training in social interaction (the collective formation and reformation of concepts and judgments in practice, with the aim of seeking self-coherence and satisfaction).

This package of commitments has, to many, considerable implausibility. Jerry Fodor has complained time and again that the appeal to capacities and to training is non-explanatory: it offers no account of either the psychological or material processes and states through which linguistic and cognitive-conceptual development occur.[28] But there is also a reply to this Fodorian criticism: the cognitive-developmental psychologist Michael Tomasello, in exciting recent work,[29] has developed a careful description of language learning as involving the grammaticalization of holophrases. For example, "Iwanna" is initially learned imitatively as an unstructured holophrase. It is *not* first "thought" by the child as a first-person pronoun noun-phrase, followed by a modal verb and then by a curtailed infinitive phrase. Only later, will the child segment the phrase and recombine its parts under grammatical and lexical categories that it is implicitly coming to be able to deploy. This development is not undergirded simply by either prior Cartesian intellectual processes or brutely material processes. (Though some material processes are causally necessary for this development, none are causally sufficient.) Rather it takes place as the child picks up on what grownups are doing *with* certain noise makings: specifically to how they are attending and calling attention to certain aspects of things. Human beings have a natural capacity to see a stick, for example, as firewood, as a tool, as a weapon, as a prop, as a bit of a wall to be built, and so on, even as a hobbyhorse to be ridden. And they further, even when very young, have a capacity to pick up on how others are attending to things: under what aspects they are seeing or making use of them. Children, according to Tomasello, learn how to understand and to use words just as they learn how to see and to use sticks in certain ways: through social interaction in which aspects of things as attended to are highlighted and shared.

This account of the process of language learning – attractively developmental, anti-intellectualistic, and pragmatic-expressivist as it is – will not satisfy everyone. It is specifically neither couched in the vocabulary of the physical sciences nor such that translation from it into that vocabulary can be readily envisaged. It makes free use of the idea of human beings having capacities for seeing things under aspects and for picking up on the aspect-seeings of others. Metaphysical materialists will find this disappointing and non-explanatory. They will then seek either provisional psychological computational explanations, in the style of Fodor and Chomsky, that can at least be imagined (they think) to describe material processes occurring in sub-components of the human brain, or they will seek more brutely causal and material explanations of such material processes, perhaps in connectionist, perhaps in directly material terms, as Quine urges us to do.

But note now that these materialist programs of explanation – despite their attractive continuity with the history and successes of physical science in rejecting free talk of capacities and powers – have their own liabilities. Fodor's semantic naturalist program faces the problems of indeterminacy and of error. That is, how can Fodor distinguish, simply by pointing to causal interactions with objects in the environment and without drawing on what the subject says in a public language, whether a subject is tokening a cat-representation, a pet-representation, a mammal representation, a furry-purry-thing representation, and so on, for the same object has all these features to be noticed. Second, and similarly, cat-representations are sometimes tokened in the vicinity of small dogs, large rats, and shadows. What makes these tokenings *mistaken*, if we are prohibited from giving an answer in terms of the socio-practically established criteria for applying a term in a public language – the supposedly surface phenomenon that Fodor wishes to explain at a deeper level? Fodor, Dretske, and Millikin, among others, have proposed various answers to this question, involving notions such as Representation R is mistakenly tokened or prompted by Object O if and only if the tokening of R by O is *asymmetrically dependent* on the tokening of R by some other object O′. It is doubtful, however, whether the notion of asymmetric dependency that is required here can be made sense of without in turn presupposing, at least covertly, the view that R applies to O′ according to the rules for the correct use of some public language expression that signifies the state of attention R. As Barry Loewer summarizes the state of the argument:

> None of the naturalization proposals [i.e. the proposals that eschew as a matter of principle talk of capacities and abilities] currently on offer are successful. . . . Theories that are clearly naturalistic fail to account for essential features of semantic properties, especially the possibility of error and the fine-grainedness of content. Where these theories are sufficiently explicit . . . they are subject to counter-examples. In attempting to avoid counter-examples, semantic naturalists place restrictions on the reference (or truth condition) constituting causes [such as the 'is not asymmetrically dependent' restriction]. But in avoiding counter-examples, these accounts bring in, either obviously or surreptitiously, semantic and intentional notions [as established in public linguistic practice], and so fail to be naturalistic.[30]

These seem to me to be devastating liabilities for any program to naturalize semantic relations in physicalist terms. The eliminativist program of simply dropping all talk of believing, thinking, wishing, hoping, or meaning anything by anything we say or do is scarcely attractive. Yet given the prestige and explanatory successes of the physical sciences, many people are likely to remain queasy about free talk of capacities and powers, and they are likely to see explanations that go no deeper than talk of training in a practice as themselves bogus or empty. On each side – naturalist vs. (let us call it) semantic autonomist and social normativist – appeal is made to considerations of overall plausibility and to considerations of self-recognition of who we are and what we do, under certain persuasive accounts, supported by examples. Here what counts as plausibility and persuasiveness, and hence what counts as argument, remain deeply contested.

John Dewey captured well the depth and lack of ready resolvability of arguments about fundamental issues in the philosophy of mind, when he wrote in 1934 that,

> Science has brought with it a radically novel [non-Greek, non Judaeo-Christian] conception of physical nature and of our relation to it. This new conception stands as yet side by side with the conception of the world and man that is a heritage from the past, especially from that Christian tradition through which the European social imagination has been formed. The things of the physical world and those of the moral realm have fallen apart, while the Greek tradition and that of the medieval age held them in intimate union. . . . The opposition that now exists between the spiritual and the ideal elements of our historic heritage and the structure of physical nature that is disclosed by science, is the ultimate source of the dualisms formulated by philosophy since Descartes and Locke. These formulations in turn reflect a conflict that is everywhere active in modern civilization.[31]

IV

What is one to do, in the face of pervasive and genuinely lived conflict that is everywhere active in our civilization between images of ourselves as "purely natural", evolved, biological-physical beings, on the one hand, and images of ourselves as responsive to norms and freely responsible for what we do, on the other hand? I have no compelling demonstrative argument to offer in favor of either image and against the other. Both talk of the supposedly historically demonstrated explanatory success of purely material science and talk of the supposedly irrepudiable Kantian fact of reason seem to me to be simply question-begging. Hegelian "persuasive" descriptions of the history of our conceptual practice offer considerable illumination of what we are up to, but they fail to satisfy a demand for *explanation*, for grounding in purely material processes. While this demand may be misplaced, it is difficult to show that it is misplaced within the framework of the all-but-authoritative terms of explanation that are set within modern physical science.

As a result, what I do, at any rate, instead of flat-out arguing for my favored picture, is redescribe and elaborate both what we are up to and what we might better be up to, in various regions of practice – of inquiry, of morality, law, and politics, and of art – and then wait. The stance that I myself favor is broadly social pragmatic, neo-Aristotelian, neo-Hegelian, and Wittgensteinian.

I hesitate to call it pragmatist *tout court* only on the ground that the term "pragmatism" is often used to describe a view within the subfield of epistemology, according to which we are to favor theories that are useful. That recommendation I generally find vague and empty, precisely because standards of usefulness will vary along with standards of plausibility and persuasiveness. In a larger sense, however, the stance I favor is social-pragmatist, in seeing human beings as social- and world-embedded embodied animals, with special and distinctive capacities and abilities. Davidson captures this stance well, in remarking that we should avoid views according to which "the mind is divorced from the traits that constitute it,"[32] where the traits that constitute it are, among other things, not only an inherited biological brain, but also training in a language that is actually in use by others, publicly.

Again, I do not have a fundamental argument in favor of this view – though I am ready with counter-considerations, at least, against rivals. What I do have is various persuasive redescriptions and elaborations of what we are up to, in various domains of inquiry, action, and artistic making. Let me conclude by sketching a few of these very briefly and abstractly.

1) Metaphysically, in making guarded use of talk of capacities and abilities, without giving any underlying substantialist account of their nature, my stance is empirical realist and transcendental idealist. To say this flirts with explicating the obscure by appeal to the unintelligible. But what I mean by this is that I take it for granted – as Hegel and Wittgenstein, Dewey, and Davidson and Brandom take it for granted – that we are biological and material beings living in biological and material circumstances. Taking seriously the epistemological problem of the external world is pretty much what Heidegger said it was: a scandal to philosophy. We should stop it. But I am not able to offer any ultimate account of what the terms "material" and "real" mean: not an atomist account, not a hylomorphist account, not a vibrating superstrings account. I am skeptical of all putative "ultimate constituents" theories – how could we ever know that our physical theory is, at long last, absolutely complete? – while of course wishing to allow that sometimes material explanations that appeal to properties and behaviors of constituents of things make very good sense. In physics, especially, we have found many very good explanations of this kind, and there is no reason to think that we should stop looking for and finding more of them in general. At the same time, we do not know that the vocabulary of physics as it stands is the ultimate vocabulary of explanation, or indeed that there is any such vocabulary, and human beings have powers of aspect-seeing and picking up on the aspect-seeings of others, which powers elude material explanation. Ordinary medium-sized physical objects – what J. L. Austin once called "dry goods"[33] – seem to me to be about as good paradigms of the real as we get, and, as Austin also remarked, "real" is not a trouser word.[34]

2) Epistemologically, I expect there to be contentions among rival theories. I expect some of these contentions to be sorted out reasonably well by appeal to Kuhnian epistemic values: explanatory adequacy, predictive power, scope, logical consistency, simplicity of vocabulary, and the like. Yet, first, rankings based on epistemic values can be very close and quite uncertain at particular historical moments, and, second, they cannot be carried out effectively when quite different metaphysical schemes are in play, as aspects of contending explanations. For example, as Hugh Lacey has argued with great subtlety and penetration, we can evaluate neutrally and impartially according to epistemic values which of several schemes for increasing crop yields under artificial, intensively controlled, single-cycle conditions of crop production is the best. But how are we to compare the results we can get here with claims about how it is best both to maximize yields and to sustain both social reproduction and usable acreage over many generations of use? Are human beings and their patterns of social reproduction and distribution part of the phenomenon to be explained? Or is which seeds can under certain artificial circumstances produce which yields itself the only phenomenon to be explained? There is, Lacey has urged, rightly I think, no way to answer this question that does not bring in both metaphysical stances and questions of social and political values as pursued and achievable within human practice.[35] Pure epistemology simply will not help us with this. Nor will purely epistemic values alone. We had better, I think, try to make the best sense we can of what we are up to and might better be up to, at once in agricultural science and in historical social practice, letting many flowers bloom and waiting to see how things turn out – in agricultural science and in social life together. The overall practice of science, or the pursuit of theories that realize well the epistemic values, and its epistemology are *not autonomous* from metaphysics, politics, and morality.

As a result, for the time being, and perhaps for a very, very long time indeed, we should in a tolerant spirit follow Nancy Cartwright in thinking of even material objects as having many different kinds of powers, the actualization of which occurs in many different circumstances and the description of which can be undertaken from many different points of view, within many different special sciences, so that there are many sciences, not one unified, ultimate, material science. If this is right, then there will not be any unified epistemology either.

One interesting consequence of this view is that it enables us to make interesting sense of work by J. L. Austin and by Wittgenstein on "I know" and "I believe." Both "I know" and "I believe" are used to express degrees of commitment. "I believe" is somewhat concessive. It indicates some commitment and readiness to discuss a claim, but absence of decisive considerations. "I know," in contrast, is more declarative and committive, almost what Austin temporarily called a performative. It indicates readiness to supply decisive considerations, against the background, of course, of shared, wider metaphysical and social commitments that make impartial and neutral assessment in terms of epistemic values possible. "It's true that p" is largely redundant for or simply endorsing of "p." It implies commitment of normal or unspecified degree. This explains why one cannot coherently say "It's true that p, but I don't believe it." Even though there is no logical contradiction involved here, there is a contradiction in commitment. One would be saying, in effect, I am committed to p, but then again I am not really committed to p.

Here to know something, or to claim to know something, is, in Brandom's terms, to have, or to claim to have, a deontic status. But the view here is far from the pale, conventionalist communitarianism of some pragmatisms. There is, as Brandom puts it, for any proposition p – and so, for the proposition *the swatch is red* – a logical gap between "p" and "the claim that p is properly assertible by me now."[36] These two claims are not what Brandom calls "incompatibility equivalent" and so not equivalent. For example, it might be that the swatch is red (and others are committed and entitled to this claim by the circumstances of their perception) but also that the claim "the swatch is red" is not assertible by me: I am color-blind or in bad light, and so not entitled to assert it. That is, these latter circumstances are incompatible with:

2) The claim that the swatch is red is properly assertible by me now, but not with

1) The swatch is red.

Brandom's point is that not only is this true, but also that we know this. We know some people are in a position to know (are entitled to, are able to offer decisive enough reasons for) some claims. But we also know that what counts as decisive enough reason can be contested and that no one is in position to know everything. As a result, "propositional contents are objective in the sense of swinging free of the attitudes of the linguistic practitioners who deploy them in assertions."[37] (As Hegel put it, we must when judging be immersed in the content and not given over to subjective fancy, not even to collective subjective fancy.) "In claiming that the swatch is red [i.e. in undertaking a certain commitment, claiming a certain entitlement] we are not saying anything about who could appropriately assert anything or who is committed or entitled to what."[38] We are staking ourselves to the having of reasons for a judgment about how things are, not claiming permission from a social group.

3) Finally, anthropologico-morally, we have good reason to see ourselves, both individually and as members of groups, as in possession of conflicting commitments. We are committed to physical science and to our educational and legal systems. We are committed to thinking and judging for ourselves, in light of reasons, and also to our own choices, to expressing our inchoately felt distinctive personalities in what we do. And yet we are also committed to judging

and cooperating with others in communities, to accepting in certain regions and at certain times, what is done: for example, to acknowledge what *we* mean by *our* words. That we are, always, caught between what one might roughly call individualist commitments and communitarian commitments is what Stanley Cavell calls the truth of skepticism: "that it names our wish (and the possibility of our wishing) to strip ourselves of the responsibility we have in meaning (or in failing to) one thing, or one way, rather than another."[39] What Cavell means by this is that the problem of negotiating individualist and communitarian commitments does not get solved, never gets solved once and for all. Sometimes there are times to be the one who goes first, the one who thinks and judges according to reason, against the conformist sways of the community. Against Rorty, I do not think that only incremental changes in what is said and done can be apt, albeit that incremental changes are often more sensible than revolutionary ones. And sometimes there are times to accept what is done, what *we* say and mean. In Hegelian terms, self-certainty is never brought to full truth; subjective particularity and social universality are never fully reconciled, and a perfected community is never achieved. But human life is at the very least very interesting, in involving this play between individuality and community.

Artistic making and responding to art are especially interesting regions of human life, where artists frequently undertake to find ways of making new, distinctive, original sense (somewhat like making a new joke), and we can sometimes follow them. This is some consolation – important consolation – that in our personal and collective negotiations of individual and communal commitment we *need not always* fall apart. I spend most of my time at the moment thinking about how certain writers, mostly lyric poets, have registered in their writing simultaneously the fact of at least some standing apartness from others and some possibility nonetheless of shared meaning and of satisfying closure in human performance. Aesthetics – if it is understood as thinking about how poets and other artists do this: how they sometimes find satisfaction in making meaning anew – is itself one central aspect of what epistemology might best now be or become, where epistemology is thinking at least about some central features of knowledge of ourselves. In thinking about the powers of art, we are thinking about what human beings might best make of themselves in some regions of cultural and material practice. And why should we not think about the powers of mind that are exercised in art as themselves just as distinctive of mindedness as the powers exercised in the unhesitating production and comprehension of single sentences? This suggestion is, to put it mildly, extravagant, yet it has the charm of urging attention to dramas of human self-orientation as they are played out within expressive media. Perhaps it is, then, not too much to think of major works of philosophy themselves, with all their examples, narrative rehearsals of histories, images, and allegories, as themselves such situated dramas of orientation. With major works, these dramas are – because faithful at once both to what we are and what we might better be – lived by an us of some significant extent. And perhaps then, there is after all something to the idea of knowing what we know.[40]

Notes

1 Richard Rorty, *Consequences of Pragmatism* (Minneapolis: University of Minnesota Press, 1982), p. 186.
2 Ibid., p. 189.
3 Ibid., p. 176.
4 Ibid., p. 180.
5 G.W.F. Hegel, *Phenomenology of Spirit*, trans. A.V. Miller (Oxford: Clarendon, 1977), para. 11, pp. 6–7.
6 Hegel, *Elements of the Philosophy of Right*, trans. H.B. Nisbet (Cambridge: Cambridge University Press, 1991), p. 14.
7 Rorty, *Philosophy and the Mirror of Nature* (Princeton: Princeton University Press, 1979), p. 3.
8 Immanuel Kant, *Critique of Pure Reason*, trans. N.K. Smith (London: Macmillan, 1933), A68 = B93, p. 105.
9 Kant, *Philosophical Correspondence, 1759–95*, ed. and trans. A. Zweig (Chicago: The University of Chicago Press, 1967), p. 253.
10 Kant, *Opus Postumum*, trans. E. Förster and M. Rosen (Cambridge: Cambridge University Press, 1993), p. 255.
11 Kant, *Critique of Pure Reason*, Bix, p. 18.
12 Onora O'Neill, "Vindicating Reason," in Paul Guyer (ed.), *The Cambridge Companion to Kant* (Cambridge: Cambridge University Press, 1992), pp. 291, 287.
13 Hegel, *Logic, Being Part One of the Encyclopedia of the Philosophical Sciences (1830)*, trans. W. Wallace (Oxford: Clarendon, 1975), § 20, p. 30.
14 Ibid., § 23, p. 36.
15 Ibid., § 22, p. 34; translation corrected.
16 Ibid., § 23, p. 35.
17 Ibid., § 163, p. 228.
18 See Robert Brandom, "Some Pragmatist Themes in Hegel's Idealism," in Brandom, *Tales of the Mighty Dead* (Cambridge, Mass.: Harvard University Press, 2002).
19 See Robert B. Pippin, *Hegel's Idealism: The Satisfactions of Self-Consciousness* (Cambridge: Cambridge University Press, 1989).
20 Pippin, "You Can't Get There from Here: Transition Problems in Hegel's *Phenomenology of Spirit*," in F. Beiser (ed.), *The Cambridge Companion to Hegel* (Cambridge: Cambridge University Press, 1993). See also C. Taylor, *Hegel* (Cambridge: Cambridge University Press, 1975), Ch. VIII.
21 Hegel, *Logic*, § 24, p. 44.
22 Donald Davidson, *Subjective, Intersubjective, Objective* (Oxford: Clarendon, 2001), p. 142.
23 Ibid., p. 144.
24 Brandom, *Articulating Reasons* (Cambridge, Mass.: Harvard University Press, 2001), pp. 47–48.
25 Ibid., p. 48.
26 Jerrold Katz, "The Problem in Twentieth-Century Philosophy," *Journal of Philosophy*, 1998, vol. 95, pp. 547–75.
27 Brandom, *Articulating Reasons*, pp. 63–64; emphasis added.
28 See, e.g., Jerry Fodor, *The Language of Thought* (Cambridge, Mass.: Harvard University Press, 1979), p. 8.

29 Michael Tomasello, *Constructing a Language: A Usage-Based Theory of Language Acquisition* (Cambridge, Mass.: Harvard University Press, 2003).
30 Barry Loewer, "A Guide to Naturalizing Semantics," in B. Hale and C. Wright (eds), *A Companion to the Philosophy of Language* (Oxford: Blackwell, 1997), p. 121.
31 John Dewey, *Art as Experience* (New York: Penguin Putnam, 1980), pp. 337–38.
32 Davidson, *Inquiries into Truth and Interpretation* (Oxford: Clarendon, 1984), p. 185.
33 John Austin, *Sense and Sensibilia* (Oxford: Clarendon, 1962), p. 8.
34 Ibid., p. 70.
35 See Hugh Lacey, *Is Science Value-Free?* (London: Routledge, 1999).
36 Brandom, *Articulating Reasons*, p. 198.
37 Ibid., p. 188.
38 Ibid., p. 203.
39 Stanley Cavell, *In Quest of the Ordinary* (Chicago: University of Chicago Press, 1988), p. 135.
40 I am grateful to the members of the philosophy department at the University of Aberdeen, especially Peter Baumann, to Hugh Lacey, to Alex Burri, and to the participants in the 11th International French-German Colloquium (Evian 2005) for their helpful comments on earlier drafts of this essay.

Part VI

From Epistemology to Art: The Philosophy of German Romanticism

13

PHILOSOPHY AS 'INFINITE APPROXIMATION'

Thoughts arising out of the 'Constellation' of Early German Romanticism

Manfred Frank

Everyone – or at least, anyone interested in the 'history of ideas' – has an opinion on Early German Romanticism. We may see in it a high point of European culture, whose power and productivity in the most varied fields can only be compared with that of Athens of classical times;[1] or we may detect in it the essence of the 'special German path' into the modern period and perhaps see it as the start of a fateful history that leads 'from Schelling to Hitler'.[2]

In truth, Early German Romanticism, at least as far as it concerns philosophy,[3] is the unknown quantity par excellence in the archives of the history of ideas, and not simply a part of the 'official' history. Part of the reason may be that sources such as Hölderlin's systematic sketch '*Urtheil und Seyn*' (May 1795), Friedrich von Hardenberg's *Fichte Studien* (September 1795–July 1796) or the *Philosophische Lehrjahre* of Friedrich Schlegel (from August 1796) were only discovered or published in critical editions a few decades ago. More importantly, there was no systematic overview of these documents, as they were mostly handed down in fragmentary form.

The research situation was not fundamentally altered until the 1990s, when Dieter Henrich and his followers founded 'constellation research'.[4] This hermeneutical procedure can be characterized in the following way: it traces the gradual formulation of (philosophical) thoughts or fundamental beliefs back to the intellectual exchanges between a number of sources over an eventful period of time. In the case in question, this is the philosophically unusually fertile period in Jena between Carl Leonhard Reinhold's publication of the *Versuch einer neuen Theorie des menschlichen Vorstellungsvermögens* (1789) and the first significant reactions to Johann Gottlieb Fichte's lectures on the *Wissenschaftslehre* (1794–95). The constellation procedure offers the opportunity of complementing the ideas of an author that have come down to us in fragmentary form with (previously unknown or unnoticed) ideas of another author whose formation or development followed (or may have followed) a similar path, like pieces of a jigsaw puzzle. This was fortunately the case for Hölderlin, Friedrich von Hardenberg and Friedrich Schlegel, who from the beginning of the 1790s either studied under Reinhold himself or were kept informed by third parties (especially Niethammer) about the ongoing debate in the circle of Reinhold's followers.

Thorough knowledge of this debate is particularly fruitful for us because it is completely at variance with the account that most historians of philosophy have given of the influence of Kantian philosophy and of the rise of German Idealism. Reinhold was convinced that Kant's philosophy lacked a highest principle that would present it as a unity rather than one that was fragmented into principles that were not reducible to each other, and into three critiques. Reinhold's followers soon began to have doubts about this foundationalist programme, and they then applied these doubts to Fichte's attempt to outdo Reinhold in foundational philosophy. These anti-foundationalist tendencies are true to Kant in a certain manner, and suggest a way in which the re-emphasis on metaphysics, which German Idealism proceeded to pursue with great effect, could have been avoided.

It is customary to classify 'Early German Romanticism' as a distinct subdivision of German Idealism. I have always disputed this classification and propose the following distinction. In my view, Idealism is a form of thought that traces the structures of reality back to the products of the mind or – conversely – derives them from the assumed evidence of a subject. On the other hand, Early Romanticism, as I see it, is the conviction that the subject itself and the consciousness through which it knows itself, rest on a presupposition over which they have no control. Telling evidence of this is Schleiermacher's reference to a 'transcendent ground' of the consciousness of self, which should no longer be called 'transcendental'. It cannot, according to him, be adequately represented in the consciousness, but can only be inferred from the (otherwise inexplicable) constitution of the consciousness. This assumption is coupled with an ontological realism that links the early philosophical sketches of Hölderlin and his circle with those of Friedrich von Hardenberg and Friedrich Schlegel and their followers. As we know from constellation research, these are themselves the product of the foundational scepticism that was first expressed in the early 1790s within the immediate circle of Reinhold's followers. This is connected with a great appreciation of the fine arts, which is characteristic of the whole movement. If 'the highest' is not accessible to reflection, only art can reveal this inaccessibility as such. It does so in the inexhaustible content of an aesthetic work.

Now that we can determine the specific character of philosophical Early Romanticism so much more clearly than previous generations, new light is shed on another line of tradition, namely that which runs from Kant through Early Romanticism to the American transcendentalists.[5] If 'the absolute' cannot be comprehended in a definitive thought, it is transformed from something possessed by reflection into a Kantian idea. We strive endlessly to attain it, but cannot 'present' it demonstratively. As Novalis famously said (in 1797): 'We *seek* the absolute everywhere, and only ever *find* things' (*NS* II, 412, No. 1).[6]

Around the middle of the nineteenth century, it was Ralph Waldo Emerson's knowledge of Early Romanticism, happily complemented by what he himself divined, that communicated to one of the younger members of the 'Transcendentalist' circle in New England the idea that was to be linked with his name thereafter: that of philosophy as an unending approach to the truth, truth being understood as the creative comprehension ('representation') of reality in the form of theory. I am referring to Charles Sanders Peirce, the originator of the expression 'in the long run' (he thought the *run* would be really *long*, indeed that it could go on 'till kingdom come').

Here he was picking up one of the core ideas of philosophical Early Romanticism. For example, Friedrich Schlegel had translated the Greek expression 'filosofiya' unusually, yet quite aptly, as '*yearning for the infinite*'.[7] The translation glosses over the particle 'sofiya', which stands for a state of mind in which the soul opens itself to the truth. As it will never gain possession of the truth, the love of wisdom becomes transformed into an eternally unsatisfied desire. With reference to himself, Novalis writes that his vocation has the same name as his fiancée: Sophie (letter to Friedrich Schlegel dated 8 July 1796). 'Philosophy,' he says, 'just like my love for her, is the soul of my life and the key to my innermost self' (*NS*, IV, 188, ll. 8–11). So philosophy also remains an unfulfilled passion – and for reasons that few have analysed with such penetration as Novalis.

I

At the age of 24 years – working full-time at the daily grind of a legal office in the district administration of Tennstedt (and with only three hours a day to spare for the luxury of asking such questions) – he wrote: 'What am I doing when I philosophize?' His answer, as exciting today as it was then:

> I am thinking about a foundation. . . . All philosophizing must end at an absolute foundation
>
> (*NS* II, 269, No. 566)

Why *absolute*? Because a relative foundation would take its place in a chain of further foundations that would never lead to a final link in the chain. But this is precisely what seems to occur. So Novalis continues with the question:

> [How would it be] if this [the absolute foundation that determines all things] did not exist, if this concept were an impossibility – then the urge to philosophize were consequently an infinite activity – and would therefore never end, because there would be an eternal need for an

absolute foundation, and this need could only be partially satisfied – and would therefore never cease? (Ibid.)

From October 1790 to October 1791 Novalis had studied under Reinhold in Jena and knew him well.[8] The main achievement of Carl Leonhard Reinhold in the field of the history of philosophy is regarded as the founding of what he called *Elementarphilosophie*. The essence of this philosophy is that we can base the previously tentative and uncertain search for knowledge – as he aptly translated the Greek word 'filosofiya' – on an ultimate foundation. He described the discovery of this foundation – rather grandly – as 'the one thing needed by humanity'. The problem that his discovery proposed to solve was described in 1789 by Jacobi in the expanded second edition of his little Spinoza book as follows. If – following the ancient, revered (and still living) tradition – we describe knowledge as a justified opinion, we get into an infinite regress.[9] We base our claims to knowledge on propositions that only express knowledge on condition that they are founded on propositions that express knowledge, and so on. This regress could only be ended by a proposition that is valid '*un*conditionally'. 'Unconditional' means: without being dependent on a higher condition. Such a proposition would have to be seen to be valid without further justification. It would have to be 'neither in need of nor capable of justification'. It would have to be evident, for 'evident' means (literally) that which is seen to be true from within itself.

Reinhold believed he had found such a proposition. He called it the 'proposition (or principle) of consciousness'. He believed that other propositions that had a claim to truth ought to develop out of it – either through logical deduction or analytically. Reinhold's definition of 'analytic' did not differ greatly from that of analytic philosophers today: it is that which arises out of the understanding of the meaning of the expressions used (including that of logical particles).[10]

Doubts soon arose concerning this project, which seemed to reach completion in 1794 with Fichte's philosophy of the absolute ego. These doubts centred on three areas. Firstly, it was disputed that a system of beliefs could be supported by evidence at all; for evidence is a private conscious experience. Intersubjective consensus building cannot take place by an appeal to evidence. It does, however, represent a criterion for what we call knowledge. Furthermore, when closely examined, evidence cannot be clearly distinguished from 'claims of the common sense'. We can usually only base it on so-called intuitions – i.e. we believe in it. Credal statements are similar to Euclidean axioms in character. If it were possible to prove them, they would immediately lose their status as highest principles – for a proposition that finds its justification in another one is not the highest principle. Thus, the justification of knowledge becomes an article of faith. Novalis says: 'It is a product of the imagination in which we *believe* without ever being able to know it according to its nature or our nature.'[11] – It was the third objection, however, that was to have the most serious consequences: Reinhold's highest proposition does not actually stand on its own two feet. To justify itself, it presupposes other propositions that supposedly follow from it.

This had damaging implications for a philosophy founded on a first principle (or foundationalism). In fact, Novalis's basic critical impulse can best be understood when we bear in mind that he was on familiar terms with those within the Reinhold circle who were critical of this philosophy. I should like to mention three as representative of the circle: Carl Christian Erhard Schmid – Hardenberg's former tutor, who helped him when he was suffering hardship; Johann Benjamin Erhard – the Jacobin revolutionary, whom he helped to obtain a position through the mediation of his uncle Karl August von Hardenberg, who later became the Prussian State Chancellor; finally, Friedrich Carl Forberg, who provoked the famous atheism controversy in Jena, as a result of which Fichte lost his professorial chair. Novalis met him for an important discussion when he was writing the piece from which I have just quoted.

II

Next we move on to the inspiration that Novalis may have found in Schmid's *Empirische Psychologie* – a lecture that he might have heard in Jena; he occasionally quotes from it,[12] indeed he owned a published edition of it.[13] With reference to Crusius, Schmid had objectively, yet sharply, criticized Reinhold for taking as his starting point the concept of representation as an elemental term of philosophy. In his view, the concept of 'representation' was unsuitable as a philosophical principle of deduction because it had only been gained by means of abstraction from a large number of mental experiences or acts.[14] To make inferences from a generic concept obtained in such a manner was inadmissible, however, as the circularity of the procedure was all too obvious: I obtain from individual events, *via abstractionis*, that from which I then claim to have derived them.[15]

Moreover, that which is defined by a concept is by no means contained in it as a part.[16] For example, the fact that someone understands the generic concept of the law does not mean that this person knows anything about present-day English legal practice, although this is a sub-category within the generic concept of law. Or the fact that someone correctly understands the concept 'mammal' does not mean that such a person knows anything about the life of the opossum.[17] The specification cannot be constructed a priori from the generic concept. For this reason, Kant wisely refrained from declaring the generic concept 'representation' to be a principle of deduction, even though he himself had shown that all concepts of mental functions and dispositions fall within it.[18] In reality, however, Reinhold had declared the 'principle' of his philosophy of elements – 'representation' – to be a 'generic concept'.[19] He had also called on philosophy to continue to follow the guideline of the species/genus distinction, i.e. to continue to infer concepts as specifications of higher ones in a hierarchy until, he says, we '[come up against] something that cannot be resolved'.[20] But even from such a concept we can, of course, only derive that from which abstractions have already been drawn, in other words that which was already known – and this is a poor deal. A similar point had been made by Novalis's teacher Karl Heinrich Heydenreich, who in 1790, with regard to Reinhold's first principle, the concept of representation, had raised the objection: '*Representation* and the *faculty of representation* are not the prius but the posterius, and can in no way give us *premises* for science.'[21] His (and Schmid's) disciple Novalis will take issue with this view. He does this in his own sequence of notes, which begin at about No. 466 and continue over several pages. They start by wondering whether that 'sphere', which contains 'essence' and 'property' as relata of the absolute (*NS* II, 251, l. 14 ff.; similarly also 241, No. 444, l. 20 ff.), can properly be understood as 'the highest genus – the genus of all genera, or the authentically absolute genus' (ibid. ll. 23–25); and the notes conclude with the thought that progressive abstraction right up to the highest genus, or rather, the search for the very first of an infinite sequence of derivations, is 'nonsense': 'it is a regulative idea' (*NS* II, 254, l. 11 f.). Central are four distinct but inter-related arguments. 1. Anything that is supposed to be capable of definition (or, as Reinhold says, 'self-determined throughout'[22]) needs for its demarcation a lower and a higher genus; this requirement, however, is meaningless in the case of the highest genus, as the highest genus does not contain 'a common and a differentiating characteristic' (*NS* II, 243, No. 445, ll. 6 ff.).[23] This leads, however, to argument no. 2, that there is no end in sight to the chain of justifications:

> In the end probably every genus necessarily presupposes a more comprehensive one[24] – a space – and if that is so, then the highest category is probably a non-entity [Nonens]. ... the concept of genus, species and individual has only a regulative, classifying use – it has no reality in itself, otherwise it would be infinite. There is no need for us to pursue the idea, as to do so can only lead us to the realms of nonsense (251 f.).

Novalis runs through some of the candidates for identification of the highest genus suggested by contemporaries; first the concept 'thing' (251, l. 5 f.; and previously *passim*), then that of 'representation' (ibid.), and finally that of the 'self' or 'subject' (No. 470, 253, l. 20 ff.). All are rejected; that of the self because it is a relatum, part of a sphere, and cannot be thought of as an absolute (253, l. 28 f.).[25] Even the concept of the (absolute) 'cause' (in the sense of the final part of Reinhold's *Versuch einer neuen Theorie des menschlichen Vorstellungsvermögens*)[26] does not find favour. Projected into 'infinity', the 'cause' would again 'be only a regulative concept, an idea of reason – it would therefore be foolish to attribute real efficacy to it. We are therefore looking for an absurdity' (*NS* II, 255, No. 476, l. 12–14; cf. ibid., No. 477, l. 25 f.). A fourth argument (added later) reminds us strongly of Heydenreich and Schmid. It emphasizes that what would be found in the course of progressive abstraction, i.e. the 'highest genus', lives from the reality of that from which it has been abstracted. It would not only be a circular argument to attempt to make derivations from a generic concept discovered in such a way; we would also be merely presupposing, rather than explaining, the individual: 'I can never get to know the individual through the genus; I can only get to know the genus through individuals' (*NS* II, 271, No. 567, l. 17 f.). 'The characteristic sphere of the genus is the species, or the individual. It exists only through these' (*NS* II, 261, Nr. 513).

Schmid – to return to him – also attacked Reinhold very effectively in a review of the *Fundamentschrift*[27] in early April 1792 (in the Jena *Allgemeine Literatur Zeitung* [ALZ] of 9th and 10th April 1792, col. 49–60). In his review, he shows that Reinhold is mistaken if he believes that the whole of the Kantian faculty can be reduced to *one* principle. An intermediate step in this demonstration is that Reinhold, instead of making his deductions from the (fundamental) principle of consciousness, tacitly presupposes that at least some of them are already valid ('that the principle of consciousness has done very little to demonstrate these propositions, but that instead [in this so-called deduction] other principles have been called upon to lend unnoticed and unspoken assistance' [ibid., col. 57 f.]). The principle of consciousness stated – in brief: 'In consciousness, the *subject* relates the representation to the subject and the object and distinguishes the representation from both.' The true agent in all the moves designated by the formula is therefore the *self-activity of the subject*. Reinhold, however, claims to have deduced this from the well-analysed concept of *representation*. To generalize, then, the objection is that Reinhold did not *deduce* the consequences from his principle, but *presupposed* them. Schmid also finds a rather technical error in Reinhold's argument. A deduction or logical derivation is typically made from a universal major proposition and a singular minor proposition that is logically dependent on the major proposition. ('All cats are furry. Kater Murr is a cat. Therefore Kater Murr is furry'.) However, the 'principle of consciousness' formulates one singular fact, nothing universal. In order to bring out the consequences alleged by Reinhold, the proposition needs the support of a major proposition, which however could only be *inferred*. In short, Reinhold's deductions have only the character of a *hypothetical* deductive process in the manner of Kant's deduction from (regulative) ideas of reason: 'But that which is only an assumed hypothesis [and not – as asserted – direct *evidence*] cannot in this capacity make any claim to universal validity, because we are not obliged to accept this explanatory hypothesis as an indubitable fact; we could accept another one or none at all' (ibid., col. 59). Finally, the set of premises from which an explicandum follows (according to one or several universal rules) is unrestricted. To put it another way, the set of premises is not sufficiently determined by the existence of this concrete explicandum. It is worth noting that Kant, Maimon and Aenesidemus-Schulze constantly stressed this very point.

III

We must now move on to the objections raised by Erhard, which carry far more weight, because they are so much more effective in developing a philosophy in the spirit of Kant. They crystallize in precise terms what those of Reinhold's followers who were critical of him believed and discussed in correspondence.

Firstly, Erhard does not dispute the fact of self-consciousness as a first principle (or starting point) of philosophy. True, Reinhold himself had not initially elevated self-consciousness to the position of such a first principle, but came to adopt this view under the influence of his critics, including the former Tübingen Repetent[28] Immanuel Carl Diez, in the summer of 1792.[29] Indeed, in the standard formulations of his theory of the faculty of representation (from 1790) it is the *subject* that appears as the sole actor in all the operations of which the 'principle of consciousness' speaks. In the consciousness, the subject at some times relates the representation to itself and the object, and at others distinguishes itself from them. If we spell out the possibilities thus opened up, we quickly reach the conclusion that they must all be characterized as conscious self-references and that only the subject is active. With regard to Reinhold's starting point Novalis observes: 'The subject is presupposed in all consciousness – it is the absolutely active state of the consciousness' (*NS* II, 253, l. 25 f.). This is also the assumption made by Erhard. He does not, however, attribute any special epistemic significance to the self-consciousness. Indeed, Erhard wrote a scathing review of Schelling's *Of the I*, which annoyed and unsettled its author so much that in a detailed and aggressive reply he went as far as to deny that this article had anything to do with a philosophy of the first principle.[30] In this review,[31] Erhard accuses those who speculate about an allegedly absolute ego of describing it in terms that distinguish it radically from any possible object of our (empirical) consciousness. We are only conscious of that which defines boundaries and thereby provides a demarcation against other things. Since, according to Erhard, such consciousness exhausts the sphere of *all* consciousness (alongside, of course, that of our moral personality [ALZ No. 319/1796, 91]), we are not conscious of the self in its absolute freedom. Its supposed absoluteness and purity rests, he says, on its objective indeterminacy (ibid., 91, bottom). Schelling, he points out, used the expression 'intellectual intuition' for this (ibid., 90). Erhard closes with biting sarcasm:

> As far as he [the reviewer] can grasp, the real object of this [namely the Schelling system] is guaranteed by nothing but a kind of intellectual intuition that is not worthy of the name, as nothing in it is intuited, for in the whole of its interior the reviewer can find nothing matching

> the predicates of the absolute ego, unless it be the deliberately unthinking condition into which we can put ourselves if we hold our imagination in check and have no feeling other than that of self-determination. There is, of course, something very mysterious about this particular feeling, because we can distinguish nothing in it, and a philosophy based on it can turn out to be nothing other than the description of the life of nobody. We can say whatever we like about it without running the risk of ever being held responsible, because what another person refutes is never what we meant by it. At the same time, we cannot suppose that in Germany a philosophy should be built up that has as its sole principle and purpose to sink into the great nothingness that some Indian sects praise as the supreme good. Something more noble must underlie it. And this can only be the feeling of our personality. ... as moral beings we are [in fact] not an object of knowledge – we must act. (Ibid., 90 f.)

True, Novalis by no means reaches the same conclusion as far as moral philosophy is concerned. He does, however, agree with Erhard in believing that 'there is no more an absolute subject than there is absolute space' (*NS* II, 253, l. 28 f.). Early in the *Fichte Studien*, Novalis had already pondered the conditions under which a transcendent being (or 'original being') could be communicated to the consciousness. For him, the highest consciousness is not self-positing, but the (passive) 'feeling' of a boundary beyond which we must assume that there is something to be believed: 'The self is fundamentally nothing ... – everything has to be *given* to it'; and 'philosophy therefore always needs something given'; 'we are born with empty categories – i.e. with containers devoid of content. – ... They need to be filled – without content they are nothing – they have an urge to be, and consequently to have content, for they are only real insofar as they have content' (*NS* II, 273, ll. 31 f.; 113. l. 30; 250, ll. 19 ff.). The content given in this way must, admittedly, be adapted to the structure of our consciousness, which Novalis sees as a reflection, and thus as an alteration and inversion of the given ('*ordo inversus*'). Reflection can, however, become aware of its 'inverted being' and thereby correct it. In the first few pages, Novalis also assumes an 'intellectual intuition', albeit one that is differently constituted from that of Schelling. It is not the fullness of being – *plenitudo realitatis* – that is presented in it, but rather our inability to recognize this: 'The spirit of feeling has departed', 'the boundaries of feeling are the boundaries of philosophy'; 'The human being feels the boundary that encloses everything for him, for himself, *the first act;* he must believe it with as much certainty as that with which he knows everything else' (*NS* II, 114, 8 f.; 114, 1 [GW1]; 107, 1–3). In the course of the *Fichte Studien* intellectual intuition increasingly loses its function and is finally abandoned in favour of a return to the Kantian doctrine of ideas and postulates, very much in the spirit of Schmid and Erhard.

Erhard shook the faith of many contemporaries in the possibility of a philosophy of the first principle even more effectively, however, by expressing doubt about the method employed:

> The philosophy [he says] that starts from a principle and takes it upon itself to derive everything from it remains for ever a clever artifice, but the philosophy that rises to the highest principle and represents everything else as being in perfect harmony with it, rather than deriving everything from it, is the true one.[32]

In the (previously mentioned) letters to Reinhold and Niethammer (July 1792 and May 1794), he calls this method 'the method of *Analysis*'.[33] Employing a language reminiscent of the school of Wolff, to which Kant also belongs, it starts from that which is founded and progresses to the foundation itself. By contrast, the deductions of Reinhold and Fichte are synthetic. Their philosophy, however, cannot progress synthetically, because the principle of consciousness, or the one that expresses Fichte's self, is not already justified, so is not self-supporting. Its truth is tied to presuppositions that do not hold for these propositions at the outset. It can only be reached by abductive reasoning, and even then only as a hypothetical claim. If moreover we assume that this process continues to infinity, i.e. that there is never any final certainty, then we have to abandon the idea of definitive justification altogether. In place of the infinite we get (romantic) 'yearning' for it; and in place of an evidential theory of truth we get one that has to show all the relationships in the world and in consciousness in the greatest possible 'harmony' (as Erhard puts it). We are talking about a kind of coherence theory, to which Novalis also subscribes, so that he does not describe the foundation by which philosophy justifies its convictions as one that is given, but as one that appears in the 'connection [of all individual things] with the whole' (*NS* II, 269 l. 27). The creation of this coherence, he continues, remains the only possible means of making his convictions plausible to one who cannot accept the givenness of an 'absolute foundation' and therefore must 'assert the actual absolute foundation ... through linking up (*completing*) the explicandum to form a whole' (*NS* II, 270, l.16 ff.). As you have just heard, Novalis calls this process 'completing' [Verganzung]. For the Romantics, the absolute is replaced by the search for the absolute. 'We seek the absolute everywhere, and only ever find things' (*NS* II, 412, No. 1).

A detailed account would be necessary to show how the foundational philosophy of Reinhold and Fichte managed to get into a position that was so open to the objections of sceptics. We have already anticipated one objection from the Reinhold followers and have come across it again in the report on Schmid's critique of Reinhold (it is most cogently set out in Paul Johann Anselm Feuerbach's 1795 essay 'Über die Unmöglichkeit eines ersten absoluten Grundsatzes der Philosophie'[34]). Evidence of a highest principle cannot be justifiably claimed; fundamentally, it shares the fate of intuitions of common sense. It requires justification by philosophical reasoning. But this is carried out with ideas, and ideas are hypotheses or conclusions offering the best explanation, not pieces of evidence. Moreover, pieces of evidence are facts; and facts are singular and at best represent the minor – or second – premise – in a formally valid deduction process by *modo ponente* (Kant sees the inference of reason, as he calls it, as a procedure of this kind; it has the structure: M = P, S = M, hence S^P).[35] The major premise, on the other hand, must be a universal conditional ('for all x, if x is F, then x is G'). Such an if-then proposition, however, has no implication for existence such as would be necessary for a real principle. But we have already seen that Erhard simply denies that the absolute ego of Fichte and Schelling has epistemic accessibility and therefore comprehensibility. Novalis concurs with his Jena friend in the matter, indeed he goes much further, following Feuerbach and (as we shall shortly see) Forberg in declaring the 'absolute in human knowledge' to be a '*non-entity*', an 'absurdity', indeed an 'impossibility'. (Once again, these audacious formulations are nowhere mentioned in the scholarly literature on Novalis; there his image is that of the youth or simpleton who is 'bathed in silvery light', who has never ceased to sit at the right hand of God Almighty, and – according to the likes of Emil Staiger, who coined the phrase – only knows Paradise from above.)

Incidentally, Reinhold admitted in his letter to Erhard of 18 June 1792 (now published for the first time by Henrich)[36] that it was Schmid and Diez who persuaded him to make a complete change to his foundational philosophy. In fact, however, Diez did no more than reinforce Erhard's objections, which – as Henrich has shown – Niethammer had already made known to him.

To repeat – as this is so important – the process of justification by the ultimate foundation is turned around into a search for the foundation, and no-one can say in advance where or indeed whether the search will end. And it is precisely this conclusion that Novalis has in mind when (as mentioned above) he defines philosophy as an infinitely open-ended search for the foundation.

Kantian philosophy had called the ultimate justification of our convictions 'ideas'. By this, Kant understood concepts that we *must* accept in order to bring unity into our system of assumptions, even though in doing so we are still a long way short of being able to accord objective reality to them. If justification becomes a 'mere' idea, it will only succeed hypothetically. If, says Novalis, we were really to 'pursue' its realization, we would find ourselves 'in the realms of nonsense'. We have seen how emphatically he must have written that when we saw that he repeated on several occasions the epithets 'nonsense' or 'absurd'. Thus, he says: 'All searching for the first [genus] is nonsense – it is a *regulative* idea.' Or: '[What we seek] however is only a regulative concept, an idea of reason – so it is foolish to attribute real efficacy to it. We are looking for an absurdity.'[37] Indeed, he wonders whether Fichte's 'self' is perhaps 'like all ideas of reason merely of regulative, classifying use – with no relation to reality' (*NS* II, 258, ll. 18 f.). We cannot be sure that such an idea will lead us to determinations of empirical reality. Moreover, factual control over the course of arguments cannot be exercised by an idea. One hundred and fifty years later, Wittgenstein will note that 'the chain of reasons has an end'. But not because we have hit upon some (intersubjectively obvious) evidence, 'but because – in *this* system – there is no ground'.[38]

But Novalis goes much further: he speaks of concepts that guarantee the unity of the system of conviction and of justification as 'necessary fictions'.[39] A fiction is not a discovery [Findung] but an invention [*Er*findung].

> Quite simply, the Highest Principle must not be something given, but something freely made, something *created*, *imagined*, if a universal metaphysical system is to be grounded on it . . . .[40]

This is not only a very strong and, in the context of the foundationalism of absolute Idealism, truly surprising conclusion to draw. The wheel has come full circle, and we are back with Erhard's method of the analysis of the faculty of representation. This method was occasionally characterized as that of 'invention', among others by the younger Reimarus (Johann Albrecht Heinrich, the son of the more famous Samuel), at that time a well known (physician and) logician, with whom Erhard corresponded. We also know that Novalis was acquainted with Reimarus through a book of logic by Johann Christoph Hoffbauer, as he makes reference to it in his *Fichte Studien* (*NS* II, 191, l. 21).[41]

Thanks to the element of inventiveness, some uncertainty creeps into the process of philosophical analysis.[42] Wolff seems to have seen this already.[43] But it is only the younger Reimarus, says Hoffbauer, who drew precisely determined conclusions from it.[44]

> *Invention*, he says, means, in effect, to reach a knowledge of what was previously unknown by the application of thought. ... The inventor does not attain what he finds through the mechanical application of a rule that gives assurance of the object of his search in advance, and *secondly*, we do not invent what we produce through the mechanical application of a rule. We can therefore say that invention means finding something that was previously unknown to us out of what we do know in a manner that does not involve merely following a rule known to us in advance.[45]

In this way, the process of the analytical search for the foundation comes close to invention, a procedure that posits rules but does not obey them, one that has always been connected with poetry (and, more generally, with art). 'How do I begin, according to the rule?' asks Walther von Stolzing in *The Mastersingers*. And Hans Sachs replies: 'You set it yourself and then follow it.'[46] It was only to be expected that this liberating advice would appeal to Novalis, the lawyer, mineralogist and poet, who gradually began to acquire a taste for leaving 'this craggy mountain of pure reason' behind him 'and living again with body and soul in the colourful and health-giving land of the senses'.

> You can hold philosophy in high esteem without having it as a housekeeper and living from that alone. Mathematics alone will never make a soldier or a mechanic, nor will philosophy ever make a human being.[47]

This, of course, applies to a universal genius like Novalis with even greater force if we assume (as Kant does not) that scientific procedures call for genius, i.e. artistic talent.[48]

It should be noted that we are not here talking about just any kind of invention. What is not given to be discovered (Findung) but has to be invented (Erfindung), is (in Novalis's words) an 'absolute foundation'. That is the only thing that could provide a solid basis for our frail life and its insecure beliefs. But such a solid foundation is, in the literal sense, fiction, poetry (Er-Dichtung).

I must now rapidly bring my sketch to an end. By defining the search for a foundation as invention we are giving a key role to artistic procedure. The arts have the task of indirectly making us aware of something ultimate that cannot be grasped by the means of rational justification. And they enjoyed this high esteem long before Arthur Danto proclaimed the end of invention and the sell-out of innovation. We are too prone to forget what the term 'religion of art' actually meant in its time, and how not only the Symbolists (right up to Stefan George) but also the provocative Expressionists and Surrealists, and even Joseph Beuys, understood their activity as artists to be a priestly function. For the thinkers of the school of Critical Theory – first and foremost Adorno – an incurably blinded humanity has taken refuge in the fictional world of art to make its final, and indeed only, universally valid claims. Heidegger and Derrida have tried to expand philosophy itself to include, indeed to flow into, the language of art. Even Wittgenstein wanted his *Tractatus* to be understood as a literary work, in which what was said excluded the area of the unsayable, even though this represented the true message of the work.[49]

And Novalis wanted art to be understood as 'presentation of the unpresentable' – the true foundation of our conscious life.[50] Elsewhere he notes:

> It is not possible to imagine the attainment of the unattainable, according to its character – it is like the ideal expression of the sum of the whole sequence and hence [only] apparently the final link – the type of every link, indicated by every link. . . .
>
> [Therefore] the supreme works of art are . . . simply not *amenable* – They are ideals, which can – and *should* – only open up to us as we approach them – they are aesthetic imperatives.[51]

Or:

> If the character of the given problem is indissolubility, we solve it when we represent its indissolubility [as such].[52]

Through the unfathomable sensuous fullness of the work of art, he says, something that cannot be subjected to the bright light of conceptual clarity speaks to us allegorically (in other words, with a meaning other than what it superficially says). It is the 'riddle of our existence'; 'the work of art is inexhaustible': 'like a human being'.[53] So art confirms the truth that the essential elements of what there is to say about us humans, something that could provide a solid foundation for our shaky beliefs, cannot be held as a possession. This is why Romantics are driven by 'yearning' – yearning is, after all, a state of not having, of not possessing.[54] We can only work our way toward what we desire in a 'never-ending approach' ('approximando'). Who would not see a certain affinity with Popper's polemic against Newton's 'Hypotheses non fingo', especially when we recall that the motto of Popper's principal work is the distich from the *Dialogues* of Novalis: 'Hypotheses are nets: only he who casts will catch./ Was not America itself discovered by a hypothesis?/ [etc.]'?[55] We are given the same promise by the work of art, which is 'not amenable', imperious and demanding because it does not press a result into our hands, but throws us into a state of agitation: into a vague striving for a foundation like that which Agathe in Musil's *The Man without Qualities* so desperately seeks and cannot find.[56]

Around the time when Novalis was noting down his thoughts on infinity, i.e. the impossibility of philosophy as the search for knowledge, he was visited in Jena by Forberg, 'who, after a long break in our friendship, showed a heart full of tenderness toward me'.[57] As we have seen, they had studied together under Reinhold. Clearly, Forberg was so impressed by Novalis's formulation, the one with which I began Section I of my text, that a year later in his *Briefe über die neueste Philosophie* he wrote:

> So I shall have to seek a last 'therefore', a last original foundation, in order to fulfil the demands of my reason.
>
> But what if such a final original foundation were to prove ... impossible to find?–
>
> Then all that would happen would be that the demands of my reason would be impossible to fulfil completely – that reason ... would have to continue its searches to infinity, without ever bringing them to an end. The absolute would then be nothing but the idea of an impossibility ....
>
> [But] is a goal any less of a goal because it is unattainable? Is the prospect of heaven less delightful because it will always remain – a *prospect*?[58]

Notes

1 This is how Dieter Henrich put it in his report on the research programme headed by him 'on the origins of classical German philosophy after Kant in Jena 1789–95': *Konstellationen. Probleme und Debatten am Ursprung der idealistischen Philosophie (1789–1795)* (Stuttgart: Klett-Cotta, 1991), pp. 217–18.

2 This was the subtitle of Georg Lukác's famous treatise *Die Zerstörung der Vernunft. Der Weg des Irrationalismus von Schelling bis Hitler* (Berlin: Aufbau, 1954).

3 In which, for reasons of structural and historical similarity, I also include the philosophical work of Hölderlin and his circle.

4 Cf. *Konstellationsforschung*, Martin Mulsow and Marcelo Stamm (eds) (Frankfurt/M.: Suhrkamp, 2005).

5 Cf. the popular but thorough work by Louis Menand, *The Metaphysical Club. A Story of Ideas in America* (New York: Farrar, Strauss and Giroux, 2001).

6 Quotations from Novalis's works will be made using the following edition, henceforth '*NS*': Novalis, *Schriften: die Werke Friedrich von Hardenbergs*. Edited by Richard Samuel in collaboration with Hans-Joachim Mähl and Gerhard Schulz. Critical edition in 4 vols., a volume with further material and a supplement in 4 vols. (Stuttgart: Kohlhammer, 1960 onward).

7 Friedrich Schlegel, *Kritische Ausgabe seiner Werke*, ed. Ernst Behler, in collaboration with Jean-Jacques Anstett and Hans Eichner (Paderborn: Schöningh, 1969), vol. 18, p. 418, no. 1168; see also p. 420, no. 1200.

8 And around New Year he went back there (according to some accounts he was still in Jena in February). On the subject of Novalis's close contact with the Reinhold and Schmid circles, see Hermann F. Weiss, 'Eine Reise nach Thüringen im Jahre 1791. Zu einer unbeachteten Begegnung Karl Wilhelm Justis und Joseph Friedrich Engelschalls mit Schiller und Novalis', in: *Zeitschrift für hessische Geschichte und Landeskunde*, 101 (1991), 43–56.

9 Cf. Friedrich Heinrich Jacobi, *Ueber die Lehre des Spinoza in Briefen an Herrn Moses Mendelssohn* (Breslau: Löwe, 1789), pp. 389–434, esp. 424 ff., 430 ff.

10 Reinhold's Philosophy of Elements and the arguments of its most important critics feature prominently in Manfred Frank, *Unendliche Annäherung. Die Anfänge der philosophischen Frühromantik* (Frankfurt/M.: Suhrkamp, 1998).

11 *NS* II, 273, No. 568, ll. 16 f.

12 *NS* III, 356, No. 524. Cf. commentary 943.

13 Cf. ibid., 1009, No. 81.

14 In these, Schmid includes the corresponding faculties or forces, seeing them also as irreducibly plural: 'The multiplicity of the phenomena of the mind leads us to the idea of the multiplicity of faculties and forces as the conditions of their determinate possibility and their existence' (*Empirische Psychologie*, Jena: Cröker, 1791, First Volume, 158, § VII).

15 Ibid., 18 f. (§ VI of the introduction); cf. – with reference to Crusius – also § XII of the First Part (164): 'that after this everything that we are supposed to explain would have to be assumed'. This is the historical origin of Nietzsche's mocking remark that Kant answered the question of how synthetic judgements were a priori possible with the words: 'By means of a faculty' (Section 11 of *Beyond Good and Evil*, in: Friedrich Nietzsche, *Sämtliche Werke: kritische Studienausgabe in 15 Einzelbänden*, G. Colli and M. Montinari (eds) (München: dtv, 1988), vol. 5, pp. 23–25). On the entire context, cf. Frank, *Unendliche Annäherung*, 275 f.

16 Cf. Immanuel Kant, *Critique of Pure Reason*, trans. Norman Kemp Smith (London: MacMillan, 1993), B40.

17 Cf. Kant's famous remark in the *Critique of Judgment*, trans. Werner S. Pluhar (Indianapolis/Cambridge: Hackett, 1987), p. 236:

> For when we point, for example, to the structure of birds regarding how their bones are hollow, how their wings are positioned to produce motion and their tails to permit steering and so on, we are saying that all of this is utterly contingent if we go by the mere *nexus effectivus* in nature and do not yet resort to a special kind of causality, viz., the causality of purposes (the *nexus finalis*); in other words, we are saying that nature, considered as mere mechanism, could have structured itself differently in a thousand ways without hitting on precisely the unity in terms of a principle of purposes, and so we cannot hope to find a priori the slightest basis for that unity unless we seek it beyond the concept of nature rather than in it.

18 Kant, *Critique of Pure Reason*, B376 f; also B676 f.
19 K. L. Reinhold, *Beyträge zur Berichtigung bisheriger Mißverständnisse der Philosophen. Erster Band, das Fundament der Elementarphilosophie betreffend* (Jena: Mauke, 1790), p. 117.
20 Ibid., p. 16 (in context 15 f.), cf. p. 358 (in context 357 f.).
21 Ibid., p. 427 f.
22 To this concept Novalis has an even more fundamental objection, one which admittedly is directed more against Fichte and immediately attacks his Idealism: 'A self-determining activity is an absurdity – all determinate activity assumes something posited, something existent' (*NS* II, 242, No. 444, l.7–10).
23 Cf. the whole section, which explores the concept of 'definition' – as 'containing the *objective concept* of the thing' (*NS* II, 262, No. 526) – against the claims of 'theory' as a whole.
24 Cf. *NS* II, 252, ll. 2 ff.: 'When we speak of genera, what do we understand by these: a basic character of commonality – but do we not find again and again that the genera are contained in more comprehensive genera [?]'.
25 Cf. *NS* II, 256, No. 478, l. 3: 'The self is an expression of the individual that has representations, makes judgements'.
26 Cf. Frank, *Unendliche Annäherung*, pp. 286 ff., 418 ff., 485 ff.
27 See Reinhold, *Über das Fundament des philosophischen Wissens: nebst einigen Erläuterungen über die Theorie des Vorstellungsvermögens* (Jena: Mauke, 1791).
28 Tutor at the Tübingen *Stift* (theological college) [Tr. note].
29 Cf. the recent monumental work by Dieter Henrich, *Grundlegung aus dem Ich. Untersuchungen zur Vorgeschichte des Idealismus Tübingen–Jena (1790–1794)*, 2 vols. (Frankfurt/M.: Suhrkamp, 2004), esp. vol. I, pp. 388 ff.
30 Friedrich Wilhelm Joseph Schellings, *Sämmtliche Werke*, K.F.A Schelling (ed.) (Stuttgart: Cotta, 1856–61), vol. I/1, p. 242. (Reprinted in *Ausgewählte Schriften in sechs Bänden*, M. Frank (ed.) (Frankfurt: Suhrkamp, 1985), vol. I, p. 132). See also Schelling, *Vom Ich als Princip der Philosophie, oder über das Unbedingte im menschlichen Wissen* (Tübingen: Heerbrant, 1795).
31 Published in the Jena *Allgemeine Literatur-Zeitung* No. 319, Tuesday, 11 October 1796, Col. 89–91. Schelling's reply (26 Oct. 1796), with Erhard's brief and cutting answer, appeared in: *Schellingiana Rariora*, collected and introduced by Luigi Pareyson (Turin: Bottega d'Erasmo, 1977), pp. 55–59.>
32 Letter to Niethammer of 19 May 1794 (in: Friedrich Immanuel Niethammer, *Korrespondenz mit dem Herbert-und Erhard-Kreis*, Wilhelm Baum (ed.) (Wien: Turia and Kant, 1995), p. 79).
33 Cf. especially the 15th and 17th lectures in Frank, *Unendliche Annäherung*.
34 *Philosophisches Journal* 34 II/2 (1795), pp. 306–22.
35 Kant, *Critique of Pure Reason*, A103 f.
36 Immanuel Carl Diez, *Briefwechsel und Kantische Schriften. Wissensbegründung in der Glaubenskrise*. Tübingen-Jena (1790–1792), Dieter Henrich (ed.), (Stuttgart: Cotta,

1997), pp. 911–14; cf. introduction by Marcelo Stamm, 898 ff. Cf. also the 15th of my lectures in *Unendliche Annäherung*.

37 *NS* II, 252, l. 6; 254, ll. 11 f.; 255, ll. 12 ff.

38 Ludwig Wittgenstein, *Werkausgabe* (Frankfurt/M.: Suhrkamp, 1984), Vol. 8, p. 342, No. 301; cf. 346 f., Nr. 314: 'The difficulty here is: to come to a stop.'

39 *NS* II, 179, ll. 17 ff.

40 *NS* II, 273, ll. 22–24. Cf. the later writing (1798–99): 'Analysis is (*divination*, or) the art of invention reduced to rules' (*NS* III, 434, No. 858). Cf. *NS* II, 442, No. 906 for what he says about the danger 'of straying into areas where no end is in sight, into infinity itself', indeed, 'like a madman', getting into a kind of 'infamous, false mysticism – the belief . . . in the possibility of fathoming things in themselves'.

41 Cf. Johann Christoph Hoffbauer's definition of the analytical method in his revised prize-winning work *Ueber die Analysis in der Philosophie* (Berlin: Hemmerde & Schwetschke, 1810), pp. 6–8. Hoffbauer makes reference to the §§ 416 and pp. 503–5 of Alexander Gottlieb Baumgarten, *Acroasis logica in Christ. Wolff* (Halle: Hemmerde, 1761).

42 Cf. pages 23 ff. of the revised version of Hoffbauer's *Ueber die Analysis in der Philosophie*.

43 Wolff, *Philosophia rationalis, sive logica methodo scientifica pertractata et ad usum scientiarum atque vitae aptata* (Frankfurt and Leipzig: Renger, 1728, 1732, reprint Hildesheim/Zürich/New York: Olms, 1983), § 885: 'Appellatur . . . *methodus analytica*, qua veritates ita proponuntur, prout, vel inventae fuerunt vel minimum inveneri potuerunt.'

44 In his '*Vernunftlehre*', § 259.

45 Hoffbauer, *Ueber die Analysis in der Philosophie*, 23 f., 25 f. Hoffbauer's own thoughts on this point are of great interest, not only with regard to the fact that Novalis, when writing his *Fichte Studien*, drew on the work of this very author, who had already expressed himself on the analytical method in previous publications. On one later occasion the 'Method of Analysis' was to be important to Novalis: in the context of the mathematical studies that he undertook in connection with his mineralogical activities as inspector at the salt works. His aim was to draw conclusions from the geometrically calculated surface structure of the finds regarding the chemical composition of minerals (on this: Irene Bark, '*Steine in Potenzen*' – *Konstruktive Rezeption der Mineralogie bei Novalis* (Tübingen: Niemeyer, 1999), esp. 420 ff.). Novalis based his *Mathematische Studien zu Bossut und Murhard* (from 1798 [*NS* III, 115–24]) primarily on a paraphrase of Maimon's essay 'Ueber den Gebrauch der Philosophie zur Erweiterung der Erkenntniß', which had appeared in the *Philosophisches Journal* (II/1, 1795, 1–35). The paraphrase was published in Friedrich Murhard's Compendium (*System der allgemeinen Größenlehre nach ihrem Zustand am Ende des 18. Jahrhunderts nach Literatur und Geschichte* (Lemgo: Meyer, 1798), 6 ff.). With reference to p. 9 of Murhard's Compendium, Novalis defines analysis in the broad sense as the 'representation of the unknown by means of the known' (*NS* III, 120, ll. 25 f.). I propose to write an essay of my own investigating what else Novalis learnt about philosophical method from Maimon's essay.

46 Richard Wagner, *Sämtliche Schriften und Dichtungen*, Volksausgabe, 12 vols., (Leipzig: Breitkopf und Härtel, 1911), vol. 7, p. 239.

47 *NS* IV, 321; Letter of February 1800 to district administrator Just.

48 Hoffbauer defends this point of view expressly against Kant, in his essay 'Ueber das Genie und die Fähigkeit des Kopfs', in: *Ueber die Analysis in der Philosophie*, 101–13, here: 102 [ff.]. Of course, in his *Logic*, Kant had called 'the analytical method . . . the method of *invention*' (AA IX, note to § 117, 149).

49 This is the subject of my 1990 Christian Gauss Lectures at Princeton. They have been published in three parts in the journal *Metaphilosophy*, ed. by Armen T. Marsobian: Blackwell Publishers Ltd., 1999 (1st Lecture: July, vol. 30, no. 3, 145–67, 2nd and 3rd Lecture: October, vol. 30, no. 4, 265–301).

50 *NS* III, 685, No. 671.
51 Ibid., 413, No. 745; No. 748.
52 Ibid., 376, No. 612.
53 Ludwig Tieck's *Schriften* (Berlin: Reimer, 1828–54), Vol. 11, LXXXIX, XC; *NS* III, 664, No. 603.
54 Kritische Schlegel-Ausgabe XVIII, 418. No. 1168; 420, No. 1200.
55 *NS* II, 668, ll. 26 f.
56 Cf. Manfred Frank, 'In search of a foundation. From epistemology to mythology in Musil', in; Karl-Heinz Bohrer, *Mythos und Moderne* (Frankfurt/M.: Suhrkamp, 1983), pp. 318–62.
57 *NS* IV, 187, ll. 23–25.
58 *Philosophisches Journal* VI/5 (1797), 66 f.

14

GERMAN IDEALISM'S CONTESTED HERITAGE[1]

Andrew Bowie

Context

Many philosophers belonging to the analytical tradition used to portray – and some still do portray – the history of philosophy as a comedy of errors, useful mainly for revealing the logical and conceptual mistakes of past generations. However, as the recent reception of Plato, Kant, Hegel and others can suggest, many figures in the history of philosophy may not actually have been concerned with what such analytically oriented philosophers thought they were. The hermeneutic insight that one cannot interpret a philosophical text just by analysing the logical role in argument of its central concepts, but must also consider the performative and other roles of the text in its historical contexts, is now becoming more widely accepted among philosophers, and such interpretation necessarily affects the construal even of the logical aspects of a text. Interpretation that goes beyond a concern with philosophy as the advancing of arguments should therefore not only be essential in considering texts from the history of philosophy, but also in interpreting contemporary texts, although one still sees few signs of an awareness of this point in many analytically oriented texts.[2] Even in the analytical camp, though, attitudes to the history and historicity of philosophy have begun to change.

One sign of these changes is that the term 'analytical philosophy' has become subject to the kind of historical reinterpretation which some philosophers regard as inimical to the purity of the philosophical enterprise. Use of the term 'analytical' had tended to rely on the idea of adherence to a 'linguistic turn' as the basis on which the core problems of philosophy were to be addressed.[3] However, some self-confessed analytical philosophers now no longer regard a linguistic turn as essential to their aims, claiming that they have returned to a substantive concern with metaphysical issues.[4] Moreover, many European philosophers, like Derrida, Gadamer and Habermas, do adhere to versions of a linguistic turn, even though what they say is in contradiction with some of the received wisdom in the dominant Anglo-American approaches to philosophy.[5]

The institutionalised philosophical landscape makes it clear, however, that there still are informative grounds for lumping together, as notionally 'analytical' philosophers, certain of those who do take a linguistic turn with some of those who do not.[6] In an essay written a few years ago, I referred to analytical philosophy as 'the ideologically dominant form of institutionalised philosophising in the English-speaking world', which 'can often be recognised, though not defined, via the questions it fails to ask and the philosophers with whom it fails to engage'.[7] As philosophers like Hegel and Heidegger are increasingly deemed worth engaging with by some who formerly ignored or dismissed them, such changes in the canon of what is acceptable have become an indication of the need for a more general re-assessment of the philosophical landscape. But which criteria are to be used for such an assessment? It is here that retaining the label 'analytical' can make some sense, as the contemporary revival of interest in German Idealist philosophy, occasioned by the work of Robert Brandom, John McDowell, Terry Pinkard, Robert Pippin and others can suggest.

This revival has helped to make apparent that much institutionalised Anglo-American analytical philosophy depends – linguistic turn or not – on empiricist assumptions.[8] The assumption which has generated the most critical attention recently is what Wilfrid Sellars termed the 'myth of the Given': the idea that there must be an immediate source of evidence which can be used to justify knowledge claims. As I shall argue later, however, criticism of this assumption needs to be complemented by criticism of the more widespread tendency to reduce philosophy to epistemological and metaphysical issues. As Donald Davidson puts it, the myth of the Given involves the claim that 'there should be an ultimate source of evidence the character of which can be wholly specified without reference to what it is evidence for'.[9] The foundational status of this idea seems increasingly to be the only real excuse for much of analytical philosophy having ignored, and still ignoring, large parts of the history of modern philosophy, from German Idealism and Romantic philosophy, to phenomenology and deconstruction.

The most significant divide in contemporary philosophy may, then, be found between those who still adhere to an empiricist epistemological project, seeking a uniform answer to what makes sentences true, by describing how they relate to an objective world, and those who think that this characterisation of the task of philosophy not only ignores the necessarily social nature of truth, but, more importantly, excludes much of the substance of human communication from philosophical investigation.[10] One advantage of this view of the divisions in contemporary philosophy is that it offers a different way of framing what has otherwise tended to appear as a rigid contrast between the orientation towards the natural sciences of much analytical philosophy, and towards the humanities and arts of certain parts of European philosophy.

A further advantage of the view is that it highlights the mythological aspect of the idea, on the part of some of those who ignore or reject most of the European tradition, that analytical philosophy is a unified project that is working towards a theory of meaning, rather than a series of often local and contingent conceptual moves, the worst of which were generated by scientistic assumptions. The historical moves in analytical philosophy from the concern (1) with the proposition (early Wittgenstein and Russell), to (2) with the (observation) sentence (logical positivism), to (3) with language as a whole (speech act theory), to (4) with a holism which no longer sees language and the world as separate (Quine, Davidson) mean that in certain respects analytical philosophy actually ends up, albeit in a very much more differentiated form, where, on the basis of their development of Kant's questioning of empiricism, Hegel and Schleiermacher had located philosophy by the 1820s at the latest.[11] Ironically, then, sustaining the idea of a unified analytical project comes to depend on the Hegelian idea – in opposition to which logical atomism arose in the first place – of a 'mediating of immediacy'. In the *history* of the analytical project the word is mediated by the sentence, which is mediated by language as a whole, and so on, to the point where the project arguably dissolves.

The new Hegel

There are obviously plenty of stories to tell about the repressions involved in the rejection of German Idealism that helped found analytical philosophy, and about the contemporary implications of the return to what was rejected. Important as these stories are, however, the interpretation of the analytical/European division in the light of the revival of German Idealist thinking must also be informed by an awareness that, along with the ideas that they shared against empiricism, there were decisive differences between Fichte and Hegel, and the early Romantics and (at times) Schelling. It is not that these differences have been absent from discussion in this area. They form, for example, a central focus of the work of Manfred Frank, which first made clear how mistaken it is simply to equate the 'German Idealism' of Fichte and Hegel with the 'early German Romanticism' of Novalis, Schlegel and Schleiermacher, as well as of some of the recent reception of Schelling and early Romantic philosophy which connects them to Nietzsche, Adorno, Heidegger and post-structuralism. My question, though, is how this divide in German philosophy looks in the light of the 'new Hegelianism' of Brandom, McDowell, Pippin *et al.*, which has sought to obviate some of the key objections to Hegel by reinterpreting his claims in terms of what Terry Pinkard calls the 'sociality of reason', rather than seeing them as a manifestation of an all-consuming speculative metaphysics that Adorno termed 'the system' as 'the belly become spirit'.[12]

The new interest in German Idealism might appear, as we have just seen, to be predominantly a result of the growing suspicion of arguments which rely on a grounding empirical 'given'. This is clearly true within professional philosophy, but that would not explain why this philosophical difference is now coming to have wider resonances.[13] If Hegel's characterisation of philosophy as 'its age written in thought' is appropriate, our age is increasingly being written in terms of a clash between scientism and those forms of philosophy which focus on what cannot be reduced to the terms of natural science.[14]

The initial issue here is whether all kinds of explanation can be reduced to a causally based account of the explanandum, especially if that explanandum is the mind or consciousness itself. The return to Kant and his successors is based in this respect on the idea that understanding a cause as a cause and taking a stance on its identification entails a judgement which cannot itself be reduced to causal terms. Causal accounts require normative assessment as to their justification, which is a socially mediated activity, and this poses, to put it in the terms of Sellars and McDowell, the question of how the 'space of reasons' is to be understood in relation to the 'space of causes'. The path from this issue to a marriage between those analytical philosophers who now are developing some of Sellars's (already confessedly Hegelian) arguments, and Hegel, is, in one sense at least, a straightforward one. For such thinkers the validity of scientific laws is established in terms of developing, socially produced norms of investigation, not by appeals to immediate evidence, because the latter must be expressed as socially interpretable and assessable claims that form the content of what Hegel means by '*Geist*'. What initially interests me, then, is how to give a credible account of the Romantic alternatives to the new Hegelian approach which does not rely on a myth of the given.

The difficulty here is that the plausibility of Hegelianism derives precisely from its insistence on 'mediation', because appeals to anything immediate involve a failure to appreciate the inherently mediated nature of concept-using activity. Robert Pippin's argument in relation to the issue of immediacy is that any philosophical attempt to transcend the normative demands of justification in a community by appeals to a ground from which that normativity ensues will necessarily be dogmatic. In this sense *both* an empiricist appeal to sense-data *and* the kind of post-Kantian speculation about the nature of subjective spontaneity which regards it as, for example, grounded in Schopenhauerian Will, or Nietzschean Will to Power, are manifestations of what Hegel seeks to avoid. In Pippin's view, upon which I will concentrate in what follows, Hegel's insistence is on the irreducibility of the demand that concepts be subject to reflective evaluation in relation to the historically developed norms which make their employment valid. What links this to the more traditional idea of Hegel is the claim that there is consequently nothing to be said about what lies 'outside' such evaluation: by positing such a limit, one has already made it an issue within thought. The Romantic tradition which interests me can be used to question the consequences of this assumption.[15]

Pippin's version of Hegel is derived from his appraisal of the contemporary philosophical situation, and so largely eschews a historicist reconstruction of Hegel in relation to the thinking of his period. His approach therefore involves interpreting theological and metaphysical terms in a manner which makes it possible to understand claims about 'absolute knowledge', 'spirit', etc., in the vocabulary of a self-authorising modernity that is no longer beholden to unexamined traditional and other dogmatic assumptions. Whether this view really obviates concerns about the historical Hegel's later conservatism and attachment to some of the reactionary directions of the era, let alone concerns about how such attachment may arguably follow from the philosophical core of his thinking, is not clear. Such decisions depend on what one interprets as the relationship between a historical figure and the content of their philosophy.[16] What matters most for contemporary philosophy is, though, that Pippin offers a way of reading Hegel which looks forwards, rather than backwards, rejecting a metaphysical construal of claims about the absolute while still sustaining the notion as essential to anything that can be called Hegelianism. He uses this rejection to suggest an alternative both to Heideggerian/deconstructionist readings of Hegel as a manifestation of the 'subjectification' and 'closure' supposedly inherent in modern philosophy, and to the use of Hegel to keep alive totalising metaphysical aspirations of precisely the kind rejected by the Heideggerian/deconstructionist view. As such, whatever the relationship is between the detail of Hegel's texts and Pippin's interpretation, what results is important to debates in contemporary philosophy.

Subjectivity and nature

The issue that can initially focus the issues here is how subjectivity's relationship to nature is to be construed. Contemporary materialist naturalism seeks to reduce subjectivity to the space of causes, rendering normative justifications and other aspects of subjective life in the last analysis just a function of causal processes. Our ability to reflect in a manner that is supposedly not relative to some prior determining ground – thus in a manner which is 'absolute' in the German Idealist sense central to Pippin – on why we should assent to judgements, or act in one way rather than another for explicit reasons, therefore has itself to be grounded in neural processing and the history of conditioning that leads a particular organism's neurons to function in the way they do. Concerns about such a reduction can be related to a structure which F.H. Jacobi already brought into modern philosophy in the Spinoza controversy, which began in 1785,[17] whose implications haunt the history of German Idealism from its inception to its contemporary revival. Jacobi himself relies on dogmatic theological arguments and on aspects of a Locke-, Hume-, and Hamann-influenced empiricism, and many of the criticisms of him in his own time and since make weaknesses in what he proposes quite clear. However, the questions he asks are by no means obviated by the often vituperative attacks of his opponents, a fact that is apparent in the way they keep reappearing in modern philosophy.[18]

For Jacobi, who is responding to Spinoza's perceived determinism, a world of 'conditioned conditions', i.e. a world consisting of regressing chains of conditions, cannot explain how the intelligibility required for cognitive, ethical and aesthetic responses to the world arises at all.[19] We can now think of an analogy to Jacobi's view in terms of structures in cognitive science: the identities of elements of a system are there seen as grounded in their differences from and relations to the other elements, so that each is a 'condition' for the others. The problem is that mere relations between elements do not constitute those elements as possessing significance or as being true: this requires intentionality, which cannot be grasped solely in terms of relational structures. Subjectivity's relationship to how significance and truth are generated from relational structures is therefore the key here, and this is where important differences begin to emerge that are crucial to the tensions in German Idealism.

Jacobi insists that

> I am not a *Cartesian*. I begin like the Orientals ('*Morgenländer*') in their conjugations with the third, not with the first person, and I believe that one simply should not put the *Sum* after the *Cogito*. I needed a truth which was not *my* creature, but whose creature *I* would be.[20]

The problem of how truth could be thought of in a non-Cartesian manner consequently leads Jacobi to the notion of a theologically grounded immediate relationship to a world whose essential nature is to be disclosed and alive, rather than opaque, and whose intelligibility is prior to the subject's cognitive determination of it in terms of relations between conditions. He talks of this relationship in terms of '*Glaube*', 'belief'/'faith', which he describes as 'holding as true' ('*Fürwahrhalten*'). '*Glaube*' can be interpreted here in terms of its familiar contrast with 'knowledge'. However, the still salient point of what Jacobi means by '*Glaube*' is that knowledge itself would not be possible without our having a prior intelligible relationship with the world. This relationship, Jacobi thinks, guards against the threat of scepticism that results from the regress of 'conditioned conditions' inherent in attempting finally to ground the knowledge of any phenomenon, as well as against solipsistic consequences which may result if the subject is supposed to be the sole source of the world's intelligibility.

Jacobi's idea will be echoed in Heidegger's claim that 'ontic' determination of what there is depends on the prior 'ontological' disclosedness of the world, without which ontic questions would not arise in the first place.[21] If thought is considered as a kind of light, Heidegger later suggests, it can only illuminate if an opening, a free space, is cleared. Light itself cannot create this free space; it has somehow to be 'given' to us. What this kind of idea implies appears in a less metaphorical form in Charles Taylor's claim that 'We are able to form conceptual beliefs guided by our surroundings, because we live in a preconceptual engagement with these that involves understanding'.[22] One way of characterising most forms of Hegelianism is precisely in terms of their rejection of the idea of 'ontological difference', because for them the truth of the preconceptual disclosedness of the world only emerges insofar as it is conceptually articulated by *Geist*.[23] The tension in the German Idealist tradition arises around the extent to which this articulation exhaustively captures our relationships to ourselves and the world.

A major motivation for Jacobi's view arises from what is implicit in his argument that, by seeking finally to ground any explanation in an 'ontic' manner, 'one ends by having to discover *conditions* of the *unconditioned*'.[24] Echoing precisely Jacobi's point, Hans Albert has referred to the 'Münchhausen Trilemma' for modern philosophy that results from the attempt to use Leibniz's 'principle of sufficient reason' to ground knowledge: one ends either with an infinite regress of reasons for reasons, or a circular argument that relies on reasons which themselves require grounding, or a breaking-off of the attempt at grounding in the name of a 'given' which is taken as dogmatically self-evident. The point of a German Idealist position is that the ability to take a reflective intentional stance with regard to the world cannot be conditioned in the same way as are the 'conditioned conditions' of the causally explicable world. Jacobi's key question therefore concerns exactly how the 'unconditioned' is to be understood. How can the legitimacy of self-legislation be established in a manner which does not fall prey to regress, circularity, or dogmatism?

Jacobi's suspicion of the attempt to reduce the world to chains of conditions might appear to put him in the same territory as Pippin, who sees Hegel's idea of freedom in terms of normatively governed self-authorisation and self-determination, thus as constitutive of the space of reasons and as not reducible to the space of causes: 'the I's relation to itself is "the Absolute", the unconditioned possibility of which explains the possible intelligibility of all else'.[25] However, the connection of the idea of the unconditioned to subjectivity is precisely what Jacobi objects to in Fichte, and will also be what leads the early Romantics and Schelling to question certain aspects of Idealism.[26] Pippin shares the anti-Cartesian premise common to Jacobi, Schelling and the Romantics, but maintains that a Hegelian account of subjectivity's constitution in social interaction can avoid many of the objections to the grounding role of subjectivity in modern philosophy that are familiar from recent European philosophy. In certain respects, the way he presents this case is highly plausible, but I think that he underestimates the contemporary significance of certain aspects of Schelling and early Romantic philosophy for parts of his project.

Freedom and reason

The most familiar objection to any Idealist emphasis on the 'persistence of subjectivity' (Pippin) is summed up in Heidegger's notion that modernity is characterised by the 'subjectification of being', and in Horkheimer and Adorno's idea of a 'dialectic of enlightenment' that results from the subject's aim of self-preservation by dominating the other via 'instrumental reason'. The dangers to which such positions advert are implicit in Jacobi's claim that, because it is grounded in the activity of the I, Fichtean reason, in which the 'I's relation to itself' is precisely the central factor, is necessarily narcissistic: 'The root of reason ("*Vernunft*") is listening ("*Vernehmen*"). – Pure reason is a listening which only listens to itself. Or: Pure reason listens only to itself'.[27] In seeking to establish systematic 'closure', the I therefore represses 'alterity' by not 'listening' to what eludes its self-generated concepts.

This kind of claim will be the core of the many objections to Hegel, particularly in recent French philosophy,[28] that Pippin rejects.[29] Jacobi's alternative to Fichte's idea of reason is itself dogmatically theological, relying on a version of divine revelation as the ground of intelligibility that transcends the subject. Hegel therefore dismisses Jacobi's alternative because it involves the immediacy suggested by the idea that the absolute in such cases is the unarticulated 'night in which all cows are black'. For Jacobi the absolute is resistant to conceptualisation, rather than being, as it is for Hegel, thought's most complete self-articulation. Hegelian self-articulation results from reason's insight into its self-determining status, which raises it above all relative forms of immediacy. Jacobi's claims about the regress of conditions that lead him to his theological stance therefore epitomise what Hegel means by 'bad infinity', which he contrasts with Spinoza's example of the rational infinity that is present in the determinacy of all the points enclosed in the space between two intersecting circles.[30]

The Jacobi-influenced question that Schelling will pose in his later work is how such a rationalist conception of infinity, which derives from necessary truths, relates to the contingency of a world which cannot, on pain of a regression to dogmatism, be shown in philosophy to be inherently rational.[31] The 'bad infinity' which results from Jacobi's reflections on the regresses involved in grounding appears again because Schelling ceases to accept that reason can ground itself by showing how it relates to being, or by eliminating the question of this relationship in the manner Hegel does in the doctrine of Being in the *Logic*. For Schelling, although there can be no grounds for rejecting the necessities encountered in logical thinking, rational thinking cannot itself explain the fact of those necessities, and so is not self-grounding.[32] In the last analysis reason is therefore in some sense contingent, and, from the essay 'On the Essence of Human Freedom' (1809) onwards, Schelling begins to connect this contingency to an idea of freedom in which the subject's capacity for self-determination in the 'absolute' sense outlined above is put in question. Freedom is 'unconditioned' in another sense: it resists conceptual determination as well, so that self-determination itself involves an irreducible contingency. 'Freedom' cannot be defined, precisely because it is the essence of a world which is not predetermined from the beginning and which transcends how philosophy (including natural science) can conceptualise it.[33] The question is now whether such criticisms of Hegelian rationalism have any purchase on Pippin's reinterpretation of that rationalism. This will turn out to be formulable in contemporary terms as a question about the scope and aims of philosophy.

Schelling's 'freedom' can admittedly be regarded in a way which falls prey to Pippin's strictures, because it can be seen as entailing a dogmatic claim about the nature of the ground of being. However, the implication that *philosophy* may not fully articulate the nature of freedom can lead in other, more defensible directions. Despite all that Pippin jettisons from the metaphysical construal of Hegel, the idea of 'self-grounding' is central to his interpretation, as the remarks on the absolute cited above make clear. The core of Pippin's objection to what he sees as Schelling's position is precisely Hegel's objection to Jacobi: unless what is supposed to be the origin of the subject's self-grounding 'is self-consciously determined as such, for the subject, it is nothing; it is "the night in which all cows are black"'.[34] Pippin argues that the early Schelling, of the *Naturphilosophie*, is aware that explaining how material nature could produce self-conscious beings will involve the dogmatism of claiming to know how the world is 'in itself', and so will fail to fulfil the demand that the explanation be 'self-consciously determined as such'. Schelling consequently contends that both material nature and subjectivity have their source in what he will, following Hölderlin, come to term 'being'. Being is prior to subject/object divisions, and so not accessible in conceptual terms.

Nature is therefore not just the causal realm, and is, in one sense, inherently 'subjective'. As Taylor puts it in his essay on McDowell cited above: 'There is something more in nature between full spontaneity and mere mechanism'.[35] For Schelling the status of nature as subjective cannot be articulated as such from the subject side, because that would be an objectification of the kind involved in knowing nature conceptually. We can, in Schelling's terms, only conceptualise 'products', the world of appearing, causally determined, objective nature, not the 'productivity' common to mind and material nature which gives rise to the fact of an intelligible, changing, differentiated world that comes to know itself in thought.

Art and Philosophy

The question is therefore what kind of access we have to this productivity, which is where a decisive tension in German Idealism becomes apparent. Because it cannot be conceptualised in the manner of nature's 'products', the productivity has to be accessible in some kind of immediate 'intuition', and this, of course, can very easily lead towards night and black cows once again. Schelling talks in this context of an 'intellectual intuition', linking the idea in the 1800 *System of Transcendental Idealism* to art as the locus of such intuition. It is, though, here that there will actually be some mileage in what Schelling is saying, despite the well-known problems involved in the appeal to intellectual intuition.[36] The idea here can be initially suggested by Cavell's remarks on the fact that, however much we may seek to convince others of our aesthetic evaluations, 'if you do not see something, *without* explanation, then there is nothing further to discuss',[37] in which there is an irreducible moment of intuitive immediacy in aesthetic experience that gives it its particular meaning.

Art appears as a 'product', as a material object like any other, but it cannot be conceptually determined, in the way that objects in general can be, without ceasing to be understood as art. – Think of what can be conveyed by a piece of music which is not exhausted by what we say about what is conveyed, and of the fact that a physical description of music in terms of frequencies, durations, etc., is not a characterisation of it as music. – Art cannot be conclusively interpreted, being a concrete manifestation of human freedom, but one which is not produced wholly through conscious, normatively assessable intentions. In line with one of the basic aims of German Idealism, Schelling is seeking in the *System* to overcome any division between mind and nature by establishing the nature of the connection between them, hence the term intellectual intuition, which combines Kant's idea of 'intuitive' receptivity to external nature with the spontaneity which characterises the active aspect of subjectivity. The nature of the connection is, though, precisely not discursively accessible, relying on means of access which are not reducible to what can be known about them. For Hegel, in contrast, this connection, as he argues in the *Phenomenology*, must be the result of the articulation of all the ways in which thought fails to be complete in relation to the world: a philosophical account of the totality of those failures can show that there is nothing else left to think. Instead of mind and nature being presupposed as identical, they are therefore articulated as identical at the end of Hegel's system. The true content of intuition is therefore to be demonstrated by philosophical reflection, art being only a stage on the way to that true content.

To the extent to which Schelling wants to found *philosophy* on intellectual intuition, Hegel is in a strong position. A philosophy which relies on immediacy is relying on something extra-philosophical, in the sense that what is at issue is not articulable in concepts, and so can justifiably be accused of indeterminacy. The criticisms of Schelling concerning the way he relies on intellectual intuition may, then, well be valid for some of his work, but they do not obviate the issue of intuition.

The question is whether the content of intuition is articulable in the absolute manner that Pippin and Hegel wish it to be, such that nothing meaningful can be said to be excluded from the articulation. In his interpretation of Heidegger's questionable assimilation of Schelling's idea of freedom (which mistakenly removes all ethical content from it, making it a wholly ontological issue), Pippin suggests that Heidegger seeks to make Kant's spontaneity, which in Pippin's self-legislating view brings the mind's thoughts and intentions under a norm which makes them '"my" thoughts and intentions', dependent rather on 'some *arche* whose unity or coherence or intelligibility cannot be articulated'.[38] Consequently 'to live freely cannot hope to be a life commonly and justifiably measured by some norm. It must be some sort of *acknowledgement* of what cannot be measured without falsifying, covering over. A kind of mythic-poetic discourse seems to keep emerging as the appropriate mode of acknowledgement'.[39] This claim may be applicable to the later Heidegger, and relates to one aspect of the later Schelling's ideas about the implications of the fact that being always transcends what we think of it, but it fails to get to the heart of the alternative understanding of subjectivity, being, and freedom present in aspects of Schelling and Romantic philosophy.

Pippin's stark alternative, between the sense of spontaneity as 'absolute' in a community of self-determining subjects, and the idea that we are essentially the objects of the history of being obscures the crucial fact in modernity that the aim of self-determination is always pursued in circumstances where the 'absolute' moment of such determination may not necessarily be transparent as such. While this does not mean we have to take the Heideggerian route of subjecting self-determination to the history of being, it should mean we introduce a strong sense, both of the fallibility of the forms of self-determination which develop in modern communities – which Pippin actually acknowledges – but, more crucially, of the ways in which we come to terms with the lack of final transparency that Schelling and the Romantics regard as part of human freedom. Pippin leaves too little place for forms of human existence which make no sense without the idea of freedom, in the sense that they are not explicable in naturalistic, causal terms, but which are not normatively governed in the ways that knowledge and action may be. These forms demand instead a preparedness to transgress norms with no guarantee that the result will actually even make sense, which is what links them to the more contingent dimension of human freedom explored by Schelling. Pippin thinks that a description of the endlessly self-correcting nature of thought, of the kind given in Hegel's *Logic*, suffices to counter objections concerning human fallibility. This seems to me too easy. Self-correction is indeed inevitable: the real question is whether we can give an exhaustive *philosophical* account of its developmental nature, of its 'logic'. While this may be possible at the level of epistemology, where an explication of processes of knowledge acquisition by the elimination of inadequate theories makes sense in Hegelian terms, the approach does seem to not offer a great deal for understanding the real course of ethical development: why does modern history so often destroy or pervert self-determination?

Art tends to be given an inflated role in much of the philosophy which Pippin opposes. However, the sense that what art – in a very broad sense of expressive production, especially including non-verbal forms of expression – reveals may be an essential complement to what can be said in philosophy can be interpreted in ways which do not give art the dogmatic status it sometimes has in discussions in European philosophy. (As Pippin points out, this is a status which it is hard to square with the actual social role of the art to which many philosophers refer.)[40] Pippin's discussion of the idea of 'acknowledgement' in Heidegger stresses the passive sense that we just undergo something which subverts our apparent self-determination. What I think Pippin underestimates is the notion, which is central to Schleiermacher's account of art's relationship to subjectivity, of actively 'responding' to the feeling that understanding of freedom is not exhausted by the availability of the reflective stance.[41] The idea of responding takes us into the realm of expressive practices which cannot be wholly grasped in terms of the normative assessments required for cognitive and ethical judgement. In such cases the point of the practice lies in participation in it which need not be formulable in terms of claims, but which is essential to the subject's self-understanding. I am thinking, for example, of the significance of music for both players and listeners.[42] Such practices do involve a kind of self-determination, but one which results from doing something which is never fully theoretically accessible, and so cannot be characterised primarily in terms of spontaneity's being brought under socially generated norms. The role of norm-oriented, reflective thought in art is, of course, vital, but what interests me are the limits philosophy encounters when accounting for art's significance in terms of propositionally explicit norms.

It is in this respect that questions of art are relevant to the issues examined earlier, concerning how the causal realm can be related to the mental realm, without the latter being reduced to the former. John McDowell's questioning of the idea of nature as just the realm of law, which he sees as rendering the fact of intentionality incomprehensible, can be related to aspects of what leads to the need for responses to human freedom which are not purely discursive and philosophical. Pippin thinks, in contrast, that we can 'leave nature out of the picture altogether', rather than seek to use nature as a means of accounting for intentionality.[43] The content of Pippin's intentionality is *Geist* which has moved beyond nature in the process of self-determination which leads to the normative sphere of giving reasons and the self-determination this involves. This sphere need not, he thinks, be regarded as McDowell regards it, namely as a kind of 'second nature' that is inherent in the fact that human being is social being, which McDowell links to Gadamer's idea of *Bildung*.

How, then, are nature and the 'other' of nature to be conceived, without regressing into dogmatism or into reductive naturalism? As Pippin sees it, there is simply the natural space of causes, and there is the social space of reasons. They relate in the sense that the latter is the location of the normative conditions for legitimate knowledge of the former, the causal effects of the former not playing a direct role in justification, because that would entail the myth of the given. In his response to Pippin, McDowell details his concern about Pippin's strong Idealist claims, which seem to him to lead to another version of the 'frictionless spinning' with no control by input from the world that he sees in Davidson's idea that only a belief (in the space of reasons) can 'count as the reason for holding a belief'.[44] That issue has formed the focus of much debate over McDowell,[45] and has led to suggestions about McDowell's proximity to Schelling's *Naturphilosophie*. In my terms it might, though, be best to interpret the debate as still tied up with the legacy of empiricism, insofar as the concern remains with drawing the line between the mind's and the world's contribution to knowledge, rather than with a wider consideration of how our relationship to nature is to be negotiated. Pippin and McDowell admittedly concur that sceptical worries generated by the idea of an isolated Cartesian subject must give way to a conception of subjectivity as formed in social interaction and interaction with the world, but the focus of their discussion still seems predominantly epistemological.

Beyond epistemology

One possible consequence of the decline of empiricism is, however, that epistemologically oriented approaches, which put the legitimation of knowledge at the centre of philosophy's concerns, may, even in the socially mediated form proposed by the new Hegelianism, become less significant, in a way I have argued that they already begin to do in Romantic philosophy.[46] One reason for the decline of the agenda which drove empiricism is simply the accumulation of reliable scientific knowledge: at some point, it becomes more important to think about what we do with that knowledge and what role it plays in interpreting human life than whether it needs a philosophical meta-justification. Making the normative dimension central to philosophy is obviously a crucial move in overcoming the worst aspects of the analytical legacy. However, the conception of freedom as self-determination does not do justice to the more expressive dimensions of human existence, which are not adequately grasped by thinking in terms of giving reasons and taking normative stances. Furthermore, there are related grounds for suspecting that philosophical approaches to explicating freedom may suffer from certain problems of the kind suggested by Schelling's criticism of the idea of reason's self-grounding. How this may be the case is, for all his faults, apparent at times in Adorno.[47]

Following in the tradition of both Schelling and Hegel, Adorno says of reason that 'emerging in an ephemeral manner from nature, reason is identical and non-identical with nature'.[48] In the lectures on *Problems of Moral Philosophy* he maintains that 'We are really no longer ourselves a piece of nature at the moment when we notice, when we recognise, that we are a piece of nature'.[49] The apparent ambivalence in the concept of nature is essential to Adorno's dialectical approach. Nature appears both as a positive and negative quantity in his reflections, and cannot be assigned either just to the space of causes or just to the space of reasons. One of Adorno's ideas is that before we recognise our natural status we may merely function as a piece of causally determined nature which shares the destructive potential of the drive for self-preservation with the rest of nature. By recognising this state of affairs, reason is able to take us beyond it, and so potentially, to enable us to become aware of when we regress into 'nature'. Thus far, Pippin can concur, via his story of *Geist* 'leaving nature behind' in its growing self-determination. However, Adorno argues that the development of modernity (and, in the terms of *Dialectic of Enlightenment*, of all human culture based on self-preservation) sees rationality become 'natural' again, in the form of the sort of instrumental – subjectively determined – control of nature that leads to what we now think of in terms of the ecological crisis, rapacious forms of capitalism, etc. This kind of 'second nature' is at least as threatening and destructive as wild 'first nature'. Adorno's strong thesis is, then, that humankind has regressed into what he terms 'self-preservation/assertion run wild' ('*verwilderte Selbstbehauptung*'). Instead of the content of modernity being rational self-determination, it becomes a potentially self-destructive drive for domination of the other. As Pippin rightly points out, this story is often hardly different from that of the later Heidegger, though it does highlight some things that Pippin underplays.

The obvious problem for Adorno's strong thesis is that there can be no location for his critique that is not already contaminated by what is to be criticised. A rational criticism of the state of affairs in question would have to stand outside what is criticised, but if rationality is itself actually a form of self-preservation, it cannot claim to do so. Pippin would therefore seem to be vindicated, because Adorno relies on what is effectively another version of a night in which all cows are black. On the other hand, the horrors of modern history seem to speak in certain respects more for Adorno's than for Pippin's conception: if modernity is so rationally self-determining, why is it so brutal?

The answer in Adorno's strictest terms has to do with the predominance of instrumental reason, thus with self-determination's becoming exclusively self-preservation. Pippin regards a collectively constituted self-determining subjectivity as necessarily prior to such claims: how else could we make apparent what may be wrong with instrumental reason in modernity? Adorno, in contrast, talks of the 'primacy of the objective' that is occasioned by social processes which make subjects blind to the consequences of their actions, so that apparent free self-determination can never be guaranteed not to be a form of self-deception. The argument is related to that of Marx in *Capital*: 'the fetish-character of the commodity is not a fact of consciousness but dialectical in the emphatic sense that it produces consciousness'.[50] If something objective produces consciousness, we might, of course, seem to be in the space of causes, as Adorno often mistakenly implies. What is thus 'produced' can, though, vary enormously, which entails the involvement of the spontaneity of the space of reasons, and this means that what is produced cannot, as Pippin argues, be as uniform as Adorno too often suggests that it is.

It is for this reason that Adorno is at his most telling when he drops the sense that the commodification of thinking is total, and deconstructs the opposition between the causal and the spontaneous in relation to social issues, rather than seeing the social as having become predominantly causal. In the lectures on history and freedom Adorno stresses that destructive forms of rationality are also what make possible the advances of modernity, and that there is no simple answer to the dilemma this entails, decisions about rationality being both ineluctable and always potentially involving catastrophic misapprehensions.[51] The stance of Adorno that offers most resources in this respect relates closely to the reasons for his concern with art. Here the dialectic between the constraints imposed on the subject by the demands of artistic expression and the subject's potential for new expression suggests a way of thinking about how the relationship between the pressure of objective circumstances and freedom can be better understood, without either making self-determination essentially dependent on something else or underplaying the problem of the transparency of self-determination.

Both Adorno's putative 'materialism' and Pippin's Kant-inspired, idealist Hegelianism articulate something crucial about the nature of modernity, and this has important consequences for how we regard philosophy in this context. Modernity offers resources for rational self-determination that have led, as Pippin argues, to moral advances like the impossibility of arguing for the inferior status of women or justifying the exploitation of children. It also, though, produces what leads to the Holocaust, arguably at least in part on the basis of the perverted forms of rationalisation that Adorno makes the target of his critique of modern subjectivity.[52] The question is therefore how the incompatibility of these accounts is to be confronted.

Pippin thinks the strength of his position lies in its giving a philosophical legitimation of moral advance, based on a narrative of how and why we arrived at the norms that inform our practices, rather than either seeking a legitimation for them in some foundational principle for morality, or seeing them just in terms of 'how we go on'. One motive for his stance derives from his justified suspicions of the results, in Heidegger and some 'post-modern' thinkers, of seeking to subordinate subjectivity to something else, such as 'mentalités, epistemés, "discourses", "fields of power", and so on'.[53] These positions lay claim to access to something that is prior to the subject and which undermines its claims to sovereignty, thus robbing claims to self-determination of their legitimation. However, if this subordination is to be put forward as a discursive explanation of the nature of subjectivity, it must be able to be 'self-consciously determined as such', otherwise it leads to the problem which Adorno has in advancing his strong claims about a world of systematic commodity-determined delusion. Theories like these consequently involve a performative contradiction, and in this respect, I am with Pippin. What he seems to neglect has to do with the Romantic idea that we cannot fully grasp the nature of our subjectivity in terms of norm-governed self-determination. This idea is not obviated by the failure of theories which seek to conceptualise the ground of subjectivity in a theory of a structure or force which motivates or underlies it.

The point here is not that subjectivity is therefore irredeemably mysterious or ineffable – though it may well be that the idea of explaining it as a determinate objective phenomenon is actually incoherent – but that our understanding of it must take account of the implications of a more ambivalent notion of freedom. The contingency which is an essential part of expressive articulation is seen in this respect as having to do with our being part of nature, in the sense Taylor indicated in his remark that 'There is something more in nature between full spontaneity and mere mechanism'. The Hegelian rejoinder to such assertions is that any appeal to nature must always recognise that what nature is understood to be is mediated by social forms, so that subjectivity has its own phenomenology, part of which are forms of aesthetic expression. However, if we think that the issue of nature cannot be exclusively dealt with in terms of its theoretical or philosophical determination, but can also be approached in terms of expressive responses to external and internal nature, a dimension opens up which Hegelianism characterises as just a form of immediacy which is to be conceptually determined. The approach I am suggesting does not reject the anti-Cartesian sense in Hegel, which Pippin shows to be so important, of subjectivity as inseparable from the world in which it emerges, but it questions philosophy's ability to render all forms of expression conceptually transparent.

We can elucidate this approach via part of Adorno's questioning of an idealist construal of nature. Adorno might seem from what has been said so far to regard 'nature', in a partly Hegelian manner, as what needs to be transcended by *Geist* in its non-instrumental forms. At the same time, however, he regards 'nature' as a resource against the rigidities involved in social rationalisation. This links him to some of the defensible aspects of Schelling and Schleiermacher, where they question reason's ability to be fully self-determining, making the aim of doing so a regulative idea that may never be achieved because the line between reason and nature cannot finally be drawn. The crucial point is that recognition that we are a piece of nature, which is essential to an adequate understanding of human freedom, is therefore not just a matter of *Geist* leaving nature behind in realising its self-determining status and consequently making a clear demarcation between itself and the 'other' of nature.

Adorno's idea of 'mimesis' offers one way of understanding what is at issue here, and it relates to his sense that nature need not be construed just as the realm of necessity. The difficulty, as we have seen, is that this change in the view of nature requires some kind of non-conceptual – 'immediate' – way of relating to nature both internal and external. Mimesis, in Adorno's particular sense, begins in the form of imitative behaviour which seeks to counter the threat of the other, and it is still apparent in the pre-linguistic behaviour of humans that is a necessary pre-condition of linguistic understanding. As such, mimesis precedes what becomes the explicit, mediated development of social norms; it is both a form of potential regression, and something which, if it is not integrated into the rest of life, can lead to a repression of vital human needs. Mimesis challenges the sense that freedom is only present in self-determining assent to social norms *both* via its relation to self-expression as the response to our impulses, and via its relation to potentially regressive collective forms of behaviour that have been mobilised in appalling forms in modernity.

Art, for Adorno, is 'mimesis which has been driven to consciousness of itself'.[54] This might seem to take us back to Hegel, but Adorno insists that 'what mimetic behaviour addresses is the telos of cognition which cognition at the same time blocks with its own categories',[55] which means that the telos of cognition is not immanent to cognition itself. On the one hand, this may be interpreted as just a version of his questionable equation of cognition and instrumental reason, but on the other, it is also a warning about what can be missed by an exclusive concentration on the conceptual. Adorno illustrates 'the mimetic ability' in terms of 'the musician who understands his score, follows its most minute movements, and yet in a certain sense does not *know* what he is playing'.[56] Adorno's contentions therefore echo part of what motivated Schelling's insistence on 'intuition' in his *System of Transcendental Idealism*: 'Art completes cognition with what is excluded from it and thereby in turn detracts from the character of cognition, namely its unambiguous nature' (ibid.). Adorno sees art as located between 'regression to literal magic, or the surrender of the mimetic impulse to reified rationality' (ibid.), and it is this in-between status which makes it important in understanding what the Hegelian position underplays or excludes, namely the enduring possibility that our conceptual resources may fail to give access to what other means of expression and articulation make possible.

Pippin has no time for the idea that the 'preflexive', either at the level of the subject's pre-conceptual self-awareness, or at the level of being's transcendence of the relationship between subjective and objective, might be important, claiming that Manfred Frank's attention to these does not go 'all that far in establishing any positive philosophical project'.[57] Frank's subsequent concentration on debates in the analytical philosophy of mind, which repeatedly recycle the issue of whether self-consciousness is inherently propositional or not, suggests that there can indeed be a problem in establishing a wider philosophical project via the idea – which Pippin, incidentally, does not seek to contradict – that there is a dimension of self-consciousness which cannot be accounted for in terms of Hegelian self-recognition in otherness.

However, as Frank has also shown by his attention to the role of art in philosophy, Romantic explorations of freedom do not fail to offer something positive, though it may not necessarily take the form of a philosophical project. They share with Hegel the sense in which mind and world cannot be thought of in isolation from each other, but do not conclude from this that self-consciousness is exhaustively characterisable in terms of self-determination by collectively generated norms. Instead, they seek to explore how subjects arrive at their particular sense of their place within things that may, for example, best be articulated by aesthetic forms of expression. Schleiermacher suggests what is meant here when he contrasts language and music:

> just as the infinity of combination of articulated sounds belongs to human thought being able to appear in language, so the manifold of measured ('*gemessen*') sounds represents the whole manifold of movements of self-consciousness, to the extent that they are not ideas, but real states of life.[58]

Similarly, Adorno's idea of mimesis cannot be regarded as a mere form of 'immediacy'. Art's mediation of mimesis does not result in its becoming something conceptual, and this need not be regarded as a defect, unless one assumes that norm-based self-determination is the key to aesthetic production and reception as well. What this assumption misses, though, is the sense, central to Schleiermacher, that the role of spontaneity in art is something that philosophy cannot capture because it has to do with individual responses to our 'being in the world'.[59]

Now this might well not appear such a big deal in relation to the wide-ranging and often impressive implications of Pippin's attempt to give philosophical dignity to assessments of modernity in terms of moral progress and self-determination. It can be asked, though, how much of Pippin's – to my mind admirable – liberal, critical stance on ethical life really needs the absolute philosophical moment which distinguishes his Hegelianism from the kind of pragmatism which echoes the Romantic idea of the absolute as just a reminder of human fallibility that may best be responded to in aesthetic production or reception. Pippin's complaint about such positions is that they lack a narrative legitimation of how we arrived at the practices that demand rational approval which constitute the substance of *Geist*. The problem is, though, that such narratives, as the example of Adorno suggests, are essentially contested.

The obvious difference between Adorno and Pippin, which, despite their shared orientation towards Hegel, produces such radically differing stances with regard to philosophy and modernity, lies in the fact that, in Adornian terms, Pippin's idea of free assent to social norms means that we can be sustaining the norms of unjust societies.[60] Both see the subject as essentially constituted in social interaction, but Adorno sees the antagonistic nature of modern society as undermining self-determination. The choice of appropriate norms can consequently become irredeemably complex, and appeals to some kind of absolute based on collective norms are in danger of becoming ideological, rather than being a philosophical answer to the problem of how to live ethically in modernity. The brutal aspects of modern history and the manipulations of the culture industry make this view hard to ignore. Adorno's extreme version of this approach can admittedly lead, as we saw, to the demand for something outside supposedly wholly dominant commodity-determined norms, or to the indeterminate aim of 'reconciliation' with nature. This can, as Pippin argues, lead to the rejection of too many of the advances of the Enlightenment. The best elements of Adorno's approach, though, involve a more cautious attitude towards self-legislation and freedom, based on the sense that reason and nature cannot be decisively separated, and a questioning, which is part of the history of German Idealism from the very beginning, of the extent to which philosophy alone can make these issues transparent.

German Idealism involves a tension between attempts at philosophical completion of the Kantian project of self-legislation, and approaches which seek in nature and art ways of responding to the loss of meaning that results from self-determination in science and the state. Neither approach can, of course, claim to have achieved its aims, and this is now reflected in questions about the role of philosophy that are manifest in the analytical/European split, and in what might now be thought of as the beginning of its aftermath. McDowell has, in line with Pippin, seen his appropriation of Hegel in Wittgensteinian 'therapeutic' terms, as an attempt to cure us of philosophical anxiety about the mind-world relationship, but this aim seems to me to raise the following question. A familiar objection to psychoanalytical therapy, which seeks to bring repressed contents to the knowledge of the subject, thus loosening their hold on the subject, is that this process does not per se enable the subject to do anything with this new or restored knowledge. What is needed are responses to such knowledge which really enable the subject to live with it, rather than simply be aware of it or acknowledge it, given that awareness of the repressed can be paralysing, rather than enabling. Analogously, establishing in the Hegelian manner that there is no gap between the world and our knowledge of it and that there is no external source of higher ethical insight is clearly an important philosophical aim. However, the Hegelian approach is, as Charles Taylor has reminded us, not enough to establish relationships between the subject and the natural and social world which are felt as tolerable and meaningful. How such relationships are to be achieved without regressing to pre-critical and dogmatic views of nature and the self, remains perhaps the central question in the contested heritage of German Idealism.

Notes

1 This essay was written with the support of a Major Research Fellowship from the Leverhulme Foundation.

2 This criticism might appear to ignore the distinction between genesis and validation, but the point is that *what* is to be validated may not be appropriately interpreted if it is not adequately contextualised.

3 The linguistic turn must, of course, itself be understood historically, given that it is arguably already part of the work of Hamann and Herder (see Andrew Bowie, *Aesthetics and Subjectivity: from Kant to Nietzsche* (Manchester: Manchester University Press, 2003)).

4 One might have thought that these philosophers would also feel the need to reconsider the interpretation of classic texts of Western metaphysics in the light of new work in the history of philosophy, but this is rarely the case.

5 As is sometimes pointed out, e.g. by Samuel Wheeler (S. Wheeler, *Deconstruction as Analytic Philosophy* (Stanford: Stanford University Press, 2000)), Derrida and Quine share rather a lot of assumptions about the nature of 'meaning', despite Quine's intemperate objections to Derrida.

6 This approach allows one to exclude from the criticisms implied here those who are analytically trained and philosophise in a manner based on the striving for argumentative precision – which is the positive aspect of the analytical tradition – but whose concerns go beyond the narrow empiricist agenda (epistemological scepticism, realism, etc.) which renders the point of much analytical philosophy obscure to all but those who are engaged in it.

7 Andrew Bowie, 'The Romantic Connection: Neurath, the Frankfurt School, and Heidegger', *British Journal for the History of Philosophy*, Part One, 8 (2) 2000; Part Two 8 (3) 2000.

8 The point being made here is perfectly illustrated by Crispin Wright's tetchy responses to McDowell, which culminate in the accusation that McDowell is no longer an analytical philosopher (in N.H. Smith (ed.), *Reading McDowell. On 'Mind and World'* (London, New York: Routledge, 2002), p. 157), an accusation to which McDowell is rightly indifferent.

9 Donald Davidson, *Subjective, Intersubjective, Objective* (Oxford: Oxford University Press, 2001), p. 42.

10 The interest of McDowell for many philosophers derives from his lying somewhere between the empiricist, and the idealist and pragmatist approaches to these issues. On the limitations of the analytical tradition with regard to questions of communication see Jürgen Habermas, *Zwischen Naturalismus und Religion* (Frankfurt: Suhrkamp, 2005), pp. 19–20. It is a source of some surprise to me that the work of Brandom now has almost canonical status in Germany, when most of what matters about his work is already present in Habermas, and Habermas takes account of far more aspects of communication than does Brandom. It is also noticeable that, whereas Habermas has engaged in detail with Brandom, the converse is not the case.

11 See Richard Bernstein, *Radical Evil* (Cambridge: Polity, 2002); Andrew Bowie, 'German Philosophy Today: Between Idealism, Romanticism, and Pragmatism', in Anthony O'Hear (ed.) *German Philosophy Since Kant*, Royal Institute of Philosophy Lectures (Cambridge: Cambridge University Press, 1999); and 'Schleiermacher and Postmetaphysical Thinking', *Critical Horizons* 5, 2004, pp. 165–200.

12 Theodor W. Adorno, *Gesammelte Schriften* (GS) (Frankfurt: Suhrkamp, 1997), Vol. 6, p. 34.

13 It is, moreover, not always the case that philosophical changes are necessarily the result of arguments between philosophers, something which is almost universally ignored in the analytical tradition.

14 The latter forms can involve a return to traditional metaphysics, but the option that concerns me here tends to see itself in 'postmetaphysical' terms.

15 See Andrew Bowie, *From Romanticism to Critical Theory. The Philosophy of German Literary Theory* (London: Routledge, 1997).

16 This is itself a normative issue concerning the goals of philosophy. It is clear from his responses to contemporary political issues that the mature Hegel was at times on the side of reaction, in contrast to the liberalism of precisely the kind of thinkers, like Schleiermacher, whom Pippin regards as failing where Hegel succeeds.

17 See Bowie, *From Romanticism to Critical Theory*; Manfred Frank, *'Unendliche Annäherung'. Die Anfänge der philosophischen Frühromantik* (Frankfurt: Suhrkamp, 1997).

18 See Andrew Bowie, 'Re-thinking the History of the Subject: Jacobi, Schelling and Heidegger', in Simon Critchley, Peter Dews (eds), *Deconstructive Subjectivities* (Albany N.Y.: SUNY Press, 1996); and John McDowell's '*Mind and World*, and Early Romantic Epistemology', *Revue internationale de philosophie*, Vol. 50, 197, 3 1996, pp. 515–54 – where I connect Jacobi's objections to Spinozism to McDowell's objections to Davidson's 'coherentism', and Bowie, *From Romanticism to Critical Theory* for a historical account.

19 Kant's realisation that there can be no rules for judging, on pain of a regress of rules for rules, can be seen as a response to what is at issue here, as can Fichte's question in the *Vocation of Man* of 1800: 'And do I really think or do I just think a thinking of thinking? What can stop speculation acting like this and continue asking to infinity?' (J.G. Fichte, *Werke* II (Berlin: de Gruyter, 1971), p. 252).

20 H. Scholz, *Die Hauptschriften zum Pantheismusstreit zwischen Jacobi und Mendelssohn* (Berlin: Reuther and Reichard, 1916), p. 52.
21 An analogous point is made by Davidson when he claims that truth cannot be explained, as all explanation depends on it.
22 In Smith, *Reading McDowell*, p. 114.
23 Brandom and Pippin offer construals of this position in more current terminology, but they do not question its basic premise.
24 Ed. Scholz, *Die Hauptschriften zum Pantheismusstreit*, p. 51.
25 Robert Pippin, *Idealism as Modernism* (Cambridge: Cambridge University Press, 1997), p. 404.
26 See Bowie, *From Romanticism to Critical Theory*.
27 F. Jacobi, *Jacobi an Fichte* (Hamburg: Friedrich Perthes, 1799), p. 14.
28 Derrida talks, unconsciously echoing Jacobi, of metaphysics of the kind he sees as proposed by Hegel as the 'absolute desire to hear oneself speaking' (Jacques Derrida, *La voix et le phénomène* (Paris: Presses Universitaires de France, 1967), p. 115).
29 The route from Jacobi to the later Schelling to Levinas is suggested by the refusal of Jacobi to see the subject/other relation in terms of reflective 'self-recognition in otherness'.
30 G.W.F. Hegel, *Werkausgabe*, Vol. 2 (Frankfurt: Suhrkamp, 1970), pp. 350–51.
31 Brandom talks of Hegel regarding 'concept using activity' as making '*intelligible*, the conceptually structured world' (Robert Brandom, *Tales of the Mighty Dead* (Cambridge, Mass., and London: Harvard University Press, 2002), p. 208), which poses the question, that is central to the later Schelling, of what it means to say that the world is conceptually structured.
32 See Andrew Bowie, *Schelling and Modern European Philosophy* (London: Routledge, 1993).
33 The link of freedom to evil which is the core of the essay on freedom is not always sustained in the later work. There freedom has more to do with the fact that the world has meaning at all, a fact that cannot be explained in terms of the meanings that develop within the world.
34 Pippin, *Idealism as Modernism*, p. 405.
35 Smith, *Reading McDowell*, p. 111.
36 See Andrew Bowie, *Schelling and Modern European Philosophy* (London: Routledge, 1993).
37 Stanley Cavell, *Must we mean what we say?* (Cambridge: Cambridge University Press, 1976), p. 93.
38 Pippin, *Idealism as Modernism*, pp. 408–9.
39 Ibid. p. 409.
40 It is worth remembering here that professional philosophy at least has an even less significant role, however much people in general may philosophise about what concerns them.
41 See Bowie, 'Schleiermacher and Postmetaphysical Thinking,' and Andrew Bowie, *Music, Philosophy, and Modernity* (Cambridge: Cambridge University Press, 2007).
42 See Bowie, *Music, Philosophy, and Modernity*.
43 Robert Pippin, *The Persistence of Subjectivity* (Cambridge: Cambridge University Press, 2005), p. 188.
44 Ernest Lepore (ed.), *Truth and Interpretation* (Oxford: Blackwell, 1986), p. 310.
45 See, e.g., the essays in Smith, *Reading McDowell*.
46 See Bowie, *Music, Philosophy, and Modernity*.
47 I neglect many of Adorno's most familiar ideas here, concentrating more on aspects which have had too little attention paid to them. Adorno's work seems to me frequently implausible, but it still contains remarkable insights.
48 Adorno GS, Vol. 6, p. 285.
49 Theodor W. Adorno, *Probleme der Moralphilosophie* (Frankfurt: Suhrkamp, 1996), p. 154.

50 H. Lonitz (ed.), *Theodor Adorno; Walter Benjamin. Briefwechsel 1928–1940* (Frankfurt: Suhrkamp, 1994), p. 139.
51 Theodor W. Adorno, *Zur Lehre von der Geschichte und der Freiheit* (Frankfurt: Suhrkamp, 2001).
52 For an attempt to substantiate such a case see Zygmunt Bauman, *Modernity and the Holocaust* (New York: Cornell University Press, 1989).
53 Pippin, *Idealism as Modernism*, p. 410.
54 Adorno GS, Vol. 7, p. 385.
55 Ibid., p. 87.
56 Ibid., p. 189. My emphasis.
57 Pippin, *The Persistence of Subjectivity*, p. 169.
58 Friedrich Schleiermacher, *Vorlesungen über die Ästhetik* (Berlin, Reimer, 1842), p. 394.
59 Friedrich Schleiermacher, *Der christliche Glaube* I (Berlin: de Gruyter, 1960), p. 26. Adorno, it should be noted, often comes close to Pippin insofar as he has a strongly normative conception of what true modern art must be. In this respect he can lose sight of the way the aesthetic either complements or sustains a critical relationship to the philosophical. (See Bowie, *Music, Philosophy, and Modernity*, Chapter 9, where I sum up the issue in terms of Adorno being at his best in creating 'musical philosophy', rather than trying to interpret music as 'philosophical music'.)
60 One does sometimes wonder why such Hegelian enthusiasm for the manifestation of freedom in civil society seems to be predominantly the preserve of North American philosophers, especially at a time when their own country seems to be exemplifying Adorno's concerns about appeals to freedom as ideology. Rather as the German philosophers of the Idealist period projected a freedom concretely missing from their own country, such Hegelianism might, perhaps uncharitably, be construed as a compensation for at least part of the direction of politics in the USA. Pippin, it should be said, admits that Hegel's demand for rational institutions to realise human freedom has been anything but realised.

INDEX